Volatility-Based Technical Analysis

Founded in 1807, John Wiley & Sons is the oldest independent publishing company in the United States. With offices in North America, Europe, Australia and Asia, Wiley is globally committed to developing and marketing print and electronic products and services for our customers' professional and personal knowledge and understanding.

The Wiley Trading series features books by traders who have survived the market's ever-changing temperament and have prospered—some by reinventing systems, others by getting back to basics. Whether a novice trader, professional or somewhere in between, these books will provide the advice and strategies needed to prosper today and well into the future.

For a list of available titles, please visit our web site at www.WileyFinance.com.

Volatility-Based Technical Analysis

Strategies for Trading the Invisible

KIRK NORTHINGTON

WILEY

John Wiley & Sons, Inc.

Library of Congress Cataloging-in-Publication Data:

Northington, Kirk, 1959–
    Volatility-based technical analysis : strategies for trading the invisible / Kirk Northington.
        p. cm.—(Wiley trading series)
    Includes bibliographical references and index.
    ISBN 978-0-470-38754-2 (cloth/website)
1. Investment analysis.   2. Portfolio management.   I. Title.
    HG4529.N6—75 2009
    332.63'2042—dc22

                                                                    2009007397

Printed in the United States of America.

10 9 8 7 6 5 4 3 2 1

For my wife Faith ...
only with her unceasing belief in me
was this book written.

Contents

Preface

For years, I have participated in regular group meetings of private and professional traders. It is always at a nighttime venue because the markets or careers occupy everyone during the daytime hours. No matter what the individual's skill level or success rate, I see a common trait in all of them. Each person possesses a strong belief that he can be successful at trading, regardless of whether that belief is well founded.

I have also observed a decided shift toward technical analysis and away from fundamental trading. It's partly because corporations have proven themselves to be unreliable information sources, but also because an abundance of vendors tout overly simplified technical analysis products and services. No matter how you slice it up, traders—professional and private—are led astray by most market services. Certainly, we all deserve better.

I wrote this book to bridge the technical analysis advantage gap between resource-rich institutions and ill-equipped individual traders. The nonutilization of volatility measurement defines this great divide. Programmable technical analysis software is the vehicle that enables the smaller professional and private trader to level the playing field.

As a beginning trader, I marveled at the many technical analysis indicators and techniques that could be applied to the chart. I longed to predict the distinct reversal points that appeared before me every week. As so many classic technical analysis methods and indicators only intermittently displayed success, I began to realize that the market-moving players were armed much differently from the way I was. I decided that on each chart there exists a structure that I could not see, but it was there nonetheless; and I was going to find out how to uncover it.

I have encountered many private traders who rely on options without ever buying or selling the actual underlying stock. These individuals today are more the rule than the exception, and yet technical analysis has left detecting option-spread trades to be largely a guessing game. This has caused many to overly rely solely on Greek values, and the plethora of graphs created to express them, while ignoring basic chart technical analysis. My belief is that volatility-based support and resistance is there to serve all traders. It is ironically the market's vast preference for options, and thus option-valuation mathematics, that actually propels the effectiveness of *Volatility-Based Technical Analysis*.

INTENDED AUDIENCE

This book is intended for those who want technical analysis to adapt to the volatility forces at work in today's markets. Most traders understand the importance of using methods that are largely unknown to the greater community. If you want to better understand the relatively simple arithmetic volatility measuring techniques, and how to incorporate them into indicators of your own adaptation or design, then you will benefit from this content. There are unobstructed processes, of which most people are capable, that enable today's programmable technical analysis software to give them an advantage. This book explains the reasons why technical analysis should incorporate volatility measurement in virtually every indicator, component, and algorithm.

WHAT'S INSIDE?

Part One gives you an understanding of the many obstacles that individual traders must overcome to level the playing field. It carefully lays out why the markets have changed since 2000, and thus produced the need for volatility measurement in all aspects of technical analysis. It also provides some important groundwork material to prepare you for understanding the purpose and usage of volatility analysis.

Part Two explores arithmetic measurements of volatility within exercises that create custom indicators. This is a calculus-free zone; only high school math is used. This section delves into specific techniques for creating indicators. It also focuses on retrofitting classic technical indicators with volatility measurement. Also, the concept of *Projected Implied Volatility* (PIV) is introduced.

Part Three continues the process of developing volatility-based technical analysis components, with an emphasis on solving some classic technical analysis weaknesses, such as trend compensation. This section delves deeply into the importance and methods of forecasting the broad market's short- and intermediate-term direction. Exact trade setups are the focus of Part Three. The concept of *Volatility Shift* in particular is introduced, along with specific ways to exploit it. Part Three culminates in the practice of using the scientific method to develop trading system components. A simple component testing routine, complete with code, is also explored.

Appendix A duplicates all of this book's code as TradeStation EasyLanguage code, complete with charts.

Appendix B explores in-depth methods for finding high probability option spread trades: Condors, Butterflies, Strangles, and Straddles. This is done using the MetaSwing system. Where feasible, care is taken to present statistically valid test results.

Appendix C explains the resources available to you at this book's companion web site, tradingtheinvisible.com.

All of the indicator examples in the book are coded in MetaStock Function Language to show the simplicity of coding, and that most anyone can do it. Over 180 charts are also included in the text, designed to be large and descriptive.

This book also lays out how finding profitable exits, within a set time frame, should be a goal of every trader. Enhancing almost any technical analysis method or calculation with volatility measurement provides the highest probability exit signals. The activity of increasing each trade's profit, or lessening its loss, has always seemed to be a universal desire of private traders.

Life as a private trader can be a solitary existence in the physical and the informational context. Understanding the broader market's short-term bias using the volatility of market breadth is perhaps the most underused gift we all receive. And yet so many look right through it every day. In Chapter 13 you will find the algorithms and source code for the MetaSwing Correction Surge system released. It provides an early warning system for the short- and intermediate-term market direction and corrective events. This system kept Northington Trading profitable during the fall market crash of 2008, and for that matter throughout all of 2008. It is a calculation and methodology that any trader can implement and use effectively.

Ultimately, the business of trading depends on your ability to make well-balanced decisions at times when the act of decision making is hardest. In Chapter 6, a methodology called the Framework is presented. When the Framework is adapted to the specifics of your trading methods, great clarity is gained, in that it more clearly identifies the pieces of a method that work or show weakness. Its strength is garnered by the proper use of component cross-verification. The net result is better trading decisions.

KIRK NORTHINGTON

Acknowledgments

C arson Dahlberg, CMT, is the head of the Charlotte, North Carolina, chapter of the Market Technicians Association. Carson contributed a significant amount of time and expertise in providing peer review for this book's original content. His insights showed me better ways to emphasize its practices. Derek Hernquist is the Chief Investment Officer at Integrative Capital, LLC, and also employed his market knowledge for peer review. Derek's understanding of the underlying logic required when creating new methods was very insightful for me as a first-time author. My good friend Pamela Dennis was quite helpful by providing the quintessential private trader's take on new market realities and the need to keep trading methods grounded.

In so many ways, my wife, Faith, deserves thanks and credit for keeping this book's content grounded and straightforward. She tirelessly listened to my endless technical explanations, only to yawn and remind me that making methods simple is always best.

I also want to thank Jeffrey Gibby, Kelly Clement, Heidi Browning, and all the good folks at Equis International for their support and assistance with the evaluation of some advanced analysis techniques, and for providing additional peer review.

On any given day, I could always rely on the master swing trader Alan Farley to enlighten me with concise and meaningful answers to some deep questions. He's never been too busy to reply to my e-mails and share his expertise.

I would also like to extend my appreciation to Megan Sordo, Janette Perez, and Jacqueline Reyna at TradeStation Securities, Inc. They are always great to work with.

My gratitude is also extended to Richard Saidenberg for lending his TradeStation EasyLanguage expertise at some critical times. Richard is available at ricksaidenberg@spitfire.net, or (914) 769–5164.

Throughout the body of this book, MetaStock charts are the courtesy of Equis International, a Thomson Reuters company. In Appendix A, all charts were created with TradeStation, TradeStation Technologies, Inc. All rights reserved. The high levels of professionalism at both of these companies make them terrific to work with.

Lastly, I want to thank my cat, Summer. It was a great help to have her always resting on my desk, giving her opinions on this book's most complex trading methods, and making the really big decisions.

K. N.

PART ONE

Are You Prepared?

ave you ever had the dream where you are unprepared for the exam? Upon showing up for a class you find out that there is an important exam scheduled for that hour. Not only have you not studied, but strangely you don't even remember having attended any of the prior lectures. This is a common "dream you can't forget" according to Gillian Holloway, author of *The Complete Dream Book*.[1]

If you trade the markets, I hope you have had this dream many times. Its nickname is "the overachiever's nightmare," because it is so common for successful people to experience it. The dream seems to occur most often when an individual assumes "responsibilities that increase what he expects of himself." It seems to signal to a person the need for accountability, performance, and preparation. Indeed, Part One of this book focuses on the need for all technical traders to adapt and prepare for the increasing role of volatility in the financial markets.

The first three chapters of this book deal heavily with the recognition of how market participants have changed, and the challenges these changes present. It should also open your eyes to your opportunity to transform your methods and prepare yourself. Perhaps it can even help you avoid those embarrassing classroom exam situations.

Chapter 1: The Challenges presents your market competitors and their daunting capabilities. The information in it is quite an eye opener for most private traders; it may even instill a splinter of fear into your psyche. A healthy amount of fear has kept mankind alive since fire was considered high tech.

Chapter 2: The Opportunities introduces the many realistic opportunities that await you, if you can adapt. Each of the specific challenges presented in Chapter 1 are initially countered. You will begin to understand the advantages possible with volatility-based technical analysis.

Chapter 3: The Foundation gives you important information to best use the balance of the book. Important technical analysis tenets are covered, along with a quickstart primer of MetaSwing.

CHAPTER 1

The Challenges

W ho wants to walk up to an ATM, put in $10,000, and then take out $11,000? I'm going to go out on a limb here and say we'd all love to do that. In a sense, though, isn't that what trading is? We buy shares of a stock through a small computer program interface to a brokerage firm. Then flip over to your browser and see what's going on at the CNN web site. "Hmm," you wonder, "I can't wait to buy that new suit I was eyeing yesterday with the money this trade will make." Later, we sell the shares and walk away with more money in our account than we started with. Doesn't that feel good?

Of course, we all know better than that. We know that there is a realistic chance that we may only get back $9,000, or less. And that's not even mentioning that we can't directly touch this magical ATM, which is the financial markets. There's a guy standing in front of the ATM, and he's going to operate the ATM for you. He's also going to take a small piece of that $10,000, going in and coming out.

So the real question is, "Do most people really know what's going on inside the magical ATM?"

Before we get to that, though, it's important to keep in mind that if you actually succeed in taking out $11,000 after you have put in only $10,000, some other poor soul is getting back only $9,000 on his $10,000 deposit. The only way a person makes money in the financial markets is if someone else loses money. This means your task is to take someone else's money. If this concept bothers you, then maybe active trading is not your brand of coffee. If that's true, then give your money to a mutual fund manager and let him attempt to grab someone else's cash. Most beginning traders don't realize this and your broker—online or flesh and blood—is in no hurry to tell you this, or the rest of what you will read in this chapter.

Trading is a battle, a competition, a game with no second place. If, at the end of the week, you realize that your trading account is $500 lower, there isn't anyone who's going to console you or tell you that everything's going to be okay. That person is busy eating lobster and celebrating the good week he had taking money away from a bunch of poorly prepared retail traders. That person is an institutional trader with a support staff of quantitative analysts who provide him with high probability strategies and resources.

My intention is not to scare you away from trading. Trading financial markets is a wonderful and often rewarding experience. Indeed, with the well-deserved death of "buy and hold," and the ever-increasing rise of systemic risk, it's the best way to get decent returns in the market. Whether making money or losing it, anyone who experiences trading will walk away an improved person. She may be richer or she may be poorer, but she will have improved in some way. She will most definitely understand things about herself she did not know before. Everyone will learn things about the world that they would not have known otherwise.

The purpose of this chapter is to give you an accurate and honest understanding of what any trader is competing with when he puts on a position. You are going to need to understand what's out there. These are facts that the retail trading industry does not want you to know. There's an entire industry in place to help you trade and charge you for it. Some of this industry is legitimate and will help you become successful.

Unfortunately, most of these trading industry vendors are more interested in your money than your success. Your online broker spends fortunes on television and print advertising trying to convince you that you can single-handedly achieve your financial goals. All you need to do is open a brokerage account with their company and use their software tools, although their print copy and commercials are sufficiently filled with enough content to legally cover themselves when someone loses his shirt. Incidentally, their software has the same technical indicators that are publicly available on the Internet for free. There are a multitude of software companies that will sell you a technical trading system that claims to ensure that you will rule the markets, with seemingly no risk.

Meanwhile, getting back to reality, here's what the business actually is, and a very serious business it is. It's the ultimate game of mind versus minds. You're not up against one MIT graduate; you are competing with thousands of them. You can't see the other minds you are up against. You don't know who they are or what they look like. At least when a fighter steps into the ring, he's entitled to a good look at his opponent.

So before we dive into the enlightening world of volatility-based technical analysis, let's understand the most important challenges you face. The pages that follow will briefly discuss some very eye-opening truths about the markets, which you will likely find both fascinating and disturbing. Use the sections that follow to better understand what awaits you when you step into the trading pits, and keep in mind that there is a specific solution for each of these challenges. I identify the solutions in Chapter 2, and explore them in the body of this book.

THE BRAIN POWER

Today all traders, and that includes you, are competing with the best and the brightest minds that the world has to offer.

Perform an Internet search and look at a job advertisement for a trading development analyst at a large institutional trading firm. The job qualifications and educational requirements are lengthy. Every type of quantitative and financial modeling methodology imaginable is housed within these firms. Many of these firms have mathematical talent in-house that could rival NASA when the United States won the space race.

Large hedge funds, mutual funds, and investment banks are staffed with incredibly bright, well-educated, and highly paid individuals. These are typically quantitative analysts and computer programmers with an aptitude for finding a single needle in five hundred haystacks. Suffice it to say these people are not paid to play with trend lines and Fibonacci grids. They use advanced quantitative methods to find inefficiencies in the markets, and develop trading strategies to capture them. They have access to the finest software programs and enormous computing power. They work with ultra-high-speed data that go way beyond high-low-open-close and volume. Market declines and financial industry layoffs have not reduced the effects of these individuals. Periods of ultra-high market volatility conveniently provide data, which enable them to more finely hone program trading algorithms.

Here are a couple of sample job requirements for the talent behind the trading strategies that are created inside the institutional firms with which all traders are competing:

Senior Quantitative Analyst—Salary/Rate: 300K+

Essential skills, experience, and qualifications:

- Two to four years of relevant quantitative research, or trading experience.
- PhD or equivalent degree in Math, Financial Mathematics, Physics, Engineering, or Computer Science.
- Very strong analytical, mathematical, and problem solving capabilities.
- Excellence in probability theory, stochastic processes, statistics, partial differential equations, and numerical analysis.

Experience in any of the following:

- Interest rate derivatives modeling.
- FOREX modeling.
- Credit derivatives modeling.
- Commodity modeling and research.
- Grasp of PDEs and Monte Carlo.
- Very good understanding of quantitative models for pricing and hedging derivatives.
- Outstanding C/C++ programming skills.

Statistical Arbitrage Quantitative Analyst / $120K+

New York, United Kingdom
Quantitative Analyst with sound skills in statistical arbitrage needed
Requirements:

- Honors degree followed by a post-doctorate degree in mathematics, finance, statistics, or similar.
- Knowledge of SAS or other statistical packages.
- C++/MATLAB and VBA along with strong quantitative skills.
- Experience in implementation of quantitative trading systems.
- Experience in high frequency algorithmic trading, P&L, and various other quantitative tasks.

Do you think you're smart now? That increase in sales you achieved last year at your job was a pretty good feat. The way you opened that new location in an up-and-coming part of town before your competitor did was a real accomplishment. The promotion you received this year was a genuine triumph over your peers. Now imagine what you could have done if you had had at your disposal a team of rocket scientists such as those just described. Just as important, suppose your competitors had access to that team of geniuses last year and you did not. Would you still have that promotion, sales increase, or competitive advantage?

Here's the question that is just screaming for an answer: Does anyone think an institutional trading firm would spend a couple of million dollars annually paying a team of Ph.D. graduates to perform technical analysis using publicly available technical indicators?

It's almost comical to imagine a room full of MIT graduates staring at computer screens, drawing trend lines and Fibonacci grids, and sending buy recommendations to the traders based on a stochastic oversold indicator. It's like something out a Far Side comic frame.

THE HORSE POWER

Institutional market participants with deep pockets have a technological infrastructure advantage.

Try to buy some of the advanced analytical software and data feeds that institutional trading firms use. You would not be able to justify the cost because you're not in the club: the billion-dollar institutional investment business. You don't manage a three-billion dollar fund. I believe you have just as much right, however, to eat steak in first class as the club members do. You will be able to see how in the chapters to come.

Inside these institutional firms real-time super computer systems run 24/7, monitoring price and volume movements, implied volatility levels, trading pairs and correlations, foreign exchange rates, right down to the tick, on every tradable financial security and instrument. The software they are executing is created by the sum of the mathematical brainpower of the most amazingly sharp minds in the entire world. As has been shown, these minds are highly paid; nothing less than six figures!

Vendors such as Thomson Reuters provide international market data feeds that propagate data into high speed databases that drive programmed trading execution. For example, their FasTick analytics suite can capture, sort, and archive 100,000 tick transactions per second in real time. These data are then used instantaneously by quantitative trading algorithms. This same vendor connects the institutional client directly to the trading exchange by T3 communication lines for automated order execution. This is a process that measures its end-to-end performance in milliseconds.

All captured tick data are routinely used to adapt and update the algorithmic trading models as markets change. For instance, the seamless integration of these tick databases with the MathWorks MATLAB application enables the quantitative analyst to model accumulation and distribution strategies quickly. The strategies are then executed by automated algorithms over increasingly shorter periods of time; days instead of weeks. This is largely responsible for the erosion of chart pattern effectiveness. These strategies are preempting their formation behavior, and post-formation behavior through recognition of the opportunities in advance of most market participants. Price action that previously signaled demand is vanishing because of arbitrage strategies and hyper-efficient programmed trading.

Do you like to trade news releases? You might want to think again. Thomson Reuters and Bloomberg offer high speed news feeds. Everyone knows that, but did you know this: Thomson Reuters, for instance, offers a software product called NewScope, which reformats the electronic news document with meta tags, which are codes that a computer program understands. It processes the document in less than 300 milliseconds; that's one third of a second.

The meta tags mark and specifically classify the pertinent facts and figures in the document so that an automated trading program can quantify that new story's effect on specific asset classes. Targeted securities are then bought or sold in real time, based on the algorithm's logic. These trading algorithms are created by those bright MIT-level graduates discussed in the previous section. This automated trading of news events happens without human intervention. Using this methodology, trades in response to news events are routinely executed within one to three seconds. Before the private trader even thinks about the news event, bid and ask spreads on actionable securities are widened and price has begun to move. By the time the individual trader is buying in response to the news event, the automated algorithm is selling and booking profit.

This is computer logic that never sleeps, does not go on vacation, and is not subject to fear, greed, or other emotions. It has access to data that aggressive individual traders can often only dream of. Don't make the mistake of trying to beat it at its own game. A butter knife will not help you much in a gun fight.

OPTIONS AND VaR ASCENDANCY

Current technical analysis leaves the individual and private trader ill-prepared to participate in today's markets because it does not adequately utilize volatility measurement.

Are you basing your technical analysis methods on the correct underlying dynamics? Or, more importantly perhaps, the question should be, why is such intense talent needed in-house at large institutional firms? These two questions are linked in a most important way. The answer to them both is simple yet subtle. Trading has changed, but no one bothered to tell the private trader-investor about it.

Trading is no longer just buying and selling of stocks. Today, the major influencers of stock prices are options trading, and the effects of Value-at-Risk (VaR) on modern portfolio theory. We look at options trading first. A careful historical examination of this volume and type of trading brings to light the forces causing this underlying market-moving shift.

Figures 1.1 and 1.2 together illustrate the tale of the equity trading metamorphosis. Here are the underlying causes for this dramatic fundamental market change:

- Although options have been traded since the early 1970s, the markets in recent years are experiencing a large divergence in the volume of options trading relative to direct buying and selling of stocks.
- Figure 1.1 shows that the Dow Jones Industrial Average has achieved significant price gains between 2002 and 2007. Its actual equity trading volume, however, has remained flat year over year. Taken alone, this is an illogical divergence.
- By contrast, Figure 1.2 shows clearly that between 2002 and 2007 the U.S. total equity options contract volume has increased by almost 200 percent.
- These data imply clearly that larger market-moving institutional players are executing their strategies with a heavier reliance on options than on direct equity trading. Option valuation is now a primary underlying influence of supply and demand in equity trading. Note that not all stock indexes show as dramatic a change in equity trading volume as the Dow Jones Industrial Average does. However, it is clear that indexes more heavily comprised of option capable stocks reflect this trend most.

This incredible shift to options trading has been largely attributed to the rise in the number of hedge funds, since, not coincidentally, the year 2000. The amount of assets under management at hedge funds grew from $300 billion in the year 2002 to more than $2 trillion in 2007.[1] An increased reliance on leverage, and the use of complex hedging strategies, have caused options to be the market's primary instrument of choice.

The reason all this is important is that options pricing and valuation is based on volatility. Determining the probability of what a stock's price may reach, higher or lower, within an ever-decreasing time window is almost entirely based on volatility. Of even greater importance is that technical analysis as it exists today rarely uses volatility in its algorithms. Rather, current technical analysis commonly available to retail traders is based on calculations of linear price movements and two-dimensional data. It depends heavily on chart pattern analysis and fixed pricing levels of support and resistance. In short, classic technical analysis delivers what the eye can see on the chart, while what is needed is only that which the microprocessor can see.

The other massive influence of volatility on stock price movement is the current use

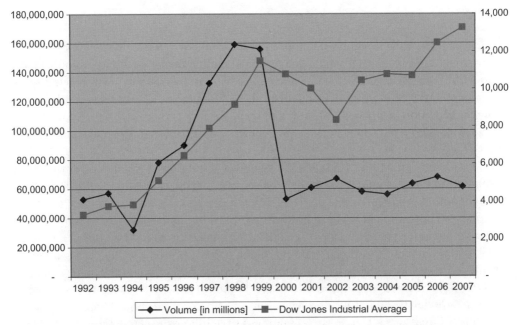

Dow Jones Industrial Average vs. Trading Volume

FIGURE 1.1 In the first decade of the twentieth century, the Dow Jones Industrial Average achieved significant price gains, while direct trading of its individual equity components experienced negative volume growth.

Data source: Reuters QuoteCenter.

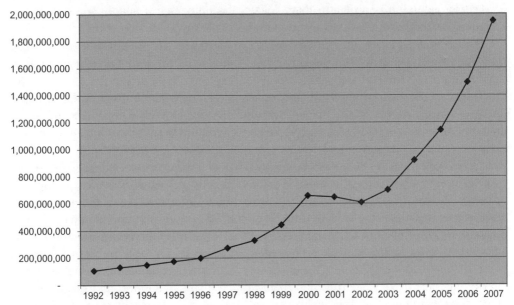

Total Equity Options Contract Volume

FIGURE 1.2 By contrast, total equity options trading has increased by almost 200 percent since the year 2002.

Data source: Chicago Board Options Exchange, 2007 Market Statistics Report.

of Value-at-Risk (VaR) modeling on modern portfolio theory (MPT). Most stock is owned by large institutions: mutual funds, hedge funds, endowments, sovereign wealth funds, and so forth. These organizations balance and diversify their stock portfolios based on VaR calculations. VaR, first developed by J. P. Morgan in 1994, is primarily a risk-modeling methodology based primarily on, you guessed it, volatility. It therefore forces volatility measurement to be a primary driver of the institutional accumulation and distribution of specific equities.

Volatility in the world of finance is usually expressed as the standard deviation of the change in value of a financial instrument with a specific time horizon. Its largest use is that of option premium pricing and quantification of risk. Volatility in its two distinctly different forms, historical and implied, are the primary inputs for determining a stock option's premium price. Simply put, volatility measurement is the key input that determines equity valuation, through the underlying stock's option pricing. The subject of volatility is quite deep and is one of the most misunderstood financial measurements.

Here's the answer, though, to why there is the need for expensive rocket science talent at large institutional trading firms, mutual funds, investment banks, and hedge funds. Volatility analysis requires the higher use of mathematics. Only quantitative mathematicians can really work in-depth with it, and to its highest degree.

In the chapters to come you will learn ways that the private trader, without advanced degrees, can work with and analyze stock volatility using today's programmable technical analysis software. There are other methods to measure it that don't require quantitative mathematics. It's one of the most important disciplines that will make you successful. Once you become an opportunist of volatility measurement, instead of a casualty of it, you will be able to see and capture market inefficiencies that were previously invisible to you.

Here is a sneak peak at how you can have volatility-based technical analysis work for you. Figure 1.3 shows us a weekly chart of Cephalon Incorporated (CEPH). The chart time span is 2007 to 2008, which was a very difficult and volatile market environment. The upper and lower trading bands are based purely on volatility measurement. Their peaks and troughs project forward key levels of support and resistance, which are shown on the chart as dashed horizontal lines. You will learn more about these technical components in the chapters to come.

The circled areas on the chart show how these volatility-based levels of support and resistance were instrumental in causing price to reverse or pause. The lines are usually determined weeks in advance and exist in most time frames. The foreknowledge of these support and resistance levels, and the best practices of their use, can be a vital part of the edge that you need to overcome the challenges faced by individual traders. This is a clear advantage of volatility-based technical analysis.

RAIN CLOUDS OR URINE?

The individual retail trader is largely unprepared to trade, but is swayed to believe just the opposite by an industry that seeks mostly the contents of the trader's wallet.

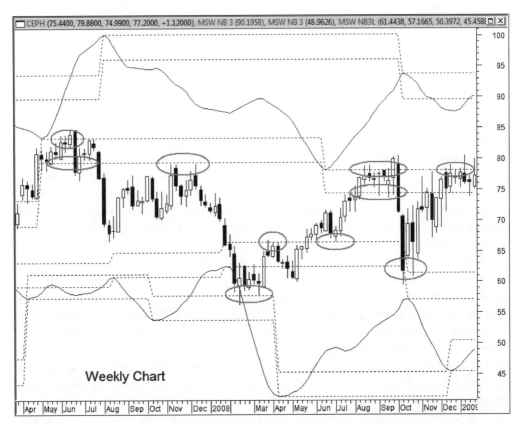

FIGURE 1.3 This weekly chart of Cephalon Incorporated (CEPH) shows how the foreknowledge of volatility-based support and resistance can give the individual trader an advantage.

Chart created in MetaStock. Chart uses the MetaSwing Add-on, by Northington Trading, LLC. All rights reserved.

As Judge Judy Sheindlin is fond of saying, "Don't pee on my leg and tell me it's raining." And that brings us to the fourth challenge that aspiring traders face today. According to an entire business sector of retail brokerage firms and software products, cool-looking technical indicators are all you, the retail trader, need to garnish dramatic returns in the stock market. The television commercials that bombard us are outrageous with oversimplification.

If you have recently entered the trading arena, you have no doubt read articles in today's trading periodicals that discuss the usage of indicators to achieve success. Many people are fascinated by looking at oscillators of all types, chart patterns, moving average strategies, Elliott waves, and multiple intersecting trend lines. "Surely," their intellect reasons, "I've found the way to buy low and sell high."

That would be an incorrect conclusion. In truth, they have found one of the keys to buying low and selling high 15 years ago; but not today. To be clear on this point, though, it is vital to understand the discipline of technical analysis, both past and present. The volatility-based technical analysis that can make it possible for you to be a profitable trader today is not all that different from so many great forms of classic technical analysis used in the past. Therefore, a thorough grasp of it can be important.

Do you ever wonder why the traditional methods of chart pattern trading are experiencing reduced effectiveness? Simple breakout methods that made many wealthy in the 1990s do not render the same performance, largely due to programmed trading. Every known and unknown chart pattern and technical indicator that we have all been taught to use is recognized immediately by the microprocessor.

When most traders and institutions can see the same trade setup, the past predictable outcome of that strategy is rendered ineffective by arbitrage. This is readily evident when consistent reading of today's technical analysis magazines reveals one after another classic setup and pattern trading strategy now produces statistically insignificant trading performance; virtually random results. Furthermore, these still currently promoted trading methods produce inferior results when compared to a buy-and-hold baseline.[2]

Here's the bottom line on this dilemma. As a retail trader, there is no end to the number of services and products that all communicate to you that you are well prepared to take on the financial markets. The only hitch is that you must pay them money for their information, software, stock picking advisory service, training and coaching services, black box system, or some other type of secret weapon. Then, if that's not enough, they then tell the hopeful trading neophyte to "Trade with confidence!" An entire industry wants you to believe that trading profits can be purchased. This is simply just not true. Trading profits can't be bought.

Profits can only be attained when you learn to trade within a viable system framework. Successful technical trading components and methods can only come to you in two ways:

1. The first is your ability to trade in your own original way, using volatility-based methods and setups that you create, with no one else privy to them. To achieve this, you must learn to think in unconventional ways when looking at the stock chart.
2. License volatility-based algorithms from a credible source, which limits their use and thereby their exposure to the markets.

NEWS FOLLY

An abundance of news media today feeds the private investor-trader an endless stream of inaccurate corporate news bits, convinces her that it's true, and then convinces her that it is actionable.

How about the other road: the one most traveled? Trading based on accurate fundamental information is the purview of the insider. Current laws and accounting practices allow publicly traded companies to do everything but tell the truth. C-level executives at today's publicly traded companies are under enormous pressure to show positive results every quarter. These corporate leaders are obscenely motivated by stock option incentives. As sure as they are human beings, and thus subject to temptation, the truth will be stretched or fall victim to *spin.*

One or two financial quarters later, that previous white lie has to be stretched even further; at this point it's based on fiction. Most often, the ugly truth ends up coming out as a complete surprise to analysts and financial commentators in the media. This is why stock prices drop so much faster than they rise. It's the "Oh, crap!" factor.

Picking stocks the old-fashioned way may seem possible, but the reality is that Warren Buffett has access to much more inside information about a company in which he invests than you could find out in 20 years. Nevertheless, the financial markets are filled with individual traders who will try to emulate the methods of market barons with only the information they hear on CNBC or read in the *Wall Street Journal.* Here's a good rule of thumb: If you think you know some valuable piece of inside information, but trading on it is not enough to land you in prison, then the information is almost certainly insignificant or too old.

One very popular news source promises its subscribers the advantage of knowing if a stock is being accumulated or distributed by mutual funds. In truth, the source of the information comes from SEC filings, which are three to nine months old. By the time the subscribers see these numbers, the mutual funds are scaling out of their positions. It's hard to tell which party benefits more, the service that sells the subscriptions, or the mutual funds that are easily able to take profits because the subscription service helped make a market for the stocks they are selling. People eat this stuff up without question. A good way to look at this is that it's okay; the mistakes of others are where some of your future profits will come from.

EYES ON THE GOAL

If you've gotten to this point and you still want to pursue trading, then congratulations—you don't scare easily. While your market opponents and their capabilities appear daunting, as an individual trader you actually have some significant advantages on your side. A more level playing field can be attained by embedding volatility measurement into core technical analysis methodology. This makes it possible for your trading talents to be much more effective when you choose the right opportunities.

The great Henry Ford once said that "Obstacles are those scary things you see when you take your eyes off your goal." It's important to be completely aware of your market competitor's strengths. But if you focus only on those very scary strengths, then you won't know how to beat him. It is therefore equally as important to understand his weaknesses, and your advantages.

Imagine yourself as a speedboat pilot. You are fast and agile. You can enter a trade and exit it all within a minute. A professional money manager at a mutual fund is the equivalent of a freighter captain. The adage that "big ships make slow turns" is seldom more applicable than in large fund portfolio management. It's not able to respond to the market nearly as quickly as you can. It can sometimes take weeks for a large fund to scale out a position.

The opportunities that a retail trader can exploit in today's markets are numerous. There are almost limitless inefficiencies available once you approach trading with the right thought processes. Also virtually all of the components and methods I will discuss apply to futures and FOREX trading. The best news of all is that you only have to create and master one or two unique methods. The next chapter discusses the spectrum of opportunities available for the private trader.

CHAPTER 2

The Opportunities

Mountaineering is the art, sport, science, and hobby of climbing mountains. Those who do it see much more than a mountain; they see a classifiable intricate series of objective and subjective hazards that can be dealt with safely. We who choose to avoid climbing the heights see the potential for a tragic fall accompanied by a slow and painful death. We see this because the central image that comes to mind is of ourselves falling. The skilled mountaineer is actually more concerned with pieces of the mountain falling on him. As you can see, there exists a very different point of view between mountaineers and nonmountaineers.

The vast majority of the investing and trading community equates volatility to risk. And by default, risk is synonymous with loss and fear. A central premise of Modern Portfolio Theory (MPT) is to diversify a portfolio using volatility measurement for the purpose of reducing risk. Value-at-Risk (VaR), a measure of portfolio risk, uses correlations of volatility. Active traders use a stock's volatility measurement to gauge their risk vis-à-vis position sizing and stop-loss levels. As you can see in the world of finance, the word *volatility* has gotten a bum rap. So many people associate it with the concept of bad.

Just as with mountain climbing, however, everything depends on your point of view. Volatility is an opportunity if you know how to use it. In fact, I would even say that the real risk exists when one does not decide to use volatility as an opportunity.

The smart analyst will change her viewpoint and belief system with that opportunity in mind. Your viewpoint must be up close and personal. This involves getting inside the grade school arithmetic of volatility measurement. If you can be on intimate terms with the math inside your personal indicators, then right out of the starting blocks you have an advantage over most other traders. It's in the math!

As for the proper belief system, it should be summed up in the following statement:

Money is to be made at the extremes.

That is your belief system. It represents the correct approach for turning volatility from a risk into a profit vehicle. In the pages that follow I briefly highlight some of the realistic advantages gained by making volatility a friend. I also believe that you will be able to see how to make these advantages your own by bonding them with your existing strengths.

CHOOSE YOUR BATTLES

The first two large challenges presented in Chapter 1 dealt with the premise that the market is dominated by large institutional firms. They have tremendous assets in the form of highly talented quantitative analysts. They also use incredibly powerful computing platforms and software, which are fed by seemingly infinite streaming financial data. With all of these resources, they are able execute arbitrage, event, and accumulation and distribution strategies at incredible speeds. How do individual traders compete with them?

The answer is simple: Don't.

In 1941, the U.S. military capability was much smaller than that of Japan. After the Pearl Harbor attack, the Pacific fleet was crippled. Within a few years, however, the United States was able to defeat the Japanese, all the while it was fighting a major war in the European theater. In the Pacific theatre of operations, it was able to achieve an advantage with the strategy of island hopping. In essence, it chose to engage the enemy only on strategically important islands that were poorly defended. The islands on which the enemy was heavily fortified were simply bypassed and ultimately cut off from their supply lines.

A private trader can't make a decision and click a mouse fast enough to outperform a well-honed quantitative trading algorithm. It is therefore foolish to even try. Concentrate your efforts in areas where you have the advantage.

Yes, the larger industry players have more expensive toys. They receive information faster. They may even have information that they shouldn't have; but that's just how the world works. Corporations filling quarterly results can distort the truth and delay bad news, or in some cases, just plain lie.

The one thing that no industry player yet can hide or lie about is the price of a security, and when those prices change. Volatility is the measurement of price change over time. Accurate volatility measurement, therefore, is something you can count on; and indeed is the equalizer. Your advantages will originate from methods of using volatility measurements. They will become clearer as you read the rest of this chapter. Therefore consider your first advantage as:

You can choose to trade only when and where the odds are in your favor.

TAKE THE OFFENSIVE

The third challenge presented in Chapter 1 states that classic technical analysis provides individual traders with methods that are declining in effectiveness because of a lack of volatility-sensing methods. While this is true, it is not a condition that you must accept. Indeed, this is the point at which to shout "Enough! I'm not going to stand for the status quo any longer." Or if that feels corny, then just think it loudly.

It's now time to use the great enabler for individual traders. Programmable technical analysis software is the key to creating your own opportunities. With it, you have the ability to redefine the data that you see. You can use it to see clearly that which is normally invisible to the vast majority of private and retail traders, but is visible to many professionals.

The great enabler I'm referring to is commercially available software products that perform technical chart analysis, and provide the user the ability to write custom formulas and algorithms in an underlying programming interface. There are many proven products to choose from. This book uses MetaStock by Thomson Reuters, and TradeStation by TradeStation Securities. Both are very powerful, each with unique strengths.

The opportunities available to you in the markets exist as somewhat of a niche. While they do exist, the greatest are those that you create, and that's the best mental approach to take as well. It is a creative process, which is how the programmable aspect of technical analysis software comes into play. This creative process is what this book is really about. Leveraging the capabilities of programmable technical analysis software gives you the next major opportunity, which is:

You can trade better than other private traders, and smaller professional firms that do not use volatility-sensing calculations and algorithms while being on par with large institutional firms that do.

Redraw the Playing Field

From the perspective of the individual trader, the market data that vendors offer can seem vast and descriptive. It isn't always enough, though, to help you gain the edge. Hedge funds certainly don't think so. They are free to trade anything that's legal in any way they choose to do so. Making the most of that type of freedom requires that they exercise flexibility. To find the right opportunities they get very creative. You should, too. This describes in general one of the important opportunities available to you:

Create your own capability to view market inefficiencies that are usually invisible to others.

Let's take a look at an example of how you can exercise some of your own vision. One great way is use a composite security. This function joins together two or more stocks into a single security. There are many benefits to doing this.

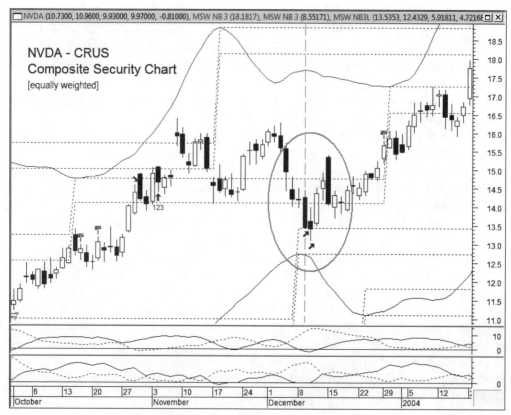

NVDA (10.7300, 10.9600, 9.93000, 9.97000, -0.81000), MSW NB 3 (18.1817), MSW NB 3 (8.55171), MSW NB3L (13.5353, 12.4329, 5.91811, 4.72168 □ | X |

NVDA - CRUS
Composite Security Chart
[equally weighted]

FIGURE 2.1 This composite chart of Nvidia Corporation (NVDA) and Cirrus Logic (CRUS) provides a clear and timely long trade setup due to the inherent compatibility of volatility measurement and positive correlation.

Chart created in MetaStock. Chart uses the MetaSwing Add-on, by Northington Trading, LLC. All rights reserved.

Figure 2.1 shows a daily chart of a composite security. The security was created by combining Nvidia Corporation (NVDA) and Cirrus Logic (CRUS) on an equally weighted basis. All values in the time series, therefore, were produced by simple summation. The circled area in the chart shows a typical long trade entry, as denoted by the upward pointing arrows. It is very clear, because the signal comes at an appropriate level of support. The signal is also well timed because it first appears on December 9, 2004, which is not a day early or late. The date is notated with a vertical dashed line.

By contrast, examine Figure 2.2. Here we see the daily charts of Nvidia Corporation (NVDA) and Cirrus Logic (CRUS) presented individually. These are the two stocks that actually compose the composite security shown in Figure 1.1. Again, the trade signals in December are circled. Notice that neither of these present crystal clear long entry signals. Cirrus Logic triggers two days early, and prior to support being reached. Nvidia Corporation never actually reaches support. Both seem, therefore, to be somewhat nebulous opportunities.

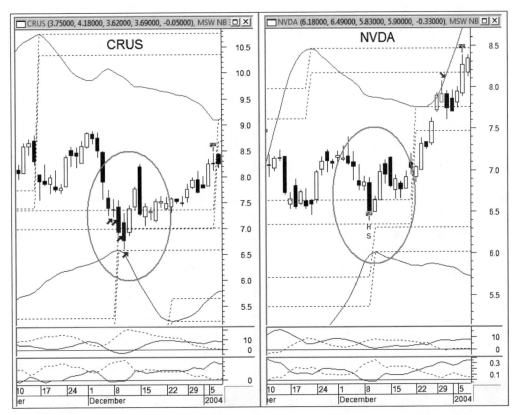

FIGURE 2.2   These two separate charts of Cirrus Logic (CRUS) and Nvidia Corporation (NVDA) each contain far less clarity than their composite chart.

Chart created in MetaStock. Chart uses the MetaSwing Add-on, by Northington Trading, LLC. All rights reserved.

By redefining the data, a good trade is identified with the NVDA-CRUS composite security. Depending on your time frame, it produced an 8 percent swing trade, or a great trend entry spot for a position trade. To trade it, just buy equal dollar amounts of each, and manage the trade on the basis of the composite chart. If you were only looking at each stock chart independently, you probably would not have taken the trade. So why does this work well?

The success of this method is built on two technical measurements: volatility and correlation. The two stocks were chosen for the composite because they are in very similar businesses. They are in the same sector, but that's not always enough. Sectors are often populated with extremely disparate stocks. When a 20-period correlation analysis is run on these two securities, it is easy to see that they correlate very positively. Incidentally, correlation is a volatility-related mathematical measurement.

Beyond the effects of correlation, though, why is the signal so clear on the composite chart? All of these charts were made using MetaSwing, which is a purely volatility-based technical analysis system. You will learn more about that system in Chapter 3. The signal is clearer because a correlated composite volatility signature contains less chart noise. It enables higher clarity when measuring:

- Overbought and oversold levels.
- Support and resistance levels.
- Hidden momentum.

That's why this trade works so well. Incidentally, classic technical analysis methods would recommend reducing chart noise by applying moving averages to effect dampening. The downside of that is to introduce lag into the analysis, and thus enter the trade late. Volatility-based measurements do not have the side effects of lagging signals. Instead, they make chart analysis much more structured, timely, and clear, as is shown in Figure 2.1.

This example illustrates a creative use of programmable technical analysis software. If you apply a little of your own ingenuity and research, you can add clarity to trading opportunities that are still blurry to others. In all likelihood, you have in the past seen opportunities that stimulated your curiosity. Combining software tools with exterior-box thinking will lead you to your own personal trading methods.

Simple Volatility Measurement

Chapters 4, 5, and 6 will help you understand volatility measurement from the inside out. Measuring price momentum with volatility, in lieu of differences, lies at the heart of highly effective technical analysis methods. Because it isn't inherently complex, it represents a great opportunity to improve your trading. The benefit of this is that you are then working with similar technical analysis methods to those of larger institutions.

The good news is that calculus need not be involved. It can all be accomplished with simple arithmetic and basic algebra. This means that virtually anyone is capable creating his own analysis components. Because you have control over your own indicator development, you can customize it for the specific sector, market, or commodity you trade.

Adaptive indicator design is used in Chapters 4, 5, and 7. This is the process of using the algorithm structure of a classic technical indicator and adapting it with volatility measurement. It's like performing indicator surgery. There exists a vast library of technical indicators published over many years by many talented market technicians.

In Chapter 7, there is an application of this practice with the relative strength index (RSI). In it, we transplant volatility sensing into the original RSI calculation. Its effectiveness was greatly improved by doing so. In Chapter 7, Table 7.1 shows how its performance changed from net negative to net positive.

Avoid Systemic Risk

With the advent of technology and globalization, the financial markets have become vastly more efficient than in previous decades. Theoretically, these advancements should produce markets with less underlying risk. Unfortunately, this hasn't been the case. The crash of 1987, the Long-Term Capital Management meltdown, and the financial crisis of 2008 are all testaments that point to an opposite truth. It appears that as we create more efficient financial networks and products, we also add to their complexity and potential for damage.[1]

It's no longer enough to be able to time the market and be on the right side of it, although that is as important as ever. Severe damage to equity and commodity positions can happen quickly. Routine countertrend corrections are becoming more severe because of these systemic risks. You now have the opportunity to:

Have a broad market early warning system.

We discuss in Chapter 13 the logic and rationale for just such a system. The actual system algorithm and MetaSwing code are released for the first time. Chapter 13 shows you just how to use market breadth to avoid hurtful or severe losses. Market breadth represents one of the most underused advantages that private traders have.

We see in Figure 2.3 an example of the MetaSwing Correction and Surge system on a daily chart of the S&P 500 Index during the market crash of 2008. The MetaSwing Total Correction events are denoted by large skull and crossbones symbols above the day's price candle. The Correction signals are most predictive when they are the first to occur within a few weeks. The three most significant signals are circled and notated with vertical dashed lines.

As you can see, these Correction signals warn the trader to go flat, or to short the market. This time, which was such a gut-wrenching period of loss for many, was a money-making time for those that used this system. Needless to say, Chapter 13 of this book represents an outstanding opportunity for you.

Hidden Momentum

If you have participated in the markets for any time at all, you know how important it is to ride a trend. In fact, identifying and profiting from the trend is really a central purpose of technical analysis.[2] A nice upwardly sloping stock chart, printing higher highs and higher lows, is a beautiful thing because of the momentum it contains. Picture-perfect trends aren't always available, however.

Momentum exits in other forms, though. The best type is when it is invisible to the naked eye. This limits the number of traders that see it in advance, which in turn provides a window of opportunity. This is where rising and falling levels of option-implied volatility come into play.

You will learn in Chapter 11 about another great opportunity, which is:

You can uncover hidden momentum with volatility shift.

A valuable aspect of volatility shift is that a trend need not be present. This method provides directional intelligence indicating that the recent trading range will change to a different level.

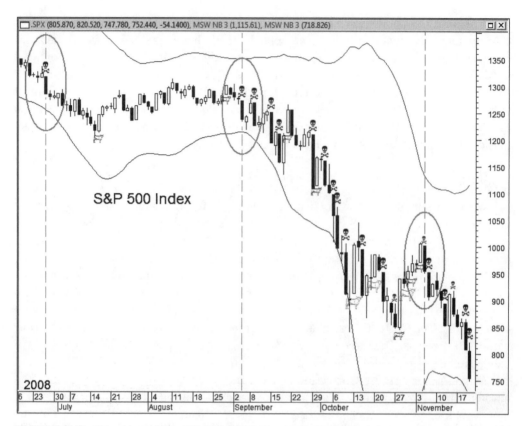

FIGURE 2.3 This chart of the S&P 500 Index shows the MetaSwing Correction and Surge system in action during the market crash of 2008.

Chart created in MetaStock. Chart uses the MetaSwing Add-on, by Northington Trading, LLC. All rights reserved.

You can in Figure 2.4 see two daily MetaSwing chart examples of volatility shift in action. The chart at left shows a long entry trade for Digi International (DGII). The chart at right gives us a short trade instance with Advanced Micro Devices (AMD). The circled area in each chart denotes the basic high slope signal. The rectangle shows the new trading range that forms as a result of the underlying hidden momentum. Each chart is shown with longer time spans at this book's companion site, www.tradingtheinvisible. com. You can find it on the page for the Chapter 2 supplemental content. You may find a wider view very interesting.

By measuring historical and implied volatility you are working with primary market moving forces. This is why volatility shift works well. It provides a major opportunity for you to identify momentum where others see none. The tools to accomplish this are within your grasp.

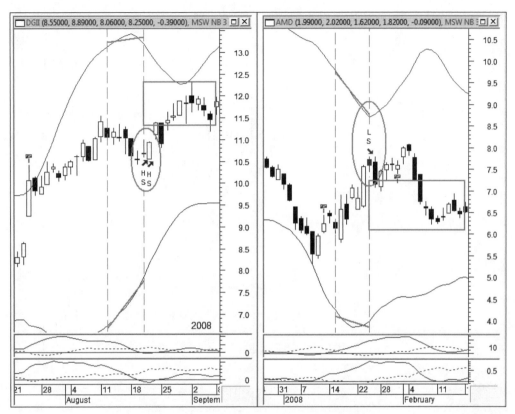

FIGURE 2.4 This dual example of Digi International (DGII) and Advanced Micro Devices (AMD) shows how the opportunity of identifying hidden momentum with volatility shift creates successful trades.

Chart created in MetaStock. Chart uses the MetaSwing Add-on, by Northington Trading, LLC. All rights reserved.

True Overbought and Oversold

A known deficiency in the overbought and oversold oscillators of classic technical analysis is their inability to work reliably during trending markets. Provided you know whether you are currently in a trading range or a trend, that isn't a problem. That knowledge, however, is often unclear.

Suppose your indicators worked well in trending and nontrending environments? This is a major advantage of inducing volatility into overbought and oversold measurement. I define it as the difference between an oversold condition and a *true* oversold condition.

The example in Figure 2.5 shows us a daily chart of Cendant Corporation during a trend rally. In the lower indicator pane a stochastic indicator is plotted. In the middle indicator pane the TTI Composite indicator is plotted. The circles represent correct readings. The rectangles represent false readings. The TTI Composite is a volatility-based

FIGURE 2.5 This chart of Cendant Corporation (CD) shows the accuracy improvement that volatility measurement can produce in overbought and oversold indicators during a trending market.

Chart created in MetaStock.

overbought and oversold component and is constructed in Part 2 of this book. You will be able to see what makes it different from the inside out.

As with any chart example, what you see in Figure 2.5 is anecdotal. It is, however, representative of the opportunity that volatility measurement creates with respect to indicators. And this opportunity is yours.

> *There are two key indicator advantages possible by incorporating volatility measurement: Accuracy and Trend compensation.*

When an indicator signals an extreme reading, is it right or is it wrong? You should be able to trust what your indicators tell you. In the world of trading, the most profitable decisions are usually made at difficult times. The accuracy of a true signal is what matters most at the point of inflection.

In Figure 2.3, the stochastic oscillator is at an inherent disadvantage because the trading direction is not range bound. At any given time, however, when you are staring

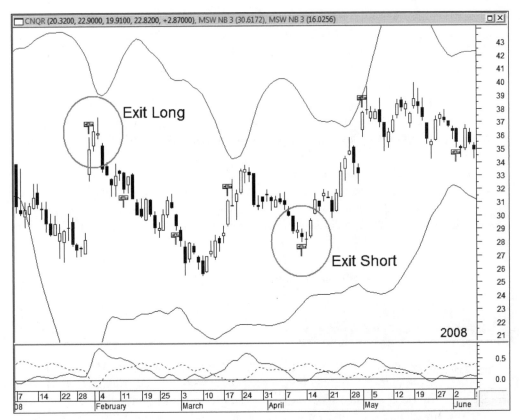

FIGURE 2.6 For many traders, well-timed exits are the key to net sum profitability. Adaptive volatility is the key.

Chart created in MetaStock. Chart uses the MetaSwing Add-on, by Northington Trading, LLC. All rights reserved.

forward into the abyss that is the future, how can you be sure if you are currently in a trading range or a trend? Creating or using technical components that are trend compensated can be a great advantage.

Exit on Cue

The reality about exiting a closing position is that any profit left on the table, within the appropriate time frame, is the same as a loss. It isn't enough to simply close the trade with a profit. Exits, therefore, are more important than almost any other aspect of your analysis. Trading is a net sum business and you've got to grab it all when the trade is a winner.

There are several effective methods for exiting, all covered in Chapter 12. One of them is shown here in Figure 2.6. The small Exit symbols shown above the price candles are for closing a long position; those below are to close a short position. Automated entry and exit systems are never 100 percent correct. I promise not insult your intelligence in this book by showing you only *perfect* examples.

In Figure 2.6, the Exit signals are generated by relative volatility levels. These are tuned for a 2-day to 10-day swing trade duration. Taken alone, most of them work. However, when cross-verified with other technical volatility measurements, some can be ignored, while the accuracy of those remaining can be startling. Figure 2.6 is a good illustration of this. The generic algorithm that produces this type of exit signal is presented in Chapter 12. Once you understand the algorithm, it is simple to interpret the signals.

When combined with volatility-based support and resistance, the art of the exit becomes quite clear. Once you begin to improve profit-taking through efficient exit methods, your trading business will become much more lucrative. This leads us to the next great opportunity that volatility-based technical analysis can provide for you.

You can improve your exits enough to cancel out a significant percentage of your losses, and thus greatly improve your bottom line profit.

PREPARE AND PERFORM

The fourth of the challenges that afflict the individual trader-investor is that she is unqualified for the markets, but is persuaded to believe otherwise. This is true because the financial markets are not like ski resorts; there are no bunny slopes. A financial market is a professional's arena only. If you step into it you assume the responsibility of competing with professionals, at their level of expertise. The barriers to entry for a private trading business are very low. The unprepared frequently wander into it, consequently, only to experience failure. This doesn't have to happen.

The ability to project the broad market direction, within your trading time frame, will prepare you to perform better than many professionals. A process for it is covered at length in Chapter 8. This ability is essential for trading success.

Developing your own trading methods will reap many benefits that you probably haven't thought of. In Chapter 6, we carefully examine the process of decision making within a volatility-based framework. Through proper cross-verification, you can learn to objectively focus on probabilities rather than emotion. Developing your trading components and methods within a procedural scientific method is the subject of Chapter 14. By defining a development process in simple terms, almost anyone can accomplish it.

Broad Market Direction

Why do we trade securities at all? Because we think that we can predict the future direction of a security's price, and by default we will garner a profit. Individuals get this wrong more often than they get it right.

In a study of 10,000 randomly selected discount broker accounts, 49,948 stock purchases and 47,535 stock sales were analyzed for profitability, over a six-year period.[3] The study showed that the individual trader tended to sell winning positions too quickly while holding on to losing trades too long. Individuals could obviously stand to improve somewhat. In my opinion, a study of this magnitude points directly to the private trader's inability to forecast short-term and intermediate-term broad market direction.

Operating in sync with the broad market's direction and swings is the single most important analysis objective that exists for the trader. We explore in Chapter 8 a simple system for anticipating the short- and intermediate-term market swings. With it, you will be better able to accomplish the most important opportunity you have, which is this:

> *Reduce your trading capital's exposure to the market by knowing three things: (1) when to trade, (2) when to be flat, and (3) which side of the market to be on.*

Stop making money and then giving it back because the broad market moved against you unexpectedly. This means trading less, but trading when it counts. It is the best preparation you can undergo before entering the market. Chapter 8 shows you how to do this. The most important pieces of MetaStock code for this are included in different chapters of this book.

A Structured Approach

Pablo Picasso said that "Computers are useless. They can only give you answers." Here was a guy who knew about creativity. I think he meant that answers are of little use to us unless we first have a desire to know something specific. To find out some piece of knowledge, the question about it must be asked. If you don't first formulate the interrogative, what good will you be able to make of the information? It is our desire to know and understand, consequently, that drives our creativity and what we accomplish with its fruit.

Creating technical analysis methods is no different. Certainly it is not easy, but it is possible. The key to turning *possible* into *probable* usually lies in approach and motivation. As for motivation I suggest money, in the form of trading profits. I offer a cheat sheet so that you may have the right approach.

The Framework is presented in Chapter 6. This is a definable and flexible methodology that identifies the specific classifications of indicators needed with which to trade. It fits on one page and guides your decision-making. Studying this framework design, and working within it, will keep you on track to creating your own components and methods. It's like a template, and you fill the blank spaces with tools for the appropriate tasks. You'll learn more about components and methods later in Parts 2 and 3 of this book.

The Scientific Method

If the Framework shows you what to build, then a correct application of the scientific method can show you how to build it. We lay out in Chapter 14 the creative development mindset and methodology for making volatility-based technical analysis components. Indeed, many chapters in this book follow this development process.

We were all able to execute the scientific method in fifth grade science class. It isn't all that different now. The truly amazing thing is how many private and professional traders do not use a sound development process when they create their own trading methods. If you follow a logical method, complete with testing, you can start out of the blocks with an advantage; this translates to less money lost while proving a new method.

There are many types of testing. Each phase of trading strategy development requires its own testing methodology. When beginning development of indicators, the more elaborate back-testing methods are tedious and not well suited to the task. A simple MetaStock exploration, complete with code, is presented in Chapter 14 specifically for the initial stages of indicator development. If you use it for the test-and-analyze phase of the scientific method, the numerical results will tell you the truth about your component's performance. Figure 2.7 shows the MetaStock Explorer application interface.

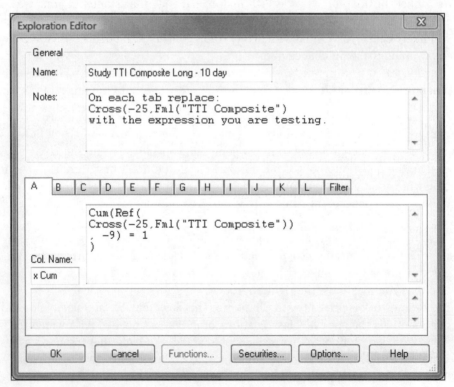

FIGURE 2.7 A simple indicator testing report, such as this MetaStock Exploration, is created and explained in Chapter 14.

Application window created in MetaStock.

Using the Explorer, we are able to conduct quick and simple testing for component profit and loss potential, along with other performance metrics.

This brings us to a very important opportunity that you should not pass up.

Your trading decisions can be made from a state of objectivity by using a proper scientific method to create volatility-based technical components and implementing those components within the Framework.

QUIET THE NOISE

Most religions around the world practice meditation, albeit in different ways, and have done so for thousands of years. All of them seem to use a process of focusing one's attention on a single point of reference. This process separates a person from the external forces that surround him, and enables his mind to exist or function in a higher state. This age-old practice has sustained great spiritual leadership, facing enormous challenges, spanning the millennia. In many ways, this same process will work to heighten your analysis and trading performance.

We looked in Chapter 1 at the fifth major challenge that stands in your way. It is how the financial news media insert themselves into your life and feed you information that will likely cause you to make incorrect trading or investing decisions. You have the choice of tuning these influences out.

I once listened to a presentation by a top mutual fund manager while attending a local chapter meeting of the Market Technicians Association. In the midst of the tumultuous stock market of 2008, this fund manager controlled a fund rated in the top 1 percent of Long-Short mutual funds for its previous 12-month performance. The manager stated that he was a very technical trader, that he used only one indicator, and that he spent very little time ingesting the financial news of the day. This market master clearly practices a form of trading meditation.

He stays focused on his own technical analysis methods and tools, and in doing so he consciously, and by default, neutralizes the biasing effects of news reporting. Regardless of his methods, his decision-making process is performing at a heightened state of capability and objectivity. You can make the same choice he has, and I hope you do.

This brings us to another very important opportunity within your grasp:

You can achieve a heightened state of trading skill and objectivity by choosing to focus on a consistent set of volatility-based indicators, components, and methods instead of the nonstop media noise and newsprint.

It is a discipline more than a practice. We all have to work at it. Just remember that neither Bloomberg nor CNBC will deposit money into your trading account if their Nielsen ratings go up.

OPPORTUNITIES OUTNUMBER CHALLENGES

It is true that the obstacles we face as private traders are scary and serious. But as you have been able to see in the previous sections, there are plenty of positive actions that you can implement to overcome them. There are actually more opportunities than challenges for the individual investor. Remember that even if trading is a part time activity for you, it must be conducted as though you are a professional.

The capabilities and examples presented in this chapter by no means constitute a complete list of the many advantages you have. You will uncover additional opportunities in Parts 2 and 3 of this book. I'm certain that if you pursue your own personal development path with volatility-based technical analysis you will discover new market inefficiencies, and make them your own.

Chapter 3 is the first stepping-stone to beginning your development path. It will help you get the most from this book. You will find in it a list of important tenets that aid in the development and interpretation of chart-based technical analysis. The rationale you derive from these tenets will help guide your comprehension as we step through the numerous sections about indicator and method development.

A quick start guide to understanding MetaSwing is also presented. As an example of a fully developed volatility-based technical analysis system, MetaSwing is frequently used to demonstrate many advanced capabilities. It will also help you understand new concepts that are possible. While I trust that you will likely want to create some of your own technical analysis methods, if you choose not to, then understanding MetaSwing will help you better source a volatility-based system for licensing.

CHAPTER 3

The Foundation

*Preparations for Exploring
Volatility-Based Technical Analysis*

On December 11, 1998, the Mars Climate Orbiter (MCO) was launched from Cape Canaveral, Florida, atop a Delta II rocket. It was part of a dual spacecraft mission, with an estimated total cost of $327 million. The MCO was a beautiful gleaming example of space technology. Packed with advanced instrumentation, its mission was to establish a stable orbit around Mars and study its climate characteristics. The redundancy of its on-board systems was a testament to the capabilities of Lockheed Martin Astronautics, the vehicle's prime contractor.

When a spacecraft approaches a planet, it executes a series of trajectory correction maneuvers (TCM). It fires rockets to alter its course in very precise measurements. When it's time to enter the orbit, it completes the Mars orbital insertion (MOI) rocket burn. Trajectory data are produced as a result of the last TCM, prior to the MOI. Rocket scientists, mathematicians, and computer programmers use these data to set up the final MOI timing. Compare it to finding the right parking spot at the mall, but you're approaching the mall at 12,300 miles per hour.

On September 23, 1999, the big day had finally arrived. All the numbers had been crunched and the MOI rocket burn started at almost 09:01 (GMT). Everything was going perfectly. Soon the MCO would be shopping at the cosmic mall.

It was also expected that during this phase Ground Control would temporarily lose radio contact for 21 minutes. The loss of signal occurred 49 seconds sooner than expected, however. It had been traveling to Mars for over a year, so what's 49 seconds one way or another, right? It's actually a lot if you are zipping along at 12,300 miles per hour; 167.4 miles, to be precise. After that earlier-than-expected loss of signal, the Mars Climate Orbiter was never heard from again.

Within six days, engineers at the Jet Propulsion Laboratory determined that the final TCM trajectory data were processed incorrectly. At Ground Control, a software program named SM_FORCES provided its output in English units. Specifically, it was to use

Newton-seconds (N-s, metric), but it actually used pound-seconds (lbf-s, English). The devil really is in the details. As a result, the spacecraft fired its rockets too late and broke up in the atmosphere; it was never designed to even touch an atmosphere.

The specification for the trajectory software clearly stated that only metric system measurements were to be used. The "Mars Climate Orbiter Mishap," as it was officially titled, occurred because someone did not follow the directions.[1] Maybe it should not have been called a mishap. When I make a similar mistake and my trading account suffers, I call it much worse things.

This chapter is designed to provide a foundation in volatility trading tenets, examples, and philosophy before we delve into actual volatility calculations and applications. Without this chapter as basic guidance, some might perceive volatility-based technical analysis and its applications inaccurately because:

- We all bring to the table different trading backgrounds, and varying perceptions of technical trading.
- Much of the content presented in Parts 2 and 3 of this book are new and not previously found in traditional technical analysis.
- Some technical analysis concepts, which are routinely assumed as valid, are not treated as such in this book.

Given this set of circumstances, I encourage you to enjoy this chapter. This book's total value will resonate much more clearly for you as a result. Think of it as reading the directions. We've seen how important that can be....

THE PREPARATIONS NEEDED

Life can be looked at as a series of choices, which use priorities as a basis. Trading, being a subset of life, is also a series of choices. To prepare well for making decisions in ways that you may not have done before, there are some important underlying beliefs that you should embrace. Those beliefs are presented in the Tenets of Volatility-Based Technical Analysis section. Understanding them will greatly help you to comprehend the many analysis exercises in Part Two of this book.

Also, the MetaSwing QuickStart section of this chapter will help you see all of the important details presented in the MetaSwing examples. Many of the more advanced tactics used in the MetaSwing analysis scenarios can be valuable food for thought when you are further developing your own methods. This makes understanding MetaSwing important for you.

I've written this book for the simple and practical purpose of helping you make money. It provides a different and realistic approach to technical analysis. Specifically, it incorporates volatility measurement into virtually all aspects of technical trading because, as expressed in Chapter 1, that is what moves prices in the post–year 2000 markets. You should be able to learn the following as a result of reading this book:

- Understand why volatility-based technical analysis should be incorporated into a successful technical trading system.
- Develop technical analysis indicators that use volatility measurement; indeed, you should feel compelled to do so.
- Fluency in various methods of swing trading and position trading with volatility-based technical analysis.
- Using volatility and market breadth to forecast short- and intermediate-term swings in the broad market.
- The concept of the way money is made at the extremes should become second nature to you.
- Source and choose a profitable and responsible technical trading system that is based on volatility; in essence, you will be a knowledgeable buyer.

TRADING THE INVISIBLE INDICATORS: ORIGINAL DEVELOPMENT

As we delve into the application of volatility measurement, custom indicators are created in almost each chapter going forward. Each begins with the letters *TTI* (*Trading The Invisible*). These are all new and original, and were created specifically for this book; they have never before been released, and their primary purpose is for teaching and demonstrating. They will be developed and refined in Parts 2 and 3.

The TTI indicators perform well; better than nonvolatility-based technical indicators, for obvious reasons. Please understand, however, that I did not create them to work extremely well. I consider them to be incomplete because they were meant to be starting points. Their structure should provide creative examples for you to begin with, but each TTI indicator can be further developed for much better performance.

Also, if any of the TTI indicators were published herein as a finished product, with outstanding performance characteristics, it would be a tragic waste. Once a technical indicator is widely released to the trading community, it becomes heavily used. Before long, its effectiveness is neutralized because of overuse. It becomes a victim of a form of technical indicator arbitrage.

This is why very effective technical indicators and methods remain proprietary to their creators. Even trading systems that are sold commercially suffer this fate when they are marketed en masse without capacity controls. A trading method should be used by a limited number of traders so that it can maintain its effectiveness. Responsible system vendors typically implement capacity control with active license management software; standard copy protection is insufficient.

For this reason it is best to practice the 3B rule: *B*uild or *B*uy, but do not *B*orrow. It means that your best avenue for trading success is to develop at least some of your own technical components. You will be a better trader because of this. If you decide to not personally build your system indicators and methods, then it is best to license a proven system from a responsible vendor. If you effectively borrow technical analysis from the public domain, then you are choosing to trade without an advantage.

TENETS OF VOLATILITY-BASED TECHNICAL ANALYSIS

Let's first focus on some important underlying foundations that I feel are important to this form of technical analysis. Here's what we are about to cover:

- *Discretionary or Mechanical:* Are we bound by ironclad rules, or do we use judgment?
- *Trading System Object Terms:* A hierarchy of terms used.
- *The Trend:* Important or a necessity?
- *Time frame:* Understanding your time frame within the mathematics of technical analysis.
- *Broad Market Cycle:* Its influence on your trading.
- *Minimum Time in Market:* Making market exposure a primary consideration.
- *Fundamental Information versus Technical Measurement:* Positioning your trading activities for minimum external influences.
- *Analysis by Cross-Verification:* Achieving high probability decisions.

Discretionary or Mechanical?

Very few private traders use mechanical trading systems rigidly. Personally, I am a discretionary trader. There isn't anything wrong with mechanical trading execution except that few people have the stomach for it. The first thing that individuals tend to do when they begin trading a mechanical system is to break the rules in an effort to improve them for that specific situation. The mechanical system, therefore, instantly becomes a discretionary system. It's human nature to behave that way.

If you want to trade a rigid mechanical system, then I encourage you to statistically back-test it properly with Monte Carlo permutation, throughout many different market environments. This is your best possible defense against the perils of data mining. It will also help you to understand if you can financially withstand the drawdown risk that the system possesses.

In all likelihood, you are a discretionary trader. With respect to development and testing of system components, Chapter 14 was created with you in mind. Many traders test a system without individually testing the components of the system, which is usually a costly mistake. It's important to first understand how the components of your system or method perform by themselves.

Trading System Object Terms

To add clarity to several terms, used frequently with respect to technical analysis as a system and parts composing it, here are simple descriptions.

- *Component, Indicator,* and *Algorithm* are terms used to describe the most basic mathematical, or logical, calculation to derive values.

- *Algorithm* is also a term used to describe a set of mathematical and logical steps as executed by technical analysis software.
- *Method* is a term used to describe a trading process for a specific trade setup and management. For instance, an Adeo High Slope is a specific trade method described in Chapter 11. A method normally contains and utilizes a set of components, indicators, and algorithms. A method can be mechanical or discretionary.
- The term *System* is used to refer to a collection of methods, components, indicators, and algorithms.
- The *Framework* is a structured three-dimensional methodology for implementing a system's methods, components, indicators, and algorithms. It achieves success by increasing profit probabilities and lowering risk. The framework depends heavily on component cross-verification. See Chapter 6 for further details about the framework.

Figure 3.1 shows us a diagram that illustrates the relationships between the terms in this list. As you can see, the Framework includes any entire system. This emphasizes the methodology of decision-making over all other considerations. That's because the Framework itself is always implemented by cross-verification. All of the other analysis objects are presented in the hierarchy.

The Trend

The majority of the best trades ride the prevailing trend like a surfboard rides a wave. According to most authorities, identifying and exploiting a trend is the primary role of

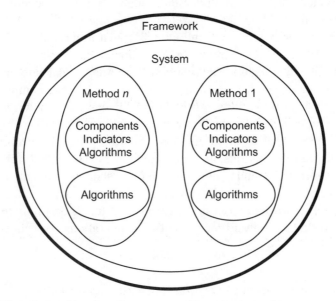

FIGURE 3.1 The relationship of trading system objects is shown here.

technical analysis. It isn't as easy as it once was, however. Trend line analysis in particular has gotten very difficult in recent years because trends are decreasingly occurring in straight lines. Pattern recognition and algorithmic trading are causing trends to take different forms, and their associated momentum to be less visible.

Using a trend's energy is a good thing to do. Trading it successfully increasingly depends on volatility-based support and resistance. But it's not the only way to trade. Many opportunities exist where trends do not, as with the volatility shift method. That does not mean, however, that you should trade against an obvious trend. That type of activity ends badly more often than not.

Time Frame

The volatility-based technical analysis methods and components shown herein are useful for swing trading, position trading, and day trading. They are fractal, and therefore function well across most chart periodicities. The real question for most traders is that of their own personal trading time frame. It's the second-largest potential mistake individual traders can make. Be sure, therefore, to know your trading time frame and execute it consistently.

Aligning the time frame of your analysis methods with your actual trading time frame may seem obvious. Many individuals assume, however, that they are doing so, or trade without even considering this facet of analysis. It's important to give attention to it, since each can be different.

The value of technical analysis is in its predictive qualities. Predictive quality can be gauged in probability. The further forward the number of chart periods (bars, candles, and so forth), the lower the probabilities become. One very specific value of developing your own components is that you understand implicitly their respective forward time period predictive values.

As examples of this, see the chart in Figure 3.2. Featured is a daily MetaSwing chart of Unum Group (UNM). There is more about MetaSwing later in this chapter. An Adeo Long signal is beside Rectangle 1. The function of an Adeo signal is to predict when the price will reverse or pause. It is normally combined with other components within a method to predict high probability reversals. In this case, it's shown in a standalone example so that we can view its predictive time frame.

In a daily chart periodicity, the Adeo has a forward predictive probability range of two to five days. After five periods, its probability declines sharply. Prior to rectangle 1, notice how the short-term trend is down. A brief and shallow reversal occurs, resulting in no more than a pause in the current downtrend. The same happens for an Adeo Short beside rectangle 2. These examples demonstrate that the Adeo predictive time frame, like virtually all technical analysis components, has limitations. Knowing the time frame of your components is essential.

Broad Market Cycle

The prices of most equities in a market tend to move with a high level of correlation to that market's index. Understanding ways to effectively forecast the broad market's

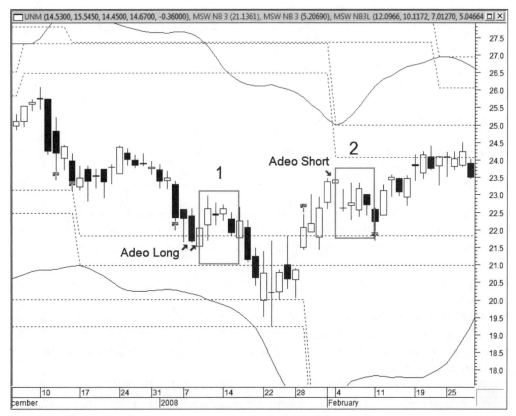

FIGURE 3.2 The predictive value for any technical analysis component is unique to itself, and can usually be measured in a forward quantity of periods.

Chart created in MetaStock. Chart uses the MetaSwing Add-on, by Northington Trading, LLC. All rights reserved.

short-term and intermediate-term swings is a critical part of trading. In fact, I believe that it is the single most important skill a trader can possess. I also believe that ignoring this process is the single largest mistake a trader can make.

Your long and short trading activities, therefore, should be conducted to correspond with the like directions of the broad market. Chapters 8 and 13 of this book deal specifically with this topic. If you do this activity well, it becomes difficult to fail as a trader.

Minimum Time in Market

To have your trading capital in a market position is to have it at risk. Having it in cash involves no risk. Therefore, making 10 percent in a trade that lasts three days should be considered more profitable than the same 10 percent made in six days. "Minimum Time in Market" should be an ongoing operating goal for two reasons.

First is the reality of limited trading capital. A single dollar can be in only one position at a time. If your money is tied up in a position that stretches on too long, then it

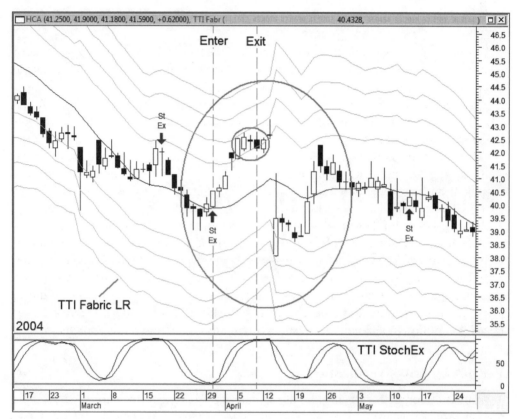

FIGURE 3.3 This example of HCA Corporation (HCA) shows how quickly a winning position can turn into a losing one, and thus emphasizing a minimum time in market philosophy.

Chart created in MetaStock.

is not available for another concurrent opportunity. The second reason is that unforeseen fundamental events happen with regularity. If a single equity or industry analyst gets up on the wrong side of the bed some morning, your existing position can, in a flash, be reversed past your entry point.

There is a daily chart of HCA Corporation (HCA) in Figure 3.3. This chart uses two components created in later chapters to generate trade entry signals. The proper entry and exit days are denoted with vertical dashed lines. Notice the unfortunate gapping price drop on April 14, 2004. This is the penalty the swing trader would pay had he not exited as he should have three or four days earlier; a winning trade would instantly turn into a losing one. This gap occurred without warning because of an analyst downgrade.

Fundamental Information versus Technical Measurement

Fundamental information and chart technical measurements each have an effect on price movement. Unfortunately for the market technician, fundamental news and information is the dominant force. Fundamental will trump technical in virtually all circumstances.

Because of this dominant force, the technical analyst should seek to trade an instrument or security that is undergoing a void of fundamental information. As best possible, seek to ensure that a very quiet news period will persist during the projected time span of the trade. This is another reason to know and adhere to your trading time frame. Avoiding holding a single-sided position during an earnings announcement is the number one precaution you can take.

This is not to say that technical analysis is of no value when fundamentally driven events occur. It is just that technical analysis performed before a fundamental event is of much less value once the event occurs. At that juncture, the analyst must reconsider her previous judgments.

When extreme fundamental events happen, however, large price movements accompany them and usually move toward extremes, which are identified by volatility-based technical analysis. The irony is that when things go really awry, fundamental price measurements are difficult to apply and volatility and statistical probability is what most staunch fundamentalists revert to. This sort of behavior is commonly witnessed during quarterly earnings announcement. The Microsoft example, beginning at Figure 4.2, is an illustration of how fundamental events are driven to use volatility measurements.

Analysis by Cross-Verification

To verify is to confirm or to substantiate something. To cross-verify is to repeat the verification process by using a separately independent means. Technical analysis makes consistent use of the primary time series data, which are the high, low, open, close, and volume. Cross-verification in technical analysis involves performing analysis with the same data but in different ways.

The most common mistake inexperienced traders make is to base decisions on several indicators of the same type. The logic for this is that if one momentum indicator reads oversold, it is three times more meaningful when three momentum indicators say the same thing. This assumption is greatly flawed. In reality, most momentum indicators function very similarly with respect to their internal calculation methods. Therefore, additional signals from similar indicators provide little additional predictive value. A method of proper cross-verification involves using technical measurements of different types, such as support and resistance or trend strength. Since these indicator types calculate their values very differently, their incremental confirming effects add real value.

Think of it in the same way that a global positioning system (GPS) works. It requires a minimum of four different satellite signals for a location to be computed by triangulation. Each satellite is far away from any of the other satellites. It would therefore be useless to have two satellites sitting next to each other. Furthermore, when a GPS receiver adds more satellite signals to its calculation, its accuracy increases. You could then say that the GPS is using a form of cross-verification.

COMPONENT TESTING

I use a process of testing the relative effectiveness of a component in several chapters of this book. The method used produces a simple arithmetic mean, and uses the price data of the S&P 500 Index components. This test process is sufficient for use only during the component development process.

It produces results designed to show a component's individual predictive value when used alone. The results show the component's potential for profit and potential for loss in the form of a raw average. Full details on this book's testing methodology are presented in Chapter 14. This simple average process can be performed by combining the report-generating capabilities of most programmable technical analysis software in combination with Excel. It is quick and simple, and the MetaStock code for it is also presented in Chapter 14.

It is not a substitute for valid statistical back-testing methods. It does not perform any statistical distribution analysis. It is not suitable for use as a basis for trading decisions. Backtesting systems such as Monte Carlo permutation and Bootstrap should be used when whole trading systems and methods are tested.

METASWING QUICKSTART

The majority of this book focuses on the construction of volatility-based technical analysis components and methods. Samples of specific MetaStock function language code are presented for your use in doing so. In fact, as the chapters progress, different components and potential methods are improved and expanded upon.

Consider the average television cooking program. As they make the featured recipe, it is shown throughout the preparation process, ending with the chef showing a finished dish so that the viewer can see how it should turn out.

For this same purpose, the MetaSwing system is featured throughout this book. MetaSwing charts demonstrate a mature and comprehensive volatility-based technical analysis system and framework in action. You should view its charts as one possible outcome of the development processes that you'll be learning in the coming chapters. The MetaSwing system is proprietary; as a bonus for having invested in this book, however, Chapter 13 provides you with the actual source code for the MetaSwing (version 3.2) Correction and Surge components. That source code has never been released before its publication in this book. The timely usage of those components can be very profitable for any trader.

What follows is a short tutorial on MetaSwing. Its major features are discussed and accompanied by examples. This quickstart is not a complete instruction manual for using MetaSwing, but it will get you started. By familiarizing yourself with this system, an important percentage of the volatility-based technical analysis presented in this book will be much more useful to you. If you are more visually inclined, there are also instructional videos that cover much of the same sections that follow. You can access them at www.metaswing.com/htm/tutorials.html. The pages that follow, however, are a quicker way to grasp the content.

N Bands

N Bands consist of lower and upper price bands (or trading bands) that serve as immediate levels of extreme support and resistance, respectively. N Bands are very different, in both composition and usage, from other forms of price bands, such as Bollinger bands, Keltner bands, or standard error bands.

The central defining composition of N Bands is that they quantify a security's most significant level of consolidated implied volatility, as plotted on the stock chart. In short, the N Band is a single price representation of the stock option's implied volatility. The N Band is fractal in nature, so it adapts appropriately across any chart periodicity.

We have in Figure 3.4 a daily chart of PF Chang's China Bistro (PFCB) with upper

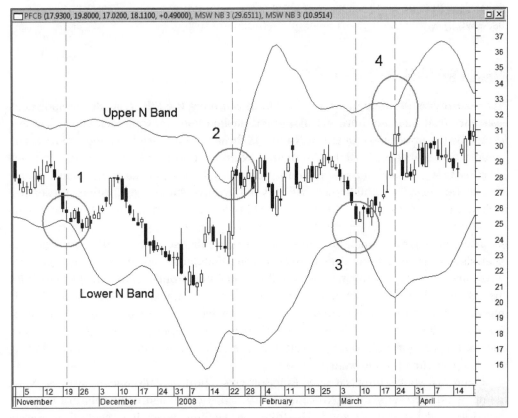

FIGURE 3.4 In this daily chart of PF Chang's China Bistro (PFCB), N Bands demonstrate how they provide immediate levels of support or resistance.

Chart created in MetaStock. Chart uses the MetaSwing Add-on, by Northington Trading, LLC. All rights reserved.

and lower N Bands plotted. The N Band is expressed in the same price units as the Y-axis at right. In circled areas 1 and 2 note how the price pauses and changes direction when it reaches the band. In circled area 4, the price pauses and reverses when it nears the one Average True Range (ATR(40)) area near the lower N Band. In circled area 4, the intraday range reaches the upper N Band resistance and reverses. The key characteristic to remember about N Bands is that the band itself represents immediate support or resistance.

Behavior characteristics include:

- When price approaches the N Band, it usually reverses or pauses.
- Moderate immediate support is reached when price comes within one Average True Range (ATR(40)) of the lower N Band.
- Extreme immediate support is reached when the price touches or crosses the lower N Band.
- The same immediate resistance relationships exist for the upper N Band.
- N Band peaks and troughs form S/R lines, which are future levels of support or resistance.

N Band S/R Lines

N Band S/R lines are hereinafter referred to as S/R lines; the *S/R* stands for support and resistance. S/R lines are horizontally plotted dashed lines on the stock chart, and are formed by the peaks and troughs of N Bands. These lines are used as technical levels of support and resistance. S/R lines function within the concept of Projected Implied Volatility (PIV). This is because they are formed by N Band peaks and troughs, which are key levels of consolidated implied volatility. As such, they project these key levels forward as support and resistance. You will learn more about PIV beginning in Chapter 5.

There are four dominant S/R lines and four matching secondary S/R lines. The four dominant lines are created directly from the two N Band peaks and troughs. The four secondary lines are exactly one unit of ATR(40) distance from its matching primary line. Just as with classic technical analysis support and resistance, each line becomes the opposite when crossed. For example, once crossed decisively, a resistance line functions as a support line. For ease of reference, S/R lines use a simple top-to-bottom numbering system. S/R 1 is formed from the peak of the upper N Band and S/R 3 is formed from the trough of the upper N band, and so on.

Figure 3.5 shows how S/R lines function as support and resistance barriers. Note the price gap across S/R 4 in November 2007. Price continued decisively in the same direction until it met resistance. Also note the trading range that resulted in March between S/R 5 and S/R 6. The other circled areas demonstrate the S/R lines functioning as basic support or resistance.

Behavior characteristics include:

- When price approaches an S/R line, without having done so recently, it usually reverses or pauses.
- Price will also experience periods of consolidation at or between S/R lines.
- Areas between S/R lines frequently form trading ranges, in the short- or intermediate-term time frames.
- Breakouts above S/R 4, or below S/R 5, indicate possible beginning trend formation or continuation.
- When price gaps over an S/R line, it is a signal of additional price momentum in that direction.
- When an S/R line from each of two time frames aligns closely, the line becomes significantly stronger.
- When price sits at or close to an S/R line, combined with other MetaSwing signals, specific trading methods are worth consideration. This is a result of proper cross-verification.

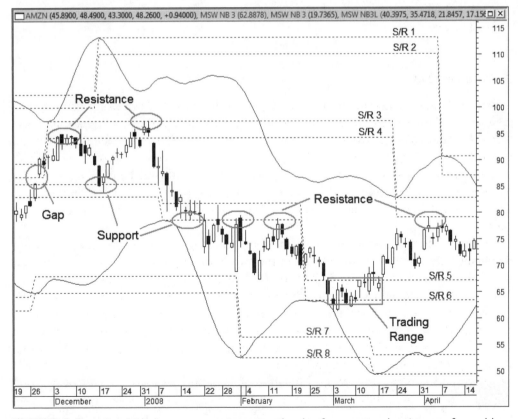

FIGURE 3.5 N Band S/R lines serve as important levels of support and resistance, formed by the forces of recent options implied volatility levels.

Chart created in MetaStock. Chart uses the MetaSwing Add-on, by Northington Trading, LLC. All rights reserved.

Adeo Long and Adeo Short

The Adeo occurs when price is at a place on the chart, at a specific time, where it should not be, as measured using volatility-based calculations. Price is statistically out of bounds. It is very much more than a typical overbought and oversold level. The Adeo is a primary MetaSwing component for reversal trading methods. Figure 3.6 shows a daily chart of Nvidia Corporation (NVDA) during an intermediate decline, a short-term base, and a subsequent intermediate rally. Adeo signals occur at key points during this price movement.

Behavior characteristics include:

- When used concurrently with other MetaSwing components, it can provide a signal of a high probability price reversal, and can thus be used to identify a trade or position entry point.

FIGURE 3.6 In this daily MetaSwing chart of Nvidia Corporation (NVDA), Adeo signals demonstrate their ability to signal short-term reversals and identify trend entry points.

Chart created in MetaStock. Chart uses the MetaSwing Add-on, by Northington Trading, LLC. All rights reserved.

- When used alone, it can serve as a high probability Exit signal for an existing position.
- The forward accuracy range of an Adeo is two to five periods.

Exit Signals

The Exit signal is derived from extreme volatility relationships of two key MetaSwing tandem indicators. The purpose of the Exit signal is to show that further price action in the current direction will be very unpredictable. Once the Exit signal has appeared, most of the profit attainable as a result of a short-term swing has usually been achieved. You will learn much more about how these exits are derived in Chapter 12. In Figure 3.7, volatility-based Exit signals are shown above and below the price candles. When positioned above the candle, it is an Exit Long signal, and those below the candle are Exit Short signals.

FIGURE 3.7 Volatility-based Exit signals contribute heavily toward closing short-term positions and capturing as much of the potential profit as is possible.

Chart created in MetaStock. Chart uses the MetaSwing Add-on, by Northington Trading, LLC. All rights reserved.

Behavior characteristics include:

- It can serve alone as a high probability Exit signal for an existing position. They should normally be used with other MetaSwing components for best results, however.
- When used concurrently with other MetaSwing components it can provide a signal of a high probability price reversal and thus be used as a trade or position entry point.

DLRL-DSRS Indicators

MetaSwing comprises over 15 different technical oscillators. Some are used directly by the user. Most are used internally as inputs to neural algorithms. Most of them function as indicator pairs, along a unique tandem construct. The indicator pair forms opposing measurements that identify an oversold or overbought condition, and then gauge its severity relative to historical levels. Together, the pair confirms to identify a true extreme level.

Figure 3.8 shows how the DLRL-DSRS indicator pair works together. The DLRL indicator is the solid line and measures the oversold level of price. The DSRS indicator is the dotted line and measures the overbought level of price. They each read a positive for their respective signal types when the indicator value falls below the zero line. The upper end of the Y-axis is unlimited and unfettered. The lower end of the Y-axis is very rigid at or just below zero; the indicator will not go far below zero.

One is not considered extremely oversold or overbought, however, unless the other is reading high levels relative to recent peaks of itself. Since both work together to confirm extreme levels, this indicator pair is called a Tandem Construct. For an example of the DLRL-DSRS Tandem indicators applied to a stock chart, consult Figure 7.17 and its descriptive narrative.

MetaSwing® DLRL-DSRS Tandem Construct

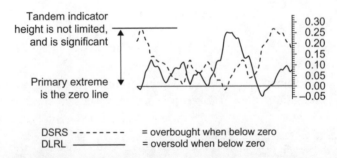

FIGURE 3.8 The DLRL-DSRS Tandem Construct indicators produce more reliable oversold and overbought readings because of their dual nature and their basis of pure volatility-based algorithms.

Chart created in MetaStock. Chart uses the MetaSwing Add-on, by Northington Trading, LLC. All rights reserved.

Behavior characteristics include:

- It identifies a true and relative, extreme oversold and overbought price level.
- The DLRL-DSRS indicators are trend compensated to work well during trending conditions.
- The DLRL measures extreme, or *true* oversold, when it is below zero and the DSRS is at its high or higher for the previous three to six months. The respective relationship exists for overbought conditions.
- When the MetaSwing Divine oversold indicator also reads below zero, the DLRL oversold reading is additionally confirmed. The Divine indicator will often lag the DLRL by two or three periods. The respective relationship exists for overbought conditions.

Correction and Surge Signals

MetaSwing Correction and Surge signals are extreme market breadth signals based on a proprietary ratio. The Correction signal in particular will help you to quickly exit long positions before profits turn into losses. These signals help you understand the likely trading direction the broader market will take in the coming days or weeks. Each of the two major U.S. stock exchanges, the NYSE and the NASDAQ, has Correction and Surge signals. When the same signal occurs on both exchanges, it is considered a Total Correction or Total Surge signal.

These extreme selling or buying days are the market's way of telling you that a potential change in direction is happening. The entirety of Chapter 13 is devoted to Correction and Surge signals. You are presented in Chapter 13 with the MetaSwing (version 3.2) source code for Correction and Surge signals. This source code has never before been released. This system is also important for understanding the intermediate-term market direction. Figure 3.9 gives you an example of these signals in action.

Correction signal behavior characteristics include:

- The signal is most significant and potent when no other Correction signals have occurred for at least 15 days.
- The Total Correction event has much greater predictive value than the individual NYSE or NASDAQ Correction events.
- The higher the close between the N Bands on the day of the Correction event, the greater the potential for downward price action in subsequent days.
- When a Surge signal appears immediately after a Correction signal, the short-term market direction is unclear.

Surge signal behavior characteristics include:

- If the Surge event occurs after an intermediate-market downtrend, then strongly consider finding exit points for any short positions you currently hold.

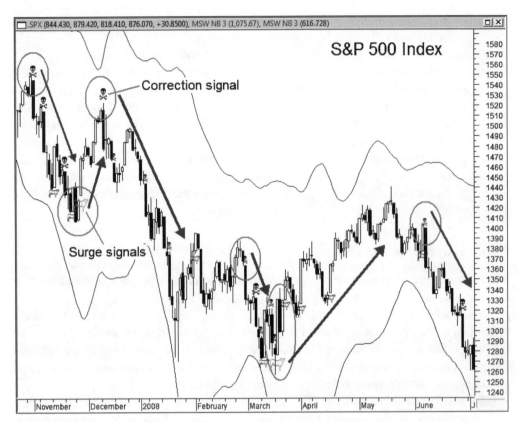

FIGURE 3.9   The circled signals and arrows in this chart of the S&P 500 Index show how
Correction and Surge signals help you forecast the broad market intermediate-
term trading direction.

Chart created in MetaStock. Chart uses the MetaSwing Add-on, by Northington
Trading, LLC. All rights reserved.

- Wait after a downtrend for a second surge event to confirm that a current
  intermediate-term bottom may be forming. Make sure that the recent Surge signals
  outnumber recent Correction signals. In other words, wait for there to be two Surge
  signals that are more recent than the most recent Correction signal. They also need
  to be relatively close together.
- The more predictive of higher prices to come the Surge signal is, the lower its position between the N Bands. This is because PIV and volatility-based support is closer,
  and thus resistance is further away.
- Consider trend strength to be the most important technical measurement once two
  successive Surge events have occurred; use a three-day periodicity for this.
- Unlike Correction signals, a stock's oversold technical reading can be important for
  short-term trading.

- Unlike Correction signals, time is not of the essence for Surge signals. Carefully choose a stock that has been showing signs of strength during the previous downtrend.
- During a bull market, if the Surge signal occurs while the market has been experiencing an intermediate-term uptrend, then consider it a continuation signal.

Trend Strength

The MetaSwing Trend Strength component is referred to in this book as TTI Trend Strength. Its purpose is to confirm the likelihood of a trend beginning, or when it may be coming to an end. This indicator is used as a confirming component in several trading methods, the most common of which is trend following.

TTI Trend Strength is also used as an indicator pair, although the pair is not an opposing construct. The pair is used instead to confirm each other. One component of the pair uses a 10-period partial lookback, and the other uses a 20-period partial lookback. You will learn more about this indicator in Chapter 6, where it is introduced. For an example of TTI Trend Strength, examine its use in Figure 3.10.

Behavior characteristics include:

- The actual numerical value of TTI Trend Strength is unimportant. The method for interpreting it is to examine a 20-period linear regression analysis of it. The positive or negative readings are derived from the positive or negative readings of the slope of the 20-period linear regression line plot.
- If both lines have positive slopes, then its logic is positive for an upward trend presence.
- If both lines have negative slopes, then its logic is positive for a downward trend presence.
- This indicator should be used in conjunction with S/R lines for trend confirmation.
- When stocks are experiencing strong trend rallies, this indicator will usually warn with negative readings just ahead of the trend's end.

Putting It All Together

MetaSwing is a comprehensive system and framework that enables volatility-based technical analysis to work for swing traders, position traders, and intraday traders. It relies heavily on a strong framework methodology that uses cross-verification by multiple components within a trading method. You will learn much more about the Framework in Chapter 6.

Figure 3.10 shows an example of a simple Adeo long trade method for a possible beginning trend breakout. The chart depicts a daily MetaSwing plot of Aaron Rents (RNT). This method serves as swing trade or a position trade for trend following. For

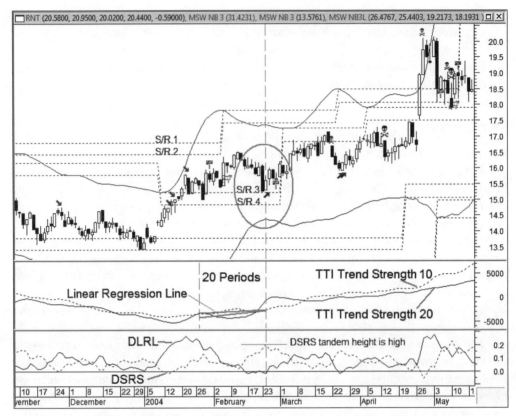

FIGURE 3.10   This daily MetaSwing chart illustrates how several different components of volatility-based technical analysis are used with cross-verification to produce a profitable long trade.

Chart created in MetaStock. Chart uses the MetaSwing Add-on, by Northington Trading, LLC. All rights reserved.

support of the trade's entry point decision, here are the more basic individual points of analysis logic that can be derived from this chart.

- The circled area shows an Adeo long signal occurring the day after the price closes right at the S/R 3 support line on February 24, 2004.
- Price has recently gapped up and traded straight through resistance at S/R 3 and S/R 4, indicating a probable change in trading direction. Research may show some fundamental reason for this. It is a classic sign of long side demand.
- In the center indicator pane, both components of the TTI Trend Strength are showing positive slope values. There are 20-period linear regression lines plotted over the indicator lines for illustrative purposes between the two vertical dashed lines.
- In the bottom indicator pane, the DLRL oversold component (solid line) level is below zero. The opposing tandem component, the DSRS (dashed line), is showing

a high reading relative to its recent levels. These two conditions confirm an extreme oversold condition for the short term.

DISCOVER BY DOING

It is my wish that when you finish this book you will know volatility-based technical analysis. I don't mean understand or recognize it when you see it; I mean really know it. I want it to be a part of you and your success.

Vince Lombardi, arguably the greatest football coach of all time, said this:

I firmly believe that any man's finest hour, the greatest fulfillment of all that he holds dear, is that moment when he has worked his heart out in a good cause and lies exhausted on the field of battle—victorious.

This quote and his other beliefs teach us that to succeed, total commitment is required. Our "field of battle" is the market in which we trade. The people we compete with are the best in the world. To truly succeed, you must achieve successive personal bests.

The time to begin actual development of your own indicators is now, right here at the completion of this chapter. The remainder of this book is devoted to creating and implementing volatility components within programmable technical analysis software. The best way for you to learn this process is by doing. If you don't already have software installed on your computer, then I recommend getting some to use while you finish this book. In doing so, you will be able to gradually see mathematical chart components take shape right before your eyes, not just on the printed page.

The list of responsible vendors is more than sufficient. These packages normally install easily over an Internet download. Here is a partial list:

- MetaStock
- TradeStation
- eSignal
- NeuroShell
- Wealth-Lab

The indicators developed herein are shown coded in the MetaStock function language. Appendix A depicts these same components written in TradeStation EasyLanguage code. You will find there the actual EasyLanguage code along with explanations of its execution particular to the TradeStation platform.

A special arrangement for access to MetaStock software has been created for this book's readers. At this book's companion web site, www.tradingtheinvisible.com, you will find links and a web page giving you the details. There is also a special offering page with details in the back of this book. This special offer provides you with an opportunity to concurrently use MetaStock software while exploring the volatility-based components that we learn in Parts Two and Three. A hands-on experience with programmable technical analysis software should greatly enhance your endeavors to leverage volatility.

I encourage you to turn comprehension into action. Parts Two and Three will demonstrate price action in ways that larger institutional players see it. I hope you enjoy it and use it.

PART TWO

Seeing
the Invisible

I once visited a specialty tire manufacturing plant that made tires for the NASA space shuttle. Upon landing, the shuttle's maximum weight can be 230,000 pounds. At the exact point of touchdown, the shuttle is traveling at 215 mph. The cost to build a space shuttle is virtually incalculable.

There was a display of an actual space shuttle tire in the lobby of this plant. Ordinary automobile tires are embossed with their maintenance specifications at the tire's rim section. Even on the space shuttle tire, there were small raised letters all around the rim with technical specifications. At one point in the text, it read "Maximum of Two Landings."

This proves one thing for sure. If nerdy, pocket-pencil-holder-wearing design engineers can have a sense humor that good, then certainly you have the ability to create your own volatility-based technical components. All you need are some fresh concepts and a cheat sheet.

The chapters that follow in Part Two should present you with ways to examine price movement that are likely new to you. They will encourage you to expand your understanding of the underlying arithmetic that drives potentially new and innovative indicators.

In Chapter 6 you will be furnished with the cheat sheet we call the Framework. It represents a proven way to employ cross-verification for all of your creativity. Who knows, you may even feel compelled to purchase your first pocket-pencil holder.

CHAPTER 4

New Volatility Indicator Design

D o you know what a sandpiper and successful trader have in common? This is not a jest, or a trick question. Before Part Two of this book is done, you will understand their common ground.

The lowly little sanderling, a type of beach-dwelling sandpiper, stands just four to eight inches tall. This small bird eats by dodging the surf and digging up tiny marine life at the water's edge. Even a very small wave is much taller than the sanderling, and this little guy can only see the next wave in front of him.

Its challenge is to gauge when to run out there into the dangerous crashing waves, and then do it without hesitation; the water will not pause for the convenience of a simple little bird. The waves come in regularly, then recede to reveal all the little aquatic invertebrates on which it feeds. The best food is the furthest out, nearest to the greatest wave height. Timing is everything!

Watch a sanderling a bit longer and you notice something even more incredible than their innate sense of wave timing. They know exactly how far to go into the surf's receding wave to dig for the best food, then dart back toward shore just ahead of the next incoming wall of bird-bone-breaking water. Think about it. They know the farthest point that can be reached before they need to turn around and come back, all the while achieving a successful bite of food necessary for sustaining another 10 minutes of life on the beach. This bird does this over and over, all day long.

Does this challenge sound familiar? When to move? How far to go? When to get out? These are all critical choices we make each time we trade. If you could make these decisions as flawlessly while trading as the sandpiper does while eating, would not riches be just around the next bend? But how does the bird do it?

Each wave comes in at a different height with varying levels of stored energy, which propel it toward the beach. But there is much more to consider if you want to get really scientific about it. After a succession of incoming waves, there is a surplus of water rushing back to sea, and thus opposing the effectiveness of the next wave. Our little feathered friend on the beach is so good at gauging all of these factors that he is actually measuring *volatility*.

Yes, somewhere in that tiny brain is a volatility computer. It's measuring all of the factors mentioned, plus more that we probably don't comprehend. The sandpiper's computational ability is able to calculate, based on what has been happening all around him, just where the next wave will break. He observes the past and predicts the future very accurately. Perhaps most importantly, the bird knows that the best food is to be had at the extremes. That is to say, the best eating is when the sea has receded the farthest.

This last concept is one that most technical traders overlook very often. The middle ground is safe but there is not much there to eat. It's out near the edge of perceived danger that the most money can be made. Maybe Wall Street should be recruiting sandpipers instead of quantitative analysts and traders.

VOLATILITY UNMASKED

We are going to begin this foray into volatility by bringing the subject of volatility down to earth. Volatility can be very complex and frightening, or it can be quite simple and easy to work with. We will be using in this book the latter version. Take a look at the following equation. It is a mathematical calculation of past volatility as expressed in calculus.

$$\sigma_T = \sigma\sqrt{T}$$

This is the first and last time you will see an equation expressed as calculus in this book. Not that there's anything wrong with calculus. It's quite useful and necessary for a great many tasks. An overwhelming majority of the people walking the earth, however, have no functional knowledge of calculus. The wonderful news is that you don't need to have ever touched calculus to perform volatility calculations. A successful completion of most high school math curriculums is all that's needed. To be specific, we will be using a few specific math concepts and calculations such as:

- Standard Deviation
- Percentage
- Mean (or Average)
- Logarithm
- Linear Regression

So then, let's suffice it to say that we will leave the advanced mathematics, calculus and such, to the highly paid quantitative analysts. We will instead take advantage of our advanced technical analysis and charting software, such as MetaStock or TradeStation, to kick in these calculations where necessary.

STANDARD DEVIATION

Set an objective for yourself. Try to spend not more than a day researching and defining *volatility* in the world of finance. Your goal is to find and produce a single definition. Good luck, because there really isn't just one.

It seems like there should be. Everyone talks about it and uses the term. When listening to financial news programs we all hear "volatility this" and "volatility that" as though it were a well-defined indication method. In truth, volatility is more of a concept applied to whatever the task at hand needs it to be. So conceptually, volatility as it applies to a tradable instrument is just a measurement of an instrument's price, in terms of rise or fall, within a given time frame.

Historical Volatility (also referred to as *Statistical Volatility*) is a measure of movement within a given period of time. Historical volatility is normally measured using forms of standard deviation and is expressed in terms of *percent*. We commonly refer to the given period of time as the *lookback period*. For the purposes of this book, we will use Historical Volatility and Statistical Volatility interchangeably. When one looks at the actual math calculation for standard deviation, the logic is fairly obvious. In plain people language, the standard deviation just tells you how much a bunch of number values *deviated* from the average of the bunch of numbers. This sounds simple, and it is. What is surprising, however, is how powerful this calculation really is.

While the software tools we commonly use in technical analysis do an enormous number of great math functions for us in the blink of an eye, the standard deviation is so centrally important to our thought process that it is important to give the conscious and subconscious mind a clear view of the actual calculation. Let's consider an example.

Standard Deviation Calculation: Relevant Data

x = one day's closing price of a stock

$\text{avg}(x)$ = the mean of all the stock's closing prices for a set of days

n = the number of days in the set

Let's assume that there are 20 trading days of closing price data to use in our example. Our objective is to compute the most common measure of historical volatility looking back at that period of time.

Calculation Steps

1. For each daily closing price, subtract the average of all 20 days of closing prices from that day's closing price.

2. Multiply the result of step 1 by itself; in math terms, square that value.

3. Add up all 20 squared values.

4. Divide the sum of the squared values by the number of values less one. In this case, it would be 19; thus $20 - 1 = 19$. Some methods call for using the entire value, but this is the most common.

5. Find the square root of this averaged value.

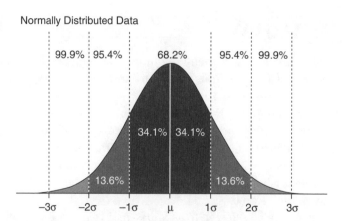

Normally Distributed Data

FIGURE 4.1   This shows standard deviations of normally distributed data.

Presto! That's the standard deviation.

Take a look at step 2. This is the most important step, from the standpoint of volatility indicator design. Step 2 squares the difference between each single value and the mean. This simple step magnifies the value that is most deviant to an even greater value than it already is. It gives the most weight to values that are the farthest from the average. By doing so, it identifies the extreme; it makes visible the fringes. Remember that it is at the extremes where the most money is to be made. Train yourself to think that way.

It may be helpful to think of standard deviation in a slightly different way. Ask yourself the question, "What does standard deviation do for me?" To answer this, first examine Figure 4.1. This is a diagram of a common bell curve expressing a distribution of data samples. It shows that if all the data samples were derived randomly, then the standard deviation calculation can accurately predict the percentage of samples that will be within one standard deviation of the mean. In fact, as the number of standard deviations increases, then the quantity of samples that fall outside of the respective standard deviations becomes quite small. The percentages are listed across the top of Figure 4.1.

For a more applicable example, consider 100 days of stock closing prices. Next, plot a moving average line of those 100 days of prices. This assumes that there are at least 100 more days of price data prior to the oldest sample. Then plot another line above that one, which is equal to the moving average plus one standard deviation. Because it is one single standard deviation, then normally 68.2 percent of the closing prices will fall below this second line plot. Do you see the value of it now? Using this calculation, we can begin to calculate probabilities of how high or low a stock price, or indicator, will likely reach. In other applications, we can measure just how far out of bounds a price or value is.

For a simple statistical calculation, this sure seems like a lot adding, subtracting, multiplying, and dividing, not to mention square rooting. That's because it is. Technical analysis usually involves a ton of raw arithmetic calculations. A single chart can contain enough calculations that it would require a human with a calculator months to complete. Computers, fortunately, just love to perform math, and all the trader has to do is type

FIGURE 4.2 A daily chart of Microsoft (MSFT) showing the value of a single 20-period standard deviation, and the 20-period simple moving average it is based on.

Chart created in MetaStock.

the following into technical analysis software. Here is the MetaStock Function Language Statement for Standard Deviation:

```
Stdev(C, 20)
```

Now that we know what standard deviation is, let's take a look at it in action. Depicted in Figure 4.2 is a daily chart of MSFT. The chart is loaded with data ending on 12/31/2007. The standard deviation on that ending date is 1.03016. In the lower pane is the indicator with the standard deviation function code shown previously. The *20* value in the code statement defines the lookback period as 20 trading periods, which would approximate the number of trading days in December.

There is a simple moving average in the upper pane shown for the purpose of clarity. That indicator line is also simple to create in MetaStock:

```
Mov(C, 20, S)
```

Internal to the standard deviation function is a moving average calculation equal to this line. As we examine the standard deviation indicator line, it's easy to see how the sudden price jump at the end of October affected the 20-period volatility reading. Since the price deviated from the mean by a significant amount, the corresponding reading of volatility also increases. Also note that movement above the average, a positive direction, or below the average, a negative direction, both produce an increase in standard deviation.

This simple math is fun, but what does it tell us about trading Microsoft (MSFT)? Notice that in the first half of October the price candles are much smaller than after the large gap up on 10/26. After that date, the average daily trading range increases, showing wider intraday price ranges. Also, prices begin to trade in up or down directions from the previous day's close. Microsoft required a week or more before the breakout to increase or decrease in price by more than 2 percent.

Prices don't move themselves. Traders move prices through the forces of supply and demand. After the breakout day, buyers outnumber sellers for a solid week. The drastic rate of change of the volatility created uncertainty in the minds of some very big money traders. It's easier for a sole swimmer doing the backstroke to tow an aircraft carrier than for an individual trader to move the price of Microsoft's stock.

Lastly, even once Microsoft's price reverts back to its mean, the daily trading range is noticeably wider. Traders are still jittery and constantly on the lookout for another sudden price move. Not wanting to miss out on a great profit opportunity, with virtually no liquidity risk, many traders take positions that are premature and doomed to fizzle or stop out.

But wait, is it really this simple? Can the pure math calculations of a statistical measure such as standard deviation give us all the trading advantage we really need? The answer is Yes and No. Remember first that the ability of this calculation to be accurate about its percentages relies on the data samples being normal, or pretty much random. The fly in the soup is that the price movement of traded securities is not random or normal. So if a predictable distribution of the data relies on randomly generated price data, our goose is cooked, right? Actually, we'll be okay because volatility measurement more accurately tracks human behavior than any other type of algorithm. And since humans and their emotions are the culprits in this nonrandom price behavior, our ability to predict the markets remains quite realistic.

If there are any true believers of Random Walk theory reading this book, right now it would be great to have a magic volatility indicator that measures how hard eyes can be rolled. If you can be sure of one thing intensely, it is that stock prices are influenced heavily by forces of supply and demand, and most appearances of random movement are not at all random. This has been proven definitively with volatility-based and mean-reversion-based testing.[1]

As to the question two paragraphs before this one, the answer to the question is No because price movement is routinely heavily manipulated by any number of interested parties for any number of reasons. If it were not so, then possibly a few algorithms would suffice to make a fortune trading the markets in relatively short order. Thus, price movement would then be truly normal and random; and I had lunch with the tooth fairy last week. The answer is Yes, because so many of these artificial price movement influences are measurable by volatility-based calculations. We will explore the thought processes and techniques necessary to validate the Yes answer in coming chapters.

EXAMPLE: VOLATILITY-BASED SUPPORT AND RESISTANCE

While these market-moving traders are being influenced by volatility measurements, it's not simple standard deviation that determines which side of the market they'd prefer. As stated previously, there are many ways to compute price volatility. More important, there are many ways to look at price movement using volatility calculations. We have focused to this point on a simple method of calculating volatility. Let's take a glimpse into your future and focus on the results of more advanced methods of volatility calculations. It's very important to note that the explanation to follow is far ahead of our progress into volatility tools. We have more basics to explore. I think you will enjoy understanding, however, that there will be ways within your grasp to identify those invisible price targets that enormous Wall Street players seem to magically know ahead of time. Yes, there is a pot of gold at the end of the volatility rainbow.

Take another look at Figure 4.2. On October 26th, why did price jump all the way up to 36.02 at the opening and then settle to close at 35.03? Why that closing price? Why not close at 33.50 or 41.25, or some other price point?

There was a frenzy of exciting information about Microsoft before the market opened that convinced traders that a majority of other traders were going to be convinced that the share price of Microsoft was going to rise significantly. They had a solid reason to bet serious money that a long position in Microsoft would ride a rising price wave and sell with a profit. With that truth determined, the last question the trader has to answer is, "How high is too high?" The trader wants to enter a long position, but so do many other traders. At what price would it be too high? Or maybe the best way to ask this question is, "How high is up?"

Let's look at Microsoft charts with the aid of more advanced volatility measurements to answer this. This is closer to what the large institutional trading firms were studying that morning of October 26th. Figure 4.3 shows a chart from MetaSwing, which is a volatility-based technical analysis trading system. Specifically Figure 4.3 is a chart set to a three-day periodicity; that is to say, each price candle represents three days. It shows the chart image as created after the market closed on October 25, 2007, the day preceding the breakout. Again, it's important to point out that this example is ahead of our discussion of volatility measurement tools.

The upper trading band in Figure 4.3 shows resistance for the current point in time. In MetaSwing, this is called the N Band. It is a measurement of volatility. The dashed lines that extend forward from the band are indicators of key levels of implied volatility. I discuss implied volatility in detail later. For now, just understand that these implied volatility lines represent key hidden, invisible if you will, levels of support and resistance.

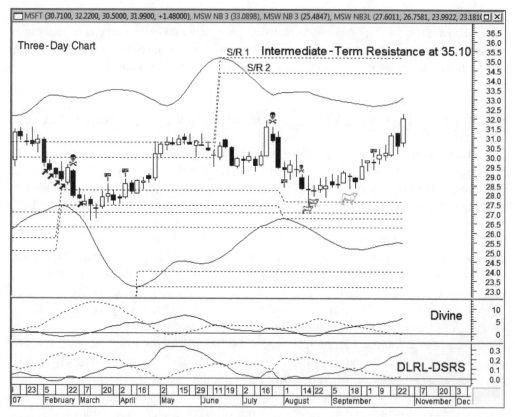

FIGURE 4.3 This view of Microsoft (MSFT) uses a three-day periodicity and identifies the outermost resistance at 35.10.

Chart created in MetaStock. Chart uses the MetaSwing Add-on, by Northington Trading, LLC. All rights reserved.

We will therefore refer to them as S/R lines. The top S/R line (S/R 1) in Figure 4.3 signifies that resistance in a three-day time frame exists at 35.10. Large institutional firms do not regularly trade in a traditional swing trading time frame of 2 to 10 days. With that in mind, we need to look at longer time frames as well.

Volatility measurement crosses multiple time frames. That's because volatility is in itself price movement across a time period. Therefore, where prices can be reasonably expected to move a maximum x distance, based on historical volatility over a week, they can be expected to produce a different maximum movement over a month. The relationship of movement across different time frames is nonlinear. Therefore the relationship of volatility measurement across different time frames is nonlinear. If it were not so, we wouldn't need to measure differing time frames.

Figure 4.4 shows the same chart view in a weekly time frame. In this longer time frame, key resistance is observed at 35.53, which is not that far from 35.10. This gives a strong degree of confirmation of resistance at a fairly tight price level. In looking out

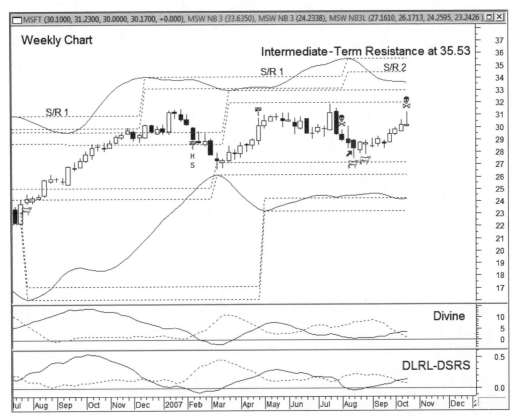

FIGURE 4.4 Within this weekly chart periodicity, Microsoft (MSFT) demonstrates an extreme resistance level of 35.53, which is virtually the same as the three-day time frame.

Chart created in MetaStock. Chart uses the MetaSwing Add-on, by Northington Trading, LLC. All rights reserved.

even further, Figure 4.5 shows us MSFT on a monthly periodicity chart. There is a significant difference in the distance to this resistance level, however, as indicated by the upper N Band. Remember that the N Band is a volatility measurement and provides an immediate indication of resistance for the current period. The monthly time frame indicates upper resistance at 37.21. This difference between 35.10 and 37.21 is a possible opportunity zone.

At this point of our analysis we have identified key levels of potential support and resistance. But the challenge before the trader on the morning of October 26th is in figuring out what to do with this information. There is little doubt that the opening price of MSFT will gap up. The trader must decide at what price she will buy and at what price she will sell. An important concept here is that a support or resistance line is just that: either support or resistance. If trading is transacting below the S/R line, then the S/R line signifies resistance, and vice versa for support. Obviously then, it's impossible to know

FIGURE 4.5 The monthly chart shows a long-term resistance at the upper N Band.

Chart created in MetaStock. Chart uses the MetaSwing Add-on, by Northington Trading, LLC. All rights reserved.

exactly what will happen at the open of the trading day, but it is important to know what should be done in specific possible scenarios. Therein lies one of the most important truths for traders: A trader does not control what happens in a market; he can only react to it.

Finally, Figure 4.6 shows the actual outcome of the trading that transpired with MSFT on a daily chart. Superimposed on this daily version of our original chart are the levels of implied volatility support and resistance. We measured these S/R levels on the charts from the other three time frames, which were three-day, weekly, and monthly. On the open, the price did indeed gap to a level above both shorter-term S/R levels. Once MSFT opened at 36.02, most of the institutional market participants felt that this price was a bit too high. This is because price was above the shorter-term S/R levels of 35.10 and 35.53. Traders wanting long positions likely scaled in with multiple orders as price dropped through the morning. Many with preexisting long positions want simultaneously to take some profits. This results in more net selling than buying interest, and thus price falls from the open. In this case, MSFT is trading above the S/R lines, which makes them

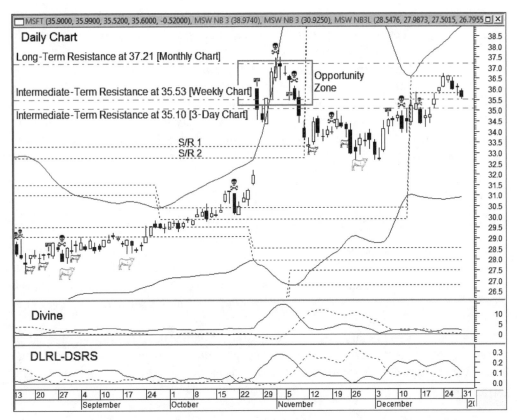

FIGURE 4.6 Microsoft (MSFT) goes on to trade within the previously identified support and resistance levels.

Chart created in MetaStock. Chart uses the MetaSwing Add-on, by Northington Trading, LLC. All rights reserved.

automatically representative of support. They were resistance on the previous day, but on 10/26/07 they become support.

As the price chart shows, the bulls outnumbered bears when the day ended, even though MSFT traded down from the open to close at 35.03. It's impossible to know for sure, but it's likely that large market participants that previously held long positions sold and took profits, only to reenter long positions when price settled back down to support.

In the days that follow, MSFT goes on to trade off of these levels of shorter- and longer-term support and resistance as defined by volatility calculations. Indeed, when its price reaches the level of extreme monthly resistance, as determined by the volatility-based N Band, the bears take over and go on to erase much of the first day's euphoric price jump. This example shows the importance of specific levels of hidden support and resistance. These levels are consistently identified with mathematic algorithms, which focus on a variety of methods to measure the volatility of price movement. This is how Wall Street trades because it is equipped with volatility-based tools; and it's how you should trade as well.

This event analysis shows just how important volatility measurement is when determining trading prices for specific stocks. As stated in previous chapters, volatility measurement is the key to the technical measurement of stock price levels since 2001. This is because actual stock trading is the junior component to stock option trading. The market of stock option trading largely determines the underlying stock's price. The price of an option's premium is determined by measurements of historical and implied volatility. While trading equities seems simplistic, it is in reality manipulated by much more sophisticated markets. You may think you are playing checkers but in reality you are playing chess.

AVERAGE TRUE RANGE

There is another very useful way to measure volatility. The actual trading range that occurs within a day can tell you only just so much. For example, the high minus the low gives a distance across a single trading period. This certainly gives you an idea of the movement a stock may experience in a single day. It's helpful for many different considerations, but is it enough?

Fortunately, a technical analyst of keen intellect named J. Welles Wilder created an extremely helpful method of expressing recent daily trading ranges known as the Average True Range, hereinafter referred to as ATR.[2] In this measurement, a single period's movement is defined as True Range. It is the greatest of:

- The distance from today's high to today's low
- The distance from yesterday's close to today's high
- The distance from yesterday's close to today's low

You can graphically view the three possible high and low relationships in Figure 4.7. True range has the ability to measure the movement of an upward trending, a downward trending, and a gapping price movement. It's this flexible methodology that gives it strength in a much shorter time frame than that of historical volatility. Also, the ability to encompass the movement attributed to gap opening is something that many indicators lack.

Knowing the range for a single day is not of much value, thus the *Average* component of ATR converts a single day's measurement to any particular time period that is significant. A simple moving average of the True Range component produces Average True Range. For example, if the True Range of today is three, and the True Range of the previous two days were five and four, then the ATR over the past three days equals approximately four. Most technical analysis software programs feature ATR as a standard function. The MetaStock Function Language Statement for Average True Range is:

ATR(14)

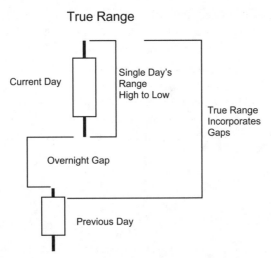

FIGURE 4.7 This diagram of True Range shows how the method incorporates gapping price action.

This will calculate the Average True Range for the past 14 trading periods. At this point, it is important to point out some potential differences in how ATR can be calculated. The original method created by Welles Wilder used a smoothing component in the average; it was not a simple moving average. The MetaStock ATR() function uses the original Welles Wilder smoothing method. If we were to write a pure simple moving average of true range in MetaStock, it would look like this:

```
Mov(ATR(1), 3, S)
```

Writing the calculation this way identifies a True Range, and then calculates a pure three-day simple moving average. You will find that this second method produces wider swings in its readings. In Appendix A both methods for this calculation will be detailed in TradeStation EasyLanguage code. We will be using the original Welles Wilder smoothing method for ATR for the balance of the chapters in this book. It is important for your own personal development to use one method of ATR calculation consistently, without variation.

The ATR calculation returns a value that expresses actual price movement. An indicated value of 1.65 therefore is equal to $1.65. In terms of a comparative gauge of volatility, however, 1.65 of average daily trading range in a stock trading at $16.00 per share is over 10 percent. If the stock is trading at $160.00 per share, then the range is only 1 percent. Certainly those two scenarios present quite different pictures with regard to expected price movement or volatility measurement.

To give a more significant and consistent meaning to an ATR indication, it's best to normalize it. This is easily done by dividing the ATR value by the underlying stock closing price. As a side note, the closing price will almost always give a sufficiently normalized

FIGURE 4.8 This daily chart of Kosan Bioscience (KOSN) demonstrates the benefits of using ATR when it is normalized by the closing price.

Chart created in MetaStock.

reading. Using the high, low, open, or even midpoint price produces little to no advantage in ATR calculations. Take a look at Figure 4.8 for a comparison of these two different methods of ATR presentation.

As you can see in Figure 4.8, volatility changes are clearly visible with the ATR indicator. In the lower pane, the pure ATR value is presented for a lookback period of 14 days. It shows the actual price movement. As a trader uses this form of the measurement, however, she will have to adjust her basis of reference each time she changes the chart to another symbol. In the middle pane, the ATR indicator is modified to normalize it to reflect the price movement in whole percentage points. A reading of 6.2 is therefore equal to 6.2 percent. This creates a consistent method for viewing ATR from chart to chart, regardless of the underlying issue's price.

The MetaStock Function Language Statement for Average True Range Normalized by Closing Price is:

```
(ATR(14) / C) * 100
```

MOLDING A VOLATILITY-BASED INDICATOR

Which part of the sandpiper's brain do you suppose computes wave standard deviation and average true wave range? Would it be two separate areas, or just one general volatility-computing subsection? Or is this why they tend to run around the beach in groups, such that there is one math-whiz sandpiper among the group that paid attention in class? That has the makings of a very expensive federally funded government research study.

Fortunately, we as traders don't need to calculate either of these functions in our heads, but suppose you could. That would really free your mind to think of the incremental effects of volatility measurement in terms of time, distance, logic, or general market conditions. We would not need to turn to the calculator, the spreadsheet, or the charting and technical analysis software for every curiosity of cause and effect. It would be much like learning a second language to the point that you begin to think in that language as well as your first one. And there you have it; you need to be able to think and see volatility-based reasoning when you look at a stock chart.

Instead of a computer screen filled with candlesticks, or patterns with statistically diminished predictive values, you will be able to see the candle at the right edge of the chart that is in an area where it just should not be. Before getting to that point, however, you need to let your brain train the synapses for this type of activity. This tends to be a creative process. It's one where you will need to think of your technical analysis software as a canvas, and of volatility measurement equations as the paint palette.

Let's make an indicator. In doing so, we would be served best to make the most useful kind of indicator, an original one that no one else is using. The best way to begin the process of creating volatility-based indicators with a genuine predictive value is to clearly identify a goal or objective. Let's be clear about this statement. The only types of technical analysis indicators that are of any value are those with predictive qualities. Some are indicators that have no predictive value alone, but are components and meant to be combined with others to create a predictive outcome. These are necessary, too. It is actually detrimental to the trader's success for him to regularly use indicators without predictive value and whose only value is to quantify what has already happened. Other than the obvious result of making poor trading decisions, regularly studying charts with these ineffective technical indicators and methods dilutes anyone's ability to develop and maintain consistency of judgment during ever-changing market conditions.

Historically, technical indicators tend to fall into different categories. Each category has its own purpose and strengths. Here are some of the most commonly accepted classifications.

- Trend sensing
- Overbought and oversold
- Momentum
- Volume
- Support and resistance
- Accumulation and distribution

FIGURE 4.9   This chart shows obvious points of short-term reversals that we would like to identify in advance.

Chart created in MetaStock.

Let's begin with the goal of creating an indicator that enables us to forecast short-term price reversals. Once completed, this indicator will likely fall into the category of Overbought and oversold. We should also be able to use this indicator to generate short-term buy-and-sell signals. We will give this indicator the name of TTI ATR Extreme (ATREx). All original indicators shown in this book will contain the prefix of TTI, which stands for Trading The Invisible.

It's easy to visually pick out the high points and low points in Figure 4.9. Isn't it amazing how easy it is to see them once they have already happened? It looks so easy. This chart shows what looks to be obvious high and low points for a daily chart of INTU in 2006. Spend a few minutes looking at the chart.

The first thought I have when I look at these circled areas is that they seem to pull away from an average quite strongly and regularly. Let's ask ourselves some questions about the observation.

- Are prices trading away from the mean significantly?
- At the same time, is the ATR increasing when it gets further away from the mean?

- Wouldn't that indicate that crowd behavior is pushing prices too far in one direction?
- How far is too far?
- How can we measure this?

For starters, we have simple tools for measuring averages. In technical analysis, several types of moving average calculations are used, depending on the task. The most common types are:

- The *Simple Moving Average* (SMA) just adds all the sample values and divides by the number of samples. It is not, however, without its drawbacks. It is the slowest of the different methods of measuring an average. All values have equal weight. It can produce a result that is overly influenced by the oldest samples in the data series. For this purpose, it tends to produce excessive lag.
- The *Exponential Moving Average* (EMA) provides a value that is representative of the more recent values in the data series. It accomplishes this by using weighting factors that decrease exponentially across the series. The EMA is the most commonly used method of producing a moving average. For very short-term smoothing, however, the SMA works best.
- The *Weighted Moving Average* (WMA) returns a value that is even more weighted to the most recent samples in the data series. WMA is used very sparingly in technical analysis.

The MetaStock Function Language Statement for EMA is:

```
Mov (C, 40, E)
```

In this statement, the *C* stands for the closing price, 40 is the lookback period, and *E* designates Exponential.

If we should choose to measure the distance of the current closing price from the moving average, however, that would look like this:

```
C - Mov (C, 40, E)
```

This statement will produce a raw price value. We can normalize this measurement by dividing it by the closing price, and thus produce a percentage value of itself. Lastly, multiplying it by 100 raises the value to a nice neat number that's easy to look at and quick to recognize. That statement would look like the next one. Just as in algebra, the sequence of execution is controlled by parentheses placement.

```
((C - Mov (C, 40, E)) / C) * 100
```

Now that we have some MetaStock function code that gives us the measurement of normalized distance from the mean, let's take a look at expressing the ATR component. Actually, we have already done that, and it looks like this:

```
(ATR(14) / C) * 100
```

What do we do with these two different measurements? If we are trying to show a measurement of the extremes, then let's multiply one value by the other. That would tend to produce an output value that truly exaggerates the circumstance when each is at an extreme. In other words:

- The further price is from the mean, the higher the value.
- The greater ATR is, the higher the value.
- When both values are at extremes, the calculated value will be truly magnified.

Here's what the ATREx function code should look like:

```
(((C - Mov(C, 40, E)) / C) * 100) * ((ATR(14) / C) * 100)
```

Each component is encapsulated by parentheses. The operation to execute is the multiplication. In its essence, we are multiplying price's distance from the mean times its average true range. This creates a basic volatility measurement. Now it is time to see what this looks like on the chart.

Figure 4.10 shows us what ATREx looks like in an indicator form. For the purposes of clarity, we have told the indicator to also plot three horizontal lines, at 0, 20, and –20. The first thing that's obvious is that the indicator identifies the extreme readings with cold precision. There are not as many extreme levels as we identified by the old eyeballing-it method. Visually, we drew six circles on the chart in Figure 4.9, and each of them seemed to be obviously extreme high or low levels worthy of a reversal trade. Now in Figure 4.10, there are only three most extreme levels reached by our new wonder indicator. Also of the six turning points we originally circled, there is only one that now shows up as an indicator high reading. We had not even identified the other two that the indicator shows. At this point Mark Twain would have asked, "How could the computer be so wrong?"

This is due to a human condition called the Hindsight Bias. David Aronson, in his book *Evidence-Based Technical Analysis*, identifies how people make visual pattern errors as a matter of how the human brain is designed. "The hindsight bias creates the illusion that the prediction of an uncertain event is easier than it really is when the event is viewed in retrospect, after its outcome is known. Once we learn the upshot of an uncertain situation, such as which team won a football game or in which direction prices moved, subsequent to a technical analysis pattern, we tend to forget how uncertain we really were prior to knowing the outcome."[2]

As a trader, you need to be acutely aware of this phenomenon. In the case of Figure 4.9, several of the reversal points chosen seemed to be such obvious extremes that we inadvertently saw the distance from the low or high to the profit target in lieu of the distance from the low or high to the mean. When the trader sees the outcome in addition to the trade setup, then he is subject to this irresistible bias. In fact, as a technical trader, this will be one of the largest challenges you will have to overcome. There are specific techniques for training your eyes and brain to be unbiased. One of these methods is just exactly what we are doing right now. By developing indicators yourself, you are forced

FIGURE 4.10 A close look at this chart of Intuit Corporation (INTU) shows that mathematical calculations resolve movement differently than human visual recognition.

Chart created in MetaStock.

to work through endless iterations of trial and error. The algorithms become part of your reasoning process. You begin to be able to look at the chart, pick a price bar in the middle of the X-axis, the time line, and ignore the price action to the right of that date. Free of processing the outcome, you are much better able to see and understand the relationships and the factors that determine the desired trade setup, which lies left of that theoretical current price bar.

The mathematical truth is presented in Figure 4.10. It's a truth that we did not really intend to see. This, however, is to be expected. It is a part of the creative technical analysis process. Our next step, therefore, is to ask some questions.

- Why were the areas of opportunity not calculated as such?
- Why did some of extreme readings identified not produce profitable trades?
- How can the desired profitable trades manually identified on the chart be better expressed mathematically so that the computer will do my work for me?

In examining Figure 4.10, perhaps the extremes can be measured better by doing just that. Certainly the High or Low of the day's bar is most often more extreme than the Close. When attempting to identify extremes, use High and Low as much as possible. So, let's change our indicator to measure High or Low instead of Close. Incidentally, when normalizing the output, dividing by the Close gives no significant difference from dividing by the High or the Low. There are algorithms that benefit from that change, but this is not one of them. Also, the ATR indicator is designed to measure maximum possible range, so no modifications are necessary with it. Here's what the new MetaStock functions looks like:

Calculating the Low:

```
(((L - Mov(L, 40, E)) / C) * 100) * ((ATR(14) / C) * 100)
```

Calculating the High:

```
((H - Mov(H, 40, E)) / C) * 100) * ((ATR(14) / C) * 100)
```

But wait, in there is a dilemma here. We have two different equations, each producing an indicator line. For the purposes of clarity and decision making, we really only need one. Now is the time to bring logic into the algorithm. Introducing logic into technical analysis is very powerful, but sometimes very limiting. We can discuss more on that topic later.

In looking at ATREx in Figure 4.10, it seems logical that we want to see the downside volatility extreme when the price is below its moving average. Likewise, it only benefits us to see the upside volatility when the price is above its mean. It would therefore be best to allow the algorithm to choose the equation based on that criterion. We will use a simple If statement to accomplish this. Here's the format for an If function:

```
If ( proof expression, expression if true, expression if false )
```

Here's the MetaStock code for our second iteration of ATREx:

```
If(C < Mov(C, 40, E),
(((L - Mov(L, 40, E)) / C) * 100) * ((ATR(14) / C) * 100),
(((H - Mov(H, 40, E)) / C) * 100) * ((ATR(14) / C) * 100) )
```

So what does our new and improved TTI ATR Extreme indicator look like? Figure 4.11 shows us how the change to the basis of High and Low bar measurement improves on the results. And it does indeed give us something of an improvement. In looking at the circled extreme at the left side of the chart, it is easy to see that it has been reduced in value. It does not reach the −20 level now, whereas before it did. We can interpret it as an improvement because it is the least-profitable trade signal of the three that were previously identified. Also, the other two extreme readings both produce profitable trades. This is certainly a step in the right direction.

It's also important to point out that our use of the term *trade signal* is theoretical at this point. I'm not advocating that anyone should make an actual trade based on a single indicator value. During the process of indicator development, however, a central

FIGURE 4.11 By adapting the ATR Extreme algorithm to incorporate highs and lows, a slightly improved signal is achieved.

Chart created in MetaStock.

method of measuring performance is to suppose that it is producing trade signals. It is a necessary part of a development process to consider it in that light.

It's certain that by now you are wondering if it is actually possible to develop a profitable technical analysis indicator, complete with genuine predictive capabilities, by working with only a single stock chart over a brief six-month period of time. Would that it were only so. For the purposes of time and space we have been performing the process with a single chart. The real process of indicator development requires that you examine many charts, hundreds really. Varying levels of volatility, multiple time frames, and different market conditions are all important to indicator design. Where appropriate, simple back-testing, in addition to statistically valid back-testing, is also required. Indeed, it's through this lengthy process that you, as the algorithm developer, learn the strengths, weaknesses, and nuances of your technical analysis component. It's a part of what gives you an edge. As stated in Chapter 1, trading is not meant to be a fair fight. You need every edge you can get.

So then it looks like we've achieved success, yes? Unfortunately, we have not yet

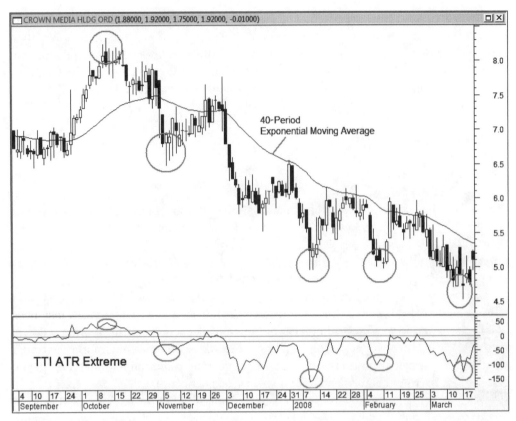

FIGURE 4.12 The TTI ATR Extreme shows here how its highs and lows can reach unpredictable levels, which can make gauging true extreme readings difficult.

Chart created in MetaStock.

done so, because reality does come into play during the process. We have chosen an extreme level reading of 20 and −20 for this chart view because it looks about right to our human eyes. And, in truth, maybe it is and maybe it's not. It stands to reason that some other stock's volatility is inherently higher, perhaps due to a higher level of risk in the company's underlying industry segment. There are going to be other stocks with higher and lower levels of ATR as well as moving average rates of change.

There is a daily chart of Crown Media (CRWN) in Figure 4.12 showing the same moving average line in the top pane and the current version of ATREx in the lower pane. As in the previous charts, the circled areas show the extreme diversions from the mean, which visually produce the best trading opportunities. Their respective ATREx indicator readings are also circled. Look at those extreme reading levels. The top reading farthest at left is 50. The others range from −65 to −162. These extreme readings are far from the 20 and −20 that made so much sense in the charts of INTU.

For indicators that are not confined to finite boundaries, the challenge is in identifying significant levels of extreme readings with predictive value. Many indicators are oscillators that have fixed ranges, such as a stochastic oscillator. The stochastic oscillator was invented in the 1950s by George C. Lane. It falls into the category of momentum indicators and produces readings between 0 percent and 100 percent. That's it, nothing lower than zero or larger than 100. Truly representative volatility indicators, however, have no boundaries. They can produce any open-ended positive or negative reading. This leads us to the most challenging questions of volatility-based technical analysis:

- How high is too high?
- How low is too low?
- How far is too far?
- How high is up and how low is down?

One particular method in technical analysis is to interpret significant levels by using moving averages. Specifically, when a moving average completes a direction reversal, then an extreme has been reached. There are whole systems of technical trading based on elaborate moving average strategies of price data. Most of them tend to have very little predictive value, but they can make for interesting viewing.

A 10-period exponential moving average of the ATREx is plotted along the ATREx in Figure 4.13. Also drawn in this chart are vertical dashed lines, which mark instances when the 10-period exponential moving of the indicator average turns up from a downward direction. These lines are the resulting signal days, which would inform the trader that because of a change in indicator direction, it's time to put on a long trade. As you can see, such a moving average method has serious drawbacks.

The trading signal happens rather late and misses the greater part of the profit opportunity because of delay. This is the single greatest deficiency with moving averages: they are simply too slow to be effective. Typically, a very short-term moving average is acceptable for smoothing purposes. Longer moving averages, however, should be avoided as primary signal-generating technical analysis components.

Another problem with the moving average direction change basis is that it still does not represent a signal generated at any particular extreme volatility level. Without this, the central objective of identifying a volatility extreme is missed.

Since it's clear that a fixed-value threshold construct is not going serve well for this indicator, we need to get a little creative. But first, there is a tenet upon which we can base our creativity. It is one that most technical analysis depends upon. Because the outside of its envelope is constantly being pushed, many traditional analysis algorithms have lost effectiveness. Fortunately, volatility measurements thrive on it. The tenet reads like this:

Lacking significant fundamental financial or market influences, a security's price should experience limited movement per unit of time based on its recent significant history.

In other words, price movement should travel only so far in a given time. Given this general truth, the question is then, which type of measurement is best suited to the task of defining how far and how fast? This is a pretty big question, and there is not a single

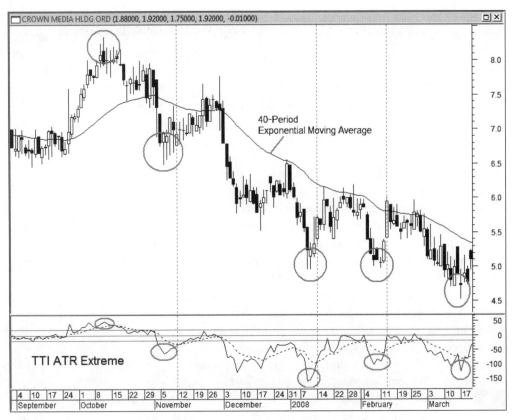

FIGURE 4.13 In an effort to detect indicator turning points, a 10-period exponential moving average of the TTI ATR Extreme is added to the indicator pane.

Chart created in MetaStock.

best answer. For now, it would be best for us to use the standard deviation. The reason to choose standard deviation is that we need a mathematical ability to:

- Set upper and lower limits that are flexible, based on significant recent price movement. These limits may be very different from ones based on more distant historical price movement within the specific security.
- Set upper and lower limits that are able to adapt to the varying levels of ATR and deviation from the mean for any trading security.

Let's add to the ATREx indicator and give it the ability to know its own boundaries. We can do this using the standard deviation function. It will be used differently, however, from how you have previously seen it used. This time, we are going to apply it to its own output, which will make itself relevant. In lieu of being applied to the price series as before, the standard deviation math will be directly applied to the value returned by the ATREx calculation.

Here is the MetaStock function code for enhanced ATREx with upper and lower extreme identification.

```
1 x:= If(C < Mov(C, 40, E),
2 (((L - Mov(L, 40, E)) / C) * 100) * ((ATR(14) / C) * 100),
3 (((H - Mov(H, 40, E)) / C) * 100) * ((ATR(14) / C) * 100) );
4 Mov(x, 40, E) + Stdev(x, 200);
5 Mov(x, 3, S);
6 Mov(x, 40, E) - Stdev(x, 200);
```

As you can see, there are some structural differences in the function code. For starters, there are line numbers shown for reference purposes. On line one, we are invoking the use of a variable named x. In this case, we are assigning the entire previous ATREx calculation to x. This is done so that we can reference this value in the subsequent statements without repeatedly restating the entire algorithm. Notice at the end of line three is a semicolon. This is how a single statement is ended manually, thus allowing the program to interpret the start of another statement. Lines four through six tell MetaStock to actually plot values independently.

Line four establishes the upper extreme limit. It calculates a value of one standard deviation of the ATREx indicator and adds it to the ATREx 40-period moving average; in essence, it adds it to itself. Line six does the same except that it uses a subtraction to define a lower extreme boundary. In this way, we are using the standard deviation volatility measurement method to establish a reasonable level of stray from its own mean.

Lastly, line five plots a smoothed version of the ATREx calculation. It does this by using a three-period simple moving average of x. Doing this with a short-duration moving average makes the plotted line much more visually enhanced by removing much of the jagged edges of the raw value. Always take care to use as few smoothing periods as possible; if anything, err on the side of fewer than more. Smoothing can delay trade signals and degrade risk-reward to the point of making a trading method needlessly unprofitable.

We can see in Figure 4.14 our new enhanced version of TTI ATREx indicator. In the top pane, all remains the same. In the bottom pane, the horizontal constant lines have been removed. The ATREx plotted value is slightly rounded. Most important, the ATREx plot exists mostly within a channel. These two lines are the upper and lower extreme limits as defined by a single standard deviation value away from a mean value. This gives us a much more realistic understanding of when and where the recent and present volatility is extended. But is it sufficient enough for us to use as a basis for trading decisions? Maybe, but at this point we have not done nearly enough to prove that. Also, it would be very helpful to visually see the trading signals it could generate in its current form.

To accomplish this system of visual trading cues, most technical analysis packages have the ability to overlay them on the chart, using indicator values and logic. This is

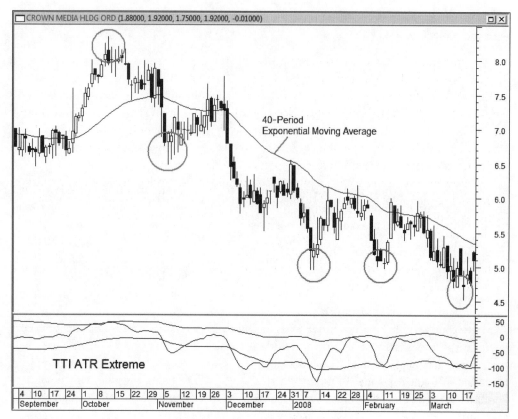

FIGURE 4.14 Creating a standard deviation channel allows the most accurate assessment of the TTI ATR Extreme highs and lows.

Chart created in MetaStock.

called the Expert Advisor feature in MetaStock. We can create some function code to drive this so as to generate some potential buy-and-sell signals.

This is the MetaStock function code to generate a buy signal:

```
x:= If(C < Mov(C, 40, E),
(((L - Mov(L, 40, E)) / C) * 100) * ((ATR(14) / C) * 100),
(((H - Mov(H, 40, E)) / C) * 100) * ((ATR(14) / C) * 100) );
Cross( Mov(x, 40, E) - Stdev(x, 200), Mov(x, 3, S) )
```

This code is identical to the indicator statements with one exception. The last line tells the program to generate a Boolean value of True when the indicator crosses below the lower extreme line.

This is the MetaStock function code to generate a sell signal:

```
x:= If(C < Mov(C, 40, E),
(((L - Mov(L, 40, E)) / C) * 100) * ((ATR(14) / C) * 100),
```

```
(((H - Mov(H, 40, E)) / C) * 100) * ((ATR(14) / C) * 100) );
Cross( Mov(x, 3, S), Mov(x, 40, E) + Stdev(x, 200))
```

As you can see, the code to generate a sell signal is the same. It returns a value of True, however, if the indicator crosses above the upper extreme limit. We can now see in Figure 4.15 the results of our new trading signals based on the latest and greatest version of the TTI ATREx indicator. Downward pointing arrows are above the candles on the day where a sell signal is generated. Arrows pointing up indicate buy signals. Note that the arrow shows the signal day as generated after the close of that trading day. The earliest trade entry can happen at the open of the next trading day.

So how are we doing so far? Four of the original areas circled are still being marked with trading signals. One visually obvious extreme area just does not measure up to being truly deviated from the mean. The sell signal generated in January, however, completely escaped our eyes, and it turns into a great trade. That opportunity was really invisible to our naked eyes. This is an example of the volatility indicator doing its job well. As traders, we need to see the transparent opportunities. These setups are invisible to our eyes, but not to math.

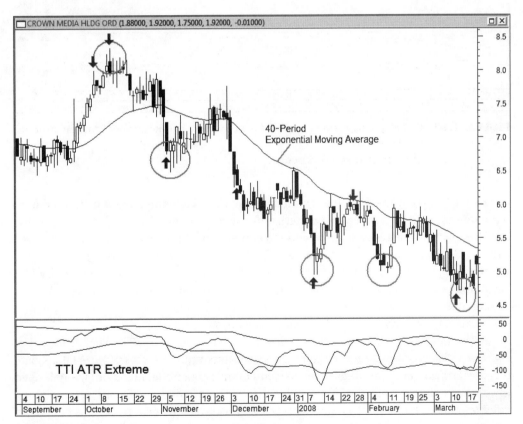

FIGURE 4.15 By using the TTI ATR Extreme signal code, trading signals can be automatically displayed on the chart for easy recognition.

Chart created in MetaStock.

FIGURE 4.16   This chart shows the current TTI ATR Extreme and how it performs on Intuit Corporation (INTU).

Chart created in MetaStock.

Examine closely the distance between the upper and lower indicator bands in Figure 4.16; we can call them bands now. Let's refer to this as bandwidth. To our eyes, the bandwidth looks mostly uniform across the entire chart. In reality, it is about 30 percent wider by August than it was in January. This translates to an expansion of historical volatility over that time period, that is to say, historical volatility as measured by this custom indicator. This brings us back to the earlier introduction of historical volatility, in that there is no single best way to measure volatility. There are more common methods, but volatility can be measured many ways.

Now in Figure 4.16, we can compare our current version of TTI ATREx to the first chart of INTU where we first started this development process (see Figure 4.9). Again, it is obvious that our eyes and brains played hit and miss. Some areas originally looked like they would be a piece of cake to identify with an indicator. Then there are some other spots that the volatility algorithm nailed. Alas, there are several signals generated that likely would have lost us some money. This is why, of course, the successful analyst does not trade on the basis of a single indicator signal.

Both of the charts used for development so far were chosen for their illustrative purposes of trend direction and trend change. The chart of INTU is dominated largely by an upward trend, which we can define as a series of higher highs and higher lows. The chart of Crown Media (CRWN) shows us a downward trending direction, which is to say that it prints lower highs and lower lows. Each chart experiences a change in trend direction as is demonstrated by the 40-period exponential moving average line in the top panes. The trading signals in each chart also exhibit failed trading signals in the mid-chart area because of this change of trend direction. Predicting intermediate trend direction change is very difficult. These two charts show just how important that detection is.

At this point of our development we have the beginnings of an overbought-and-oversold indicator based on volatility measurements. Any system that is sufficient for trading requires much more, though. Markets and individual securities frequently reach oversold and overbought levels only to continue trading in the same direction without pause. It can leave the trader standing there scratching her head wondering just where she went wrong. Trends end, mutual funds and hedge funds quietly exit positions in a single security, and the broader trading population looks for more than just a tight rubber band. Short-term price reversals require compelling arguments to persuade a majority of interests to jump in and push prices in the opposite direction. For this reason, your trading system needs to be designed to detect and measure the various technical conditions that can make this compelling argument. Comprehensive trading system components require volatility-based algorithms, and need to cover the following seven areas of measurement as a minimum.

1. Oversold and overbought levels
2. Trend detection
3. Broad market integration
4. Support and resistance
5. Historical volatility
6. Implied volatility
7. Multiple time frame verification

THE WHOLE PICTURE

So, as you can see, the process of trading system design is just only getting started here. Let's take an in-depth look at a complete system, which includes these areas of functionality. This will enable you to attach some tangible meaning to these necessary concepts. In Figure 4.17 is a daily chart of Crown Media (CRWN) for the identical time period as our previous examples. This chart shows Crown Media as it is analyzed by MetaSwing, however. By looking at the circled areas of the chart, it is clear how a trading system,

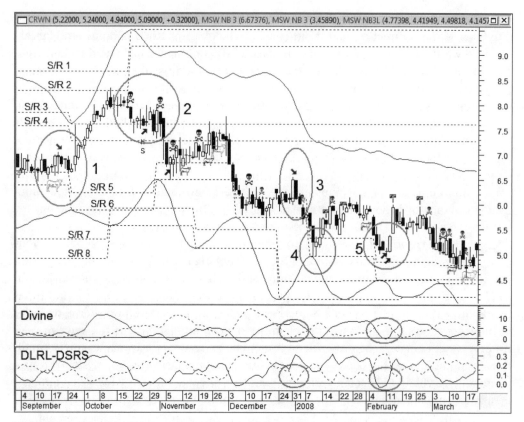

FIGURE 4.17 This daily MetaSwing chart of Crown Media (CRWN) demonstrates the analytical performance of a complete volatility-based framework. For comparison purposes, it uses the same time span as the earlier figures.

Chart created in MetaStock. Chart uses the MetaSwing Add-on, by Northington Trading, LLC. All rights reserved.

constructed within a good framework, should be able to guide the trader, thus limiting the emotional interference levels that plague us all.

Circled Area 1: Shows that price is trading sideways on a support level. An Adeo Short signals to consider a short side trade. There is conflicting market information, however, and a lack of confirming indicator cross-verification. The day before the short signal appears, a broad market Surge signal appears. This means that there was a very wide breadth buying day across the NYSE and the NASDAQ. This is a very bullish market signal. In the lowest indicator pane, the DSRS overbought indicator has not dropped below zero, thus denying us of an overbought confirmation. All of this tells us to stand aside and not trade this one. This turns out to be the correct decision because it would have been a losing short position. This setup demonstrates components 1, 2, and 3 from the preceding measurement list.

Circled Area 2: This would normally be a great setup for a long trade. There is an Adeo Long signal, which occurs right at the N Band S/R 3 support level. These two signals give us implied volatility-based support. There are also some solid oversold indications on both the DLRL and Divine indicators, which are the solid indicator lines in the bottom panes. This would normally be a go for a long trade. There is one big problem looming. On 10/19/07, four days before the Adeo Long signal, there is a Total Market Correction signal. This is a very powerful market breadth selling event. It was also the first such correction signal in over two months, and occurred high relative to the N Band spread. This occurrence and its circumstances predict that we will see a downward market trading direction in the days to come. It would therefore be unwise to enter the long trade here. As indicated by the Total Correction signal, the market subsequently begins a downward trend, and it was a good thing we allowed our MetaSwing system to curtail the temptation to trade. This setup demonstrates components 1, 2, 3, 4, and 6 from the measurement list.

Circled Area 3: On 12/31/08 we are presented with an Adeo Short signal. This stock and the broader markets have been in a solid downtrend for almost three months. Both the Divine and DSRS indicators at the bottom also show solid overbought conditions, and confirm the Adeo Short signal. This setup presents as a low-risk opportunity, in other words, a favorable risk-reward ratio. With no other conflicting system readings, we take the short trade on 1/2/07. The first primary sell target is the S/R 6 line at 5.73. The trade turns out well and continues until it finds support at the rising lower N Band on 1/9/08. This trade works very well. This setup demonstrates components 1, 3, and 6 from the measurement list.

Circled Area 4: At the conclusion of the trade in circle 3, price approaches a rising lower N Band. This means that price is on track to run into a fairly solid wall of support. Upon reaching the lower N Band, the Divine indicator in the center pane shows an oversold situation. Countertrend trading is not without risk, however. At this juncture, the trader can choose a short exit, or he can turn it around to a long trade. This long trade would be considered higher-than-normal risk because of the recent presence of the Correction signals and a strong opposing intermediate trend. This setup demonstrates components 1, 4, and 5 from the measurement list.

Circled Area 5: On 2/8/08, an Adeo Long signal is printed, with price approaching the S/R 6 support level at 4.96. Bear in mind that the rising N Band does not form a sufficient 3 percent peak until 2/12/08, and therefore, the S/R 6 line would still be displayed on 2/8. Also, with the N Band rising and the price falling, a natural immediate support level of 1 ATR above the N Band is forming. So in this case, the N Band represents immediate support in the form of historical volatility, and the S/R line represents horizontal support on the basis of implied volatility. In both indicator panes at the bottom of the chart there are solid oversold readings. There has not been a market Correction signal for over two weeks. Lastly, price is testing the same S/R 6 support line a second time, as it did on 1/10/08. All this is combined support for a long trade. A long trade should be entered beginning 2/11/08. The trade goes on to work out well. A MetaSwing Exit Long signal is generated on 2/13/08, along with a DLRL-DSRS cross, both making a good case to exit the trade. This setup demonstrates components 1, 3, 4, 5, and 6 from the measurement list.

BUILDING BLOCKS

Most of us can't effectively run into the surf, grab something to eat, and run back out. This is true even though the brain of the human far outweighs that of the sanderling. The little beach-dwelling bird does it all day, and even decides to avoid the activity in advance when the weather presents too much danger. These are capabilities that traders actually need, among many others.

On the other hand, watch a small child play with blocks, or for the current generation, make that a box of LEGOs. Look at the child's creativity as she pieces together components to ultimately craft what her mind desires. As people, we accomplish many things through secondary creation. We extend our capabilities by creating tools.

In this chapter, we began our tool-creation process. We experienced a step-by-step course of visual problem solving. Mathematical volatility measurements are the blocks that we piece together. Chapter 5 takes us deeper into more types of volatility calculations and how they can fit together. I believe you will find that process empowering.

The end result will be much more effective if you emulate the creativity of a child at play. They succeed because they do not know what they cannot do.

Integrated Volatility Indicator Design

The combination of various disciplines of physics into a single theory is generally referred to as the *unified theory*. While a single theory explains part of the world around us, no single theory explains everything. Indeed, Albert Einstein devoted much of his later career to searching for a unified theory of physics. As of this writing, none exists. Physics, it would appear, is not as simple as combining different meats, breads, and condiments to form a new sandwich.

How about technical analysis? Can it be combined like so many ingredients in a deli restaurant? Life would be easier if there were one single grand algorithm that explained and predicted all price movement, with you its sole possessor. To date, that does not exist either. But certainly, new combinations of algorithms arise as markets change.

In this chapter, we continue our component development efforts, using volatility measurement tools. They can be combined effectively where logic supports their use. Only by understanding the actual arithmetic ingredients is it possible to create effective components. If you can make the jump from being just another user of technical indicators to one that actually understands the underlying simple math, then you can grow and profit.

VOLATILITY POINTED FORWARD

Historical volatility was and is fairly simple. Look down at your bare feet. Count the number of toes. We hope you have 10. If you don't, well, don't feel so bad; you can still be a great trader. Provided you had the same number of toes yesterday and the day before, then your historical toe volatility is fairly low, as there was no change.

From that standpoint, your toe Implied Volatility is simple as well. Look around you. If you don't see a group of emergency medical personnel working on your feet, then it is likely that you will have 10 toes tomorrow. Thus, the expected, or *implied* volatility level of your toes is also very low.

Of course, stocks are not toes, so we have more to discuss. Here's the basic difference between *historical volatility* and *implied volatility*. Historical looks back and performs calculation on the prices people actually paid. Implied volatility predicts, or looks forward, by factoring in what people are actually paying for options at that instant in time. Let's be as clear as possible here. In the world of options trading, the following two definitions are specific:

- *Historical Volatility:* A measure of past movement of the underlying stock's price, as measured over time, expressed as a percentage. It is usually measured using standard deviation.
- *Implied Volatility:* A measure of possible, or expected, movement of the underlying stock's price, as projected forward through time, expressed as a percentage. It is created by any of many options pricing models. These pricing models use all known options trading factors in addition to the actual current trading price of the option's premium.

The central defining ingredient in implied volatility is the component derived from the actual pricing of the option's premium. This is a very big difference. We're talking about when people take their hard-fought-for money and lay it on the table. It's not an analyst's opinion, or a sentiment poll or anything else. It's someone's money, and more importantly, their willingness to risk it. That's the difference. Therefore, while historical volatility can be concrete, implied volatility can and does change at any given time based on:

- The particular option pricing model being used
- The option's premium price at that time; what people are willing to pay for an option
- Or both

Therefore, implied volatility is not concrete. Any expression of option volatility will be either historical or implied. The former is generally fixed, whereas the latter is not; it is open to interpretation based on the option pricing model being used. It's probably easiest to understand these two relationships if we look at how theoretical option pricing is performed. Figure 5.1 shows all of the values required to calculate an option's theoretical value, or price.

As you can see, all the seven price factors needed for the theoretical price of an option are known and quantifiable. After some math calculations are performed, it's all neat and clean. Consider this: When it's time to buy that call option, suppose its price is trading higher than its theoretical value. What gives? "I'm ready to trade," you say. "Why is the price incorrect?" It is the human element. Yes, that pesky human element again. It's the part that gives all those Efficient Market Hypothesis proponents fits...but we digress.

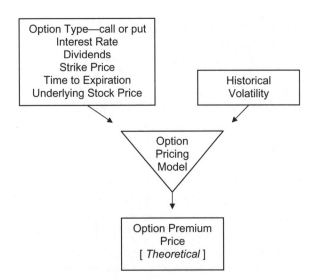

FIGURE 5.1 This is an example of theoretical option pricing.

Let's look at it another way. Suppose you have owned a home for 10 years. You have poured your heart and soul into this house. You have in it some of the fondest memories of your life, along with a sizable portion of your take-home pay. It's time now to sell the family nest and buy a larger home. You know this home well. After considering your original purchase price, the improvements made, and the prices that your never-short-on-advice next-door neighbor swears that the area has been commanding in the past two years, you have a pretty good idea of the price you can sell the house for. Your real estate agent then computes five different comparable properties that have sold nearby in the previous two months. That brick-in-the-chest feeling you get is when your agent discloses that the highest price any of the recent comparables have sold for is 17 percent lower than your own estimate of your wonderful home's value. Enter implied volatility.

Figure 5.2 shows us how implied volatility is derived. First note that this methodology has really nothing to do with historical volatility; as you can see, it's not even in the picture. Once again there are seven factors to compute. The difference in this calculation is the substitution of the option premium price in place of the historical volatility value. The options pricing model is adapted to accept the price data in lieu of historical volatility. As a result, the output is a value for implied volatility.

Historical and implied volatility can be considered mutually exclusive, which is one big reason that stock traders and options traders tend to exist in somewhat different worlds. That is unfortunate, because both are absolutely linked. Stock traders tend to take historical volatility into consideration only in passing, and ignore how critical it is. This leads some stock traders to be unprepared for the effects that options trading has on stock prices. Some options traders likewise focus very heavily on implied volatility without adequate technical analysis being performed on the underlying security. This is

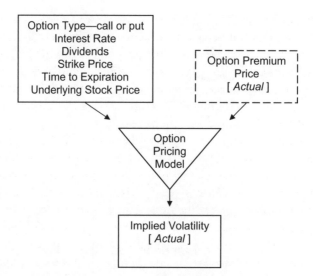

FIGURE 5.2 Here is an illustration of deriving implied volatility.

probably due to how very little classic technical analysis is expressed in the Greek measurements they are accustomed to.

An old adage states that something's monetary value is only worth what someone will give you for it. In this discussion, historical volatility is of only so much value; it is the implied volatility that gives us the magic beans. As technical analysts, we are searching to project the most, or the least, that the market will pay for a security; therefore we need implied volatility values before they happen. But if implied volatility requires that we get real money offers in the form of Bid prices for options, then how can we know implied volatility ahead of time?

That's a really good question. The answer may make some in the field of technical analysis cynical, disturbed, or amused.

PROJECTED IMPLIED VOLATILITY

Suppose you could identify ahead of time the hidden levels of price support and resistance that are created by options traders. As we discussed in Chapter 1, options trading volume is much greater than actual equity trading volume.

Options premiums define the value of the probabilities for an underlying stock's price to reach an extreme limit within a given time frame. The premiums paid for options spreads define exact trading ranges that the underlying stock will likely trade within, above, or below. These are obviously safe assumptions. It's important to drill deeper into the rationale. What's important is why an options trader thinks a given trading range will remain intact for the option duration. It's the *why* that really matters.

Most of the equity trading conducted by individual traders and smaller professional firms is fixated on support and resistance created by prior price levels, Fibonacci ratios, trend lines, or any number of other outdated tactics. Trading activity from this subgroup can move prices only to a limited degree. They just don't have the horses for it. The vast quantity of trading volume, in both shares and dollar volume, is conducted by larger institutions. These large players are the smart money that is so often referred to. It's the smart money that can enter positions on the right side of the market, and then exit just before the end of the move. Why is this money so smart?

The answer is simple. These large financial institutions have an abundance of smart people working within them, and they are well paid. A large percentage of these smart people are quantitative mathematicians. As a reminder, take a look once again at their qualifications listed back in Chapter 1. Given virtually unlimited computing and data resources, these teams of people create algorithms to identify this *why* just referred to. The options pricing model(s) that determine options premiums and implied volatility are their playground. More important, they design direct equity trading programs that operate in real time and have direct access to an underlying stock's implied volatility. Yes, implied volatility is used in real time. By identifying specific price and volume moves, with direct cross-functioning relationships to option premiums and implied volatility, they are able to instantaneously identify specific, hidden levels of price support and resistance. Therefore, we can clearly state that:

> *The prices at which stock option premiums trade, directly and indirectly, determine the key price levels, and extreme price levels, to which the actual underlying equity will trade.*

Are you feeling a little vulnerable now? You should be. Imagine yourself in Las Vegas at a blackjack table. In a casino you are competing with the house, which is the dealer, and all the other players at the table. Metaphorically speaking, then, the market is the house and the other players are one and the same, at least from a volume standpoint. Imagine yourself playing blackjack where all the players at the table and the dealer are on the same team, and are communicating telepathically. What do you think your odds are in that scenario?

As an active trader, you are facing a very similar competitive disadvantage. These big guys actually have the implied volatility component that you do not have. They have the voices of masses of options traders whispering into their ears, telling them exactly what price levels they are willing to bet money on. You don't have this.

But let's suppose for a minute that you get your hands on implied volatility values. You could open up an options trading account with a broker that furnishes you with an options trading interface. On that interface, you have real-time access to all option Greek values, up to and including implied volatility. This is not imagination gone wild. You can certainly do this. Some excellent options trading platforms are awaiting you.

However, if you had that implied volatility value, for whatever stock you manually key up, what would you do with it? Is it integrated into your technical analysis methods, charts, or custom indicators? Extreme price levels are often reached, but are only maintained for a few minutes before prices reverse. Were you able to run a market scanning report and perform calm, level-headed analysis on the chart the evening before? Are you using implied volatility to be prepared at that instant when the trading opportunity is before you?

Are you now beginning to understand the importance of *Projected Implied Volatility*?

Integrating the Solution

While it lies beyond the practical capabilities of today's advanced technical analysis platforms to import live implied volatility data, there are ways to equalize the current competitive disadvantage. The extent of the normal data feed for technical analysis is confined to High, Low, Open, Close, Volume, and Open Interest. This is enough to provide a significant method of finding the invisible levels of support and resistance derived from implied and historical volatility.

This method is called *Projected Implied Volatility* (PIV). I use specific examples from MetaSwing to show that this new technical capability is for real. You will then see, later in this chapter, some of the basic mathematics used as building blocks for PIV.

Let's first look at why Projected Implied Volatility is needed. If you drew a line representing support and resistance on a chart for every method within traditional technical analysis, you could end up with so many lines drawn that you could not see the price bars. There are a myriad of strategies and tactics, ranging from Fibonacci, to Gann, to horizontal levels, gaps, and more. Traditional fundamental traders make fun of technicians, regularly claiming that we draw enough lines on a chart such that we can't ever be wrong. Select a chart and a price movement, and you are guaranteed to find a line drawing strategy to support it. This does not solve the problem of knowing in advance which strategy is correct.

A trend exists inside another trend, which in turn exists inside another one. This happens across multiple time frames. It's very easy to get lost inside the maze of embedded trends. Trend lines can be drawn everywhere like spider webs.

Support and resistance based on PIV adds significant definition to predictive technical analysis. PIV is primarily necessary to:

- Identify current and future support and resistance levels that truly have significant profit and loss price levels for options traders. These are the only primary support and resistance levels that exist in equities trading; all others are secondary.
- Identify and confirm the beginning of a trend.
- Identify and confirm the continuation of a trend in its latter stage.

Visual PIV

In order to quantify PIV it is first necessary to measure the current implied volatility for a given chart periodicity. Then you must identify historical highs and lows of the implied volatility levels. The significant extremes of the implied volatility levels will tend to serve as good PIV values. In MetaSwing, PIV is achieved with N Bands, N Band peaks, and N Band troughs. These indicators give structure and logic to much of the trading direction

FIGURE 5.3 This daily chart of Invitrogen (IVGN) shows little or no apparent reason for price direction or reversal points.

Chart created in MetaStock.

that price takes as it satisfies supply and demand. Look first at Figure 5.3 and you will see a daily candlestick chart of Invitrogen (IVGN) for the second half of 2005. Why does the trading price reverse at key places and make whole gaps to others? There could be many reasons for each spot. Perhaps the more meaningful question at any given point on the chart is, where is the next spot that price will rethink its trading direction?

In Figure 5.4, N Bands and N Band S/R lines are overlaid onto the chart. The N Bands appear as trading bands meandering around above and below the price action. The S/R lines are plotted as horizontal dashed lines. Only the primary S/R lines 1, 3, 6, and 8 are plotted in this chart.

The N Band is an algorithm that calculates an immediate level of volatility-based support and resistance, and contains implied volatility characteristics. When an N Band rises to form a significant peak, or falls to form a significant trough, then an important level is created. The peaks and troughs represent extremes for their current time. These levels represent key measures of implied volatility in a composite form when projected forward. Since N Bands are presented in the form of price values, the N Band significant peaks and troughs form the price level equal to the key implied volatility projected

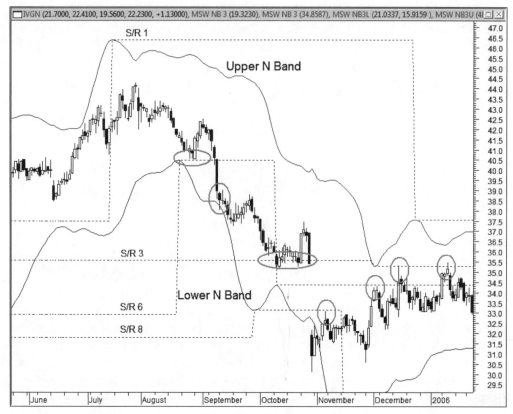

FIGURE 5.4 N Band peaks and troughs identify volatility-based support and resistance areas that explain short-term price reversal points for Invitrogen. N Bands are immediate boundaries of support and resistance, and S/R lines are future levels of support and resistance.

Chart created in MetaStock. Chart uses the MetaSwing Add-on, by Northington Trading, LLC. All rights reserved.

forward. It is in this way that the N Band peaks and troughs perform the function of Projected Implied Volatility. The N Band S/R lines directly represent the most important levels of price support and resistance.

Support and Resistance

Just as important, the Lower N Band provides a very strong level of support in the present period, and likewise, the Upper N Band provides a very strong level of resistance. The support and resistance will begin at about one ATR value from the N Band itself. In looking at the S/R lines, you can see that there are four of them plotted, but they number up to eight. This is because there are actually eight N Bands. The four most dominant lines are formed by the peaks and troughs. The other four S/R lines are not shown on this chart so that an initial level of clarity can be presented.

The circled areas of Figure 5.4 show instances where price reaches the S/R line and stops to either reverse or trade sideways. S/R lines in these cases confirm entry and exit points, which in effect raise your success probabilities when trading.

- When entering a trade at a support line, the odds of entering at the actual reversal point are greatly improved.
- When entering a long reversal trade above a support line, there is an increased level of stop protection at the S/R line below it. The opposite is true for a short reversal trade.
- When exiting a trade at an S/R line, there is an increased level of maximizing the profit, and thus increasing trade efficiency.

But wait, how about the gap down event shown on October 28, 2005? Why did it gap to that particular point? It is well below the Lower N Band, after all. A quick look at Figure 5.5 shows the same chart in a weekly time frame. Circle number 2 shows that on the day of the gap, price closed right at the lower N Band on the weekly chart. Large gapping moves will generally default to volatility reference points in higher time frames. This is because there are decisions to be made at the time of trading. There is generally no specific quantifiable fundamental value identified in market-moving news events for a specific stock. Traders, therefore, default to technical measurements. See the Microsoft scenario in the previous chapter for an additional example.

It's also important to note that trading prices were finding strong support at the N Band S/R lines in circled areas 1 and 3. Weekly charting periods can be very powerful because they can provide trading ranges that are wide enough to make some significant profit percentages. It is clear in circle 3 that a support line exists at 33.53. Even though prices consistently close above the support line every week, the noise of daily price action on the daily chart does not enable the trader to see it in that time frame. This is just another example of volatility-based technical analysis enabling the trader to see the invisible.

You may recall from Chapter 4 our list of seven necessary trading system capabilities. Here they are presented again.

1. Oversold and overbought levels
2. Trend detection
3. Broad market integration
4. Support and resistance
5. Historical volatility
6. Implied volatility
7. Multiple time frame verification

We have covered items four, six, and seven in the examples just shown for N Band support and resistance. It's important to always keep this list at the forefront of your

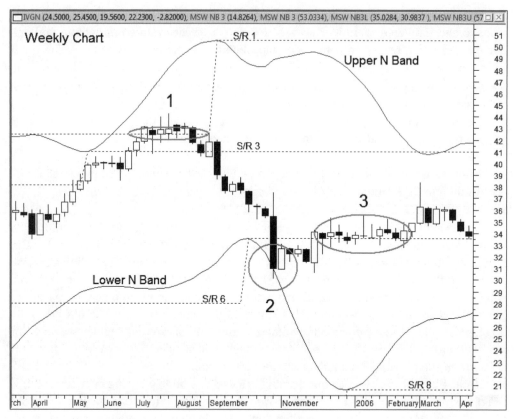

FIGURE 5.5 Invitrogen shows in this weekly chart how S/R lines guide support in a larger time frame. In circled area 2, the large gap down on the daily chart shown previously is easily explained by its close at support (at the lower N Band) in this larger time frame.

Chart created in MetaStock. Chart uses the MetaSwing Add-on, by Northington Trading, LLC. All rights reserved.

mind. Your risk-reward ratios will consistently increase to the good if you use as many of them as possible when making trading decisions.

There is another classic scenario happening in Figure 5.4. It is actually the primary reason this particular chart was chosen as an example. Perhaps you have already noticed it. Chart pattern traders should immediately see the classic head and shoulders pattern. The right shoulder occurs at the September 1, 2005, candle. This could lead some to believe that it was not volatility-based support that caused price to reverse upward on August 29, 2005, but that it was an obvious right shoulder forming. The truth is that this particular pattern setup is present in abundance all over the charting landscape of every stock.

The vast majorities of the H&S pattern setups show no particular predictive value at the potential formation of the right shoulder, and go on in any direction. It's generally only pointed out when it continues on to actually complete the entire H&S pattern. In an even larger sense, this is an example of an obscure technical analysis technique chosen to explain the past, but offering little to no predictive value. You will see throughout the examples shown in this book many instances that can be explained by other technical analysis methods. I reiterate at this point that large financial institutions do not pay large salaries to Ph.D.-level quantitative analysts to play with trend lines, look for Fibonacci grids, or identify H&S patterns.

Trend Confirmation

According to virtually all responsible texts on the subject, identifying and trading the trend is the basic purpose of technical analysis. That's a fancy way of saying buy low and sell high. How does PIV help us to accomplish this?

The beginnings of a trend happen frequently. Every zig has a zag, yes? A new trend is just one strong zag away, which means that a chart is a series of failed trend beginnings. Don't think about that too deeply. The important thing to focus on is, how do the largest players in the market agree that a trend is solidly in place and then believe that prices will continue to trend in that given direction? After all, the big money, the smart money, must be on board to maintain trend direction. If not, then all bets are off.

Figure 5.6 shows a daily chart of Dell (DELL) during the first half of 2007. In this chart, all of the MetaSwing N Band S/R lines have been turned on. This adds S/R 2, 4, 5, and 7 to the others. These additional lines are all positioned 1 ATR value from their corresponding dominant S/R lines. Lines 2 and 4 are one ATR value less, and lines 5 and 7 are one ATR greater. This second line single ATR distance from the primary accomplishes multiple purposes.

When price is trading higher, for example, it will see resistance at S/R 3. The one ATR distance is commonly an area over which trading will retrace and consolidate before attempting to venture above the resistance level. The area between the pairs of S/R lines frequently experiences short-term consolidation. Under some circumstances, it makes for very quick and simple trading opportunities. For example, look at the January-February trading on Figure 5.6, where price finds a range between S/R 5 and 6.

The S/R 3 line is an important PIV level. A strong sign of a trend's beginning strength is when price can trade above it and then confirm that ability. Also important is that the stock's trading found support at the S/R 5 area. This is important to exhaust those still holding long positions, and entice short holders to take profits. Now, understand that this latter quality flies in the face of many methodologies that believe that it's important for a stock to base for an extended period so that it may undergo accumulation.

DELL trades down to S/R 6 in March in this example. It then reverses up to a resistance level at S/R 3 in April. In May, it confirms the trend strength by demonstrating support at S/R 3. It has, in effect, turned S/R 3 from resistance to support. It has climbed above a key area of implied volatility. This level of implied volatility was identified six weeks before because of Projected Implied Volatility.

Just for fun, take a look at the complete MetaSwing chart in Figure 5.7. The two circled areas show the trading opportunities in the trend. The first occurs as a part of

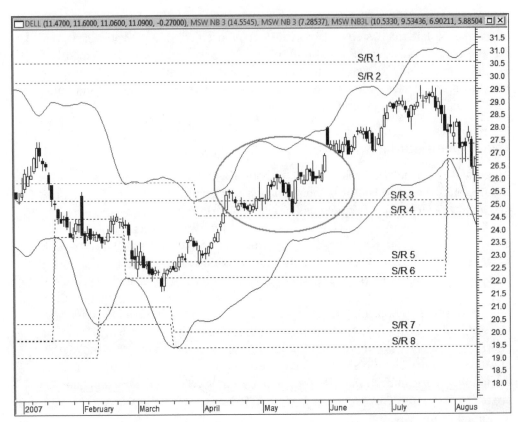

FIGURE 5.6 The beginning of a strong trend is confirmed in this partial MetaSwing chart
when Dell (DELL) finds support at the S/R 4 line, a function of Projected Implied
Volatility.

Chart created in MetaStock. Chart uses the MetaSwing Add-on, by Northington
Trading, LLC. All rights reserved.

the trend confirmation. An Adeo Long signal is generated right at S/R 4. On open the
next morning, price confirms the trend continuation by gapping up on the open. This
makes for a very good entry point. The second circle shows complete indicator verification of oversold conditions. There is a clear and strong trend in place. This is a no-brainer
entry to the trade the trend, or a quick swing trade. Be on guard in July, however, when
the Total Market Correction signals enter the scene. We cover that topic in depth in
Chapter 8; stay tuned.

What happens when things don't work out so well? In many circumstances, all of
the proper signs show themselves. In the case of Fastenal (FAST) in Figure 5.8, the trend
fails to confirm. In short, this is what a failure looks like. On November 3, 2006, price
closes below the S/R 4 line. This signals a trend failure. Fastenal advanced before this
date, confidently finding support at S/R lines. A long trade entry was well warranted in
this case. S/R 5 was fortunately close by for support. That's why it's called risk.

FIGURE 5.7 By contrast, this complete MetaSwing chart of Dell (DELL) isolates the two long trading opportunities in this confirmed trend; see the circled areas.

Chart created in MetaStock. Chart uses the MetaSwing Add-on, by Northington Trading, LLC. All rights reserved.

Trend Continuation

The third broader use for PIV and S/R lines is to confirm the continuation of a long-term existing trend. If a trend has begun and is currently ongoing, when will it end? This is extremely difficult to predict. Perhaps it is more realistic to ask, "Will the existing trend continue in the short-to-intermediate term?"

PIV can contribute significantly toward answering this question. There are some caveats, however, that accompany the prediction. The method involves looking at the chart in a weekly time frame. Just as we look for a trend beginning, it is necessary for price to trade and close above S/R 1. After trading above the S/R 1 level, the price must confirm itself by finding support at S/R 1 or S/R 2, and then continue to trade in the direction of the trend.

We see a weekly MetaSwing chart of Nordstrom (JWN) in Figure 5.9. As a side note, always remember the ever-present, and extremely annoying, same store sales results report that retail stocks generally undergo on a monthly basis. Most retail company

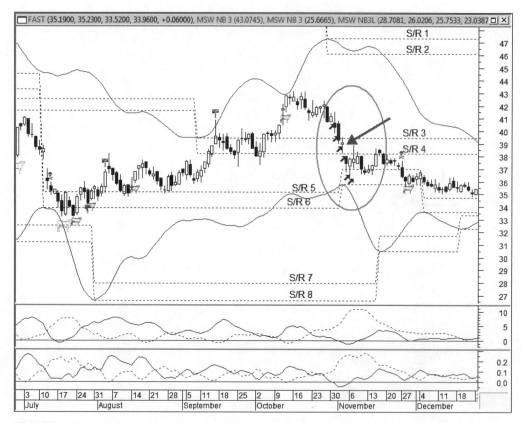

FIGURE 5.8 It is just as important to recognize a trend failure as when one confirms. Here, Fastenal (FAST) attempts a breakout but fails to confirm at S/R 4.

Chart created in MetaStock. Chart uses the MetaSwing Add-on, by Northington Trading, LLC. All rights reserved.

CEOs have great difficulty predicting the results of same store sales reports; traders stand even less of a chance of doing so. Many short-term traders avoid holding retail stocks during that event; some swear off retail stocks completely. In the circled area 1, it is clear that Nordstrom finds support at the S/R 2 line before trading higher. This is a good signal that the trend occurring on the daily chart for nine months will continue.

Here is the caveat to beware of, however. Once the trend has begun to produce profits for enough parties holding long positions, the profit-taking motive becomes a stronger influence. There are certainly always other additional factors present affecting the trend's continuation. But at this point, the larger players begin to get protective of the profits they need to hold on to. Partial positions frequently begin to be taken off the table. The rationale is that if the trend continues, it can be repurchased during the inevitable price dips. So, it is for this reason that mature trends become more volatile in their behavior. Thus, the price action after the S/R 2 confirmation shows an increasing level of choppy behavior.

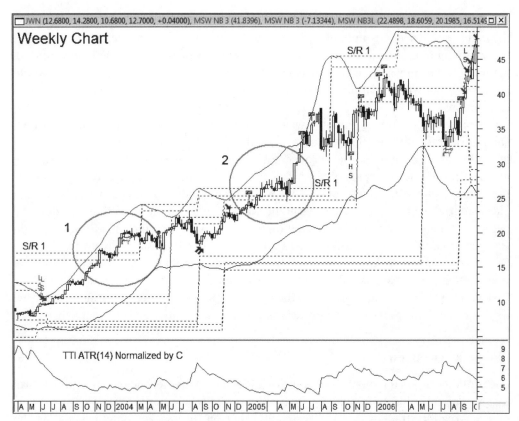

JWN (12.6800, 14.2800, 10.6800, 12.7000, +0.04000), MSW NB 3 (41.8396), MSW NB 3 (-7.13344), MSW NB3L (22.4898, 18.6059, 20.1985, 16.5149)

FIGURE 5.9 Nordstrom (JWN) confirms its strength in a longer-term trend in this weekly MetaSwing chart by rising above, and finding support at, upper S/R lines.

Chart created in MetaStock. Chart uses the MetaSwing Add-on, by Northington Trading, LLC. All rights reserved.

In the circled area 2 of Figure 5.9, Nordstrom shows another trend continuation confirmation, after consolidation along the S/R 1 line. The ATR(14) indicator is in the bottom indicator pane. If you recall, it is normalized by the stock's closing price, so it is displayed in percentage points. Visually, the stock's price action becomes more volatile, but appearances in an arithmetic chart can be deceiving. A careful look at the ATR indicator shows that volatility truly increases in the latter stages of this trend, beginning with the large price drop in August of 2005. With ATR continuing at a high level, it is evident that this long-term trend is likely getting to its end point.

MORE FROM THE MATH TOOLBOX

Think back to the day when you were sitting in high school math class. If this causes you to feel joy, then you may already be a quantitative analyst at a large Wall Street firm.

For the rest of us, the images are probably closer to boredom or dread as we counted the minutes and seconds until class was over. If only our teachers had related statistics to something real, such as closing out a three-day short position trade and pocketing 12 percent on the transaction. Had that been the case presented to this author, he would have surely shown a great deal more interest in those seemingly abstract concepts and calculations.

Some years later as a parent, I was urgently called to an ad hoc meeting with my son's third-grade teacher. She was concerned that he was not performing to his potential in math, and was doing so on purpose. She went on to describe the exercise that he underperformed on as a task to glue M&M candies to a sheet of paper and form an equation. Each child was given a total of 50. When he consistently added one M&M to one M&M to produce a sum of two, she said he was doing so on purpose, thus avoiding the exercise. I then asked what he was instructed to do with the other 48 M&Ms. She said each child could keep the leftovers. I explained to her that M&Ms were his favorite candy. The teacher was transferred to a different assignment before the end of the school year. To this day, my son is still one of the most motivated kids I've ever met. Therefore, I ask you to pay particular attention to the upcoming sections. These volatility-measuring techniques will be your best friends as you go forward to analyze price movement.

Linear Regression

The profit motive is the most compelling of influences. Whether the payoff is in the thrill of a successful trade, money, or chocolate, it is usually what drives us. We must recognize as volatility traders that we are capitalizing on the market's inefficiency. As the pendulum of price swings to and fro, we must be able to measure how far is too far. Possibly the best statistical measure of a series of data points, price points if you will, is called linear regression.

Simply put, it is the math process of fitting a straight line most efficiently to a series of data points. There is really no need to go into all of the longer definitions of linear regression, although there are many dry and abstract methods of describing it. All of them seem to be last stabs at us by those torturous high school math teachers.

Figure 5.10 shows us two lines, each surrounded by 14 data points. The dots plotted on the left could easily represent a series of 14 closing stock prices. The process of linear regression draws a straight line through this series of price points most efficiently. To focus a bit more on how it does this, look at the line plotted on the right side of the figure. The series of values is positioned more horizontally. If you were to duplicate the process of linear regression and best draw the straight line, your task would be to connect each data point to the horizontal straight line by using string made of chocolate. Chocolate is your favorite candy. You love eating chocolate more than almost anything. After completing the task, you get keep the leftover chocolate string to eat. So, you are obviously going to want to use as little chocolate string as possible in connecting these price point dots to the line. That is how the line is positioned most efficiently. That's linear regression.

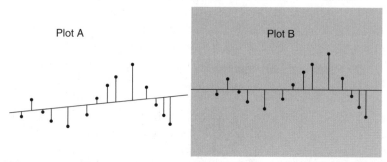

FIGURE 5.10 Linear regression uses the least squares method of plotting a straight line through a series of data points, using the most efficient path. Plot A shows the line as it would naturally be displayed on a chart. Plot B shows the line plotted in a theoretical horizontal least squares calculated method.

Linear regression uses a process called least squares to most efficiently fit the line to the data. Can you imagine drawing the line a hundred times and measuring exactly how much chocolate string you just used each time? Then you repeat the process a hundred times or more, each time measuring the string, until you are sure that you can't improve any further on the line efficiency. Now imagine that you were not given chocolate string for this task. The string is actually made of 36 carat gold and you get to keep the extra string. The profit motive is a beautiful thing.

Let's now look at Figure 5.11 to see a chart example of linear regression in action. Here is a chart of Merck (MRK) showing two 60-period linear regression lines. You can see how the straight lines are drawn through the series of the closing prices for the 60-trading day durations. By comparison, we have also plotted a 60-period simple moving average on the chart. The difference between these two types of indicators demonstrates quite obviously that they are very different types of measurements. The moving average is a lagging method. Unless price movement shows very low volatility for the majority of the moving average duration, it will then likely be above or below the moving average line. Not so with linear regression. As soon as the price trend starts to change direction, the linear regression line hugs the actual price bars more closely.

This is why linear regression is used for different purposes than are moving averages. Remember that the linear regression line does not represent a mean. It represents an efficient pathway. It is not encumbered with past values. If the time period is shifted forward by one period, then the oldest data point is dropped and the new data point is added. This is true for both a moving average and linear regression. The difference for the linear regression is that the entire line is recalculated; the whole thing shifts. With a moving average, only the most recent point assumes a new value.

The linear regression calculation has many strengths, and it differs significantly from what we've looked at thus far. The important points to note about linear regression are:

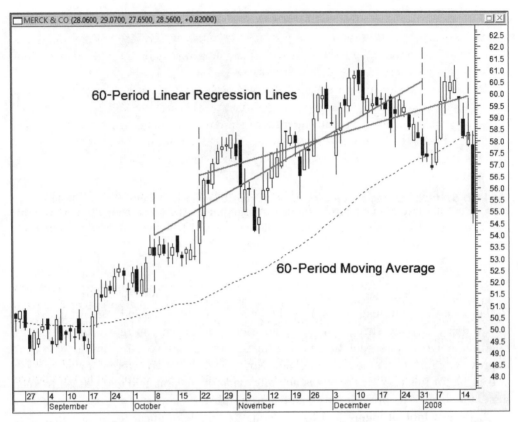

FIGURE 5.11 A 60-period linear regression line is plotted to best represent the most efficient straight line path of the closing prices over the 60-day time frame. Linear regression is a great tool for measuring central tendency because it is so highly responsive to price direction.

Chart created in MetaStock.

- It represents an efficient pathway for the specified period of time.
- It is highly responsive to price direction.
- It is more representative of the *central tendency* for the specified period.
- Its use results in greater levels of accuracy when prices are trending.
- Algorithms that use it properly can experience the ability to project or forecast.

R-Squared

Imagine that you are running the hurdles in a track and field event. As you start out of the blocks you clear the first three hurdles well with proper form and maintaining a great stride. The next three hurdles are more difficult in that you hit the hurdle with your trailing knee all three times. Ouch! During the first half of the race, you had high levels of R-Squared. In the second half of the race, your R-Squared rating declined to ineffective levels. Your ability to properly project the energy necessary to clear the hurdles was much better on the first three, and it was much worse on the latter hurdles.

For our purposes, R-Squared is to linear regression as standard deviation is to the moving average. In math terms, it is a coefficient; you can't have one without the other. More important, the R-Squared, just as with the standard deviation, is a good ingredient to add to the volatility technical analysis tool set.

Linear regression draws the most efficient path, or line, through a series of data points. It does the best job it can for such a difficult task. But how well does it perform? Can you visually see how well one linear regression line represents its data points versus a different linear regression line plot? Not really. One important thing we have learned thus far about charts and prices is that looks can be deceiving. Eyeballin' it is not what it's cracked up to be.

R-Squared is actually a measure of how well linear regression is doing its job at any given time. It's great because it's like having a judge on the sidelines with a scorecard, ready to comment on the line's current performance with a score of zero to 10. In technical analysis, R-Squared accomplishes two things:

1. It gives a value that measures the degree of efficiency to which the linear regression line represents the series of data points. The official explanation is that it gauges what percentage of the data point movement in the series can be explained by the linear regression statistical method.

2. It provides a quantifiable means to predict, or forecast, the likelihood that coming data values will continue in the same direction with the same slope. It has predictive value.

That's right, you read it correctly. R-Squared actually enables us to measure the strength and probability of directional movement. So now, not only can we use linear regression as a means of measuring volatility in difficult trending markets, we can gauge to a certain degree how well it is likely to work.

To best understand this new capability, let's examine closely Figure 5.12. We see in it a daily chart of Marathon Oil (MRO), with a collection of measurements that will help us see the relationships between linear regression, R-Squared, and price volatility. All of the indicator lines are using 40-period look-back time frames, and are using closing prices as the data series. The straight lines nearest the price candles are linear regression lines. The dashed line is an exponential moving average. The solid line in the upper pane is a different form of linear regression indicator designed to identify that current day's value. This is evident when looking closely at both the linear regression straight line and the variable line. See how they intersect at the first day's value on the straight line. The variable line, therefore, represents a continuous first-day plot of the 40-period linear regression straight-line plot. The two dashed vertical lines are markers that denote the first period of the linear regression straight lines. Lastly, the bottom indicator contains the R-Squared indicator plot. It is expressed in a value between zero and 1. Think of it as a percentage from zero percent to 100 percent.

Here are the important observational points for this chart and comparison of methods:

FIGURE 5.12 R-Squared, which is plotted in the lower indicator pane, shows the mathematical strength of the linear regression measurement. Higher readings show deliberate directional movement, and lower readings indicate more random price movement.

Chart created in MetaStock.

- In the bottom chart pane, the R-Squared value rises when the linear regression calculation can more accurately account for the price movements. Its value reads lower when the linear regression method statistically explains fewer of the price point movements. In the circled example 1 on 11/13/07, the leading day of the linear regression flat line plot, the R-Squared value is .2621. This directly means that the linear regression method can account for 26.21 percent of the price movement over the previous 40 days. So, the higher the R-Squared value, then the higher confidence you can place in the linear regression calculation at that time.
- Look at the linear regression line plot for circle 1. For the first half of the line, the R-Square value is rising to or above 70 percent. During the second half of the line plot the R-Squared value begins to taper off. Now look at the price direction and short-term volatility over that 40-day period. As price starts to jump around in late October and early November, the R-Squared value declines. Then on 11/12/07, the

price drops and changes the trading direction. To some degree, the R-Squared value warned of this before the move.

- Now look at the 40-period linear regression line plot and the indicator line plot, near circled example 2. It is easy to see how the R-Squared value increases as the price moves back to the linear regression line and then trades in its direction. The correlation is very obvious.
- On the last day of circled area 2, the R-Squared reading is 45.25 percent. This is almost 20 percent higher than the same point in circled area 1, yet there would appear to be much more price deviation from the linear regression line in this second example. Note that past this last day in circled area 2 price does continue to trade upward, which is the short-term direction of the linear regression indicator. The higher R-Squared value of 45 percent in circle 2 versus 26 percent in circle 1 shows the increased probability of directional movement with a higher value.

USING TOOLS TO LEVERAGE TTI ATR EXTREME

Our TTI ATREx indicator has been developed thus far for oversold and overbought conditions. It seems to work fairly well, but as technical analysts, we believe that our tools can always be improved upon. Indeed, we recognize as aspiring market technicians that the markets we trade evolve constantly. It's up to the individual to improve and adapt her tools and maintain the competitive edge. So let's take a further look at ATR Extreme and see how some of this chapter's math tools can be applied to it for better results.

The most recent version of TTI ATREx looks like this:

```
1 x:= If(C < Mov(C, 40, E),
2 (((L - Mov(L, 40, E)) / C) * 100) * ((ATR(14) / C) * 100),
3 (((H - Mov(H, 40, E)) / C) * 100) * ((ATR(14) / C) * 100) );
4 Mov(x, 40, E) + Stdev(x, 200);
5 Mov(x, 3, S);
6 Mov(x, 40, E) - Stdev(x, 200);
```

Lines one through three define the indicator, as it is embedded inside of a conditional If statement. Line five plots the indicator. Lines four and six establish flexible upper and lower limits by adding and subtracting a unit of one standard deviation to and from the indicator value. This sets a threshold of limits to be set for possible trading decisions.

The first approach to making indicator improvements is to examine it for visible deficiencies. But always be careful when visually looking at indicator performance. We humans don't always see what is really there. So far, the progress made with ATREx has been visually good. We are about to see, however, some shortcomings that need to be addressed.

We see in Figure 5.13 a daily chart of Occidental (OXY) in a very volatile broader

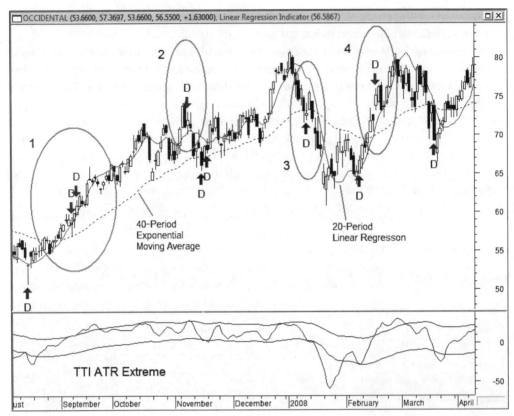

FIGURE 5.13 This daily chart of Occidental (OXY) during the subprime financial mess that began in late 2007 shows a very marked increase in volatility. The current version of TTI ATREx will require some volatility compensation for it to self-compensate for these conditions.

Chart created in MetaStock.

market period. This is during the subprime credit crisis that began in late 2007. Take a look at all of the trading signals generated by the ATREx MetaStock Expert around the price plot. The signals have been modified to show a transaction up or down arrow with the letter D above or below it. This is to designate it as a signal generated by the current version of ATREx.

There are a total of 10 signals generated. The circled areas show the four trade signals that will likely produce trades that stop out and lose money. The remaining six would likely produce profitable swing trades. Mind you, we are not trying to be highly scientific at this stage of our indicator development. It is important to preserve your time when doing indicator development. If you test and quantify the performance level for each possible iteration of a prospective indicator throughout its development cycle, it would be all consuming. We must have time left to devote to actual trading. It is therefore best to develop visually throughout the major part of the process. Examine performance by looking at a representative sample of charts across multiple market environments.

You will find this part time-consuming enough. Once through the strategic stages, it is best to use statistically valid back-testing and optimize the code.

So then, let's focus on the conditions under which ATREx fails in the Occidental chart. Circle 1 shows a solid short-term trend change. Perhaps if the signal had occurred 5 to 10 periods later, the trade could stop out without so much loss. This takes us to a tenet that is needed to guide the logic of technical analysis indicator and system design. It goes like this:

A profitable trade missed is acceptable. An unprofitable trade taken is not acceptable. A trade without profit or loss is tolerated.

This has everything to do with what so many successful traders and investors call Rule Number One: Don't lose the money. Remember that a 100 percent gain is required to compensate for a 50 percent loss.

If ATREx had reached an extreme level at a higher reading in circled area 1, then the trade could have been salvaged as a small to zero loss, using an exit rule based on inactivity. In circle 2, the trade signal generated is just plain bad. It bleeds red beginning on day 2 and does not look back. Once again, this seems to happen because of a change in short-term trend direction. Circled area 3 shows a trade signal seven days after a short-term trend change. The theme that is surfacing here seems to be one of extreme limit response. In oversold and overbought indicator development, the nature of extreme limit quantification depends on those limits being appropriately flexible. The degree of flexibility needs to reference volatility adjusted for trend or range-bound conditions. This way, you can rely on your indicator at times when price is trending or not. It's time to brainstorm a bit. What are the three possible changes that can be made to eliminate some of the unprofitable signals without sacrificing the profitable signals?

1. Add a higher quantity of standard deviations to the upper and lower indicator bands. This would push them outward a bit more.

2. Shorten the length of the look-back period of the standard deviation measurement that defines the upper and lower extreme limits. It is currently set to 200 periods. Shortening it would make it more sensitive to current price volatility. This would enable it to react faster to increases and decreases in volatility.

3. Give the extreme limits some degree of predictability, and simultaneously enable it to statistically compensate for its actual ability to predict price direction. In other words, find a way to push the extreme limits outward when it's more likely to need pushing, and affect them less when they are less likely to need pushing. Hmmm, what might be able to do that...?

The first suggestion has only a minimal amount of merit because it fails to react to changing volatility conditions. It does not increase the degree of flexibility. The second idea has some advantages. It does add to the indicator's capability and is probably one where performance improvement can be made. It is merely, however, an optimization of an arbitrary value. Optimizing is one of the most difficult processes to perform manually. It involves quantifying a whole lot of results based on back-testing. That sort of activity is what microprocessors are for. The human brain is better suited to innovation.

At the early stages of technical analysis indicator development, you need to strive for innovation, and to do it boldly! It's not enough to just think outside the box. It's not enough to build larger boxes and then think outside of those. You must think outside of the entire box factory.

Suggestion number three is obviously the optimal one. It offers the most needed type of flexibility. It offers some prospect of prediction. As technicians, we are striving for tools with predictive value. Also, number three seeks to find an additional dimension of volatility measurement and adjustment. That makes it more innovative. Innovative growth of methodology is the focus of the early stage of indicator design. We can let the computer chips and software shake out the numbers later.

So then it's settled: we will do number three. The extreme limit needs to flex on the basis of current volatility increases. It needs to be more elastic when price is heading toward it with a definite and trending force. It is when price moves toward the extreme limit because of a trend change that it is likely to continue in that direction with less probability of subsequent reversal. When the trend changes, the trader needs to avoid trading the reversal. When the price movement is due to what is more likely to be random noise, however, then there is a higher probability of turning a short-term price reversal into profit.

What is needed in this case is a mathematical method for distinguishing between trend strength and random price movement. Wow, it's a good thing we just learned about linear regression and R-Squared because they are about to come in very handy.

The following line of code in the ATREx indicator currently adds one unit of its 200-period standard deviation to itself to establish an extreme level.

```
Mov(x, 40, E) + Stdev(x, 200);
```

Since linear regression can more accurately and closely track the movement of a price series, it will be a good basis for adding or removing additional value to the current standard deviation. R-Squared measures how accurately linear regression is explaining the price series. In a way, it predicts linear regression's ability to predict. Suppose, therefore, we change the MetaStock code for the extreme limit calculation to be:

```
Mov(x, 40, E) + Stdev(x, 200) + (RSquared(C, 20) * Stdev(x, 200))
```

Which can be shortened to:

```
Mov(x, 40, E) + ((1 + RSquared(C, 20)) * Stdev(x, 200))
```

This change takes the original extreme limit and adds more standard deviation value to it. It will add between zero and one whole standard deviation to the existing level. By using the R-Squared calculation, we are assuming that price is trending toward the extreme. R-Squared gives a higher value when the confidence level of the standard deviation is high. In other words, if the probability of the price movement is deliberate, then R-Squared will read closer to 100 percent than zero percent. This higher R-Squared value will result in the extreme boundary being further away from the indicator line. It then provides price with more room to travel before reaching the extreme point.

Inversely, when the price movement is less deliberate, which would more likely be statistical noise, the R-Squared value is lower. This condition causes the extreme line to be closer to the indicator line. Having the indicator cross the extreme threshold in circumstances of random market fluctuations will produce more profitable reversal trades. This lessens the probability of trading against the trend. So that's our hypothesis at this point.

Well, how does this theory and indicator code change actually play out? In Figure 5.14, we have added the new version of ATREx to the middle indicator pane. It is the

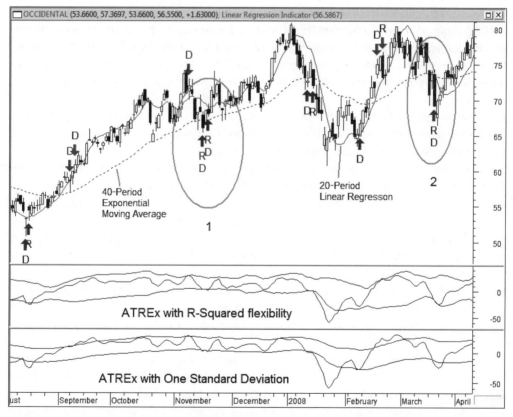

FIGURE 5.14 The addition of R-Squared compensation in TTI ATREx creates fewer signals and greatly improves accuracy. Those signals designated with R and RD use R-Squared. R-Squared helps calculations to discern deliberate and directional price action versus random movement.

Chart created in MetaStock.

one with the R-Squared calculations that add to the extreme threshold measurement. In the upper price plot pane, the MetaStock TTI Expert has been broadened to give trade signals on three different long and short conditions. They are:

1. Long or short entry based on the past ATREx version using only one standard deviation. These signals are shown with a new designation of D beneath or above the arrow symbol.

2. Long or short entry based on the current ATREx version using one standard deviation plus an R-Squared adjusted portion of one standard deviation. These signals are shown with a new designation of R beneath or above the arrow symbol.

3. Long or short entry based on the current ATREx version and the past version of ATREx. In other words, on days when both conditions 1 and 2 signal, this combined signal will show. These signals are shown with a new designation of RD beneath or above the arrow symbol.

All of the original 10 D signals are still in place; three of them are now included in the RD signals. In the middle indicator pane, compare different dates to see how the ATREx extreme thresholds expand as price moves decisively in one direction, such as the months of September, October, January, and February. The newer version does not seem to avoid all of the unprofitable trade signals. It clearly sidesteps the train wreck signal previously generated in September. It lines up right beside the two poor trade signals that occurred in January and February, however, and commits virtually the same error, each delayed by two days. The delay caused by moving outward the extreme limit is not a bad thing, but it's rather hard to gauge sometimes.

There is, however, one important phenomenon that jumps out at us. In the two circled areas are the combined RD trading signals. These are the situations where both the previous and the current versions of ATREx signal on the same day. Three signals are generated and they are all profitable. Actually, the two in November should be considered as one because of proximity. Nonetheless, the score is good guys two, and bad guys zero.

This gives us something new to think about. Is it possible that the combination of the two differently measured circumstances signaling simultaneously creates a higher probability of trading success? Does that combination have higher predictive value? It creates another condition to observe visually as you go forward to observe these indicators and trade signals in a hundred charts or so.

It is obvious at this point to see the value of easily configured indicators on chart-based trading signals. While it would be possible to visually pick out the indicator line crosses and see trade signals without the chart-based arrows, it is certainly a lot more work and error prone to do so. Since your system development time and trading time are very valuable, it is important that you learn to use all of the tools at your disposal.

So that you can see how these signals were generated, the following is the MetaStock code that automates the buy and sell signals in the onscreen MetaStock Expert.

Sell signal down arrow for both versions of ATREx:

```
Name: TTI ATR Top with R and D
Symbol: Sell Arrow
Color: Red
Label: RD
Condition:
x:= If(C < Mov(C, 40, E),
(((L - Mov(L, 40, E)) / C) * 100) * ((ATR(14) / C) * 100),
(((H - Mov(H, 40, E)) / C) * 100) * ((ATR(14) / C) * 100));
Cross(Mov(x, 3, S),
Mov(x, 40, E) + ((1 + RSquared(C, 20)) * Stdev(x, 200)) )
AND
Cross(Mov(x, 3, S), Mov(x, 40, E) + Stdev(x, 200))
```

Buy signal up arrow for both versions of ATREx:

```
Name: TTI ATR Bottom with R and D
Symbol: Buy Arrow
Color: Blue
Label: RD
Condition:
x:= If(C < Mov(C, 40, E),
(((L - Mov(L, 40, E)) / C) * 100) * ((ATR(14) / C) * 100),
(((H - Mov(H, 40, E)) / C) * 100) * ((ATR(14) / C) * 100));
Cross(Mov(x, 40, E) - ((1 + RSquared(C, 20)) * Stdev(x, 200)),
Mov(x, 3, S) )
AND
Cross(Mov(x, 40, E) - Stdev(x, 200), Mov(x, 3, S))
```

Sell signal down arrow for ATREx using R-Squared:

```
Name: TTI ATR Top with R-Square
Symbol: Sell Arrow
Color: Red
Label: R
Condition:
x:= If(C < Mov(C, 40, E),
(((L - Mov(L, 40, E)) / C) * 100) * ((ATR(14) / C) * 100),
(((H - Mov(H, 40, E)) / C) * 100) * ((ATR(14) / C) * 100));
Cross(Mov(x, 3, S),
Mov(x, 40, E) + ((1 + RSquared(C, 20)) * Stdev(x, 200)) )
```

Buy signal up arrow for ATREx using R-Squared:

```
Name: TTI ATR Bottom with R-Squared
Symbol: Buy Arrow
Color: Blue
Label: R
Condition:
x:= If(C < Mov(C, 40, E),
(((L - Mov(L, 40, E)) / C) * 100) * ((ATR(14) / C) * 100),
(((H - Mov(H, 40, E)) / C) * 100) * ((ATR(14) / C) * 100));
Cross(Mov(x, 40, E) - ((1 + RSquared(C, 20)) * Stdev(x, 200)),
Mov(x, 3, S))
```

Sell signal down arrow for ATREx using only standard deviation:

```
Name: TTI ATR Top
Symbol: Sell Arrow
Color: Red
Label: D
Condition:
x:= If(C < Mov(C, 40, E),
(((L - Mov(L, 40, E)) / C) * 100) * ((ATR(14) / C) * 100),
(((H - Mov(H, 40, E)) / C) * 100) * ((ATR(14) / C) * 100));
Cross(Mov(x, 3, S), Mov(x, 40, E) + Stdev(x, 200))
```

Buy signal up arrow for ATREx using only standard deviation:

```
Name: TTI ATR Bottom
Symbol: Buy Arrow
Color: Blue
Label: D
Condition:
x:= If(C < Mov(C, 40, E),
(((L - Mov(L, 40, E)) / C) * 100) * ((ATR(14) / C) * 100),
(((H - Mov(H, 40, E)) / C) * 100) * ((ATR(14) / C) * 100));
Cross(Mov(x, 40, E) - Stdev(x, 200), Mov(x, 3, S))
```

DEVELOPMENT EFFICIENCY

When working to develop your own personal indicators you will need to review countless charts throughout a logically progressive process. Most advanced technical analysis
software platforms have the capability to display signals as symbols in the area of the
price bars. Since this book is using MetaStock for the demonstrable presentation of

charts and trading logic, it would be prudent to expand on how it is done. Equivalent code is presented in Appendix A. In MetaStock, this display functionality is done using the Expert system. It enables many features that are too numerous to explain here. The embedded chart symbols are configured on the Symbols tab of the Expert Editor.

We are presented in Figure 5.15 with a view of this tab. Each onscreen symbol has its own line item. By choosing to edit or create a new symbol, you can enter programming code, such as that shown earlier. Use of this feature is intuitive. Clicking on the tabs in the Expert Symbol Editor enables you to name the symbol, program its conditions, and define the selection of the actual symbol and its appearance. This makes it possible to quickly and visually scan charts to observe the effects of your code changes. It is very important to make use of this capability so that it becomes second nature to your development process.

INVENTING WHEELS: YOU'RE NOT ALONE

How long did it take to invent the wheel? It's certain to have taken some trial and error with logs and other round things. It can cause one to wonder how many prehistoric deep thinkers were ridiculed for playing with circular objects instead of hunting for food. More importantly, the question is, how many times disparate groups of early humans' predecessors suffered this learning curve all over the planet? Long-range communication did not exist, so Ig could not exactly get on the phone and call Thag and tell him about this new thing he made that rolls.

Fortunately, in the world of technical analysis indicators, you don't have to re-create the wheel. The good news is that stock data have been calculated and reasoned to the nth degree with some very sound analytical basis. High, Low, Open, Close, and Volume have been sliced and diced about every way that they can be cut up. This means that existing technical analysis indicators are a rich source of indicator design logic. The key is to adapt an existing indicator's logic to use volatility as a prime measurement in lieu of its current method. That is exactly what we do next.

Performing TA Surgery

There are so many technical indicators that have come and gone it can be difficult to make choices. Let's start with one that has stood a test of time. The stochastic oscillator is a widely used indicator today. It is a momentum measurement invented by George Lane in the 1950s. To understand the stochastic oscillator's exact math and uses, research can be conducted very easily on the Internet, or in countless books on technical analysis. It would not serve any purpose to repeat what has already been written about the stochastic oscillator here. For our purposes, we are interested in the internal logic it is based on.

The stochastic is calculated as follows:

1. First consider that there is a look-back period and a slowing period. These are two separate values.

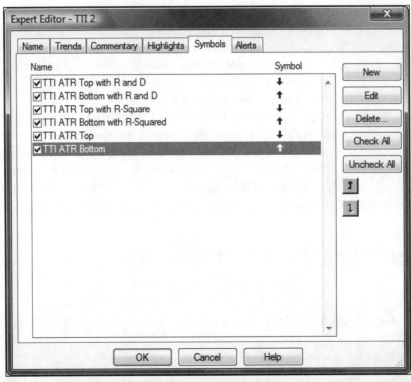

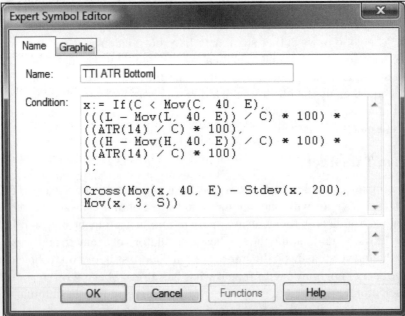

FIGURE 5.15 In MetaStock, the onscreen Expert system enables visual signals generated by the coded instructions of your choosing, which makes manual chart review much faster.

Created in MetaStock.

2. Value one is today's close minus the lowest low value within a set look-back period.
3. Sum value one for the previous price bars over the quantity of bars designated by the number of slowing periods.
4. Value two is the highest high value minus the lowest low value during the look-back period.
5. Sum value two for the previous price bars over the quantity of bars designated by the number of slowing periods.
6. Divide the summation of value one by the summation of value two. Then multiply by 100.

Here is the classic stochastic calculation expressed in a MetaStock internal function statement:

```
Stoch(5, 3)
```

Here is the same stochastic oscillator written in a more arithmetic format, but still in MetaStock code:

```
( Sum(C - LLV(L, 5), 3) / Sum(HHV(H, 5) - LLV(L, 5), 3) ) * 100
```

This code contains a few things that you have not yet seen. It contains some new functions, and also a programming technique called *nesting*. Here is an explanation.

- `LLV(L, 5)` is a function that computes the lowest low value over the past five price bars.
- `HHV(H, 5)` is a function that computes the highest high value over the past five price bars.
- `Sum(C, 3)` would add the closing prices of the last three price bars. Therefore, `Sum(C - LLV(L, 5), 3)` simply adds together the result of the `C - LLV(L, 5)` calculation for the previous three periods. This is called *function nesting*. It is a common structure used in function-based programming languages, such as Microsoft Excel and MetaStock.

Take a moment and study the line of MetaStock code that expresses the stochastic oscillator calculation. Break it apart and study the pieces. Study it until you understand the arithmetic. This is important. You need to be able to reason the indicator in your mind. This ability is key if you want to be successful at making logic-based development changes. It is also critical if you are going to profit from performing surgery on the existing indicator.

The stochastic is measuring, in essence, the relative level of the current price to an entire price range, over a given look-back period. In the case of the code stated thus far, the look-back period is five bars. The slowing period's duration is a value of three. The most commonly accepted method of manipulating the stochastic oscillator is to adjust these values lower or higher. This makes the stochastic more or less sensitive to price movement, respectively.

Modify the Base

We know that when price moves to extremes, so too does its short-term volatility. The stock's very characteristics of movement change. Many existing technical analysis indicators attempt to measure this. Changes in short-term volatility characteristics are most often the dominant base predictive value.

Given this tenet, the question then becomes how can we change the existing stochastic algorithm to reflect a volatility basis? Suppose we change the existing expression from:

```
( Sum(C - LLV(L, 5), 3) / Sum(HHV(H, 5) - LLV(L, 5), 3) ) * 100
```

to

```
1 x1:= Stdev(C, 14);
2 x2:= ( Sum(x1 - LLV(x1, 5), 3) /
3 Sum(HHV(x1, 5) - LLV(x1, 5), 3) ) * 100;
4 Mov(x2, 3, E)
```

Line one assigns the value of the standard deviation for the past 14 days to the variable *x1*. The use of these variables saves us from a lot of repetitive code segments. Lines two and three are the stochastic algorithm, which substitute the *x2* variable for the closing price. The indicator is therefore no longer using the closing price as the measured value; it is now using standard deviation. Line four converts the stochastic calculation, *x2*, to a three-period exponential moving average, for smoothing purposes.

With these changes, the calculation will now measure increases in volatility, as expressed in standard deviation, relative to a recent window of time. The calculation will still output a value between 0 and 100. In Figure 5.16, there is a daily chart of JPMorgan Chase (JPM), and this new indicator is plotted in the lower pane. Let's name this indicator TTI StochEx, for TTI Stochastic Extreme. As you can see from the corresponding circled areas, the algorithm seems to measure extreme price swings. There is one characteristic of note in that a high reading occurs regardless of the direction of the price swing. This will require that some logic be applied when generating buy and sell signals.

The TTI StochEx is an indicator with a signal confined to a fixed range. It will never read greater than 100 or less than zero. Given this constraint, how should the extreme level be defined? If you recall Figure 4.1 in the previous chapter, it shows the normal percentage of sample distribution as indicated by the multiple of standard deviations. For simplicity's sake, let's choose two standard deviations, which would be roughly 95 percent. This is, after all, a measurement of volatility. This translates to the upper horizontal line at 95 that you see in Figure 5.16.

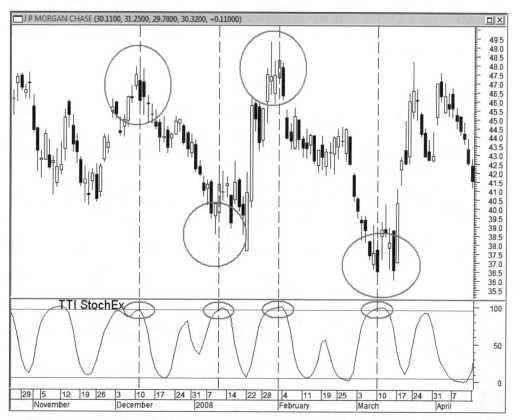

FIGURE 5.16 Here, a daily chart of JPMorgan Chase (JPM) shows us that the first version of TTI StochEx seems well suited to detecting oversold and overbought levels in a volatile and range-bound market.

Chart created in MetaStock.

The chart of JPMorgan Chase shows a sideways cycling price movement. How does TTI StochEx fare when prices are not very cyclical? Figure 5.17 shows a chart of ITT Industries during 2006. The price action is not very cyclical or trending. A new onscreen expert has been set up. There is also a 20-period exponential moving average plotted. The expert is programmed to:

- Show buy arrows when the close is below its 20-day exponential moving average, and the TTI StochEx crosses above 95.
- Show sell arrows when the close is above its 20-day exponential moving average, and the TTI StochEx crosses above 95.

There are six trade signals shown. The three to the left appear to be timely and potentially profitable. The three to the right, however, seem ill-timed and most likely to lose money. This is not what we are shooting for. What is different about the price action on the right side of the chart compared to the left?

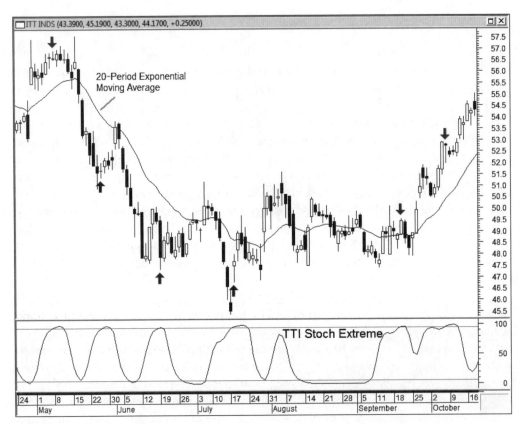

FIGURE 5.17 This chart of ITT Industries (ITT) shows a market that is not range bound, and TTI StochEx has some difficulty discerning profitable points from unprofitable ones. Overbought and oversold indicators suffer most with this type of meandering or trending price action.

Chart created in MetaStock.

We see at left that ITT Industries is visually demonstrating a greater degree of trading range. It is showing a tighter price channel at right. An adjustment that can be made is to detect more recent trading range activity. One possible change to the StochEx indicator therefore could be to add the ATR accelerator. This could add the ability to differentiate movement that has an increase in more recent volatility characteristics.

Here is the proposed change to the TTI StochEx MetaStock code:

```
1 x1:= If(C > Mov(C, 14, S), Stdev(C, 14), -1 * Stdev(C, 14));
2 x2:= ( Sum(x1 - LLV(x1, 5), 3) /
3 Sum(HHV(x1, 5) - LLV(x1, 5), 3) ) * 100;
4 x3:= x1 * ATR(5);
5 x4:= (Sum(x3 - LLV(x3, 5), 3) /
6 Sum(HHV(x3, 5) - LLV(x3, 5), 3)) * 100;
```

```
7 Mov(x2, 3, E);
8 Mov(x4, 3, E);
```

In this new version of code, we have doubled the indicator by creating a dual plot with the addition of line seven. The existing version is calculated along with the new version, which uses the ATR accelerator. Line one includes an `If` statement that converts the standard deviation measurement to a negative when the closing price is below the 14-period moving average. This is because regardless of the direction of the standard deviation, it is always expressed as a positive, which just wouldn't do. In line four, an additional variable called $x3$ is created to represent the measured value that is accelerated by ATR(5). Note that the standard deviation look-back period is 14 and the ATR look-back period is 5. The ATR period is shorter so as to measure a more recent change in true range volatility. In line 5, the same stochastic algorithm is used but with the new $x3$ value instead of $x2$. Both versions are plotted in lines six and seven. Plotting both of them next to each other will give us an immediate visual performance comparison when viewing charts.

The result of the new version of TTI StochEx, containing the ATR accelerator, is shown in Figure 5.18. The same chart of ITT Industries also shows us modified trade signals. The onscreen expert now displays signals for the standard deviation method with an SD. The ATR-enhanced signals are tagged with ATR. Signals that are generated with both methods are marked with a C, which is short for *combined*. The dashed line plot in the lower indicator pane shows the new ATR accelerated indicator.

As you can see, the ATR accelerated signal avoids the trap that the two poor SD signals on the right fall into. It measures a lower level of recent daily trading range and thus causes the StochEx value to stop short of reaching the 95 threshold. In fact, the ATR accelerated version on this chart example is present in three signals. The two circled on the left seem potentially profitable. The new signal circled at center is very interesting because it shows a quick reaction to the short-term swing, even though the trade would likely be a flat stop with little to no loss. On balance, the change seems positive on this chart because the win-loss ratio is greatly improved.

That analysis may seem simple or even potentially flawed. At this stage of indicator development, we can only make broad assumptions. It is the task of the developer to choose progress that moves toward innovation and new methodology. Granted, it is necessary to be as quantitative as one can. Study 50 to 100 charts for each iteration over multiple market years and through different market conditions. It is time-consuming work. Even after all this, you will need the help of back-testing software to know for sure if one version actually performs better than another. However, and this is important, if you rely solely on back-testing between indicator revisions, then you will not develop the reasoning required to find the best overall algorithm designs. Think things through and understand the math. An overreliance on back-testing in the early stages will cause one to revise without logic. Sometimes it's important to try what-if calculations, but don't rely on the process of throwing bubble gum at the wall and hoping it will stick.

With that said, then we should eat our own dog food. Because of space limitations,

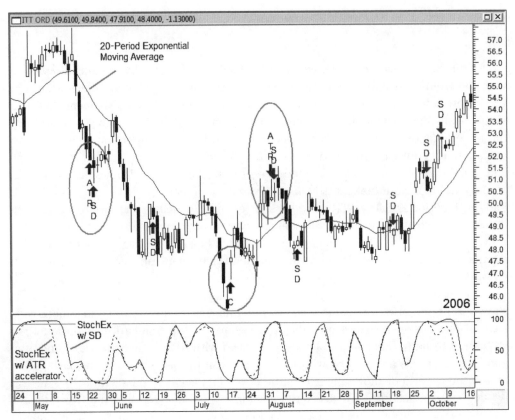

FIGURE 5.18 By enhancing TTI StochEx with an ATR accelerator, it is better able to find profitable overbought and oversold levels. While the quantity of signals is reduced, the accuracy is greatly improved.

Chart created in MetaStock.

it isn't possible to display and analyze 100 charts in this book just for a comparison. It is important, however, to compare the TTI StochEx indicator's performance in a different chart. It is imperative to discover its strengths and weaknesses.

Break the Wheel

Now it is time to look for chart examples in which TTI StochEx falls on its sword. This is not fun. Here is an indicator that you have just poured the talents of your intellect into and you have to break it. It has to be done, though. Just remember that your trading account is worth more than your pride.

Figure 5.19 is a daily chart of Thomas & Betts (TNB), showing us a well-defined uptrend. Notice that price movement is straight, with very little oscillation. This is a swing trader's nightmare. It is also the worst scenario for an oversold and overbought indicator. Indicators of this classification need real highs and real lows. This chart gives

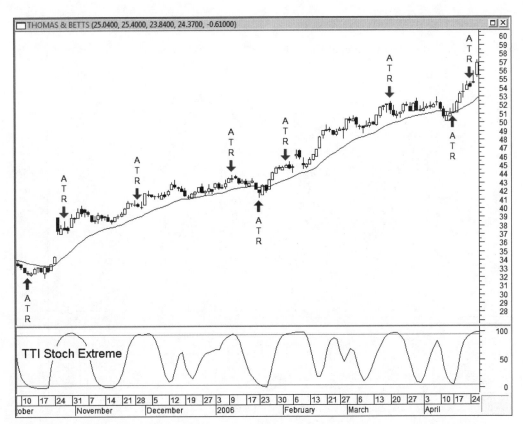

FIGURE 5.19 A daily chart of Thomas & Betts (TNB) shows a clear trend rally. This sort of price movement without oscillation is the most difficult for detecting overbought conditions.

Chart created in MetaStock.

us highs without lows. As you can plainly see, all of the overbought signals give disastrous entry timing. The upward price movement is relentless.

This chart of Thomas & Betts teaches us a valuable basic lesson. You have certainly heard this many times before, and nowhere is it more true than in technical analysis.

Use the right tool for the right job.

Brilliant, yes? Successful traders make a lot of money by taking it from other traders who are misusing technical indicators and methods. Oversold and overbought indicators are the most challenged in the market conditions shown in Figure 5.19. The key to always remember is that a wide selection of tools and hardware is required to build a house. The technical tools and methods required for profitable trading are likewise not confined to a couple of indicators. Because of its importance, we repeat the list of capabilities that volatility-based trading requires.

1. Oversold and overbought levels

2. Trend detection

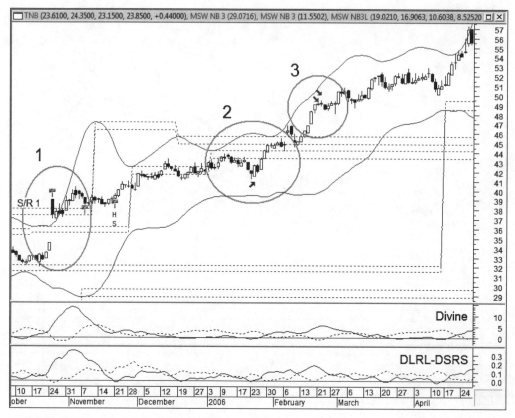

FIGURE 5.20   A MetaSwing chart of Thomas & Betts (TNB) shows a confirmed strong trending rally in place beginning in October 2005.

Chart created in MetaStock. Chart uses the MetaSwing Add-on, by Northington Trading, LLC. All rights reserved.

3. Broad market integration

4. Support and resistance

5. Historical volatility

6. Implied volatility

7. Multiple time frame verification

The lesson here is that we cannot expect one indicator to provide a complete basis for trading decisions. In this exercise, only one of the capabilities in our list is being addressed. Actual trading entries and exits should be made using cross-verification with most of the capabilities in this list.

Trend detection was shown earlier in this chapter using Projected Implied Volatility. A close look at Figure 5.20 shows that Thomas and Betts was in a well-defined trend. (This figure shows the same time span as Figure 5.19.) In circled area 1, this MetaSwing

FIGURE 5.21 Thomas & Betts (TNB) actually began the trend three months earlier.

Chart created in MetaStock. Chart uses the MetaSwing Add-on, by Northington Trading, LLC. All rights reserved.

chart has price gapping up past the upper N Band and S/R lines, and proceeding to trade above S/R 1. This is a strong breakout to trend signal. Trading continues to push upward in circles 2 and 3 through all S/R lines. Once again, it is a strong bullish trend, and so, therefore, it would be foolish to attempt trading to the short side.

If we are bringing trading decisions into this discussion, then it is imperative to look further back in the chart. In Figure 5.21, it is clear that the trend started earlier. Thomas and Betts actually began the trend in question in circled area 4. There is another important symptom to note. In MetaSwing's indicator panes, examine the period from mid-November through late March. The reduced height of the indicator oscillations shows reduced volatility relative to the months previously. In MetaSwing, visual indicator volatility is an important signal of hidden price intentions.

Therefore, let's not go hard on ourselves about the inability of TTI StochEx to successfully trade the swings in Figure 5.19. TTI StochEx is currently designed for more sideways moving price action. Just the fact that it is confined to output readings of a fixed range, between 0 and 100, puts it at a disadvantage in a trending chart environment. Alas, don't sell it short. It works well for the task for which it has been designed. Also, there may yet be more capabilities that volatility-based math can do for it....

ONWARD

As we have focused on continuing the efforts to apply volatility-based math to indicator design, it becomes more and more apparent that technical analysis for successful trading is a team sport. The team consists of the seven primary capabilities of volatility-based technical analysis. Each of the seven plays an important role.

Projected Implied Volatility (PIV) plays an important role in defining the invisible levels of support and resistance that define reversal points, trading ranges, and trend confirmations. Implied volatility is no longer solely the domain of options traders. Stock traders must participate in the equities markets, understanding all of the dimensions in which they exist.

As a system developer, you must work without end to innovate your methods so that they are original and often unconventional. The thought processes needed to accomplish this exist within an overall volatility framework. It is this framework inside of which we climb and swing from capability to derivation in the next chapter.

CHAPTER 6

The Framework

*A Structural Approach
for Cross-Verification*

J ust south of Lafayette, Louisiana, and down a bayou there lived two Cajun farmers named Boudreaux and Matherne. They had been friends since childhood. It came time for Boudreaux and his wife to celebrate their twenty-fifth wedding anniversary, so they went on a romantic weekend trip to New Orleans. While there they went to the horse races, where Boudreaux's wife was fascinated with a beautiful white Arabian stallion on display. Boudreaux gathered much of his savings and bought the horse for his love.

When he returned to the farm, his longtime hunting buddy Matherne came to see the horse. "Boudreaux," he proclaimed, "dat is da bes horse I ever done seen!" Matherne decided that he wanted a horse just as magnificent for his family, but could not find one.

As time passed, Boudreaux's wife tired of the stallion. One day while duck hunting, Boudreaux said, "Man, dat horse, he's gettin' lazy, yeah. My wife done stopped ridin' him and dat horse jus sits around and eats." Matherne saw his chance and offered to buy the horse from Boudreaux for $1,500. This was $500 more than Boudreaux had originally paid, and so a deal was made.

Matherne and his family loved the horse and rode him often. Before long, though, Boudreaux's wife decided that she wanted her beautiful white stallion back. Boudreaux offered Matherne $2,000 for the horse. Matherne, who was able to separate business from his passions, agreed, and the horse once again belonged to Boudreaux.

It seemed that Boudreaux's wife was a fickle woman who only wanted what she did not (or could not) have, so the magnificent stallion was once again idle. And Matherne's children missed the horse so much he offered Boudreaux $2,500 for it. Boudreaux was very happy. "Aaiiii!" he exclaimed to his wife. "I jus sold dat horse to Matherne again!"

Boudreaux's wife was not happy about losing something she possessed. Before long,

Boudreaux again repurchased the horse, only to have Matherne buy it back again. This went on for over a year, and each time the price was increased by $500.

One afternoon, Matherne was tending to the beautiful white horse when he was approached by a traveling salesman from Texas. The Texan desired to own the horse, and a price was negotiated. Matherne turned a healthy profit over what he had last paid Boudreaux.

When Boudreaux heard of the transaction, he rushed over to Matherne's farm very upset. Matherne explained to Boudreaux that he was offered a good price for the horse, so he took it. No longer able to contain himself, Boudreaux exclaimed, "Can't you see what you done did? You and me, we was makin' a damn good livin' off o' dat horse!" Boudreaux's thought processes were too constrained; he was trapped into thinking of value only in the context of what it meant to his longtime friend. He also allowed his emotions to play a large role in decision making. Comparatively, Matherne was easily able to see the relative value of his holdings and made better decisions.

Cajuns and horses aside, it is important for all traders to structure their thought processes—beginning with their technical analysis methods. With so much information upon which to base trading decisions, it is easy for one's judgment to be inconsistent, and unknowingly incorporate emotion. A trader must understand what is relevant and significant, and what is not.

How can the technician choose the best underlying data to process? What is relevant to what? How can you build a technical analysis methodology that cuts through the fog? How can you think more like Matherne and less like Boudreaux?

ADOPTING A STRUCTURE

We all have life experiences. Whether we want to or not, these experiences follow us everywhere, even when we are in front of the trading screen. One of the main purposes of technical analysis is to trump our emotions, and thus the experiences they are based upon, so that we can trade more objectively.

A principle of Neuro-Linguistic Programming (NLP) states that our memories have structure.[1] Because we all store memories differently, we relate to experiences differently. By changing the structure of our thinking, the outcome will be more uniform, and less affected by our individual memory structures.

In technical analysis, this structure needs to be presented as a visual presentation and analysis methodology. It should at least be a set of conditions and criteria, in print, and in front of you at your analysis workstation. This produces consistency. It produces trades that make sense instead of trades that feel good. Good trade entries don't necessarily feel good, but they should make sense. Once you decide to trade, structured trading is a must. Here's the rub, though: Structured thinking while developing technical indicators, and a trading methodology, can be counterproductive.

To a large degree, we must think like children when developing analysis tools. Here's what you should emulate:

Child: What makes the car go?

Parent: The engine.

Child: Why?

Parent: Because it runs and turns the drive shaft, which turns the wheels. (The parent mistakenly thinks that the completeness of the answer closes the topic.)

Child: But why does the engine run?

Parent: Gasoline burns inside of the engine.

Child: Why?

Parent: Because a spark plug ignites it.

Child: Why?

Parent: A computer-controlled ignition system makes the spark plug produce a spark. (Still mistaken.)

Child: Why?

Parent: So that the engine will run smooth and control the speed of the car.

Child: Why?

And on it goes ...

Anyone who is a parent, or has ever cared for a seven-year-old child, has had one of these conversations. At first it is cute, but it soon gets to be very tiring. The child always wins. But do understand that when you have this conversation you are witnessing brilliance at work. This child knows nothing of the flammable nature of gasoline, or the precise timing of a computer-controlled ignition system, and yet she can understand much of what makes a car propel itself down the highway, after only a single conversation.

Why, you ask? (Pun intended.) The child is able to learn new concepts well because:

- They want to understand root causes.
- They accept information objectively without the prejudices of prior experiences.
- They are not afraid to probe for an answer.

This is how you need to conduct yourself and thought processes while building volatility-based technical analysis indicators and methodologies. Do not let past market absolutes constrain you. Financial markets have undergone tremendous changes in the past 10 years alone. New significant correlations with predictive qualities come into being every year. You can find and exploit them only if you think without boundaries. Think like a child, but trade like Matherne.

THINK AND SEE VOLATILITY

Consider the blank chart with only candlesticks representing price movement. To a technical analyst, it is a beautiful site. Within it is complete freedom to see all the important volatility-based measurements that matter most. A blank chart begins to give you the ability to think and see price movement differently. This is exactly what you need to do. So far we have focused most of our volatility measurements on indicator development. It is important to be able to look at a price chart without the aid of indicators and feel something. The best traders can do this. It often presents as the ability to look at a price point and feel that a point of inefficiency has been reached.

This ability to visually comprehend is not innate to humans like it is to sandpipers. We have to work at it. We will use here onscreen indicators that are displayed in the price plot area, just like we did with linear regression lines. Think of the price chart as a piece of cloth. Cloth is made of fabric. All sorts of threads can be stitched and woven into the fabric. We will refer to it herein as *Volatility Fabric*.

Standard Deviation Volatility Fabric

Let's start by doing some weaving. Look first at Figure 6.1, where we see a clean, daily chart of Motorola (MOT). What's visible is price moving up, down, and all around. And

FIGURE 6.1 Motorola (MOT) January to July 2004 is illustrated here.
Chart created in MetaStock.

even worse, there is a gap right in the middle. In general, gaps are awful things. They mess up technical indicators and add pure short-term unpredictability to the process of technical analysis. In retrospect, however, gaps give us information that would otherwise be difficult to attain.

A volatility fabric is a continuous series of volatility-based mathematical relationships shown as a backdrop to the price chart itself. Chart fabrics are not new. They have been presented in years past as many types of indicators, such as moving average ribbons. We will start with a fabric composed of standard deviations.

To display a standard deviation fabric, we will create it as an indicator. If you recall from Chapter 4, a standard deviation is built around a mean. The TTI Fabric SD indicator will begin with a 40-period exponential moving average to maintain consistency with our previous work. Quantities of standard deviation are then added to, and subtracted from, the moving average to create the fabric.

We see in Figure 6.2 what the TTI Fabric SD looks like. The darker central line is the 40-period exponential moving average. Each line successively moving away from the

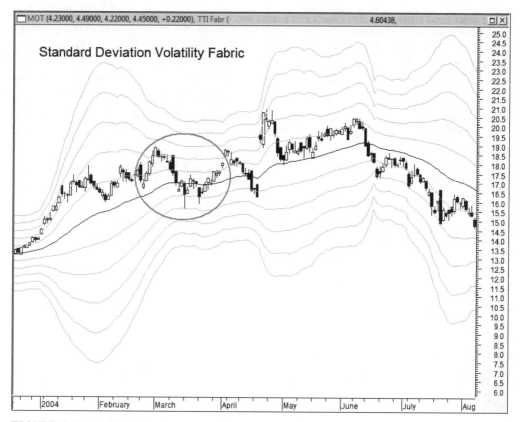

FIGURE 6.2 Standard Deviation Volatility Fabric is a variation of Bollinger Bands used to present an interactive background for the price and volatility relationship.

Chart created in MetaStock.

central moving average represents one additional standard deviation. The standard deviation lines are colored a light gray so that they present more of a backdrop, and avoid interfering with the primary trading signals that will ultimately be displayed. Study this chart for a moment. You may be wondering what the point is to this.

A fabric is not meant to be a primary indicator, or to generate buy or sell signals. Its purpose is to train your mind. With it consistently on the background of stock charts, your eyes begin to see price movement in a different way. The lines themselves show your eyes the distance price has traveled in units of that particular stock's standard deviation, in lieu of dollars or percentages. Your brain will begin to recognize movement by volatility measurement standards.

Relativity is added to price movements that might not be seen otherwise. For instance, it would appear in the circled area that Motorola trades downward during the month of March. In reality, it was a return to the central tendency of its trading range as measured by standard deviations. Yes, it did trade downward, but relative to its trading range, it did not do so. The fabric gives us a more important basis for normalizing price movement.

It's now important to point out that the example of volatility fabric in Figure 6.2 is actually a form of Bollinger Bands. The most basic form of a Bollinger Band is a measure of standard deviation around a simple moving average. You will most commonly see them presented as a 20-period simple moving average, with upper and lower band lines that have default values of two standard deviations. Even though our example uses an exponential moving average, it is the basic construct of Bollinger Bands.

John Bollinger created them and permanently changed the way the markets looked at short-term volatility. Many traders use Bollinger Bands without truly understanding how they are calculated. You should have an inherent advantage because the previous chapters presented the basic mathematical mechanics of this legendary volatility measurement tool.

Here's what the MetaStock code for TTI Fabric SD looks like:

```
 1  x1:= Mov(C, 40, E);
 2  x2:= Stdev(C, 40);
 3  x1 + (5 * x2);
 4  x1 + (4 * x2);
 5  x1 + (3 * x2);
 6  x1 + (2 * x2);
 7  x1 + x2;
 8  x1;
 9  x1-x2;
10  x1-(2 * x2);
11  x1-(3 * x2);
12  x1-(4 * x2);
13  x1-(5 * x2);
```

Line one establishes the 40-period moving average and assigns it to the variable $x1$. Line two calculates the value of a single standard deviation based on a 40-period moving average and assigns it to the variable $x2$. Line three displays the first fabric line from the top. It is a measurement of 5 standard deviations above the 40-period moving average. Lines four through seven do the same with different quantities of standard deviations. Line eight plots the 40-period exponential moving average. Lines nine through 13 plot the fabric lines below the moving average.

Linear Regression Volatility Fabric

Perhaps a more useful volatility fabric is one based on linear regression. Linear regression more closely tracks price movement. It is a better indicator of short-term central tendency. Also, average true range is a better measure of short-term volatility. Therefore, let's try a volatility fabric that is built on a 40-period continuous linear regression line.

We see once again in Figure 6.3 a daily chart of Motorola. But this time there is a linear regression volatility fabric on the chart. The fabric threads consist of average true range (ATR). The thread nearest to the center 40-period linear regression line is exactly two ATR(14) values away. After the first thread, each one thereafter is one additional ATR(14) value. Therefore, working from the inside out, the threads are at two, three, four, and five ATR(14) amounts from the interior linear regression line.

This author's preference is a Linear Regression Volatility Fabric for these reasons:

- There are fewer telescopic swings within the threads than with other measures. This is because its components are better measures of trader behavior.
- Expanding or contracting short-term volatility is generally obvious.
- Most price movement will be contained within two ATRs of deviation from the inner linear regression line.
- Most valid overbought and oversold levels are reached between two and four ATRs deviation.
- A value outside of five ATRs deviation indicates a very abnormal situation and should be looked at in a higher time frame.
- Short-term price movement across key thread levels can give valuable indications of short-term trend changes.

Examine the Linear Regression Volatility Fabric in Figure 6.3 for a moment. One of its best qualities is its ease of displaying expanding and contracting volatility. As volatility expands, the threads widen. It's impossible to miss. When volatility is expanding, your trading tactics must adapt to the condition. So many traders don't notice conditions when a little extra room on a sell stop is needed, due to an increase in short-term volatility. It's clear later that they got shaken out by a very small amount. When their position was sold at the stop level, it is likely that the buyer of their shares was more in tune to the current volatility environment. Motorola's volatility has expanded in Figure 6.3, and

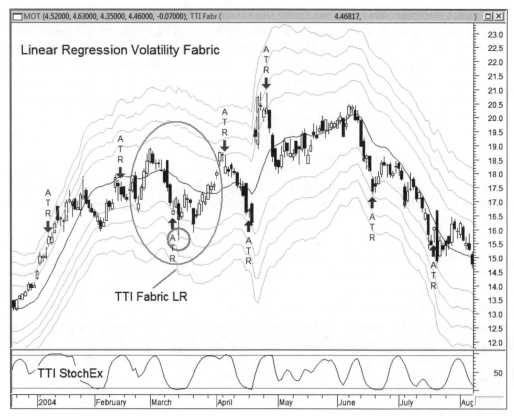

FIGURE 6.3 Linear Regression Volatility Fabric is shown here on a daily chart of Motorola (MOT). There is a center line, which is a 40-period continuous linear regression line. Built on the center line are threads separated by one ATR(14) value. The threads are at two, three, four, and five ATR(14) multiples. Also included for comparison is the TTI StochEx and its trade signals.

Chart created in MetaStock.

is obviously contracting by June 1, as noted by the vertical dashed line. By basing volatility on average true range, the threads show it as directionally neutral; price can rally, decline, or trade sideways and the volatility measurement is not affected. This is important for short-term traders.

You see, it's just as important to gauge the trading direction of prices as it is to understand the direction of volatility. This is an invisible dimension so often overlooked by traders. The importance of expanding and contracting volatility is an important concept that John Bollinger originally taught so well, and is truly universal.

When price movement is displayed over the backdrop of threads separated by increments of average true range your eye will become trained. You will begin to automatically gauge the length of movement over time in quantities of daily trading ranges. Trading becomes more significant when many ATRs are covered in a short period of time.

Perhaps most important, true overbought and oversold levels are more clearly defined when price has reached three or more ATRs from its linear regression line. Examine the circled area in Figure 6.3. This same price move in Figure 6.2 seemed to be a simple return to its central tendency. The Linear Regression Volatility Fabric paints a different picture, however. The negative two and three ATR levels tend to show some support because prices are lining up with them in an expanding volatility climate throughout February, March, and April. The smaller circled area inside the larger circle shows a great intraday trade entry opportunity as price reaches all the way out to the negative three ATR level.

The one particular example that makes fools of us is the signal in mid-January. Motorola has traded above the positive three ATR level, and TTI StochEx shows an overbought condition. However a strong short-term trend is under way. Shorting there is a pure crash and burn. Look closely at some other signs, though.

There is contracting volatility before the breakout. This is a nuclear-grade signal of the strong price move about to potentially happen. It is the same principle as a Bollinger Band squeeze. We will revisit this phenomenon later. Lastly, the upward price movement before the signal shows gaps. Gaps are powerful signals of the intent of the trading crowd. Trading against them is not recommended.

Here's what the MetaStock code for TTI Fabric LR looks like:

```
1 pds:= Input("Linear Regression Length", 5, 1000, 40);
2 x1:= LinearReg(C, pds, S, 1);
3 x2:= ATR(14);
4 x1 + (5 * x2);
5 x1 + (4 * x2);
6 x1 + (3 * x2);
7 x1 + (2 * x2);
8 x1;
9 x1-(2 * x2);
10 x1-(3 * x2);
11 x1-(4 * x2);
11 x1-(5 * x2);
```

In this fabric indicator version, we are using a new capability called an *Input statement*. The effect of the Input statement is to assign a value to a variable named *pds*. The *pds* variable enables a user input for the length of the linear regression measurement. The Input statement shown earlier establishes a possible low value of 5, a possible high value of 1,000, and a default value of 40. Line two establishes the linear regression line but uses *pds* as the look-back length. The overall effect of this enhancement is the ease of changing the linear regression parameter. Figure 6.4 shows how a simple right click of the indicator brings up a dialog box enabling you to easily change the value. Speed is very important when you want to examine many charts in the post-market segment of your day.

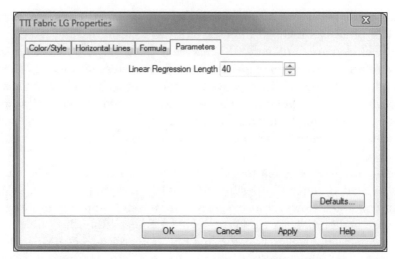

FIGURE 6.4 An Input statement enables the user to change program parameter values quickly for better analysis.

Created in MetaStock.

In general, the code lines for TTI Fabric LR are almost identical to its cousin, the TTI Fabric SD indicator. Obvious differences are that lines two and three establish the 40-period linear regression line and the ATR(14) value, respectively. Also there are two lines of code less in this indicator. The thread for one ATR value above and below is not needed.

Thread Significance

Let's take a look at another example of volatility fabric. Figure 6.5 shows a daily chart of Sanmina-SCI (SANM). This chart is equipped with the TTI Fabric LR. It also has the TTI StochEx plotted in the lower indicator pane as well as the TTI StochEx expert system trade signals show in the chart display area.

The circled areas show the overbought and oversold signals identified by the StochEx indicator, but only when price has reached three ATR(14) deviations from the central regression line. These three examples illustrate the significance of trading closer to volatility extremes. The other two examples, isolated with rectangles, show that there is less of an aggressive tendency for price to trade back toward the regression line, when price has not traveled far enough from the center.

Understand that this example is not that of a well-defined trend or a range trading range. It is a fairly common price chart. The direction of the linear regression lines enables the trader's eye to effortlessly understand the short-term slope. Location of the price relative to the thread adds significance to the degree to which it has reached a significant extreme. By leaving this fabric on your charts, your eyes will become trained to it. Set the colors of the lines to a very light gray so that they sit in the background

FIGURE 6.5 This daily chart of Sanmina-SCI (SANM) is another example of Linear Regression fabric in action. Note that when price action deviates from the central regression to the second thread or further, then short-term reversals are more likely.

Chart created in MetaStock.

and not clutter the chart. Consistent attention to this short-term volatility relationship will move the trading odds more toward your favor.

Volatility Contraction and Expansion

Have you ever noticed how life seems travel at different speeds? Sometimes things are normal, sometimes they are boring, and occasionally life is like getting shot out of a cannon. The saying "when it rains it pours" must originate from the times when daily routines suddenly cut loose and reach a breakneck pace. There must certainly be many aspects of human nature from which this phenomenon originates.

This same dynamic pace exists within traded securities, and it can be expressed through volatility. Many attempt to isolate it to a measurable cycle. While that may be possible, it need not be as complicated as waveform analytics. It's actually as simple as a signal from an extreme relationship.

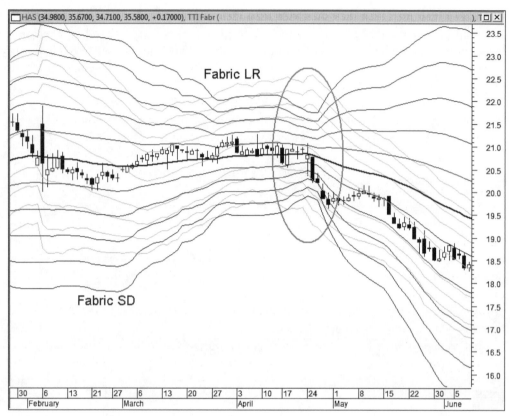

FIGURE 6.6 The relationship between Linear Regression Fabric and Standard Deviation Fabric shows a particular measurement of extreme contraction of volatility, which precedes larger price moves.

Chart created in MetaStock.

Let's be specific about the price scenario being described. Consider when a stock has been in a very flat trading range. Volatility as measured in a variety of ways contracts. The price action usually shows almost no cycling and is largely dominated by the average daily range. Then, price suddenly proceeds to trade strongly in a different direction. The average true range value expands, along with the overall trading range.

This is a commonly observed occurrence. It happens visually to almost all stocks and across most time frames. It is important to note that the visual nature of the pattern does often not coincide with the underlying mathematical relationships. Most often today the low volatility phase is detected by an extreme narrowing of Bollinger Bands. John Bollinger refers to this as a trading opportunity known as the *squeeze* method. What you will see presented in the following is detected differently, and has a limited degree of overlap with a Bollinger Band squeeze.

Figure 6.6 shows a daily chart of Hasbro (HAS). In the circled area, a sudden shift in the trading range and price volatility occurs on April 24th, 2006. The stock traded sideways before that day just beneath its linear regression line. We have plotted on this chart the Linear Regression fabric in the light gray lines, and the Standard Deviation fabric in the darker black lines. The purpose of these two simultaneous plots is not to create spider webs, but to show an important relationship. The relationship is the width of the LR fabric to the SD fabric.

As you can see in this case, the standard deviation fabric has contracted in such a way that it is enclosed well within the boundaries of the linear regression fabric. SD fabric is normally stretched much wider than LR fabric. In times of significant volatility contraction, however, the SD fabric exterior lines are much narrower than the LR fabric span. An extreme level of this ratio usually foretells a shift in the trading direction, and the possible beginning of a trend.

So do we need to have both LR fabric and SD fabric plotted on the chart to recognize these volatility contraction events? The answer is obviously no because we can express this relationship with simple math in a custom indicator. Logically, one can easily observe that the ratio is the difference between the LR fabric upper and lower lines, divided by the difference between the upper and lower SD fabric lines. The LR fabric difference will always be 10 times the ATR(14) value. The SD fabric difference will always be 10 times the standard deviation around a 40-period moving average. This can be reduced to a simple ratio of one to one.

Let's make a custom indicator that calculates this for us automatically and call it TTI Fabric Ratio LR-SD. The MetaStock code that turns this into an indicator is:

```
ATR(14) / Stdev(C, 40)
```

The chart of HASBRO has been modified in Figure 6.7 to by adding the TTI Fabric Ratio LR-SD indicator in the middle pane. Horizontal threshold lines of 1.0 and 1.5 are drawn for clarity. At a value of 1.0, the width of the threads are equal. If any value is greater than 1.0, it means that the SD fabric has contracted to less than that of the LR fabric. Also in Figure 6.7 the StochEx expert signals are displayed and circled.

A vertical dashed line is drawn on April 24, 2006, showing the candle where the daily range suddenly expands and the trading direction changes. TTI Fabric Ratio LR-SD values in the vicinity of 1.5 seem to more often predict these types of sudden, volatility expansion–oriented breakouts and breakdowns. Because this ratio is now an indicator, we can automatically reference it many ways, without the need to have the SD fabric plotted on the chart; too much stuff on the chart is counterproductive. Possibly the best way to see the ratio value going forward would be to make it a part of the Expert system. This would give an onscreen signal on the day that the ratio crossed above the value of 1.5. The MetaStock code that signals the event of the TTI Fabric Ratio LR-SD crossing above a level of 1.5 is:

```
Cross( Fml("TTI Fabric Ratio LR-SD"), 1.5)
```

This is a Cross statement. It compares two arguments separated by a comma. It renders a Boolean value: a one or a zero. The syntax is simple. When the first argument

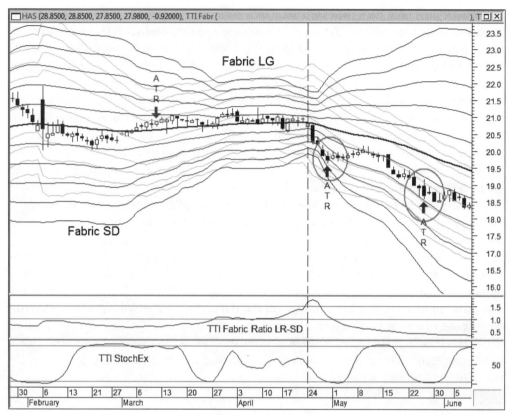

FIGURE 6.7 A second look at Fabric Ratio event shows how its best purpose is to alert the trader to possible beginnings of a new trend. This means that it's best not to trade against the direction of the price expansion.

Chart created in MetaStock.

value exceeds the second argument value, the statement returns a value of one, or else a value of zero. Another new statement type shown here is a Formula reference statement. It is used as the first argument within the Cross statement. Instead of duplicating the programming of the TTI Fabric Ratio LR-SD indicator, this method uses the actual indicator we previously created. This statement is nested within the Cross statement. The advantage of this type of programming is twofold. First, there is no need to duplicate programming. The programming for the indicator could be lengthy, and thus be very laborious and messy to rewrite time after time. Second, any changes or maintenance to the original ratio indicator need only be performed once, at the original formula itself. The change is thus implemented anywhere the formula is referenced.

The contraction of volatility and its sudden expansion, a Fabric Ratio event if you will, is very interesting and significant. But how do we use it to make money? It would be necessary to display a few dozen or two charts to show all the circumstances and nuances that Fabric Ratios create.

Most of Fabric Ratio events occur before some catalyst, the most common of which are earnings announcements. The event shown in Figure 6.7 is due to the premarket quarterly earnings release on April 24, 2006. Hasbro disappointed the Street's expectations, and pow—down it went. Volatility will contract at other times and trading will quiet down for any number of reasons. The great thing about being a technical trader is that you don't need to care why exactly. The math is what matters. We will save you at this point some research and give you some useful guidelines on this topic.

At first glance, Fabric Ratio events look like great opportunities. It seems like it is as simple as looking for the signal, then trade in the direction of the price expansion. It's not quite that simple. Price will often begin in one direction and reverse to the opposite direction. This sort of a fake can cost a lot of money in stopped-out positions. It is best not to trade with a breakout or breakdown purely on this signal, even though it looks so tempting to do so.

In Figure 6.7, the oversold signal shows that trading reversals in proximity to a Fabric Ratio event is hazardous. In the circled area on May 1, 2006, an oversold signal shows itself. If the event turns out to be the beginning of a new trend, such as in this case, then you are swimming upstream in the rapids by trading against it. In reality, the benefit of the Fabric Ratio event is to warn you off of trading just this type of situation. Trading is a net sum occupation. Reducing losses has the same effect on profitability as increasing gains. The greatest benefit to the Fabric Ratio therefore is to alert you to the possible beginning of a trend.

THE FRAMEWORK COMPONENTS

How do we, as technical analysts, make basic market data relevant? More specifically, how do we make it predict? The answer is fairly simple: The analyst must take meaningful market data and (through the way it relates to other meaningful market data) find valid logical correlations.

If this is what we must do, then is any specific piece of market data alone significant? Certainly, but it rarely counts for much in technical analysis. If we must analyze market data in relation to other market data, then how are these relative comparisons and calculations constructed? This is the question that brings us to the topic at hand.

In the pages that follow are various types of methods for making chart and market data relative. The formats proposed herein are not meant to represent all possible expressions; they do form, however, a complete start of the subject.

In an attempt to keep this as interesting as a possible, and to keep you from sticking a pencil into your eye, we will use a fictitious spousal relationship between Phil and Suzie. There will be some stock charts and indicators, too. Mainly though, you should gain an expanded ability to define exact ways to analyze chart data for volatility-based correlations, which is to say that it will make it easier to create indicators.

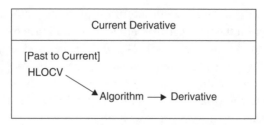

FIGURE 6.8   This is an example of a current derivative diagram.

Current Derivative

All simple indicators are derivative in nature. An indicator produces a value that is derived from some measurable property of the underlying stock. The indicator is therefore a derivative. A *current derivative* is a value that measures some property of the underlying stock in the time frame that ends in the present time period. A current derivative diagram is shown in Figure 6.8.

Let's make a current derivative out of an everyday life situation. It's Tuesday night, which means bowling for Phil. Suzie is fine with bowling just as long as Phil is home by 8:30 to help put the kids to bed. It's a tough job alone, and the kids respond well to Phil's bedtime stories.

Suzie thinks that reading bedtime stories to the kids with beer breath sends the wrong message to them at such an early age. Phil likes to keep up with the guys and forgets how important an alcohol-free bedtime can be. Phil arrives home at 8:50 and Suzie is upset. Phil tries to determine just *how* upset Suzie is. Phil thinks about the factors. He got home just in time to read stories, and not soon enough to help with baths; that's kind of bad. Phil abstained from beer tonight; that's good. Phil computes this evening's "uh-oh" indicator as a 3, on the scale of 1 to 10.

In the financial trading arena, an example of a derivative would be Average True Range. The expression of ATR(14) computes the average true range for today and the look-back period of 14 total days.

Historical Derivative

A *historical derivative* is one that measures some property of the underlying stock in a time frame that ends before the current time, and is shown in Figure 6.9. One week later, it's Tuesday night again and Phil is home at 8:15, and he has not had any brewskis. The uh-oh indicator's current derivative value is 0. However, the uh-oh historical derivative is still 3 because of Phil's past performance.

Another example of a historical derivative is the expression of ATR(14), which was calculated on the price bar 20 periods ago. In MetaStock language, that would be written as follows:

```
Ref( ATR(14), -20)
```

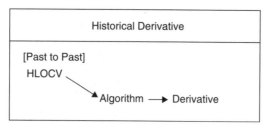

FIGURE 6.9 An example of a historical derivative.

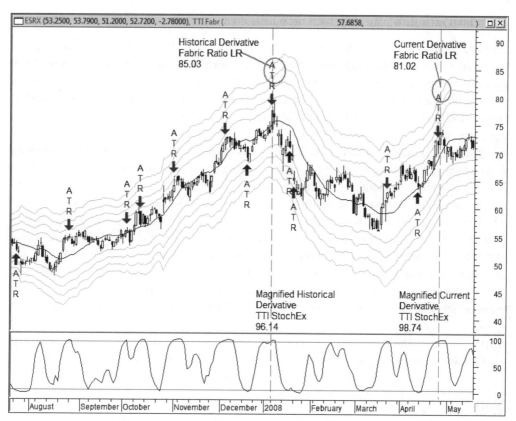

FIGURE 6.10 This daily chart of Express Scripts (ESRX) shows us that chart analysis depends on past-to-current comparisons, using Historical and Current Derivatives.

Chart created in MetaStock.

This code is shown using the Reference statement. It enables you to calculate the value of an indicator on a previous price period. In this case, ATR(14) is nested within the Reference statement. The –20 value tells MetaStock to calculate the requested value as it would have been calculated 20 days before.

Historical derivative indicators are critical because they provide the ability to make important comparisons of past levels versus the present. See Figure 6.10.

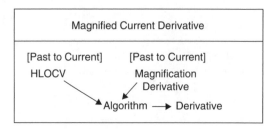

FIGURE 6.11   An illustration of a magnified current derivative.

Magnified Current Derivative

Bowling night is here and Phil is late coming home. As if that's not enough, two beers were consumed, and he's not likely to get credit for them being light beers, either. The real kicker, though, is that somehow the new SUV that Phil and Suzie just bought has a dent in the front fender. Phil has no idea how that happened. As Phil comes through the front door, his brain is calculating the uh-oh indicator as being all the way up as high as it will go.

The normal factors of time and alcohol that Phil has to be concerned with on bowling night are positively magnified by the dent in the new car. It would certainly be better for Phil if there were no dent and he had a dozen red roses in his hands. Then the normal factors would be negatively magnified by the romance dimension. Poor Phil...

A *magnified current derivative* is a current derivative that is magnified positively or negatively by an external effect based on some set of logic or market participant behavior. A diagram of a magnified current derivative is shown in Figure 6.11. The TTI StochEx indicator created in Chapter 5 is a good example. If you recall, the indicator started out as a current derivative. The second version was changed to use an ATR(5) value as an accelerator. This step turned it into a magnified current derivative. Because of this, the final value of the indicator increases or decreases if traders and market participants change the recent level of daily trading range volatility. The underlying logic is that if the recent daily trading range volatility increases near an extreme level, then the current short-term price move is likely nearing an end. The indicator should thus reach an oversold and overbought level sooner.

Magnified Historical Derivative

Just as with a historical derivative, a *magnified historical derivative* is simply the past-to-past version of a magnified current derivative. It serves the same basic value of relativity. It is depicted in Figure 6.12.

Meanwhile, back in suburbia, two months before, Phil had come home late with beer breath on bowling night as well. That night, Phil had forgotten that it was Valentine's Day, and also the obligatory candy and flowers. He subsequently needed his heavy coat outside because it was winter; inside, he needed it because of the Suzie-induced chill factor. So, by historical comparison, the bowling night with the dented car is not worthy

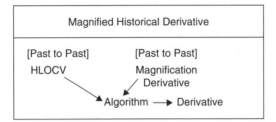

FIGURE 6.12 Magnified historical derivatives are useful in times when multiple past comparisons need to be considered.

of a score of 10. Perhaps it's only as bad as a 9; after all, what's worse: a dent in the car or a dent in the feelings?

In looking again at Figure 6.10, a daily chart of Express Scripts (ESRX) current and historical versions of simple and magnified derivatives is shown. This particular example does not give us any particular informational value other than to see the potential for derivative relationships. This is really the meatiest part of system development. Individual components are a necessary ingredient to any trading methodology. However, true synergy is gained when relative comparisons based on sound logic are used. This is just what compound derivatives do.

Compound Derivative

If having one beer is good, then having a second must be better, yes? That certainly makes sense to Phil. The logic seems more and more sound as the number of beers consumed increases; and that logic makes sense to most of us when caught up in that situation. So then, if one derivative is good, is adding a second derivative better when building an indicator?

The answer is yes, so long as the selection of the second indicator is based on logic, and oriented in sound market dynamics. For instance, if two oversold indicators are reading extreme, then it must be time to buy, correct? The answer to that is no. That is to say that internally, neither substantially improves the other, because each is a close variation of the other.

The *compound derivative* is a single indicator that is composed of two derivatives at the algorithm level. Figure 6.13 shows us a diagram of a compound derivative. Furthermore, the presence of both indicators needs to be rooted in market, price, or trader behavior that when combined creates a synergy. Be sure that you understand not only the underlying math of the two or more components, but the logic as well. If it is not so, then it runs the risk of producing results based on chance, or some unknown correlation. Market conditions change on a nonstop basis. Knowing the logic that your system is based upon is critical to realizing what its weaknesses are. Therefore, when, not if, market conditions change, you will be better able to gauge the reliability of your system components.

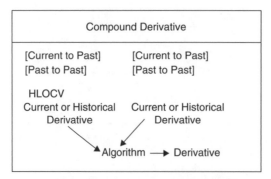

FIGURE 6.13   Combining the complementary logic and volatility measurement of two or more separate derivatives creates a compound derivative.

CONSTRUCTING A COMPOUND DERIVATIVE

Since we have not yet built a compound derivative, this is a good opportunity to do so. It would also be great to take a crack at measuring the most important market condition in technical analysis: the trend. Indicators that measure trend strength are by far the most difficult to create. The trend is of the utmost importance to trading success. Regardless of any trading style, time frame, or methods, the trader needs to be able to predict the general trading direction of the security and the broader market.

As we have constructed our TTI indicators thus far, they suffer most in trending markets. They seem to work well when price is trading in a range-bound direction. When a trend is occurring, however, these overbought and oversold indicators usually fail. They prompt the analyst to take countertrend positions in lieu of joining a profitable trend.

The Market Technicians Association is the preeminent organization for technical analysts today. *Technical Analysis*, by Charles D. Kirkpatrick, CMT, and Julie R. Dahlquist, Ph.D. (FT Press, 2006), is a comprehensive basis for most of this organization's body of methodologies, and is required reading for all members seeking the CMT certification. It clearly states that the primary method of successful trading is to exploit the trend.

The key to profiting in the securities market is to follow these three steps:

1. *Determine, with minimum risk of error, when a trend has begun, at its earliest time and price.*

2. *Select and enter a position in the trend that is appropriate to the existing trend, regardless of direction (i.e., trade with the trend—long in upwards trends and short or in cash in downward trends).*

3. *Close those positions when the trend is ending.*[2]

So then, let's tackle the trend. Figure 6.14 is a daily chart of Radio Shack (RSH). In the first half of 2007, Radio Shack breaks out from a four-month period of volatility contraction and range-bound trading. The TTI Fabric Ratio LR-SD reached a high of 1.25

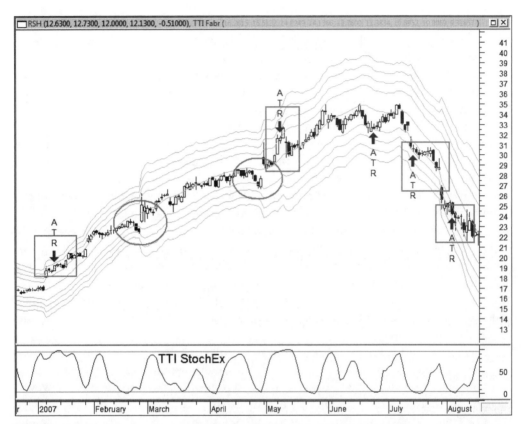

FIGURE 6.14 This classic example of a breakout to a strong unyielding trend shows us how a long position in Radio Shack (RSH) would have been very profitable. It would require, however, that the trader be able to anticipate the true strength of its trend at key decision points.

Chart created in MetaStock.

in late December 2006. The high Fabric Ratio reading, along with the gap up on January 8, 2007, helps to confirm the beginning of a trend. From January through June the trend stays intact to complete a 100 percent price increase.

What is it like to trade a trend without good technical confirmation of its beginning, or its strength? How does it feel to watch and have no alternative but to guess? I think most of us know what this feels like; it's very uncomfortable.

Remember that the future is uncertain on each day between January and June. The aggressive price advance could end suddenly the next day. That is certainly what it feels like at the end of the day when you look at an updated chart. It's tempting to just jump on the train, but at the same time there is fear that price will correct downward as soon as you enter the long position. It's much safer to wait for a price dip is what you tell yourself. When price does retrace slightly, as shown in the circled areas of Figure 6.14, there is once again fear that this could be the beginning of a downward cycle. So you wait a bit longer for price to pull back more; except it doesn't and tears on skyward.

This leaves most of us sitting there feeling like everyone else is getting wealthy, and we are not. Strong trends do that to everyone. What is needed during the trend is an understanding of trend strength.

In the later stages, after most traders have missed two or more good trend entry opportunities, the fear factor is becoming muted. This stock just keeps on going up! Indeed, in May, traders jumping on to the Radio Shack trend push prices consistently above the 40-period linear regression line, which is the center of the LR Fabric. By late May to early June, many are sure that it's safe to enter. After doing so, they see new highs in price fail to materialize. Sure that this is just a pause prior to price resuming the trend, they sit on their long positions. On July 13, they are caught in the stock's gap down and subsequent major trend correction. What is needed in the later stages of the trend is some type of warning that true trend strength is weakening.

This classic example of Radio Shack in 2007 shows us some capabilities needed in a trend-strength indicator. But how can we achieve this with a compound derivative? A simple look at Figure 6.14 shows us some volatility measurements that are already quantified in the form of the indicators plotted on the chart's upper and lower panes. The TTI StochEx and the LR Fabric for the present are current derivatives, magnified and nonmagnified, respectively. All of these same indicators' past readings are their historical counterparts.

Relying on the TTI Fabric LR algorithm alone will not help us much. But the relationship between the closing price and the fabric is a more useful value. This relationship is probably useless all by itself. If it is correlated to the TTI StochEx reading, however, then maybe there is a relationship that expresses strength. We can therefore introduce the TTI Trend Strength indicator. It is a compound derivative that comprises, among other things, the TTI StochEx and the TTI Fabric LR components. Its purpose is to confirm the beginning and ending of trends, as well as trend continuations.

TTI Trend Strength Logic and Rationale

Now let's look at the rationale for this algorithm. Why is this indicator needed? To assist in answering that question, think about the following scenario.

First, imagine yourself driving down an interstate highway. You are following a four-door sedan with two passengers in it. You do not know these people and have never seen them before. You do not know where they live, where they entered the interstate highway, or when they last got gas. You know absolutely nothing about them. Your task is to be able to predict their exit off the highway, just before they actually do exit. How could you do this with no knowledge of their intent?

This is what it is like to try to predict that a trend is about to come to an end. It's not easy. Let's continue with the automobile and highway scenario.

Perhaps when observing the car you are following you see the driver wake the passenger. This could be a sign that they are stopping for food. Suppose you see that even though the driver is usually using all lanes available equally, he is now sticking to the right lane without passing. It would be easy to assume that he could be looking for his upcoming exit. Any number of subtle clues could tip the driver's hand. So too are the changes in price action that occur during the late stages of many trends. Sometimes there is no price action or volume changes at all. It takes only one unexpected critical report from the FDA for a biotech stock price to drop like a rock.

We can't show you exactly how the TTI Trend Strength accomplishes its readings. To do so would cause them to become ineffective, because of statistical arbitrage. We can look, however, at some examples of it, which show clearly how compound derivatives are the most powerful components.

The TTI Trend Strength in Use

We once again see, in Figure 6.15, the daily chart of Radio Shack (RSH) with its strong trend in the first half of 2007. It must have been quite a time for selling electronics! In

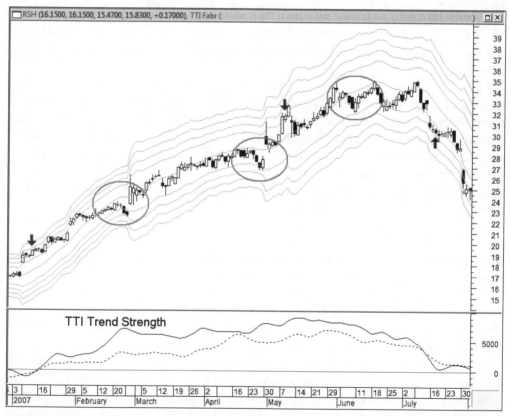

FIGURE 6.15 The strong trend produced by Radio Shack (RSH) is measured by the TTI Trend Strength indicator shown in the bottom pane. The indicator begins to diverge from the trend's trading direction just before the end of the trend.

Chart created in MetaStock. Chart uses the MetaSwing Add-on, by Northington Trading, LLC. All rights reserved.

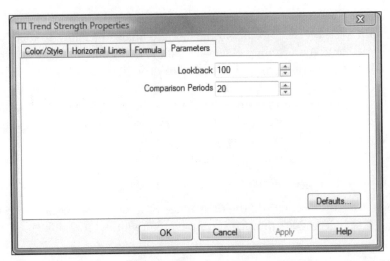

FIGURE 6.16   Input statements make adjusting time period variables easy and fast. Right click on an indicator and this simple screen gives you quick access to configuration changes.

Created in MetaStock.

the bottom indicator pane is the plot of the TTI Trend Strength indicator. There are two different lines because the indicator is plotted twice. The solid line uses a 20-period change comparison in its algorithm, and the dashed plot uses a 10-period change comparison. When possible, it is helpful to plot multiple instances of the same indicator with different time frame measurements, and this one is a good example. In this case, both plots are shown using a 100-period look-back duration. Figure 6.16 shows how both of these parameters can be user-defined.

It's easy to see in Figure 6.15 that TTI Trend Strength tracks upward with the trend. It's also visible that in this case it begins to flatten out during the month of May while the price is still rising, thus producing some price and indicator divergence. Then in June, there is definite visible indicator decline while the price trades sideways, which is a further divergence.

Let's pause for a minute, however, and think about what is visible and invisible with respect to the price advance. First and most obvious is the correlation between price trading above the TTI Fabric LR's central linear regression line and an increase in the indicator's reading. This is because trading on either side of the central linear regression line happens for extended periods. This gives the indicator time to measure strength against at least one full cycle of the TTI StochEx. To a significant degree, the law of large numbers is what makes this indicator work. The look-back period in Figure 6.15 is set to 100 days.

One of the invisible aspects of the chart is actually the net sum calculations occurring. The human eye and brain are not able to accurately count within, and then correlate to, the significant time durations. Also invisible is the actual mathematical volatility that occurs around the linear regression line within meaningful time frames. Invisible is okay

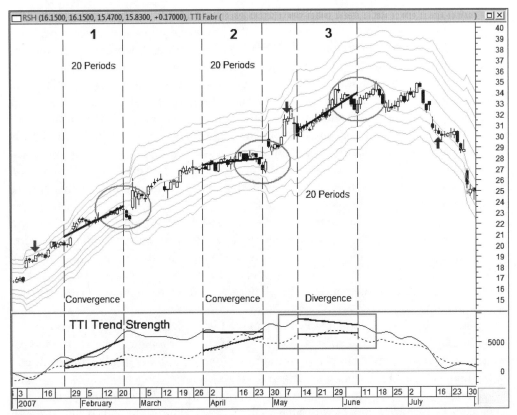

FIGURE 6.17 Careful analysis of the convergence and divergence between price and the TTI Trend Strength indicator provides a significant level of predictive information.

Chart created in MetaStock. Chart uses the MetaSwing Add-on, by Northington Trading, LLC. All rights reserved.

as long as we can enable the volatility-based technical analysis software to see through the fog.

Now let's get more specific on how to use the TTI Trend Strength to exploit the trend. In Figure 6.17, a full analysis has been applied to the same chart of Radio Shack and its 2007 rally. There are three opportunity zones identified. Each was chosen because price receded to the LR Fabric negative one thread level. This means that it was two ATR(14) increments below its 40-period linear regression line. That's a good beginning qualifier for a trend entry. Each opportunity is circled.

In the upper chart pane is a 20-period linear regression line plotted through the price candles. The same duration linear regression line is drawn through both time frame versions of the TTI Trend Strength indicator in the bottom pane. To be consistent, the up and down arrows that show the StochEx expert buy and sell signals were left in place.

Opportunity zone 1 shows us three upward slanting linear regression lines. We can see visually that the trend has been running for two months and began with a significant price gap, which was never tested. This is a good trend entry spot. Opportunity zone 2 demonstrates once again that price is trading in a positive direction. One of the TTI Trend Strength regression lines, however, is flat while the other is decidedly positive. This is still a good trend entry, but it will not carry quite as high a probability rating as the first, because of one of the flat readings. A tighter stop is therefore warranted.

In opportunity zone 3, Radio Shack continues its solid advance. With the TTI Trend Strength indicator, however, the tables have turned. There is now one time frame that is reading flat and one that is shouting negative. This gives us the all-important price and indicator divergence. For reasons that our eyes can't pick out, the trend's strength is beginning to wane. This opportunity is one to stand aside from. In fact, by July, the price has failed to rise above $35, and is actually cycling below the central linear regression line. The TTI Trend Strength indicator in both time frames is decidedly negative. Maybe it's time to do some trading on the short side.

It is important to point out that both successful entry points in February and April were on the days before earnings releases. Trading during earnings announcements can be risky for the balance in your trading account. The trend strength indication was very strong, however, and so it correctly identified the market belief in this stock's future value. Whether entering before or after the announcement, it was profitable either way.

Lastly, with the strong trend indication on the Radio Shack chart, we have the directional intelligence needed to correctly ignore all of the overbought and oversold indications. Knowing if a trend is in place is vital to picking a profitable trade strategy at any given time. Leave the swimming up stream to the salmon.

A Word of Caution: This example of Radio Shack and its trend is quite perfect and somewhat idealistic. It shows with almost flawless execution the TTI Trend Strength indicator pulling off a very difficult feat. Admittedly, we all know that charts and trading are virtually never this neat and clean. This example was chosen for clarity. Please don't misunderstand: TTI Trend Strength works well. It is just not always so perfect and obvious, as this example demonstrates. It will be used in more examples in the coming chapters. You will see there more realistic portrayals of how it fares with everyday trading challenges. No single indicator works in all situations. The key is to design and use algorithms that work when you need them to. They should perform specific tasks with predictive capabilities. You as the trader and technical analyst need to understand their strengths, weaknesses, and logic inside and out. You will know this way when to place your money on the table and when not to.

A MetaSwing View of the Trend   MetaSwing can see the trend with some specific advantages because of its ability to measure Projected Implied Volatility (PIV). The support and resistance lines created around key areas of PIV are very telling signs of the behavior of smart money players equipped with advanced quantitative mathematical tools. It enables them to pick precise conditional entry points before the critical fundamental information is attained, and before the resulting trading range defines itself.

In Figure 6.18, the MetaSwing chart of the Radio Shack rally shows some specific advantages to the trader.

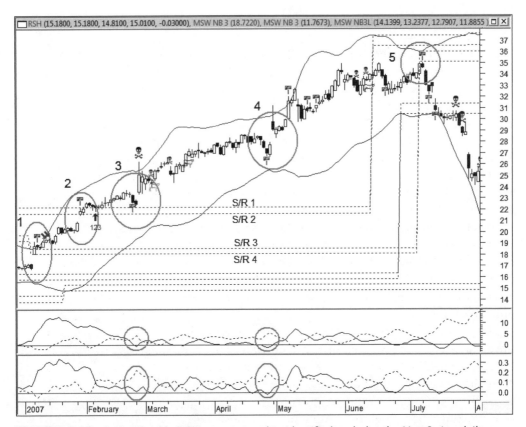

FIGURE 6.18 Radio Shack's (RSH) strong trend is identified early by the MetaSwing daily chart. Its initial January breakout is flagged accurately by price action, basing itself on S/R lines that use Projected Implied Volatility.

Chart created in MetaStock. Chart uses the MetaSwing Add-on, by Northington Trading, LLC. All rights reserved.

- *Circle 1:* The trend begins with a bang. The opening trade on January 8 is at 18.09; that's just two cents above the one ATR buffer zone, beneath the upper N Band. This is significant in that it forces the formation of a new S/R 4 line, with that new S/R line and the opening being one and the same. Serious resistance begins at one average true range beneath the upper N Band. The first week of the breakout ends with price trading to the S/R 4 line on Radio Shack's weekly chart; see Figure 6.19. On the daily chart, price pushes above the N Band in the first week. This is subtle, but it is huge in importance. This means that the smart money is paying more attention to the weekly chart in the planning of their position. Thus, their commitment and hold time is significantly larger and longer. In this way, MetaSwing S/R lines transmit market intent.
- *Circle 2:* After Radio Shack experiences an Exit Short signal on the daily and weekly charts, it pushes on. Before this time, you would want to see price retrace to

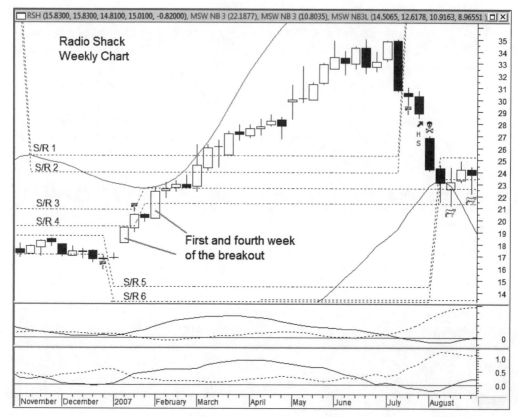

FIGURE 6.19 On the MetaSwing weekly chart, the first and fourth week of the Radio Shack January breakout show highs that tightly conform to S/R 4 and the upper N Band, respectively. The accurate trading conformity with these weekly calculated values telegraph the intentions of institutional traders, and their extended time frames beyond those of the swing trading crowd.

Chart created in MetaStock. Chart uses the MetaSwing Add-on, by Northington Trading, LLC. All rights reserved.

successfully test support at an S/R line, or do something bold. On January 30, Radio Shack chooses bold, and price once again gaps up to close above the S/R 2 line; indeed, the opening price was one penny above the S/R 2 line, which was set more than two months previously. This is a clear trend entry signal for January 31.

- *Circle 3:* Radio Shack retraces some to test the daily chart S/R 1 line, and also shows an Exit Short signal. With an earnings announcement one day away, however, the decision is to hold, or to exit with a reentry upon a good report relative to the Street's expectations. The weekly chart, in Figure 6.19, shows the S/R 4 line below price at 21.33, which is pretty good support. The price opens at 22.79 on February 26. The upper N Band represents overhead resistance at 25.40 on the daily chart. This makes for a swing trading risk-reward ratio of 1.78; not wonderful. The decision to stay or take profits depends on the trader's time frame and risk profile. Results then turn out rosy with the earnings report, and the trading prices reflect it. On

February 27, the markets signal a broad market Total Correction event and the decision to reenter the trend is still on the table. It's probably best to delay and see what the market will do. Four days later, the market signals with a Total Surge event and trend reentry is a no-brainer.

- *Circle 4:* Late April presents a similar situation to that in circle 3, with another earnings release due. Radio Shack is trading above all S/R lines on both the weekly and daily charts. Once again, the decision should depend on time frame and risk profile. Certainly the strength it displayed during the brief March correction should count for something, to say the least.
- *Circle 5:* The trend thus far has been good to the trader if she has previously heeded MetaSwing's PIV signals. We see here, however, a lack of price advance, an Exit Long signal, and the upper N Band is one ATR above. Were the trend still as strong and resolute as in the past months, price would have pushed up to the upper N Band on July 9. This is a clear warning to exit.

Market Derivative

The last of the framework component types is the *market derivative*. This is an algorithm based on data not from a security, but from a market sector index, or an entire market, or exchange. The model for a market derivative is shown in Figure 6.20. For example, a market derivative could be an algorithm that uses the high, low, open, and close data series for the semiconductor sector. One using a data series that includes the most recent period would be a *current market derivative*; of course, one using past data up to a point in the past would be a *past market derivative*.

Market derivatives are necessary if the trader is to achieve an acceptable probability of predicting the price direction of the broader market, or a specific sector. The daily trading direction of the majority of stocks occurs in the general direction of the greater market. I'm sure you may be tired of hearing that statement. It's one of the first things we learn as traders. It's also a mantra that we should recite 10 times each day we participate in the markets.

One such current market derivative is the MetaSwing system of Correction and Surge signals. These algorithms use broad market breadth data to issue important outlooks concerning the immediate trading atmosphere. In Figure 6.21, PACCAR (PCAR) is

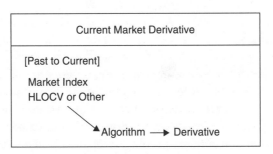

FIGURE 6.20 This shows the current market derivative.

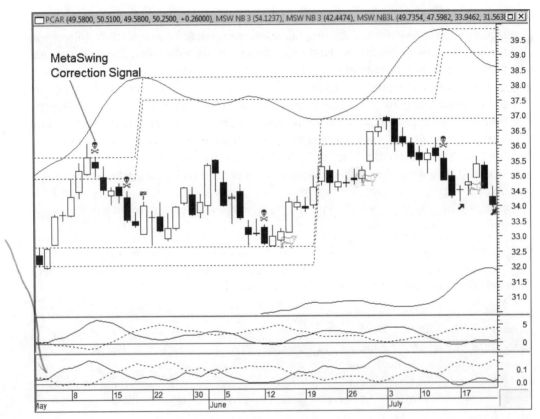

FIGURE 6.21 In MetaSwing, a system of very profitable Market Derivatives make up its Correction and Surge signals.

Chart created in MetaStock. Chart uses the MetaSwing Add-on, by Northington Trading, LLC. All rights reserved.

on a long-term cycling uptrend. Even the nasty NASDAQ correction that occurred in the summer of 2006 did not stop the trend. The MetaSwing Correction signals (skull and crossbones) were very helpful with trading the swings between the N Band S/R lines. The MetaSwing code for this highly accurate signal is disclosed and explained in Chapter 13.

THE FRAMEWORK

It appears at this point that we have developed some good tools to trade the markets. We have put together six different indicators composed of various volatility-based algorithms. These six work in some market conditions, and not so well in others.

But is trading that easy? Can we simply use a handful of relatively effective math calculations on charts and accurately predict which direction a stock's price will trade?

Remember the first time you learned what the term *sophomore* actually meant? Its direct translation of "wise fool" is usually explained to young males entering their 10th-grade level, when they are caught between the later stages of puberty and trying to shave. It's no secret of just how much trouble a kid at that age can get into once he acquires a small amount of knowledge, sans wisdom.

Without the discipline to organize and execute a technical analysis methodology, the trader is sure to be slowly, or quickly, devoured by competent market players. For this reason, he must use his own trading system framework. It is the most important step one can take toward profitability in trading the financial markets.

The major benefits of consistently using a well-defined technical analysis framework are that it:

- Forces you to trade with logic and probability rather than emotion and chance
- Ensures that trading decisions are well balanced across all of the seven important capabilities of a volatility-based technical analysis trading methodology
- Enables you to trade within your risk profile using risk-reward ratios on the basis of historical volatility, and volatility-based support and resistance
- Makes visible the time frame of the trade, using multi-time frame analysis and volatility-based support and resistance
- Gives you the advantage when using specific trading methods in which you specialize
- Provides a granular and quantifiable basis for diagnosing finished trade success or failure

Creating the Framework

It is time to take an inventory of what we have and what we know. Capabilities have been identified. Indicators with volatility-based algorithms have been created. We know the importance of applying the appropriate analysis assessment, and subsequent trading decisions, within the underlying trend and prevailing broad market conditions. Sandpipers are cool.

Your personal *Technical Analysis Framework* is the net sum of your volatility-based technical analysis components, organized within a logical three-dimensional structure, which enables and enforces a repeatable process of analysis and trading.

Herein we have *components* composed of simple volatility measuring mathematics, in the form of six different indicators. They are:

1. TTI ATR Extreme
2. TTI StochEx
3. TTI Fabric SD
4. TTI Fabric LR
5. TTI Fabric Ratio LR-SD
6. TTI Trend Strength

It is clear to us that there are seven absolutely important *capabilities* that our trading methodology should invoke when determining each trading decision. Usually, not all seven can be applied to each decision, but the capability needs to be available if applicable. The golden list of seven capabilities is:

1. Oversold and Overbought levels
2. Trend Detection
3. Broad Market Integration
4. Support and Resistance
5. Historical Volatility
6. Implied Volatility
7. Multi-Time Frame Verification

We have seen through examples that the application of our components needs to consider the absence or existence of a trend. Also important are the broader market conditions from which our trades are rarely isolated. Lastly, the actual bag of volatility-based tools we use in our framework dictate many different trade methodologies that we would like to put on. All of this means that we are well aware of an application layer that exists just before actual trade execution.

Based on the definition of a technical analysis framework, we have just identified everything needed to make one. Table 6.1 is a basic framework based on all of the components created in this book so far. A framework consists of three dimensions, or layers. The first dimension is the *capabilities level*. This is the only part of the framework that is fixed. The column to the far left represents the seven important capabilities that need to be applied to each trade.

The second dimension is the *application layer* as is shown by rows that begin in column two. Since every analyst and trader will use his components in both trending and nontrending market conditions, both of them are always listed beneath each capability. This dimension is very flexible. For each trading method you use, a row is added under each of the seven capabilities. In this way, the framework table expands downward.

The third dimension of the framework is represented in the columns beginning at number three. Each column is populated with a component of your technical analysis methodology, and together composes the *component layer*. It's also flexible, in that for each indicator in the tool box, a column is tacked on to the right. Your personal trading framework can therefore expand downward and to the right for as far as is practical for you.

Each box cell in the body of the framework is representative of the components composition and application value. For instance, the TTI ATR Extreme has an x next to Non-Trending, in the Oversold/Overbought section. This is because it is an indicator whose primary use is to detect overbought and oversold conditions in a nontrending market condition. The rows in the Historical Volatility and Implied Volatility are

TABLE 6.1 The Beginning Framework Format

Capabilities Components Application	TTI ATR Extreme	TTI StochEx	TTI Fabric SD	TTI Fabric LG	TTI Fabric Ratio LR-SD	TTI Trend Strength
1 Oversold/overbought						
Trending			x	x		
Non-Trending	x	x	x	x		
2 Trend Detection						
Trending					x	x
Non-Trending						x
3 Broad Market Integration						
Trending						
Non-Trending						
4 Support and Resistance						
Trending						
Non-Trending						
5 Historical Volatility						
Trending			x	x	x	x
Non-Trending	x	x	x	x		x
6 Implied Volatility						
Trending						
Non-Trending						
7 Multi-Time Frame Verification						
Trending				x		
Non-Trending	x	x	x	x		

necessary to identify components being used that use either or both of these types of volatility.

It is easy to see upon examining the TTI Framework that some of the capabilities have component representation, and some are very bare. The Broad Market Integration, Support and Resistance, and Implied Volatility capabilities currently have no indicators to draw upon. Trades, therefore, that depend on measuring price movement with these capabilities in mind will be at a higher risk for failure.

Using the Framework

Nothing alone is relevant in technical analysis. This holds true for technical measurements as well as fundamental and news events. As an example, political turmoil and terrorist attacks are considered universally bad for short-term trading of stocks. That's logical, yes? On July 7, 2005, a series of terrorist bombings hit London's underground subway system, tragically killing many innocent people. The U.S. markets were unfettered by the news and rose that day; the NASDAQ composite rose by one-third of a percent, and by 1.79 percent the next day. This demonstrates how there were many other dynamics at work in the markets at that time, and that specific events, or information, are not usually singularly important.

On a smaller scale, but just as significantly, when your overbought indicator reads the highest extreme level reached in several years, it does not mean that the stock is overbought. You have within your own trading methodology the potential for a comprehensive system of checks and balances, which is your framework. The good news is that it's really simple.

Let's consider again the Radio Shack trend entry opportunities in Figure 6.17. If this is a type of a trade that you want to put on, and I can't imagine why you would not, then you should have a regular trade method for it. It should be named and it should have a permanent row in your framework. For now, let's call this trade method TTI Trend Entry. Table 6.2 shows our framework with the TTI Trend Entry trade method added. As you can see, each of the seven capabilities has the method listed beneath it. This is because

TABLE 6.2 A Framework with the TTI Trend Entry Method Added

Capabilities Components Application	TTI ATR Extreme	TTI StochEx	TTI Fabric SD	TTI Fabric LG	TTI Fabric Ratio LR-SD	TTI Trend Strength
1 Oversold/overbought						
Trending			x	x		
Nontrending	x	x	x	x		
TTI Trend Entry			x	x		
2 Trend Detection						
Trending					x	x
Nontrending						x
TTI Trend Entry					x	x
3 Broad Market Integration						
Trending						
Nontrending						
TTI Trend Entry						
4 Support and Resistance						
Trending						
Nontrending						
TTI Trend Entry						
5 Historical Volatility						
Trending			x	x	x	x
Nontrending	x	x	x	x		x
TTI Trend Entry			x	x	x	x
6 Implied Volatility						
Trending						
Nontrending						
TTI Trend Entry						
7 Multi-Time Frame Verification						
Trending				x		
Nontrending	x	x	x	x		
TTI Trend Entry				x		

each of those capabilities needs to add its strengths to the decision for the trade entry when a position is taken. If any particular capability is not represented, then you are vulnerable in that area.

The single largest benefit of using this framework as an integral part of your decision-making process is that it gives you a repeatable set of logical criteria to apply to trade entry, profit targets, and stop levels. This framework will protect you from your emotions, which can be your worst enemy. For instance, your risk profile can be protected by applying the TTI Fabric LR component to your entry criteria. This is because when long trade entries are done at the negative two thread, the probabilities of further price decline are much lower. The probability of a short-term price reversal is higher. Because the threads are based on average true range, should the trade suddenly go against you, then you can better gauge your potential loss if you hit your stop loss. You will even be able to decide before trade entry how the stock's volatility affects the position size you should take. Notice, though, that Table 6.2 is currently devoid of components that identify support or resistance; Fabric LR does not. Support and resistance identification is necessary for a proper risk-reward calculation.

GOING FORWARD

As we progress into the coming chapters we will have ample opportunity to apply this practical framework for trade methodology. We will be able to see firsthand the benefits of a structured approach to trading with volatility-based technical analysis. An overarching development that occurs naturally for all technicians is how this framework process points you in the right direction. Necessity is the mother of invention, and so it is when there are voids in your component mixture.

Conceiving compound derivatives to improve specific trade setups is much simpler when you can rely on your framework to show specific component needs in the capability dimension. Each trade can be reviewed for success or failure with greater clarity. The repetitive nature of observing and measuring the individual framework component performance, by specific trade method, will give you a level of quality control that most traders strive years to attain. Most of all, applying your framework to the market's opportunities will enable you to think and trade like Matherne.

CHAPTER 7

Traditional Technical Analysis

What Works, What Doesn't, and Why

O ne chapter can't even begin to do the topic justice, but we will overcome this by focusing on the aspects of technical analysis that are the most meaningful to trading profits. A wealth of top minds at the academic level have been consistently publishing papers providing scientific proof of successes or failures for the most credible of individual technical analysis methods. The list of books that are written by capable and responsible authors that promote many of these methodologies is long and continues to grow. For each scientific paper published that supports a particular methodology, there is another equally well done that refutes it. Unfortunately, the average trader is left to his own devices to believe what will make him successful, and what will waste his time and money.

From 2003 to 2005, I noticed a consistent increase in classic pattern failures and method ineffectiveness, such as Fibonacci retracement. Comments from fellow traders tended to support my observations. During these shifts, however, many long-standing technical trading practices seemed just as relevant as ever.

Traditional technical analysis has evolved, and has been used very successfully by many over previous decades. Much of the technical analysis that made many wealthy trading in the roaring bull market of the 1990s has diminished value today. The point that can't be denied is that if you know the direction of the market, as everyone did during the 1990s market bubble, it did not matter whether your trading was based on sun spots or changes in the rabbit population; you were going to stay long and usually make money. There were many skilled traders then, however, who today do not reap rewards using the same analysis methods. As we discussed in Chapters 1 and 2, it isn't the skill of those traders that changed; it's the markets that have morphed into volatile beasts. The most influential underlying forces of supply and demand are no longer the actual stock traders themselves.

The basic tenets of the many past forms of technical analysis are sound. Support and resistance works very well today. It's the methods of successfully deriving the locations of support and resistance that have changed. For instance, we all listen to music today. The difference between now and 30 years ago is that the music resides on a digital medium instead of vinyl. In the same way that digitally based music is played only by audio equipment containing computer chips, it's now necessary to use a microprocessor to access support and resistance. Primary support and resistance is no longer visual on the chart. It is mathematically derived, and we need a computer and software to find it.

Our analysis and comparisons will focus on:

- Line Studies
- Support and Resistance
- Chart Patterns
- Oscillators

This chapter is meant to be practical, not academic, so we review some of the more common technical analysis methodologies popular today. When using volatility-based technical analysis methods versus the traditional methods, care is taken to focus on the differences in results and trading opportunities that are created. Most important, the basis for success is determined by the degree of practical utility to the individual trader.

LINE STUDIES

Imagine that it's New Year's Eve and you have an invitation to a spectacular party. It's going to be great; all the cool people are invited. Suppose, though, your handwritten invitation to the party at 500 28th Street was scribed incorrectly. Upon showing up fashionably late at 500 128th Street, which is the address on your invitation, you knock on the door and are greeted by a pot-bellied 70-year-old man in boxers who knows nothing about a party. Wanting to make sure you're not kissing him at midnight, you call the host on your cell phone for the correct address. By the time you get a cab on New Year's Eve to drive you 100 blocks, it's 1:35 A.M., and the party's mostly over. You have missed out on a great time.

This is what it's like to rely on typical line studies that are based on visually linear alignment and two-dimensional thought processes. You will miss the party, or find yourself at the wrong one.

Trend Lines and Channels, Moving Averages, and ratio-based plots such as Fibonacci and Gann lines, all comprise line studies. All of these techniques lack the ability to adjust for volatility. Without a volatility dimension, they enforce trading decisions that are based on irrelevant price movements. These generally obsolete measurements are no longer aligned with the primary sources of supply and demand. In a nutshell, these types of technical analysis methods distract the trader with busy work, and keep his mind focused on the wrong data.

Trend Lines: A Straight Line to Where?

The basic trend line uses a straight line. You have to hand it to the trend line; it certainly is simple. Actually, most people get it right when they draw them, too. They even occasionally produce a profitable trade, but not nearly as often as is needed to maintain profitability. Perhaps I'm being a bit hard on this method. It's still somewhat useful when measuring the long-term price direction, which is generally years or longer. The difficulty with a two-year time frame is that it's not used for trading; that's investing.

A trend line in Figure 7.1 has been drawn along the base of a breakout of BMC Software (BMC). The trend line is initially defined by the low of the beginning of the trend and the lowest linear point in July. By July 24, 2007, BMC Software had made two consecutive higher highs and higher lows. This can define the beginning of a trend. This chart, however, shows a common difficulty with trying to trade a linear trend line, regardless of whether the chart is arithmetic or logarithmic. The trend picks up speed

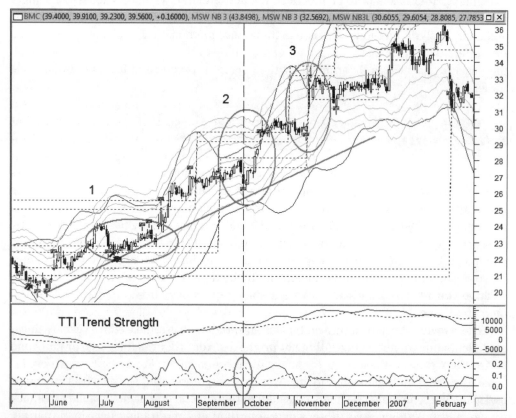

FIGURE 7.1   The basic trend line is ill-equipped to identify well-timed entry points in most trends. Two excellent trend entry points are missed by the trend line drawn from the trend base through its confirming higher low.

Chart created in MetaStock. Chart uses the MetaSwing Add-on, by Northington Trading, LLC. All rights reserved.

in August. Because its volatility increases, so too does its rate of rise over run. Thus the angle of ascent gets steeper, and as a result of that, the best trend entry opportunities are missed.

Most of MetaSwing's components are displayed on the chart of BMC Software, along with the TTI LR Fabric and the TTI Trend Strength indicators. Circle 1 shows the confirmation of a trend beginning when price rises above the S/R 3 line, and then drops to test it successfully at the S/R 4 and the S/R 3 lines, in July and August respectively. During August, the TTI Trend Strength indicator confirms that the breakout looks strong.

Circles 2 and 3 both show the optimum trend entry points. Each shows an Exit Short signal aligned close to or past the negative one LR Fabric thread. Circle 2 is a genuinely great opportunity with oversold indicator support. There is also no earnings announcement due for over a month. Circle 2 is aligned with an earnings event, so a long entry there carries some additional risk.

The single most obvious weakness that trend lines have is a lack of ability to adapt to changing volatility levels. The chart of BMC Software in Figure 7.1 clearly shows an expanding volatility atmosphere, as evidenced by the ATR threads in the Fabric LR indicator. The shortcoming of the trend line is really as simple as that.

Moving Averages: Center, Bottom, or Top?

The most common uses for moving averages are as support and resistance, or as a trend-following method using a crossover as a trading signal. Perhaps an awareness that this same mathematical measurement is used for two distinctly different purposes demonstrates how ill-suited it is to either use. First, it is a well-known fact, and needs no further explanation, that moving average crossover trading methods work when the broader market is moving decidedly in the same direction as the position. Since moving averages are lagging computations, with no real ability to predict, then it's no surprise that over the long run, the well-disciplined trader achieves breakeven. This leaves the greater majority of other traders, which fall into the less disciplined category, to lose money.

The second way that technical traders, fundamental traders, and hybrid traders of all types use moving averages is for support and resistance. It is very common to hear the financial news media explain that a market index reversed when it reached its 50-day moving average. This usually occurs when there was no other convenient basis to explain the market action that day. They do this because they think it could be true, and if they don't overuse the term, it can make them sound smart. For instance, one popular subscription service uses various moving averages to explain the market's behavior routinely. It keeps the subscribers satisfied that their money is being well spent. What's missing are the explanations for each of the majority of other instances where the market indexes and stock prices traded right through those moving average lines, like they just don't exist.

That is exactly the problem with the moving average. Everyone pays attention to it for explaining market behavior when it's convenient. But a predictive tool it is not.

Theoretically, if every trader of a particular stock believed that it would reverse its trading direction when it reached its 200-day simple moving average, then it surely would, if it reached it at all.

However, here's the real-world flaw to the whole group consensus of moving averages. There is no real agreement of moving average intervals that work. Each technical trader expert who uses them will tend to employ a different combination of moving average configurations. What follows is a list of moving average interval settings that this author has encountered more than twice from different sources: 50, 200, 100, 21, 13, 20, 14, 31, 65, 42, 26, 15, and 9. Most of these are used as simple and exponential variations, which doubles the quantity of variations. All too often a specific moving average that works on a particular chart is offered visually, while others that don't are ignored.

Figure 7.2 shows a daily chart of Molex (MOLX) responding to market conditions during the summer of 2006. This chart shows three different commonly accepted moving averages: a 50-period exponential moving average, and also 13- and 26-period simple

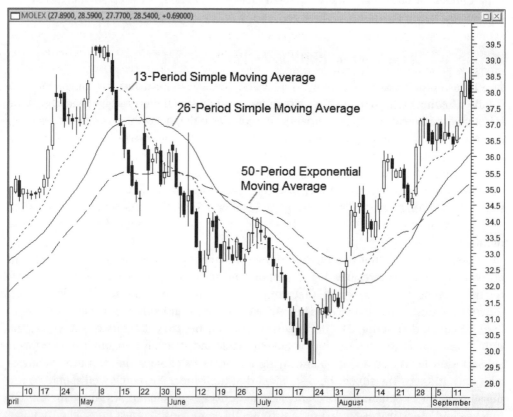

FIGURE 7.2   In this daily chart of Molex (MOLX) during 2006, the inaccuracy of the moving average as a form of support or resistance is exposed. Price trades right through all of the averages at virtually all points on the chart. Any visual resemblance of price support is due only to coincidence.

Chart created in MetaStock.

moving averages. Anyone trading this stock with these indications as support and resistance could have easily lost a lot of their trading account. Price moves routinely right through all of these lines. Only in some instances does price seem to respond to the 13-period average, but this is purely coincidence. Ask yourself this question: On any given day, how would you know to use a specific moving average interval as support? A trader would do better to find a casino and play roulette with his money.

Here is the logical question: If all of these moving averages are being used consistently as technical analysis measurements, how can any single one of them have genuine predictive performance capabilities? And its follow-up: The next time you analyze a trend, which moving average interval will you use? That is a major flaw with using a moving average as a measure of support or resistance. No one, or two, or any other combination of moving average intervals are used consistently by enough traders to constitute a market-moving consensus.

The moving average can really only be used for two functions in technical analysis: central tendency and smoothing. As a form of central tendency, it lacks responsiveness. It is a generally slow and lagging indicator. When it is used as a major component of algorithms, it will introduce these lagging characteristics into the indicator. As you have seen in previous chapters, linear regression is a much better measurement of central tendency. Besides which, a central tendency is just that: the center, or the mean. The measured component, by definition, will return to the mean and cross over it frequently. It will do this too often, therefore, to be relied upon as support or resistance.

In situations where there is a need to remove some of the noise that is produced by short-term, choppy price action, a short-duration moving average is useful. Be very careful, however, to limit the sample size to two or three, and certainly less than 10, as a general rule. When trading the extremes long, moving averages as components of indicator algorithms will cause you miss the profit opportunity.

By comparing Figure 7.2 to Figure 7.3, you can see more clearly how support and resistance are not defined by moving averages. In Figure 7.3, the same price chart of Molex is shown with MetaSwing.

Circled Area 1. Shows that when price rises to the upper N Band, it hits significant immediate resistance. An additional volatility trigger results in an exit long signal. Price reverses to form a minor consolidation area.

Circled Area 2. Price trades down rapidly because of broad market conditions, as evidenced by the MetaSwing Correction symbols (skull and crossbones). The decline reverses itself, however, when the lower N Band is reached. It then forms an area of consolidation above support at the S/R 5 level, as shown by the circle within the circle.

Circled Area 3. Again the market-induced decline is slowed at the lower N Band and the S/R 7 level.

Circled Area 4. Price rises rapidly due to extreme market breadth–induced buying, as is shown by the MetaSwing Surge symbols (bulls). Once Molex reaches resistance, beginning at one ATR beneath the upper N Band, it pauses for short-term consolidation before continuing with its rally.

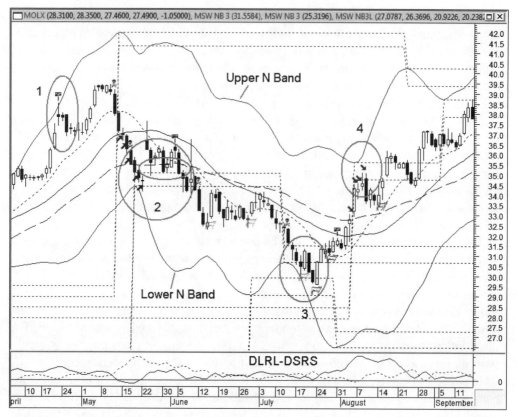

FIGURE 7.3 Another view of the Molex (MOLX) chart can accurately explain the locations of volatility-based support and resistance using true volatility-based technical analysis methods.

Chart created in MetaStock. Chart uses the MetaSwing Add-on, by Northington Trading, LLC. All rights reserved.

Fibonacci: The Party's Over

In all of traditional chart technical analysis, there probably is not a more visually convincing technique than Fibonacci retracement and projection. The golden ratio embedded within the Fibonacci grid is amazing. Prices seem to continuously be ever mindful of the next ratio level so that they can stop and reverse just where line tells it to. It is also quite probably the most deceptive analysis method as well, causing most traders using it to fall prey to hindsight bias. Fibonacci chews up the trading accounts of beginning technical traders on a regular basis; it is a shell game.

Duke Energy (DUK) is shown on a daily chart during 2007 in Figure 7.4. We have attempted for this example to choose a chart that a real Fibonacci user would likely pick to prove the method successful. There is a Fibonacci grid plotted from the top of the decline in April to its bottom in late July. Beginning at the vertical dashed line, it would seem that Duke Energy trades upward in concert with the major retracement levels.

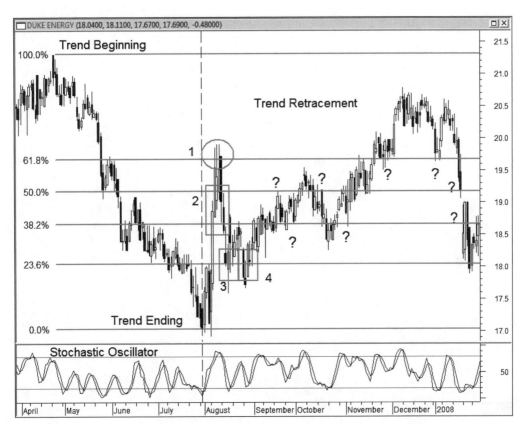

FIGURE 7.4 The Fibonacci retracement grid is visually pleasing to beginning technical traders. It provides an easy method for explaining price movement. When careful examination is given to detail, however, it's another matter all together.

Chart created in MetaStock.

Certainly the first two major moves in August look great. In circle 1, bounce to the 62 percent line at 19.68, with a confirmation from the stochastic oscillator for entry and exit, is a profitable trade. True Fibonacci believers will stop right there and shout "Aha! You see, it works!" But look further.

What follows after the initial trade is a series of questionable trade decisions that are difficult to interpret. Each retracement level offers an opportunity to trade a reversal. The trader is therefore confronted with a directional decision at each level. The squared area 2 shows that price blasts right down through the 50 percent and 38 percent levels. The stochastic oscillator does not confirm the exit at the 24 percent level, and given the downside market volatility occurring at that time, most traders stayed short in their positions. Price then reversed upward from September onward. What followed was a long series of trade decisions and miscues from oversold and overbought indicators. In all likelihood, depending upon one's trade entry and exit rules, these trades added up to net losses. At each question mark in Figure 7.4, there is a potential reversal at a retracement level.

FIGURE 7.5 The time duration of Duke Energy's (DUK) price retracement is shown in this MetaSwing chart. Only one valid trading opportunity presents itself as an Adeo Short in August. Going forward from there, while price action pauses and sometimes reverses at S/R line support and resistance, that alone is not sufficient reason to put on a trade.

Chart created in MetaStock. Chart uses the MetaSwing Add-on, by Northington Trading, LLC. All rights reserved.

The Fibonacci grid is a shell game because it moves the focus of your analysis to its ratio levels in lieu of thoroughly using your own well-balanced framework.

Trading Duke Energy during this high volatility period does not have to be such guesswork. The same retracement time duration for Duke is shown in the MetaSwing chart in Figure 7.5. This chart shows that by keeping the analysis well grounded in the seven important capabilities of volatility-based technical analysis, it is clear that there is only one good trading opportunity for the duration. In circled area 1 of August, there is an Adeo Short signal right at the upper N Band. This short-selling opportunity fits with the extremely bearish market climate that prevailed at the time, which is evidenced by the MetaSwing Total Correction signals that preceded it.

As this chart example continues into the fall of 2007, it is easy to see the price swings between the real levels of support and resistance, which are delineated by the circled areas at the S/R lines. The moral for this chart is that it is not filled with good trading opportunities, because support and resistance do not alone provide an adequate basis for a trade. In short, Fibonacci should not be a component of your framework.

Support and Resistance: Flat Is Out

Perhaps the most effective method of detecting support and resistance in the markets of old was a horizontal price line. A simple straight line sits at a previous significant high or low price. In the correct circumstances, using this extreme price point of a past swing functioned well. Its strength was clearly in high volatility environments. In this first decade of our new millennium, a previous high or low has given way to volatility-based support and resistance.

A chart of Gilead Sciences (GILD) in Figure 7.6 shows a horizontal alignment of prices at two levels. In circle 1, the low price for the day is set at 16.03 after a sizable gap down the previous day. Going forward, it set the extreme low for over two months. In circles 2 and 3, this same low is touched and used as support. In circle 4, an upward

FIGURE 7.6 Horizontal price levels are commonly used as support and resistance. This form of analysis is still valid but is becoming less reliable as time progresses.

Chart created in MetaStock.

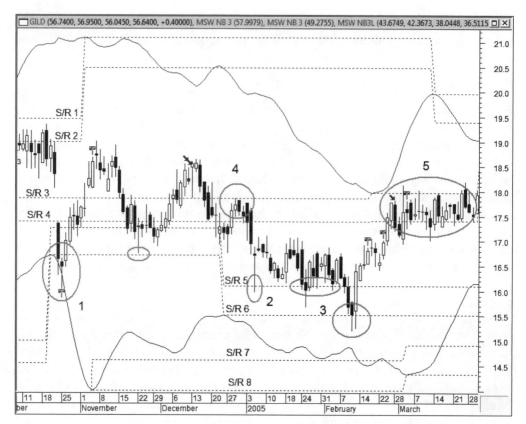

FIGURE 7.7 Upon careful examination, the same chart of Gilead Sciences (GILD) as in Figure 7.6 shows that support and resistance is most often a result of volatility levels, as shown by the S/R lines in this MetaSwing chart.

Chart created in MetaStock. Chart uses the MetaSwing Add-on, by Northington Trading, LLC. All rights reserved.

price swing sets a high of 17.85. Two months later, it appears to be used as a level of resistance. These horizontal alignments appear to be straight and true.

The same chart as viewed in MetaSwing (Figure 7.7), by contrast, shows that support and resistance levels were due to different causes:

Circled Area 1 shows that price closes at the lower N Band locations. This price action sets the peak in the N Band volatility measurement. A new S/R 6 level is consequently set. One month later, it serves as support for the low on November 22nd.

Circled Areas 2 and 3 make it clear that the dominant support areas are due to S/R 5 and 6. It certainly does not hurt that there was a previous low price set that lines up with the S/R line. S/R 5 and 6 were set because of the price action that occurred during December, which caused the lower N Band to turn down and form a peak.

Circled Areas 4 and 5 show a very interesting distinction. The highs in area 4 line up with S/R 3. Months later, S/R 3 is reset higher and is a bit more accurate at defining resistance.

It isn't that previous price levels don't have an effect on current levels of support and resistance. They do, but it is very limited, and is declining as time pushes forward.

It's important to note that many high and low prices, represented by long upper and lower candlewicks, are present because of a few transactions. There is often only a tiny fraction of the day's volume that sets this extreme, and therefore renders the price action at that level as insignificant. Just as often, there were no actual transactions at that those prices; it was a data error reported by the exchange and remains uncorrected by your data service. If we have to wonder if the price was real or significant, it makes it that much more difficult to rely on a previous price level.

CHART PATTERNS

It's fair to say that most of us would like to be a kid again, at least for a short time. Remember how long summer vacation was? It seemed to go on forever. It was a time when imagination could rule the day. Lying in the grass with friends and pointing out which white puffy cloud looked like a rabbit, or a football, was an activity most of us remember well. Your best friend often saw an elephant, and you could just not see it the same way, no matter how hard you looked at the cloud. To each of us a cloud can still resemble a different shape or object, but it can be something else entirely to another person.

Now that we are all grown up we still play the same game, but we do it with price patterns in stock charts. Chart patterns have been a form of technical analysis for many decades. Many analysts are fervent believers in chart patterns as a genuinely predictive form of analysis. Many others, in the meanwhile, deny the very existence of chart patterns. The source of this disagreement is rooted in the interpretation of what constitutes a pattern. One person's double bottom is another person's noisy consolidation area.

Bar Chart Patterns: Clouds Everywhere

Perhaps the person who has conducted the most comprehensive and scientifically responsible work on chart patterns is Thomas N. Bulkowski. In his two books, *Encyclopedia of Chart Patterns* and *Trading Classic Chart Patterns*,[1] Bulkowski statistically identified and cataloged chart patterns and their behavior. While there is no need for a lengthy discussion here, it's important to state that this author believes that patterns do exist. It is also possible to trade patterns profitably, but it is very difficult.

When a pattern develops and completes, it is recognizable. When one sets up and fizzles, however, it is very difficult for most to see. In reality, a chart is filled with partial chart patterns that fail to develop. It's this interpretational aspect of chart patterns that keeps most traders from profiting from them. Pattern recognition is an acquired skill that is all too often demonstrated by magazine articles and books as an obvious capability for anyone who attempts it. It is because of these difficulties that I can't recommend chart pattern trading as a primary form of swing or position trading. Chart pattern trading should not be a component of volatility-based technical analysis.

But let's turn the table and look at things from the other direction for a moment. There are very important improvements to pattern trading that can be realized with volatility analysis. What follows are chart pattern examples that show how volatility is not the primary cause for their formation. That's okay, because it's not really necessary to identify why patterns develop or exist. The exploding field of behavioral finance is focusing heavily on discovering the *why* aspect of patterns. Let's leave that endeavor to the academic world.

The really bright spot here is the increase in trade efficiency—that is to say, the extra cash that volatility measurement adds to each pattern-based trade. Here's what I mean. It is not difficult to recognize a pattern breakout point, the point at which to enter the trade. The art of finding the most profitable exit is not nearly as simple or exact. Most profit targets are defined as a distance measurement proportional to some aspect of the pattern itself. For instance, a flag pattern defines the height of the formation as the Flagpole. When the upper or lower trend line, which identifies the flag part of the pattern, is crossed, then the trade is entered in that direction. The exit target is calculated as a portion of the Flagpole. There are also different flavors of flag patterns. The exit point can thus be calculated differently, depending on which variation of the flag pattern is being traded.

Volatility measurement adds a much greater degree of accuracy to exit point identification. This is exciting because highly accurate exits are the best way to increase profits. It's as simple as that; leave no money on the table. In lieu of estimating or approximating the profit target, just take it all if you can. The charts that follow will illustrate these types of more profitable exits while featuring three common bar chart patterns. They are the double bottom, the flag, and the triangle.

The Flag   In Figure 7.8, there is a small flag pattern present in this MetaSwing daily chart of Boeing (BA). The flag components are marked along with the breakout level. As the flag pattern forms, there is no particular conformity to MetaSwing's S/R lines, which are formed by Projected Implied Volatility–level algorithms. The profit target is a different story entirely. As Boeing's price rises, it reaches the S/R 1 line decisively, and then promptly reverses. It is easy to see here that the optimum exit point was defined four weeks before when S/R 1 was formed as a result of the peak in the upper N Band. The existence of well-defined, accurate levels of support and resistance make it possible to trade with a greatly reduced level of estimation and guesswork.

The Double Bottom   The double bottom is one of the easiest patterns to identify. They occur all over charts in the form of success and failures. Perhaps for this reason

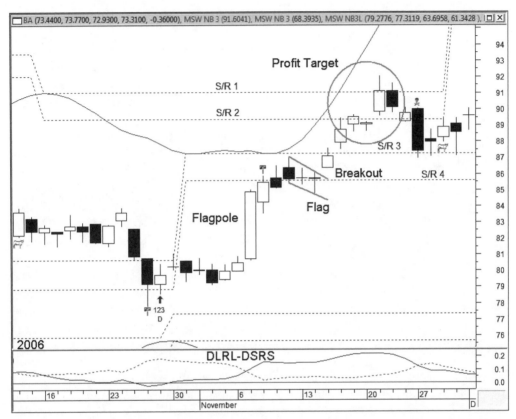

FIGURE 7.8 Boeing (BA) forms a quick flag pattern on this daily chart. Its breakout from the flag is obvious, but classic technical analysis calls for an estimate to define the trade exit point. The S/R 1 line in this MetaSwing chart shows how a solid profit target can be defined weeks in advance, and thus the maximum profit achieved.

Chart created in MetaStock. Chart uses the MetaSwing Add-on, by Northington Trading, LLC. All rights reserved.

they are considered to be among the most unreliable of bar chart patterns. In Figure 7.9, Cummins (CMI) shows a typical double-bottom pattern with a breakout. Zigzag lines have been added to show better definition of the pattern. The breakout level occurs at 15.00 on June 7, 2004. It's important to note that the N Band trough and corresponding S/R 3 level did not really begin to form until the next day. In the two weeks after the breakout, Cummins finds resistance at the S/R 4 line, until it finally climbs to reach the S/R 3 level. Can you see how knowing in advance a specific and logical price target will increase the net gain?

Many prefer to trade the throwback leg of a double bottom. In the case of Cummins, the short trade moves in a solid downward channel, and even picks up speed once it passes through the S/R 4 line. When its price reaches the one ATR distance to the N Band, it begins to encounter resistance. It also generates an Exit Short signal on July 7. The oversold and overbought indicators at the bottom pane are showing extreme

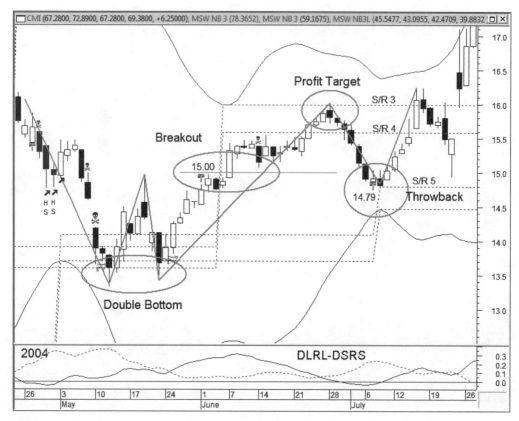

FIGURE 7.9 A very common double-bottom pattern forms during March of 2004 on this chart of Cummins (CMI). The MetaSwing S/R 3 and S/R 4 resistance lines provide accurate profit targets. The S/R 5 later furnishes the short trader a perfect exit if he chooses to profit from a typical throwback leg.

Chart created in MetaStock. Chart uses the MetaSwing Add-on, by Northington Trading, LLC. All rights reserved.

readings. All of this means that the downward price move is likely to pause or reverse. Figure 7.9 makes the trade look easy, but it actually never is.

A very important point of focus is that many traders would exit the throwback portion of the trade at the breakout level of 15.00, or slightly above it. By understanding where resistance exists, this example shows that price did not encounter resistance until it got to 14.79. That's 1.3 percent lower than the breakout line. In early July, one ATR for this stock is just 2.1 percent. Since this stock is not very volatile, an additional 1.3 percent gain is significant. This illustrates that by knowing where real volatility support and resistance exists, trade management is free to consist of less guesswork and more profit.

The Symmetrical Triangle The third and final chart pattern example is the ever-unpredictable symmetrical triangle. This pattern is fraught with fake breakouts and

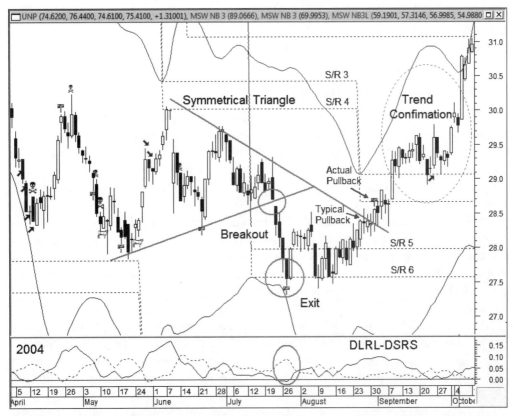

FIGURE 7.10 This symmetrical triangle chart pattern shows that a solid identification of the significant support and resistance levels defines the most profitable trade exit points.

Chart created in MetaStock. Chart uses the MetaSwing Add-on, by Northington Trading, LLC. All rights reserved.

pattern failures. If you choose to trade it, however, then arm yourself with an understanding of the locations of the nearest levels of support and resistance.

A symmetrical triangle is shown in Figure 7.10 with its defining upper and lower converging trend lines. The breakout downward occurs on July 22, 2004, and trades downward to a strong support level at the MetaSwing S/R 6 line. An Exit Short signal is also generated, with close proximity to the lower N Band, accompanied by a serious indicator confirmation of an oversold condition. This is an overwhelming combination of volatility mathematics that shouts "Take Your Money Now!"

If the trader feels so inclined, she could have reversed her position to profit from a possible pullback. This is where it gets really interesting. To calculate the classic pullback level, the upper trend line is extended forward. The pullback should terminate there on August 26, 2004. Classic pattern technical analysis dictates an exit at that point. Price continues to trade upward unimpeded, however, until resistance at the S/R 4 line. If the trader is a believer in volatility-based technical analysis, then she takes her money off the table at 28.66, just above the Exit Long signal day. A little extra money made by nailing the exit is always deserving of the victory dance.

Japanese Candlestick Patterns

Specific candlestick combinations have long held many traders' fascination, and have been believed to be reliable harbingers of short-term price action. Usually specific two-, three-, or four-pattern configurations are touted as high accuracy predictors. Unfortunately for many beginning traders, the hype surrounding Japanese candlestick patterns leads them down the wrong path. The ease of memorizing specific combinations and rules is just too tempting.

The truth is that most suggested trading tactics and rules, promoted by the many experts on the subject, are nebulous at best, and reckless at worst. For the swing trader and the position trader, candlestick patterns are of little use. Components of your frame-work need to consist of indicators and tactics that put the odds in your favor. Here are the logical reasons that support this position:

Too Many: There are easily over 100 Japanese candlestick patterns. Many are obscure and occur very infrequently. Remember, successful traders master a handful of setups, and execute the resulting trade better than 99 percent of the other market participants. Having so many candle patterns makes this difficult, to say the least.

Infrequent: Those that show positive statistical results are seen only sporadically. This makes it difficult to trade them repetitively, and thus gain experience with any specific setup. Most candle patterns that are seen with a sufficient degree of repetition have been rendered ineffective in years past because of overexposure.

Lack of Statistical Performance: Simple performance measurements show that potential losses are greater than potential gains; see the study in this section.

Trade Entry Delay: Most of the promise of Japanese candlestick patterns are for short-term reversals. While much of the published statistics on the probability of reversals may be true, what is not stated is that the pattern itself tends to consume much of the potential profit of the reversal, prior to the trader's oppor-tunity to enter.

A Limited Statistical Look   Before he lays money on the table, the intelligent trader wants this question answered: What are the odds? When trading the financial markets, this is always a more difficult question to answer than one might think. The whole area of back-testing trading strategies is more complex than most realize. The advertisements make it look like a slam dunk.

Remember that a computer is an inanimate object. In reality, it is as dumb as a brick. You have to actually think for it. When working with back-testing software, don't envi-sion that you will be talking with the computer on the Starship Enterprise. It won't even be like working with HAL 9000 on a good day, when he actually does open the pod bay doors. When back-testing a trading strategy, every single variation of the trade setup, entry, and exit, must be meticulously quantified and explained in the appropriate software's code and interface. To be clear about what we are about to do, this exercise is not complete back-testing.

This research will focus on revealing the potential for profitability. Furthermore, this analysis is not being applied to a trade setup or method. It was performed at the component level. For instance, when an aerospace company builds an advanced jet fighter, each component is tested individually first, then again as a part of its respective system. The manufacturer needs to make sure that the component's performance characteristics meet the needed requirements for that component's tasks. The candlestick pattern will be treated only as a component. That is essentially what we are doing at this stage. We are individually testing two candlestick patterns for their probability for potential profit, as well as potential loss. We are testing only two patterns, so this analysis should not be considered a comprehensive study of all candlestick patterns. I do feel, however, that it is representative of Japanese candlestick pattern trading in general.

Most trading is discretionary. Even when traders use mechanical trading systems, they rarely follow them to the letter. The human element endeavors to inflict itself on the whole process. Regardless, it is important to have some numbers on your side when you take a stance on one side of the market. Let's treat a typical Japanese candlestick pattern, therefore, as though it were a component of our framework. Not all components of your framework can be measured mathematically, but this one can.

The objectives of our analysis are to answer these questions:

1. After the pattern or signal is identified, how do the potential profits weigh against the potential losses within a given trading time window?
2. How do the trade signals perform relative to the broader market within the same given trading time window?
3. How frequently do these patterns and signals occur?

To logically attain the answers for these three questions, our method will be as follows:

1. The sample population consists of the S&P 500.
2. The periodicity is daily, with the duration being for 2,000 trading days, beginning on June 29, 2000, and ending on June 13, 2008. This equates to approximately eight years of data, which occur during bear and bull markets.
3. The trigger day consists of the candlestick pattern completion day.
4. The potential trade profit or loss begins at the closing price of the trigger day. This is done because many traders have the ability to recognize the pattern just before the close of that day on an intraday chart. Choosing the closing price of the trigger day in lieu of the opening price on the following day should give the benefit of the gap to the candlestick pattern's probable reversal direction.

5. The test periods are for 5 days and 10 days. The 5-day and 10-day periods conform to swing trade and extended swing trade time frames, respectively. The trigger day is not included in the test period.

6. The potential trade profit for a long trade is calculated as the difference between the close on the trigger day and the highest high price during the test period. The reverse is true for a short trade.

7. The potential trade loss for a long trade is calculated as the difference between the close on the trigger day and the lowest low price during the test period. The reverse is true for a short trade.

8. The percentage profit or loss is added into a net sum. The total quantity of trigger instances is added into a net sum. The net sum total of all profit or losses is then divided by the net sum total of all trigger instances, to produce a total (simple) average potential trade profit or loss.

9. The broad market comparison performance of potential profit or loss is calculated with the same method as an individual stock, but with the values of the S&P 500 Index. When each stock instance is tested, a duplicate test of the S&P 500 is also performed. This answers the question of whether the signal has general predictive value.

It is very important to point out that this method is not a complete statistical analysis. There is no analysis of the actual distribution of the results being performed. This method will compute a raw average only. We use it at this point because it is a valuable step in determining a component's initial level of predictive value.

There are two specific Japanese candlestick patterns shown in Figure 7.11 that we will be testing in this research. The Bearish Engulfing is widely believed to be a high probability reversal pattern, used as a setup for a short trade. The Three Line Strike is also rated as a high probability bullish reversal pattern, used as a setup for a long trade. These two patterns are representative of the best that this art form of trading has to offer. They were chosen because multiple popular candlestick researchers and promoters state them as high accuracy signals. Because the research results that follow is contrary to what other individuals promote, I feel that it is most appropriate for those individuals to remain unnamed.

In addition to the two Japanese candlestick patterns, two trade signals from MetaSwing will be also measured in our analysis. The Exit Long trade signal for short trade entry and the Exit Short for long trade entry are also shown in Figure 7.11. These two volatility-based trading signals will be put to the same analysis as the candlestick patterns.

A MetaStock exploration was written to perform the analysis. The MetaStock code, along with the code to specifically identify the candlestick patterns, is available at the companion web site for this book at www.tradingtheinvisible.com. There, among the support content for this chapter, you will find an Excel spreadsheet file for each signal tested. Each has all of the code and the full numerical contents of the exploration results.

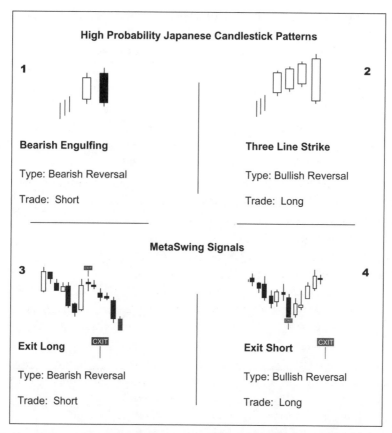

FIGURE 7.11 The Bearish Engulfing pattern is shown in quadrant 1 and the Three Line Strike is shown in quadrant 2. Both of these short-term trading patterns are widely believed to predict reversals with a high degree of accuracy. The images of each depict with relative accuracy what the candlestick configuration resembles in its most perfect form. The MetaSwing Exit Long and Exit Short signals are also included. These signals are derived from historical volatility comparisons, and do not depend on any type of visual candle or bar pattern. They are pure volatility-based algorithms.

It would be somewhat lengthy to print and explain the exploration code here, as we have in earlier chapters. We encourage you, however, to visit the site and retrieve it. It is modular, in that you can use it to test any trading system component that can be expressed as an indicator or function, returning a one or zero. By accessing the site and downloading the file, therefore, you will have code that you can adapt for your own testing. The MetaSwing Exit Long and Exit Short signal code is proprietary; if you are a MetaSwing subscriber, however, then you can test those signals in various circumstances as well.

So after all this methodical introspection of thousands of potential trade entries, how do the numbers fare? More important, what do they mean? Table 7.1 shows the tabulated results of this study. Let's examine the performance characteristics with our original analysis objectives in mind.

TABLE 7.1 Analysis Results for Two Japanese Candlestick Patterns and Two MetaSwing Reversal Signals, for Short-Term Profit versus Loss Potential

Test Event	Sample Size	Profit Potential	Loss Potential	Duration	
1					
Bearish Engulfing	4,524	4.5%	−5.3%	10 Days	−16.7%
S&P 500	4,524	2.3%	−2.1%	10 Days	5.0%
Bearish Engulfing	4,524	3.0%	−4.0%	5 Days	−34.3%
S&P 500	4,524	1.5%	−1.6%	5 Days	−8.6%
2					
Three Line Strike	583	6.1%	−4.9%	10 Days	19.5%
S&P 500	583	2.3%	1.1%	10 Days	146.8%
Three Line Strike	583	5.1%	−3.5%	5 Days	31.5%
S&P 500	583	1.8%	0.5%	5 Days	124.8%
3					
Exit Long	21,858	5.4%	−4.9%	10 Days	8.1%
S&P 500	21,858	2.6%	−2.2%	10 Days	17.8%
Exit Long	21,858	4.0%	−3.4%	5 Days	14.8%
S&P 500	21,858	1.9%	−1.5%	5 Days	20.1%
4					
Exit Short	18,638	6.2%	−5.0%	10 Days	20.2%
S&P 500	18,638	2.7%	1.4%	10 Days	152.2%
Exit Short	18,638	4.5%	−3.6%	5 Days	21.3%
S&P 500	18,638	1.9%	0.5%	5 Days	126.8%

After the pattern is identified, how do the potential profits weigh against the potential losses within a given trading time window? The purpose of this question is to identify the trading direction of the sample population. Remember that this analysis is shedding light on the price extremes of highs to lows. With that in mind the answer to this first question is simple, because the numbers don't lie. If the profit potential is larger than the loss potential, it is good. The opposite is bad.

In the case of the Bearish Engulfing pattern, the loss potential exceeds the profit potential, 4.5 percent to −5.3 percent, for the 10-day trade duration. Directly, this means that the raw average of potential profitable short trades initiated solely on this signal have the ability to achieve a profit of 4.5 percent. The same short trades can likewise also experience a loss of 5.3 percent. This equates to a −16.7 percent differential, which is to say that your potential for profit is 16.7 percent less than your potential for loss. Okay, all rocket science aside, this is not good. This measurement indicates that by using the Bearish Engulfing pattern as a component, within a multicomponent trading decision, a trader would be building in a starting disadvantage. The trader needs probabilities that work with her, not against her.

In the case of the five-day duration, the Bearish Engulfing potential performance is even bleaker. There is an average potential profit of 3 percent versus an average potential loss of 4 percent. This is a −33 percent differential, or profit disadvantage, if you will.

It's also important to note that the five-day trading window is more applicable to swing trading than the 10-day duration.

Note that we keep referring to the results in terms of potential. Whether the word *potential* is stated or not it is certainly inferred, because this study uncovers only the signal's raw average potential. There are other, more applicable, methods for determining actual performance. Discovering the signal's potential is the necessary first step to qualifying it as a valid component for your framework.

The Three Line Strike candlestick pattern exhibits some more promising potential performance numbers. Its profit to loss potential is positive, at 6.1 percent versus –4.9 percent for a 10-day duration, and 5.1 percent versus –3.5 percent for the five-day duration. These are respectable numbers. Its overall numbers, however, show its Achilles heel, which I discuss shortly.

The MetaSwing signals, Exit Long and Exit Short, both show positive potential profit numbers in 5- and 10-day time durations. Using these as components of your framework will add positive outcome probability to your trading odds. They also exhibit two other very positive performance characteristics. I discuss those in the next few paragraphs.

How do the trade signals perform relative to the broader market within the same given trading time window? While the Bearish Engulfing pattern has a negative performance in both time windows, the cumulative stocks of the S&P 500 actually have a greater profit potential than loss in the 10-day analysis. In the five-day time window, however, the S&P is also somewhat negative.

This category is one in which the other three signals perform well. The Three Line Strike, Exit Long, and Exit Short signals each outperform the S&P 500 in both time durations. This is very important. While a positive profit potential is critical, the ability to make more profit than the broader market is a key characteristic necessary to determine if a trading signal has genuine predictive value. If a trading component can't beat other stocks chosen at random, then what is the point of using it?

The Three Line Strike possesses an additional valuable trait. Notice that for each, the S&P 500 also has a positive profit potential. This means that the signal has a tendency to support trading during favorable broad market conditions. In short, it seems to promote trading in the right direction, at the right time, for the right duration. Think about it; this is huge. This means that it has a positive raw probability to make money, outperform the broad market, and encourage trading at a more advantageous time period.

When the signal analysis shows confirmation for positive broad market participation, the trader has an advantage in market timing, if he chooses to use it. What I mean by this is that by observing the repetitive daily signal count, on the same batch of stocks, it's easy to track higher levels of signals. When these higher levels of signals occur, outside of extreme contradicting fundamental events, then it serves as a valuable part of timing the market swings. When the rabbit population is high, the hunting is best. Keep your eye on the woods, however, to make sure that all those rabbits aren't running from a forest fire.

How frequently do these patterns and signals occur? Positive profit potential is important. There is another characteristic at the same time that is of a practical nature. If the given signal is very rare, then it is difficult to identify. It is also harder to trade successfully because of a lack of experience and practice with it. In the case of the Three Line Strike pattern, its profit potential was good, but there were only 583 signals in the S&P 500 in eight years. This means it happened an average of once every seven years on the typical stock in the S&P 500. While it is possible to identify it on occurrence, and become proficient with its particular trade characteristics, it's just highly improbable. It is a pattern that simply does not happen often enough to be practical. It's also important to remember that there is an abundance of Japanese candlestick patterns, each with very specific rules and peculiarities. The learning curve for this art form is no easy task.

The Effect of Analysis Results   The chart of Louisiana Pacific (IPX) in Figure 7.12 shows a real-life example of trading with Japanese candlestick reversal patterns. The Bearish Engulfing pattern completion candle is marked accordingly on the chart. It is widely regarded as a high probability reversal signal for a short trade setup. This pattern

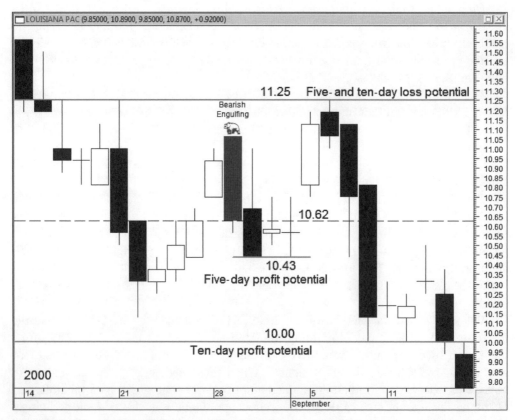

FIGURE 7.12 This daily chart of Louisiana Pacific (IPX) shows the Japanese candlestick pattern known as the Bearish Engulfing pattern.

Chart created in MetaStock.

suffers because much of the potential reversal profit is included in the confirming candle-stick, and is thus missed as a piece of the opportunity. The maximum profit and loss levels, for 5- and 10-day trade periods, are marked as well. With a possible trade entry at 10.62, the potential loss and profit for the 10-day period are virtually the same. The five-day profit-to-loss potential is really awful. This stock is on a downtrend, and a short trade still fails to make money in normal trading time durations.

The reason for this is obvious. By the time Japanese candlestick reversal patterns signal, they usually chew up profits within the pattern itself. It is this shortcoming that most proponents of this methodology fail to point out in their performance statistics. Remember, money is to be made at the extremes. Once price reverses significantly from the extreme, then the risk-reward ratio is adversely affected.

There is a significant number of candlestick patterns that are believed to signal a continuation. In theory, most of these patterns show a price retracement before a trend continuation, which would likely not sacrifice profits. That's the theory that is promoted. These patterns usually suffer from interpretation. Beginning and intermediate traders trying to place faith in technical analysis too often try to use a candlestick pattern in all markets and underlying directional conditions. This usually leads to losses as well as a mixed bag of feedback for the trader when he tries to make sense of the results. In truth, candlestick patterns need to be applied differently in disparate situations. It can add up to a very complex set of rules; rules that change according to which one of the many candlestick patterns is being used.

In her article "Counting Crows,"[2] Sharon Yamanaka methodically explores the conflicting advice of several well-known experts on the topic of Japanese candlestick trading. In the end result of her findings, that particular pattern has a set of guidelines that are at best subjective. That she finds a potentially profitable method for trading the specific pattern is not really the point. What's important is that the excessive complexity of trading this art form is brought to light.

The Japanese candlestick patterns that do have the potential to work well tend to occur very infrequently. Those that happen with an acceptable frequency tend to have negative profit potential. There are more than 100 patterns to choose from, which makes the practice complex. The overwhelming majority of traders who attempt to use short-term candlestick patterns as a form of technical analysis are never able to overcome its intricacies. This is both because of the size and scope of the required learning and experience, and because of the conflicting instruction and advice that comes from expert sources. It is for these reasons that I cannot recommend that this technical analysis methodology becomes a part of your framework.

OSCILLATORS

Most of us who practice technical analysis have a first love within the range of tools that we use. You know what I mean. Remember that initial look at a form of math that was going to tell you exactly when to enter and exit trades. It was love at first sight because you were going to be rich within a year. Your job was going to be history, your Yugo was to be replaced with a BMW, and your taste in restaurants was about to change drastically, all because you alone discovered the magic and wonder of the squiggly little curvy line at the bottom of the chart. Alas, it turned out to be more wonder than magic. Slowly, or quickly if you were fortunate, reality replaced those grandiose dreams with the understanding that your wealth was not to be attained through a superior indicator.

Indicators are absolute necessities to technical analysis. But if you find yourself conducting trades that are garnering less profit than you achieved in years past, don't fret. It's not your skills that are waning; it's more likely to be your tools that need upgrading. The appropriate set of algorithms can make a huge difference for you. I caution you, though, that what's needed are not your father's oscillators.

Many traders today repeatedly make profitable use of the most common indicators. They swear by the MACD. To them, the RSI and the stochastic oscillator seem sufficiently advanced to do the job. It isn't that these tools are completely ineffective. They work; just not well enough to give you the odds you need. The huge sums of institutional money today are not relying on these outdated calculations to move the market. Wall Street uses quantitative mathematics, based real-time volatility, to identify opportunities. What's amazing is how they do so with sufficient time for them to build a $50 million position before putting on your relatively tiny 1,000-share purchase.

We discussed in previous chapters how important it is for indicators to have a primary foundation rooted in volatility. There are almost as many indicators as there are stars in the sky, so we will focus on those most commonly known. Now let's take a little time to dig into the differences between them and what you should be using. Since we focused heavily on the stochastic oscillator in Chapter 5, there is no need to open up that indicator again. Lastly, we will closely examine the construct of a true volatility-based, trend-sensitive indicator. In the pages that follow, I focus specifically on the:

- Moving Average Convergence Divergence (MACD)
- Relative Strength Index (RSI)
- MetaSwing DLRL-DSRS

Moving Average Convergence Divergence (MACD)

It's unfortunate how most traders who use technical indicators don't try to understand the actual math equations to be executed within them. Virtually all indicators use the math that we learned in middle school. The MACD is possibly the least understood of these. The MACD is just a couple of moving averages, that's all. Here's the MACD calculation using the most commonly accepted default settings:

MACD = 12-period exponential moving average—26-period exponential moving average

Signal = 9-period exponential moving average of the MACD

Moving averages are lagging indicators. The MACD is a pure moving average calculation. The moving average period settings can vary, but it is still just a moving average. For a long trade, the classically accepted method for its use is to identify a potential trend beginning when the MACD line crosses above the slower signal line. A short trade would be indicated when the MACD crosses below the signal line.

For the reasons stated previously in this chapter, moving average–based trading cannot consistently produce profitable trades. The trader who uses a moving average–based system will experience periods of profitability and loss that are not due to the system. They are only symptomatic of broader market conditions. Losses from trades that stop out will surpass profits.

The MACD consists purely of moving average relationships. Thus, for reasons previously mentioned, the MACD is fundamentally fraught with lag, and can't really be salvaged by making it volatility sensitive. Therefore, no further discussion of it is warranted.

Relative Strength Index (RSI)

The Relative Strength Index (RSI) has long been an oscillator on which traders have relied to gauge overbought and oversold conditions, as well as bullish and bearish divergences. There is a very long list of indicators to choose from for both of these same tasks, but the RSI is about as good as any of the well-worn, and publicly available, technical algorithms. The RSI is an indicator that will always read between the values of 0 and 100. It suffers from being directionally vulnerable. When prices are cycling in a range-bound market, it works well; but then again, what doesn't? Most stocks spend very little time in range-bound patterns. Instead they wander from one direction to another without actually trending. This limbo state of trading takes its toll on the trader relying too heavily on overbought and oversold oscillators that do not incorporate volatility-based math.

Old School Refer to Figure 7.13 for an illustration of changing market conditions, where a daily chart of Stryker Corporation (SYK) transitions from a six-month range-bound pattern to a trending rally beginning in July 2007. This chart shows a wide date range and is therefore a bit crowded, but it is necessary to show the changing market conditions. This chart shows trading signals plotted with the price candles based on conventional trading practices for the RSI. The RSI with a lookback of 14 periods is plotted in the lower indicator pane. It has horizontal boundaries plotted at 30 and 70, which are the most commonly accepted levels. The trade signals shown are generated when the RSI crosses from above 70 to below it for a short trade. For a trade signal on the long side, the signal travels upward from below 30 to cross above it. The middle indicator pane displays a modified RSI indicator, which I discuss in the coming paragraphs.

This change in price direction, from range bound to rally, causes the traditional RSI(14) indicator to give consistent overbought readings throughout the duration of the

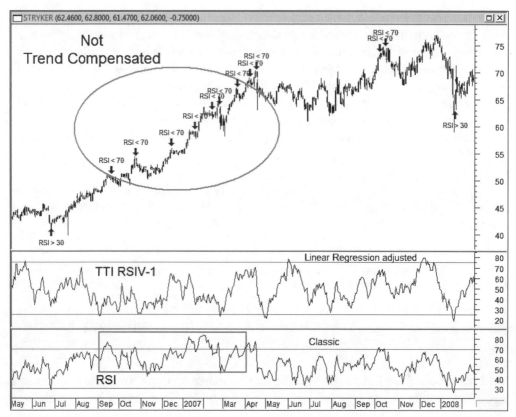

FIGURE 7.13 It is clear in this chart of the Stryker Corporation (SYK) that the classic form of the Relative Strength Indicator has difficulty adjusting to a trend.

Chart created in MetaStock.

rally. As you can see, the indicator would encourage the trader to repeatedly take losing short-trade positions. This is typical of oscillators that do not incorporate volatility or trend compensation. As the saying goes, "That dog just won't hunt."

At the end of the trend in May 2008, the indicator requires months of time to adjust to a more sideways trading environment. This delay can cause you to miss opportunities. It actually happens frequently in today's markets because the larger sources of buying and selling are not using tools such as the RSI. They are using quantitative mathematics that compensate for trend direction and volatility. This leads to the obvious question: What can be done to level the playing field?

New School   The classic Relative Strength Indicator as created by J. Welles Wilder Jr. is based on sound logic, and was a groundbreaking technical tool in its day. When it was introduced in 1978, computational hardware was not widespread, and it is thus reflective of that limitation. In those days, the trader could not just flip the computer On switch and crank out a hundred million operations per second whenever she felt like it. But when this chapter was written, and for some years now, the trader who avoids using tools of mathematical sophistication is shooting herself in the proverbial foot.

So let's give the RSI a volatility transplant. Here is the equation that best describes the RSI calculation:

$$100 - \left(\frac{100}{1 + \left(\dfrac{U}{D} \right)} \right)$$

where U = An exponential average of upward price changes
        D = An exponential average of downward price changes

- The U component computes a net sum of the individual price increases for each day that has a closing price that is higher than the previous day's close. It then converts them to an exponential moving average.
- The D component computes a net sum of the individual price decreases for each day that has a closing price that is lower than the previous day's close. It then converts them to an exponential moving average.
- The rest of the arithmetic functions to convert the results of U divided by D into a real number are between 0 and 100.

This model is a test of logic. It asks the question "How are our up days compared to our down days?" It assumes that if the up days compute to a larger number than the down days, then the Relative Strength Index reading should rise, or else it should go down. In its well-known form, the U and D components are based on changes in price. There's no reason that we can't let them calculate changes in something else, though.

Our new RSI indicator needs to be able to give accurate readings when price is trending up or down. We therefore need to depart from the basic comparison of prices to itself. Linear Regression computes a line that reflects direction in the most efficient and accurate manner.

Contemplate for a moment that you are walking up a hill. You are exerting extra effort to walk forward and rise higher. After each step, you achieve a higher elevation relative to sea level. But also after each step you are still the same distance to the ground. This is the difference between a price-to-price comparison, and a price-to-linear-regression comparison.

But how can we also adjust the equation to be sensitive to volatility changes? To a limited degree, linear regression achieves that. When price changes direction, so too does the slope of the linear regression line, in the direction of the move. This compensates to some degree by allowing extra movement before reaching an oversold and overbought level. It isn't a comprehensive method of recognizing volatility changes, but it's a start. The primary effect of using a linear regression line in this case is that it adjusts for changes in price direction.

The following is MetaStock code for expressing a version of the RSI, with linear regression used for the reasons we've just discussed. We will call this new indicator the TTI RSIV-1:

```
1 {User inputs}
2 pds1:= Input("Lookback", 2, 1000, 30);
3 pds2:= Input("Linear Regression Periods", 2, 1000, 40);

4 {Defines the difference between the day's closing price and the
5 linear regression line, and assigns the value to the variable x1}
6 x1:= (C - LinearReg(C, pds2, S, 1) );

7 {Conditional logic to define an Up day for x1}
8 x2:= If(x1 > Ref(x1, -1), 1, 0);

9 {Conditional logic to measure an increase in x1 on an Up day}
10 x3:= If(x1 > Ref(x1, -1), x1 - Ref(x1, -1), 0);

11 {Conditional logic to define a Down day for x1}
12 x4:= If(x1 < Ref(x1, -1), 1, 0);

13 {Conditional logic to measure a decrease in x1 on a Down day}
14 x5:= If(x1 < Ref(x1, -1), Ref(x1, -1) - x1, 0);

15 {Multiplies the sum of the increases on Up days by the number
16 of Up days}
17 x6:= Sum(x3, pds1) * Sum(x2, pds1);

18 {Multiplies the sum of the decreases on Down days by the number
19 of Down days}
20 x7:= Sum(x5, pds1) * Sum(x4, pds1);

21 {Calculates the ratio of trend adjusted increases to trend adjusted
22 decreases, and then converts it to a value between 0 and 100}
23 x8:= 100-(100/(1+(x6/x7)));

24 {Plots the TTI RSIV-1)
25 x8;
```

You can see if you follow the comment line explanations in this code that there are two principal differences from the original RSI method:

1. In line six, the change in price is calculated as a change of the closing price's distance to the linear regression line. This is different because the original RSI calculated the change between the closing prices of the two periods.

2. The second major difference is that U and D are calculated differently from the classic RSI method. This is evidenced in lines 17 and 20. The original RSI method

calculates an exponential moving average of the increases and decreases for U and D, respectively. The TTI RSIV-1 version computes a simple product of the two, using multiplication. The process of multiplication emphasizes larger movements more decidedly, thus magnifying volatility. It is because of this change that the threshold triggers should to be changed to 25 and 75.

A look at Figure 7.14 shows us the same chart of Stryker (SYK) as in Figure 7.13, with the exception that this one has trade signals generated by TTI RSIV-1. The long entry signal is generated when the indicator value crosses below 25. The short entry signal is generated when the indicator crosses above 75. Notice how different these trade signals are from those generated by the RSI indicator in Figure 7.13. When looking at the actual RSIV-1 indicator plotted in the middle pane, it is easy to see that it does not rise to overbought levels and remain there.

This version is able to maintain a more unbiased ability to identify the overbought

FIGURE 7.14 This chart clearly illustrates trade signals generated from a volatility adjusted, trend neutral version of the RSI. Observe how it is able to maintain an appropriate lack of trend bias.

Chart created in MetaStock.

and oversold levels regardless of the trend direction. It is able to give accurate signals to enter in the trend's direction. When the trend ends in April 2007, the RSIV-1 is able to adapt quickly to the change in trading direction and thus give back-to-back long and short signals. The RSI, meanwhile, needs more time to adjust to the range-bound market condition. The primary reason that the RSIV-1 can adapt quickly is due to the nature of the linear regression it uses. Linear regression can adapt to direction changes relatively fast.

In giving credit where it is due, I want to point out that Donald Dorsey created an indicator within a similar logical progression. It's called the Relative Volatility Index (RVI), and he first published it in the June 1993 issue of *Technical Analysis of Stocks and Commodities*. Dorsey also used the underlying RSI algorithm, but he substituted price changes with changes in the standard deviation of price. Mr. Dorsey was a very forward thinker.

A Second Variation   The TTI RSIV-1 does depart from the original indicator that Welles Wilder created. It induces a bit more recognition of short-term volatility. But what happens if we stay true to the classic method of calculating RSI? This would involve using an exponential moving average to resolve the U and D components in lieu of the multiplication step. Let's call this second version the TTI RSIV-2; how about that for originality? The indicator code would be identical except that lines 17 and 20 would look like this:

```
17 x6:= Mov(x3, pds1, E);
20 x7:= Mov(x5, pds1, E);
```

Once again the same chart of Stryker (SYK) is used as a true comparison. The middle pane in Figure 7.15 shows TTI RSIV-2 just above the classic RSI(14). Because this new version is not as sensitive to volatility, the average readings are less extreme. For this reason, the threshold levels are the same as the classic version at 30 and 70.

One thing for certain is that it really seems to be trend neutral. Regardless of the trading direction, the TTI RSIV-2 stays centered as well as a yoga master. This is purely due to the linear regression component. It also generates only one trade signal in June 2007. It's always easier to control your emotions as a trader when you can have confidence in your tools and methods. In the case of TTI RSIV-1 and TTI RSIV-2, it is somewhat comforting to have an indicator that is not led astray by the constant ramblings of a turbulent market.

So far, though, we have looked at the three iterations of the RSI on just a single chart. In truth, we could look at many charts and still have only a fractional level of insight into the actual reliability of these potential components. So at this point, it is prudent to test them in the same way we tested the Japanese candlestick patterns. Table 7.2 shows the results using those same research procedures. Just as before, this will give us a gauge of the component's profit and loss potential. It is for a 5- and 10-day trading window. Also, as before, please note that this process produces only a raw average. There is no statistical analysis of the distribution of the results.

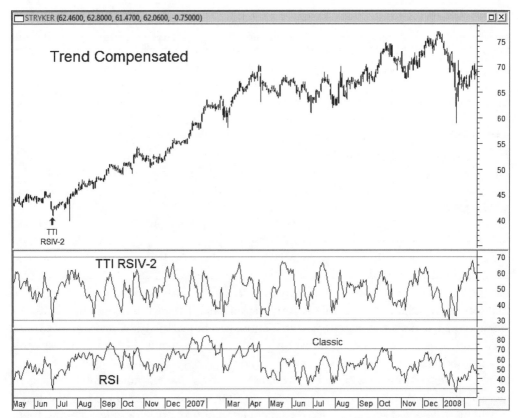

FIGURE 7.15 This is another version of the modified RSI indicator shown on the Stryker (SYK) chart. The RSIV-2 is plotted in the middle indicator pane. Its profit-and-loss potential testing performance is slightly better, but the instances of signals are far fewer.

Chart created in MetaStock.

These results reveal some very important performance characteristics. As we suspected, the classic RSI has a negative profit-and-loss tendency because it averages a 6.8 percent potential profit, but a −7.2 percent potential loss for a 10-day period. The five-day window is also negative. There's no sense in starting a trade with the odds against you, right?

Both the TTI RSIV-1 and the TTI RSIV-2, however, have both positive profit and loss potential. One big difference is in the quantity of trades generated by each. The TTI RSIV-2 produces about one-third as many opportunities. Note that this study uses all of the stocks in the S&P 500 over a period of eight years. Since these two indicators use different math, and each have positive potential performance, it would be a good decision to add them both to your framework. The original RSI, however, is probably too dated for today's volatile markets, and should be passed over.

In the way that we have evaluated and adapted the classic RSI indicator, so too

TABLE 7.2 Results of the signal analysis for the RSI, TTI RSIV-1, and TTI RSIV-2

Test Event	Sample Size	Profit Potential	Loss Potential	Duration
1 Long Trade				
RSI(14)	10,649	6.8%	−7.2%	10 Days
S&P 500	10,649	2.8%	1.4%	10 Days
RSI(14)	10,649	4.6%	−5.4%	5 Days
S&P 500	10,649	2.0%	0.5%	5 Days
2 Long Trade				
RSIV-1	10,572	5.6%	−5.2%	10 Days
S&P 500	10,572	2.3%	1.1%	10 Days
RSIV-1	10,572	4.1%	−3.6%	5 Days
S&P 500	10,572	1.7%	0.4%	5 Days
3 Long Trade				
RSIV-2	3,523	7.0%	−5.8%	10 Days
S&P 500	3,523	2.7%	1.3%	10 Days
RSIV-2	3,523	5.7%	−4.4%	10 Days
S&P 500	3,523	2.0%	0.5%	5 Days

should you approach the vast body of traditional technical analysis algorithms. Do not trust each and every technical indicator simply because someone writes a magazine article about it. There are an abundance of trade journals with a lot of space that needs filling. Be very skeptical of general-purpose indicators that do not adapt to changing market conditions and time frames. Waste no time in researching their internal logic, providing it does not violate copyright or intellectual property law, and adapting them with volatility-based math. Your trading account balance will thank you for the effort.

Suppose, though, that we want to really think outside the box factory and design or choose an indicator design that is truly volatility sensitive. What would it look like? This next section shows one construct that fits the bill.

MetaSwing DLRL-DSRS

After the indicator development work of the previous chapters, and the testing and analysis efforts of this chapter, we have a good understanding of the desirable traits for an overbought and oversold indicator. As an example of an indicator designed to correctly deal with the challenges of today's volatile markets, we examine the functioning characteristics of the MetaSwing DLRL-DSRS indicator system. I refer to this indicator as a system because it is actually two oscillators that are designed to work in tandem. The design of these two indicators creates a tag team concept. Extreme conditions are measured finitely, while the relative historical volatility of the opposing indicator is free to rise and fall on the basis of significance. This tandem capability is a design dimension that is new to technical analysis.

The basic method of the construct is shown clearly in Figure 7.16. The two indicators are based entirely on volatility-sensing algorithms. Each focuses on a different side

MetaSwing DLRL-DSRS Tandem Construct

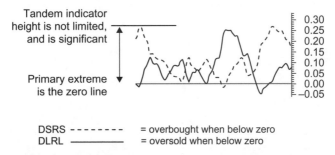

DSRS - - - - - - - -	= overbought when below zero
DLRL ———————	= oversold when below zero

FIGURE 7.16 This diagram shows the DLRL oversold indicator, working together with the DSRS overbought indicator, to see through the fog that shadows the short-term volatility within the price bars.

Chart created in MetaStock. Chart uses the MetaSwing Add-on, by Northington Trading, LLC. All rights reserved.

of the market. The best way to measure market forces in play is to make visible how they compete.

Within this philosophy an oversold condition is measured when the DLRL indicator falls below zero. An overbought level is shown when the DSRS crosses down below zero. Just sensing an extreme condition, however, is not really enough to interpret when a true oversold or overbought level exists. The height of the opposing indicator component is the key to determining a true extreme condition. This height is only relevant to the previous peaks of itself. By comparing the tandem component's past energy required to lift it to its own highest levels, a true measurement of the extreme condition is made visible. In this dual role, each indicator contributes to the identification of the true extreme.

As a real-world example of this tandem system in action look at the Cisco Systems (CSCO) chart in Figure 7.17. There are two examples in this chart. The first is delineated by a number 1 on the left side of the chart, and the second shows the number 2 on the right side. On June 6, 2005, Cisco achieves an oversold condition with the DLRL dropping below zero, which is shown at the first vertical dashed line. In the circled area below, the value of the opposing DSRS indicator is shown with two horizontal lines. Price begins to consolidate at that point. The reversal does not begin until seven days later, however, when the DSRS component reaches a height that is closer to past levels. Meanwhile, the DLRL remains below zero.

On the right side of the chart in Figure 7.17 is a second example showing a true overbought extreme. The DSRS reaches the zero line on September 6, 2005. Its teammate, however, the DLRL, is still at a low level of volatility compared with recent historical levels. The line showing the tandem indicator height shows that on September 9, 2005, the DLRL surpasses its own significant levels set in May and July. Bullish mathematical characteristics reached an extreme three days previously on September 6. By

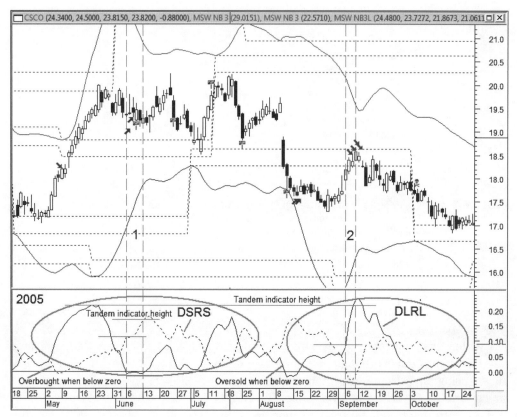

FIGURE 7.17 This MetaSwing chart of Cisco Systems (CSCO) shows two examples of the DLRL-DSRS tandem system of opposing indicators. Real clarity is gained with dual volatility measurement when measuring true extreme conditions, which is otherwise invisible to the trader's eye.

Chart created in MetaStock. Chart uses the MetaSwing Add-on, by Northington Trading, LLC. All rights reserved.

September 9, it is likely that bearish math, rooted in volatility, has run its course. The short-term rally consequently runs out of steam. It is this dual form of measurement from which the DLRL-DSRS system draws its strength.

Trend direction causes the vast majority of oscillators to consistently skew their readings. It can be a difficult problem to overcome. Like stocks, however, NASCAR tracks don't run in straight lines, either. The driver cannot run around the track constantly scraping the railings to win the race. It might be what fans like to watch, but it's a very short race for that car. The race teams in that sport have exacted the science of placing and controlling a car at exact locations within the boundaries of the track, all at over 200 miles per hour. Also, because they essentially go around in circles, the never-ending centrifugal force means there is no tendency for reversion to the mean. If they can keep their car in the middle of the track through all that, then we should at least be able to keep an indicator from scraping its own railings too often.

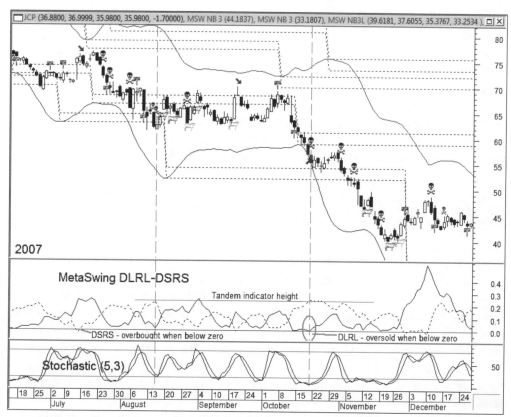

FIGURE 7.18 This example of JC Penney in a long, steady downtrend clearly shows the difference between a trend-neutral oscillator and one that suffers when the stock is not in a trading range.

Chart created in MetaStock. Chart uses the MetaSwing Add-on, by Northington Trading, LLC. All rights reserved.

An oscillator needs to be as trend neutral as possible so that its predictive value is not eroded. Just as with the RSIV indicators, the DLRL-DSRS indicators are able to withstand steep trend directions without introducing an unwanted bias into their results.

In Figure 7.18 JC Penney (JCP) is on a long, protracted downtrend during the subprime meltdown of 2007. Note the bottom indicator pane, which shows a stochastic oscillator. The stochastic consistently gives oversold indications for months on end. The middle indicator pane shows the DLRL-DSRS pair of indicators.

Only once throughout the entire six-month duration of the chart does the DLRL go below zero. It did so on October 19, 2007, as shown by the circle on the indicator. Also on that date, the DSRS component reached a high level from 10 weeks earlier on August 15, 2007. Both of these dates have vertical dashed lines on the chart. JC Penney's price decline stopped on August 15 and began to trade sideways for eight weeks. The point here is that price then begins another dive and stops when the DLRL goes below zero and the DSRS reaches the height set at the previous true oversold level.

This is significant for two reasons. First, it shows how important the combination of a below-zero reading with a sufficiently high tandem component reading is. The height of the tandem indicator is the best measure of short-term volatility. The second reason is that it is evident that the DLRL is very trend neutral. Unlike the stochastic, it is able to avoid false oversold readings, and show only the true oversold conditions.

When you are selecting oscillators to guide your trading decisions, be sure that they are first and foremost volatility based. Second, be sure that your indicators are not shoved around by the trend. If your overbought and oversold indicator choices can pass those two tests, then they deserve consideration for your framework.

CHOOSE THE BEST

The potential quantity of existing technical analysis components available for addition to your framework is vast. In this chapter we have covered only a handful of the most common forms of technical tools. We have adapted existing indicators to the challenges presented by today's more volatile markets. There is little reason why you can't develop many of your own. After all, so many bright and capable developers have gone before us and have left us a rich library from which to choose. They have contributed technical algorithms with very sound logic, well rooted in the market demands of their day. There is no reason to discard their work, or to fail to recognize them for their contributions. But none of us owe anyone a debt that would cause us to risk the balances of our trading accounts by using outdated methods.

If technical analysis development is not your bag, then buy the best available, and learn to use it well. Just like *The X-Files*, trust no one. Make a vendor prove performance before you license their technical tools. Do not waste your time or money using any technical analysis tools that are free today. That only means that they are worth what you paid for them. If an indicator is included with your charting package, and included with many others as well, consider it free and of little predictive value.

Most of all, ensure that your technical tools are truly volatility based. There can be no substitute for this. Go back and read Chapter 1 again. The forces that move the markets are using quantitative mathematics based on volatility. You need to do the same.

PART THREE

Trading the Invisible

This part of the book is about decision making. The coming chapters explore methods for specific types of trades that succeed by leveraging volatility measurement, which is another way of saying trade decisions. No matter what your style of trading, your methods involved, or your philosophies, it all boils down to your brain making decisions based on probabilities. The combination of computer and software perform this activity with clean, cold efficiency. Your brain, however, does not always do so.

It appears that we do not have the ability to be computers, no matter how hard we try. Richard L. Peterson, M.D., in his book *Inside the Investor's Brain*, describes flawed decision-making tendencies that are an inherent part of each of us. He cites many scientific studies that all agree that "Emotions such as fear also lead to the overestimation of the likelihood of low probability events that are vivid or emotionally weighted. Ego attachment to particular outcomes increases the severity of such biases. Self-awareness of risk-perception biases is challenging due to the thought distortions that arise from unconscious emotions."[1]

Understanding your limitations in trading only matters if you take positive steps to overcome them. Those positive steps are the trading methods, and new volatility-based components in the chapters that follow. Chapter 8 presents the most important decision-making process of all, determination of the broad market direction. All other methods must work well within it.

Even though you are not capable of perfectly balanced decision making, you can strive for that goal with improved odds. This is achieved by relying on your methods and your intimate understanding of their underlying mathematics. That firsthand comprehension of the exact makeup of your trading components will best enable you to overcome the emotions and biases that we all possess. If you use that strength within a well-established, cross-verifying framework, you will perform at your finest.

CHAPTER 8

Bull Bear Phase Prediction

The Intermediate- and Short-Term Market Swing

D o you ever find yourself talking with a group of friends, or perhaps members of your family, and the majority of them are down about something? One person remarks about the high price of gasoline, while another speaks of the difficulty his company is having competing with overseas competitors. The conversation progresses down a sort of negative pathway and before too long you find that you're feeling a bit down. Despite the fact that your current life's situation is rosy, your immediate surroundings have affected your mood and outlook toward the downside.

How about the average 30-minute situation comedy you routinely watch on television? We are so accustomed to the laugh track that plays along with the show that we hardly even notice it anymore. You are not particularly crazy about the program but you still laugh while viewing it. There's a good reason why the producers go to extra work and expense to carefully edit the content and achieve a perfectly timed blend of dialog and laughter. It has its roots in the same reason why most people will immediately exit a theater when someone yells fire.

It is basic human nature to participate with other humans that surround us. We laugh if others laugh, whether something is funny or not. We feel down when others do, despite our own situation being fine. Indeed, we can even panic for no reason at all if others around us are doing so. Because humans behave this way, financial markets do as well. When the broad market is doing well, most stocks trade higher, regardless of its outlook statement or recent earnings announcements. Stocks trade with a herd mentality. The herd is the entire broader market. To add yet another dimension, they trade in a similar fashion with their specific market sector.

Regardless of why it happens, it is important that you understand that this is a fact. No amount of stock-picking skill is going to insulate you from the effects of the overall market direction, in any time frame. You will need to do the market technician equivalent of being the first to laugh, or detecting when everyone is about to be feeling down, and even being the first to smell smoke.

In this author's opinion, detecting the swing of the market *in advance* is the single most difficult part of trading. Very capable and intelligent people fail at the business of trading because they lack the ability to do this or they simply underestimate its importance. This is especially true of options traders who get lost in the Greeks and pay little attention to market direction. If you are going to prevail in the net-sum business of trading, it is critical that you learn to time the swing and phase of the broader market. And if you can master this one single aspect of trading, then it's pretty hard to fail.

WHY SWING WITH THE MARKET?

As the saying goes, timing is everything. Too true. There is a very comforting feeling that a trader gets when she is lying in bed at night knowing that her trading account is flat; she has not a single position in the market. She feels great because her recent trades are closed, and their net profits are booked. Meanwhile, as other traders nervously sit on their positions waiting for the next market move, they are hoping that they don't have to give back much of their recent gains. During this off time, the competent market swing trader patiently waits until the next high probability directional signal sets up. It is really a sheer joy to watch the indexes slip back down the hill after you have just closed your long positions.

There are really eight primary pieces of intelligence that are needed to make money trading.

1. Know when to trade
2. Know when to be flat
3. Know which side of the market to be on
4. Know what to trade
5. Know your time frame
6. Know your position size
7. Know when to enter
8. Know when to exit

This chapter deals with the first three items on the list.

While it is not absolutely necessary for a stock to trade in lockstep with the market indexes, the ones that don't are certainly in the minority. It is a tricky situation when a particular issue moves in its own direction, completely isolated from the forces of the market around it. This happens and often lasts for a month or two, only to end abruptly and lose all semblance of individuality. When this occurs, there is no warning. This is why it's best to stay in step with the broader market swings and phase.

A typical relationship of a stock to its respective index is shown in Figure 8.1. Here, a daily chart of Compuware Corporation (CPWR) demonstrates an upward trading direc-

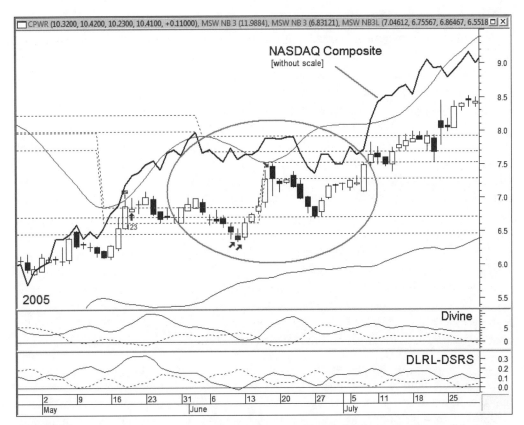

CPWR (10.3200, 10.4200, 10.2300, 10.4100, +0.11000), MSW NB 3 (11.9884), MSW NB 3 (6.83121), MSW NB3L (7.04612, 6.75567, 6.86467, 6.5518)

NASDAQ Composite
[without scale]

Divine

DLRL-DSRS

FIGURE 8.1 A daily chart of Compuware Corporation (CPWR) demonstrates very well how a stock will trade in the same direction as the short-term swings in its market index.

Chart created in MetaStock. Chart uses the MetaSwing Add-on, by Northington Trading, LLC. All rights reserved.

tion. The solid rising jagged line plotted alongside the price candles is the NASDAQ Composite Index; it is plotted without a scale. It's plain to see how the stock price directly correlates to the moves of the other stocks in the NASDAQ Composite Index. The movement of Compuware is generally the same as the composite index; it does find, however, its own levels of volatility-based support and resistance within the MetaSwing N Bands and S/R lines.

The two most common uses for identifying the broad market swing are:

1. *Trading Stocks.* The optimum price point for entering a long or short trade of a stock is mostly due to chart analysis of the actual stock. The timing of the entry, however, has everything to do with the market swing. The optimum method for stock trading, therefore, is to enter at the best point on the stock's chart, at a time just before the market is about to move in the direction of the trade. With this in mind, it is imperative that whatever method you use to measure broad

market swings, it is one with predictive value. You need for it to give you advance warning of a probable swing so that you can look for stocks trading toward proper setups.

2. *Trading Indexes.* Many traders prefer to stick with market index exchange trade funds (ETFs), or index option contracts, such as the S&P E-mini. It goes without saying then that predicting the market swing is everything to this individual.

Before we put the short-term market swing under the microscope, there is another important time frame that we must first understand: the intermediate term. In this discussion, we are conforming to the traditional short-term, intermediate-term, and long-term conventions of market cycle identification. Here is a clarification of the time definitions:

Short Term = One to two weeks
Intermediate Term = Two to six months
Long Term = Nine months to x years

INTERMEDIATE-TERM MARKET DIRECTION

Markets oscillate throughout all time frames. Multiple short-term cycles occur within a longer intermediate-term trading direction. It is this directional tendency where we must first direct our focus. Also, for the purposes of this discussion, it is best to clarify that a qualified change of trading direction for the intermediate term is 5 percent when looking at the S&P 500 Index.

There are two types of trading that occur profitably within the intermediate term. The first is position trading, which is based on identifying a trend and participating in its rise or fall during some portion of the intermediate term. Position trading involves holding a position through multiple short-term cycles. The second is best known as *swing trading*. This is simply entering a position for the 2- to 10-day time duration. Swing trading is based on exploiting the short-term market swing.

If you have the ability to time the short-term swing of a market, then why is it so important to be able to identify the current intermediate-term direction and turning points? This is a simple question to answer; doing so identifies the direction that you should be trading. There is no use in swimming upstream. Swim with the current. If you are going to trade the swing, then do so in the direction of the broad market. Of course, if you are going to position trade, then it's even more critical not to buck the intermediate-trend direction.

Exceptions to this practice do exist. For instance, stocks that are heavily rooted in a given commodity market, such as oil field services, routinely trade independent of the broader market. Stocks driven by commodity markets are accompanied by challenges of their own. So be sure to know the circumstances that influence that particular commodity. Also be prepared to devote your best effort to understanding any particular commodity market's forces of supply and demand. The underlying factors involved in commodity trading are complex.

Intermediate-Term Overbought and Oversold

Since the shortest normal time duration for the intermediate term is best understood in weeks, then that is the periodicity that we should be using for chart analysis. To use daily charts for indicator analysis across this time duration subjects the technical analyst to excessive noisy readings. It will also frequently outrun the indicator. This occurs when the cycle duration exceeds the look-back period used in the calculation. We will therefore perform our analysis on weekly price bars.

Figure 8.2 shows a weekly chart of the S&P 500 Index for a four-year period. Plotted with the chart is our friend, the TTI Fabric LR. In the indicator pane is the TTI RSIV-1, using 30 and 70 horizontal thresholds. The objective of this chart is to predict a swing of the S&P 500 Index that will exceed 5 percent. Plotted on top of the price candles are

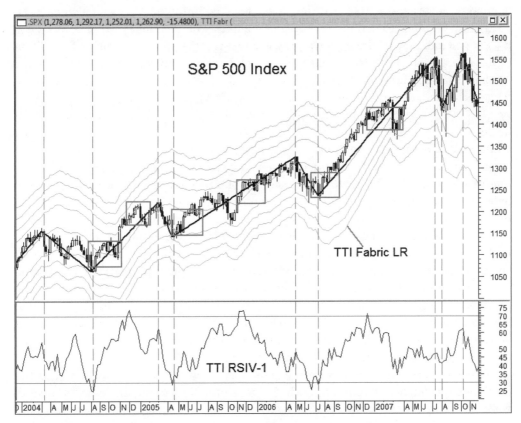

FIGURE 8.2   This weekly chart of the S&P 500 Index shows us one part of a method to measure the intermediate-term swings in the broad market.

Chart created in MetaStock.

zigzag indicator lines that are set to a 5 percent minimum, close to close change. To delineate each 5 percent change, there are vertical dashed lines plotted from the top of the chart to the bottom. Also, each time the indicator crosses the 30 or 70 threshold, a rectangle is plotted on the price chart. This highlights the indicator's ability to, if not signal a reversal, foretell a trading range.

Upon initial observation of Figure 8.2, it is obvious that predicating the intermediate-term swings of the market is not going to be a piece of cake. Whole markets are far too complex for a single oscillator to accurately call the tops and bottoms. There are a total of nine different swing pivot points shown; four bottoms and five tops. Of the four bottoms, the TTI RSIV-1 identifies three of them. It strikes out completely for calling the tops. This is a good opportunity to point out something that is already widely believed in the field of technical analysis. Identifying bottoms in the intermediate term and long term is much easier than identifying tops. Keep that in mind when using this form of analysis for those time durations.

It would make anyone's efforts to amass a fortune much easier if using this oscillator worked extremely well. Unfortunately, no one is going to become wealthy using this method. It is very useful, but it is only a single piece of the puzzle. Note also how the TTI Fabric LR tends to confirm overbought readings when the index drops to the negative one thread. Both of these indicators are useful in determining the current condition of the intermediate-term trend, but they do not form a complete method for detecting intermediate-term tops and bottoms.

Intermediate-Term Market Breadth

While walking across a demolition zone you hear someone shout, "Fire in the hole!" What should you do? You should hit the deck immediately is what you should do. Do not waste time or ask questions. That statement is shouted only by someone who knows something important that you don't. He has been generous enough to give you one last warning before something goes boom.

We all conduct trading in an equally explosive place. And in the stock market, there is also a voice that will shout out to you when it is appropriate to do so. Imagine that voice to be market breadth. The total intent of all active market participants is made visible by the simple number of stocks on an exchange that, when compared to the previous day's closing prices, close higher, close lower, or close unchanged. It is one of the most honest voices you can listen to. It can't and won't lie to you. Volume reporting on stocks should often win a Pulitzer Prize for best fiction, but price combined with the law of large numbers is quite hard to fudge.

Often at market tops, a downturn begins with a day of heavy selling. It causes the quantity of declining stocks to go just high enough that it is of parabolic importance. A well-calculated measure of broad market selling, under the right circumstances, will very accurately tell you that the coming days will see stock prices decline significantly. It is exactly this type of high-volatility event that the MetaSwing Correction and Surge signals are designed to detect. Later in Chapter 13, which is about designing an early warning correction system, you will learn exactly how MetaSwing does this.

FIGURE 8.3 The MetaSwing Correction and Surge signals show us a system designed to detect statistically significant market breadth events.

Chart created in MetaStock. Chart uses the MetaSwing Add-on, by Northington Trading, LLC. All rights reserved.

For right now, we will observe how the MetaSwing Correction and Surge system can help to predict the intermediate-market turning points. As we stated earlier in this chapter, market tops are more difficult to measure than are market bottoms. Correction events can make it easy to spot the top that you have missed in previous days or weeks.

In Figure 8.3, a daily chart of the S&P 500 Index is shown for February through September 2007. Five percent zigzag lines are drawn on the price plot to identify actual tops and bottoms. The skull and crossbones symbols represent MetaSwing Correction signals. The bull symbols show the MetaSwing Surge signals. We are not going to delve into the exact art of interpreting these signals here. Those details, and actual MetaStock code sets, will be saved for Chapter 13.

The first Correction signal will generally form after a significant advance. It is a wide market-breadth selling day. The big money, and the smart money that has not yet faded the advance, are reacting to some catalyst that is just large enough to push the boulder over the side of the mountain. These events usually signal the beginning of an intermediate-term market downtrend. It's that simple.

The Surge signal is the opposite of the Correction signal. It is not traded the same way, however. Because stocks and markets rise differently from the way they fall, the surge signal is traded more patiently. When Surge signals begin to appear with more frequency than their Correction counterparts, a bottom has likely formed. In Figure 8.3, the month of August shows that three separate Surge events occur, signaling an intermediate bottom. Once again, it is as simple as that.

The tremendous voice, consisting of the world's largest financial institutions, has spoken. It has told you what it thinks that stock prices are going to do in the days and weeks to come. This is when you should listen carefully and follow the crowd.

A Combined Approach

We have looked so far in this chapter at two methods of forecasting the intermediate-term market peaks and troughs; the swings, if you will. Using a simple volatility-and-trend-compensated overbought-and-oversold method produces incomplete results, but shows some promise. A well-calculated approach to market breadth is more reliable and historically solid. Another important aspect to the methods explored so far is that the oscillator is inherently better at detecting bullish reversals, and market breadth is slightly better at signaling bearish reversals.

Clearly the best method for applying volatility-based technical analysis to the intermediate term is by using a hybrid approach. The goal of this combination of methods is to use the best that each has to offer. This method uses the higher accuracy of market breadth when identifying the beginnings of a downturn. The strength of a good trend-neutral oversold indicator can be used to detect bottoms. The strongest capabilities of each can assume the role of the primary indication.

Taking it one step further, we will make an improvement to our method of overbought and oversold measurement by using the MetaSwing Divine components. The MetaSwing Divine indicators work very similarly to the DLRL-DSRS tandem indicators. They are different, though, because the internal algorithm is neural. The Divine algorithm is designed to measure different dimensions of price movement, with specific sensitivity to time-versus-cycle logic. With a much broader array of input data, the Divine indicator system is a complex compound derivative that is less sensitive to noise, but still able to react quickly. This enables it to measure levels over longer time frames more accurately. Figure 8.4 shows a four-year history of this methodology in practice. This chart is information-rich, with many signals, so take some time to examine it carefully. It is a weekly chart of the S&P 500 Index with MetaSwing applied to it. Plotted in the lower indicator pane are the Divine indicators described earlier. The solid line is oversold and the dotted plot is overbought. Top to bottom dashed lines show the application of the oversold readings to price. Top to bottom dotted lines show the application of overbought readings to price. Just above the lower indicator pane are smiley-face and frown-face symbols that represent an interpretation of the indicators' success. A smiley-face corresponds with a successful outcome; a frown-face means not so good.

In the price plot area are 5 percent zigzag lines to outline intermediate-term market

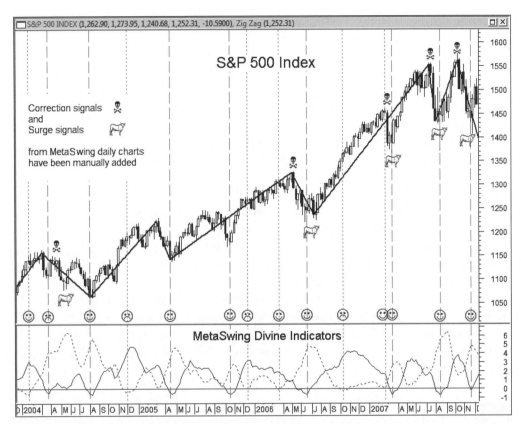

FIGURE 8.4 This weekly chart of the S&P 500 Index presents a hybrid approach to broad market peak and trough identification.

Chart created in MetaStock. Chart uses the MetaSwing Add-on, by Northington Trading, LLC. All rights reserved.

swings. Plotted above and below the price candles are the Correction and Surge symbols that identify extreme market breadth events. Note though that these signals were not generated from a weekly chart analysis. The signals came from the daily S&P chart, and have been added manually to this weekly chart. In this way, Figure 8.4 is a product of multi–time frame analysis. In the weekly time frame, the MetaSwing Divine indicator performs best at identifying the reversal points for market bottoms. While on a daily periodicity, the Correction events, combined with the weekly Divine overbought indicator component, identifies market tops.

It is important to point out the absence of consistent Correction and Surge signals prior to 2006. This is due to changes in the way the NYSE and NASDAQ exchanges reported the data related to unchanged issues traded. Exploring the details of these changes would be beyond the scope of our current topic. If data from those years were available, and were collected and reported in the same way, then there would certainly be more such signals on the chart for that time period.

The following are the performance explanations for this balanced method of intermediate-term market swing analysis:

- There are four troughs of 5 percent or greater identified on the chart. The Divine oversold indicator successfully detected each of them. Three of the four troughs were also accompanied by multiple daily Surge signals.
- The Divine oversold indicator signaled eight instances of extreme readings below zero. Seven of them yielded profitable trading intelligence.
- There are five different periods where Surge events occurred. Each of them yielded profitable trading intelligence.
- There are five peaks of 5 percent or greater identified on the chart. Correction events accompanied four of them. As previously mentioned, data reporting inconsistencies cloud the accuracy for the time before 2006.
- There are five different instances of Correction signals on the daily charts. After four of the signals, the S&P traded downward to a trough. The exception was the short market pullback in March of 2007.
- There are six instances of the Divine overbought indicator reading extreme levels below zero. Three of the instances were successful and three were unsuccessful.
- The final score equates to a 100 percent accuracy of identifying the troughs, and an 80 percent accuracy of identifying the peaks, for the years 2004 through 2007.

Clearly this combination of overbought and oversold measurement on a weekly chart, and market breadth events on daily charts, can produce relatively accurate outcomes. Similar mixtures of your own framework components are likely to yield profitable intermediate-term forecasting. It is absolutely critical that you are able to approach this with tools and a method that have genuine predictive value. Create your own method well, or buy the best tools available. Don't cut corners in this department; you would be stepping over dollars to pick up nickels.

Intermediate-Term Reality Check

The approach we have been taking is somewhat different, and it warrants some further explanation. Some technicians believe that it is not really possible to identify a market top or bottom in the present time. Many analysts focus on identifying only the direction and strength of the intermediate-market trend. If that is your approach, then you simply trade the direction identified until the direction of the market changes. This traditional approach is followed by many. It certainly has its deficiencies, though.

Take a moment to try to remember some of the days that occurred during some intermediate-term peaks or troughs. You know that feeling when the market has been selling off for weeks. You wonder, and possibly agonize over, when it will end. The talking heads on the financial news shows feature industry experts that each present very plausible cases for many different possible scenarios. What evidence that the market will cease to sell off is real, and what is not? Fear and uncertainty rule the day.

You wonder, "Should I exit, or should I hold my position? Could this sell-off continue, and thus, this is the start of the next bear market?" You just don't know. Doubt is the only resolution around every turn. The method of trading the trend until it ends subjects the trader to this type of darkness. Excessive stress is also a major factor in ending one's time as a trader.

The approach and method presented in the previous section offers a different way, and much more peace of mind. In this author's opinion, peace of mind has a place in trading. It is derived from using tools and methods that render an adequate level of probability of an outcome. Would it not make more sense to rely on methods that deliver a 75 percent probability that an intermediate-term market bottom is happening at the present time? If you had that type of broad market intelligence then the decision to cover or hold a position would be easy to make. Much more peace of mind would also accompany it.

The best method for dealing with the intermediate trend clearly involves identifying tops and bottoms and peaks and troughs. By keeping your decision making grounded in the reality of volatility-based algorithms, trading decisions can be made with an appropriate degree of calm. Enable your emotions to listen to the results of the mathematics in lieu of listening to the emotions of others.

SHORT-TERM MARKET SWING

If you really want to learn to make money trading, then it is best to begin with a week-long vacation in Hawaii. Seriously, it's the best way. When departing Hawaii once, my flight ticket showed me assigned to a window seat. Looking down at the water's surface when taking off from the Honolulu International Airport's Lagoon runway is a truly stunning sight. As the plane ascended though 500 feet, I gazed down at the shallow waters of Oahu's southern coastline and saw the lines of a well-defined wave pattern and direction. The colors of the coral reef below held me in a trance. So by 1,000 feet of altitude, I could not help notice that the wave pattern was disappearing before my very eyes. Another larger wave pattern was forming as the smaller one was disappearing, and it was pointing in a completely different direction. Still spellbound by the sheer beauty of the island, when we passed above 5,000 feet, my view produced yet another wave pattern in yet another direction. It wasn't that the different wave patterns ceased to exist. Each one simply existed inside of the next larger one.

I don't think I really understood the relationship between market trading direction and time frame until that experience. The 500-foot view essentially told me which way the wind was blowing. At that height, however, I could not see the underlying current that formed the waves visible at the 1,000-foot vantage point. The wind typically makes the waves we see when standing at sea level. In exactly the same way, the short-term market swing happens because of market winds. Lesser-level catalysts cause short-term market swing cycles. We all witness how on some days a single set of earnings results for a particular large cap stock, such as General Electric or Wal-Mart, can move an entire index. More often than not, it happens on a day when there is a void of other meaningful data to digest. But it also happens because of the market's technical overbought and oversold level, and that particular fundamental news of the day takes credit for the move.

Larger news and economic factors cause the intermediate-market movement. Each of the two market time frames, short and intermediate, has appropriate distances from which they are visible. In that same way, different dimensions of wave patterns are visible at varying altitudes. As we have seen in the prior section, we should view the intermediate-term market as more of a whole, or a single entity. Any deviation from that approach would take us into sector analysis, which is outside of the scope of this book.

That viewpoint, however, can be deviated from when trading an individual stock within the short-term market swing. The short-term swing is not as dominant as the intermediate. The true relative strength of an individual stock is considered more heavily when swing trading, albeit with great care. We will look deeply into those signs of individuality in the coming chapters. For the balance of this one, we will focus on the short-term market phase. It is tricky and very difficult to forecast.

Changing the Vantage Point

While we use similar thought processes throughout all time frames, there has to be a well-defined change when we shift to the short term. The best way to illustrate it is to look at the intermediate-term market as a *stock market*. However, when analyzing the short term, consider it a *market of stocks*. This play on words is not an uncommon way of marketplace thinking. It has long been a basis of adjusting one's philosophy in trading and investing. It's hard to imagine a better place to use this mental shift than when you shorten your time frame and analyze the short-term market swing.

Figure 8.5 shows an overview of the thought process shift and supporting tools for making the change to the short term. The intermediate term should be approached as a stock market, and therefore, it can be analyzed as single entity. Different market indexes can be viewed with individuality, but they are each still a singular unit. The most important result of our intermediate-term examination is to derive the primary trading direction. Use well-founded market directional intelligence as a basis for risk management, as well as the other more obvious implications for the trades we put on. Most important, though, is to remember that short-term analysis without intermediate-term examination is like driving while extremely intoxicated: it can have hazardous consequences.

The lower row of Figure 8.5 highlights how the short term is a market of stocks, in that we look at overbought and oversold indications of the market index, and stocks individually. Just as with the intermediate term, the short-term oversold and overbought level is important, but is more difficult to measure. There is much more daily noise in terms of erratic volatility. News events that seem important in the moment may drive a trading session, but are better rethought by the big market players when the information is digested overnight.

The aspect of the market swing that is most overlooked by traders and analysts is the phenomenon of the raw quantity of stocks that are reaching ideal trade setup levels.

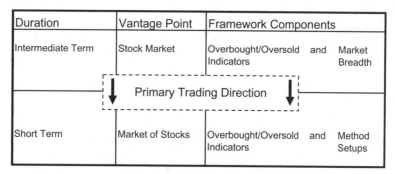

Duration	Vantage Point	Framework Components	
Intermediate Term	Stock Market	Overbought/Oversold and Indicators	Market Breadth
		Primary Trading Direction	
Short Term	Market of Stocks	Overbought/Oversold and Indicators	Method Setups

FIGURE 8.5 This shows the market swing cycle thought transition.

It happens when you have run your daily market exploration for some of your favorite trade setups. After reviewing 20 or 30 charts, the signals are there, but few or none of them are set up just right. A good rule of thumb is that if there aren't at least a few that are begging to be traded, then the market as a whole is just not yet ready to swing in the predicted direction. The spring has not yet been wound tight enough. It is important, however, to have your entry levels identified ahead of time.

The swing is typically ready when there are sufficient quantities of trade setups that are hard to resist trading. Maybe some have already failed at a move a few days earlier when the index as a whole seemed ready. An effort to quantify this degree of readiness is usually tricky or impossible. The best traders do develop the ability to tell, though. They do so by consistently trading the same methods and setups, and being the best at those specific trades. This practice of studying charts and looking for setups that are your trades is a critical component for which there is no substitute.

The Rubber Meets the Road

Now that we've had enough explanation of the theory of applying volatility-based technical analysis to market swings, it is time to actually do it. To begin, we will use two of the indicators developed in previous chapters. The TTI StochEx and the TTI RSIV-1 will be our tag team of indicators for measuring the short-term market swing. We are using a slightly different parameter setting for the RSIV-1. It is set to a look-back period of 20, with the same linear regression length of 40. The RSIV-1 thresholds are 25 and 75. The StochEx threshold levels are 10 and 90.

Figure 8.6 shows us a daily chart of the NASDAQ Composite index from August 2005 to March 2006. During this time, a consensus approach to using both of these indicators shows us five different points at which the short-term swing is predicted. The best criteria for evaluation is to determine if the signal is given prior to, or current with, successful trade setups or market directional movement. In other words, what we ultimately want from our analysis is some degree of advance indication that the market will be more likely to experience a reversal of direction. This gives the trader time to find the best setups that develop for his methods.

FIGURE 8.6 Proper analysis of the short-term market swing can be very challenging. Chart created in MetaStock.

With that evaluation basis in mind, then it looks as though signal lines 1, 2, and 4 are good. These three each give us a two-day heads up before a significant reversal. Signal lines 3 and 5 occur a bit too late. By being a day or two behind, it is likely that the better part of most trades have already passed, leaving you with poor risk-reward ratios.

It is necessary for overbought and oversold indicators to be volatility compensated in order to isolate opportunities just before short-term reversals. In Figure 8.6, the NASDAQ Composite index has five different turning points identified by the TTI StochEx and the TTI RSIV-1 indicators. Three of them work well and two of them are a bit late. It is clear that additional criteria need to be added to the process.

Let's then assume that the date is October 11, 2005. Based on our analysis of the short-term market, we believe that a reversal is expected in the next one or two trading sessions. It is therefore now time to start looking at charts listed on the NASDAQ that are showing some good, long trade setups. We can find potential trades by running a MetaStock exploration to find oversold stocks. The MetaStock code to find this could be as simple as:

```
1 Fml("TTI RSIV-1") < 25 AND
2 ((Mov(V, 10, S)*100) * C) > 250000 AND
3 C > 1.50 AND
4 C < 800 AND
5 (Mov(V, 10, S) > 1500)
```

This MetaStock code will instruct the MetaStock Explorer to find stocks that meet certain criteria. Here's how it works:

- Line 1 says that the stock's TTI RSIV-1 value today has to be less than 25.
- Lines 2 through 5 are present to ensure that only stocks with a minimum level of liquidity are chosen. Line 2 states that the stock's 10-day average volume multiplied by today's closing price must be more than $250,000.
- Line 3 says that the stock's closing price must be higher than $1.50 per share.
- Line 4 says that the stock's closing price must be less than $800 per share.
- Line 5 states that the stock's average daily trading volume over the past 10 days must be higher than 150,000 shares.

With the minimum and maximum closing price stipulated in lines 3 and 4, the implication of line 2 is that at $1.50 per share, the average day's volume over the preceding 10 days would have to be greater than 166,666. Therefore, as the closing price increases, then the volume can decrease. Because of line 5, however, it can never be less than 150,000. Thus, lines 2 through 5 form a flexible filter to ensure minimum liquidity based on the parameters.

When an exploration with this MetaStock code is run on all NASDAQ-listed stocks on October 11, 2005, about 230 of them meet the selection criteria. After reviewing them in alphabetical order, we simply must stop at Bio-Reference Laboratories (BRLI). It looks too good to pass up. While the rest of the broader market has been in decline, this stock has been showing excellent strength.

Figure 8.7 shows us that on a daily chart Bio-Reference has broken out of a lower trading range and is possibly beginning a trend rally. The RSIV-1 is reading oversold, but the StochEx has not yet gotten to its oversold extreme. The vertical dashed line shows the first day it comes to the trader's attention. At this point, it is difficult to pick an entry point without a support and resistance component in the framework. There is one very important condition present on the chart, though. Look carefully at the TTI Fabric LR threads. Do you see how they are getting noticeably wider? This means that volatility is expanding. When volatility is expanding, it is important to loosen up the entry and exit points. Be more aggressive by moving the long entry point lower and the exit point higher.

By the end of the next trading day, the close is below the negative one thread of the fabric; a good entry point is therefore likely near. Anywhere between the negative one and two thread will be a good place to enter, with a stop placed just below the negative three thread. This produces a favorable reward-to-risk ratio as well. Within three days,

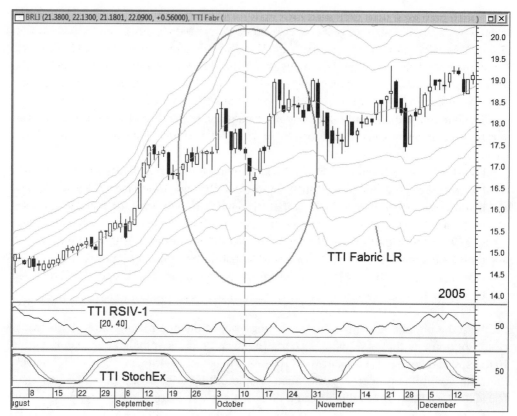

FIGURE 8.7   This daily chart of Bio-Reference Laboratories (BRLI) presents an opportunity to enter a developing trend rally.

Chart created in MetaStock.

the market begins a sharp reversal, as is evidenced in Figure 8.6. Likewise Bio-Reference Laboratories continues its volatility expanding rally and racks up a wonderful gain. Some sort of an intraday trailing stop strategy would likely enable an exit for the trade, between the center Fabric thread and the positive one thread.

Analysis with a Complete Framework

When we perform technical analysis using the volatility-based framework components created herein, we are still using only a partial framework. Not all of the seven important capabilities of volatility-based technical analysis are used. In an effort to show you how a comprehensive volatility-based trading methodology can work, one with all seven capabilities present, we will continue to demonstrate the same or similar technical analysis performed by the MetaSwing system.

The Bull Bear Phase   We will analyze in this example the same NASDAQ index for the short-term broad market swing, and also the same stock trade, Bio-Reference

Laboratories (BRLI). Care will be taken to point out the differences that the additional framework components can make with respect to trade entry, management, and profitability. You will see in this first chart a new MetaSwing feature called the Bull Bear Phase Predictor (BBPP). The BBPP is a mechanism that gives an outlook or forecast to the trader. It is designed to recognize the signs that typically occur before the broad market makes a short-term reversal. The BBPP is essentially a neural algorithm, which by design takes into account many differing volatility relationships. Within its algorithm it uses all seven of the necessary capabilities of volatility-based technical analysis. It is considered a primary indicator on the chart.

Figure 8.8 is a daily chart of the NASDAQ Composite index with the same date range as in Figure 8.6. This NASDAQ chart shows 11 different market swing signals by the MetaSwing Bull Bear Phase Indicator (BBPP). Each is notated with vertical dashed lines. The BBPP is the trend ribbon at the bottom of the chart. The darker shaded area with a bear signals an impending downswing. The lighter shaded area with a bull signals an impending upswing. Specific observations are as follows:

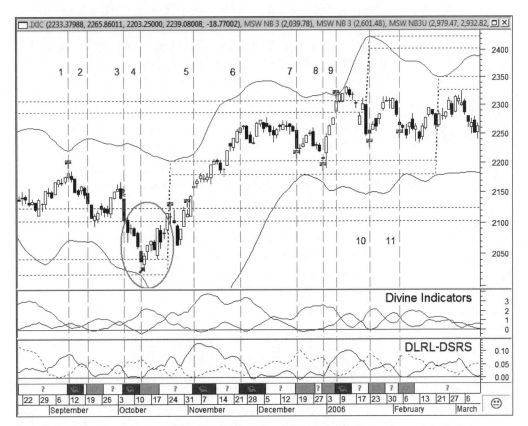

FIGURE 8.8 This MetaSwing chart shows how the Bull Bear Phase Predictor (BBPP) gives advance indication of the short-term market swing.

Chart created in MetaStock. Chart uses the MetaSwing Add-on, by Northington Trading, LLC. All rights reserved.

- BBPP instances 1, 3, 4, 7, 8, 9, 10, and 11 are each accompanied by MetaSwing event signals. Most of them are exit signals, which on an index chart are both exit signals as well as a basis for a reversal. The circled area represents the number 2 swing signal from Figure 8.6, and the same stock trade dates from Figure 8.7.

- When using the BBPP, the significant part of the signal is when the phase changes from any state to bullish, or from any state to bearish. If the phase remains at a steady state for longer than five periods it only means that general market conditions have not changed, but the reversal should have already occurred. Remember that the main benefit of the BBPP is to notify the trader, in advance if possible, to look for stock swing trading method setups.

- The Divine indicator tandem system is in the middle indicator pane. The DLRL-DSRS indicator tandem system is in the lower indicator pane. Most BBPP signals are accompanied by overbought and oversold confirmations. Those that are not generally take a few days longer to set up for an actual reversal, such as instances 9 and 11.

- When viewing instances 4 and 9, note how important the lower and upper N Bands are, respectively. When the index comes within one ATR of the N Band, significant resistance is incurred.

- There are a total of four Exit Long and four Exit Short signals on the chart. All but one is accurate in predicting an impending reversal of at least three trading periods. A properly coordinated stock swing trade can generate a significant profit in three days.

- Only the number 5 BBPP signal fails. There are some guidelines in the MetaSwing User Guide on how to avoid this particular situation.

The chart in Figure 8.9 is an expanded section of Figure 8.8. It shows the circled area in greater detail. There are four significant technical measurements that can be taken into consideration regarding the signal day denoted by the number 4 vertical dashed line. Each of them is very important. Remember that up until the market close on October 12, 2005, the trader has only experienced a market selling to lower levels for almost seven straight sessions. Indicators or no indicators, catching falling knives is not a pleasant experience. You need real confidence in your methods and solid mathematical evidence at a time like that.

1. An Adeo Long signal is shown.

2. The distance from the close of the index to its N Band is less than one ATR(40). The close is now within heavy resistance.

3. The BBPP has just clicked over from bearish to bullish.

4. While the DLRL and Divine indicators show oversold conditions, the height of the opposing DSRS tandem indicator exceeds its own previous significant high. That means that the volatility level of the [bearish] overbought measurement is high relative to the recent past.

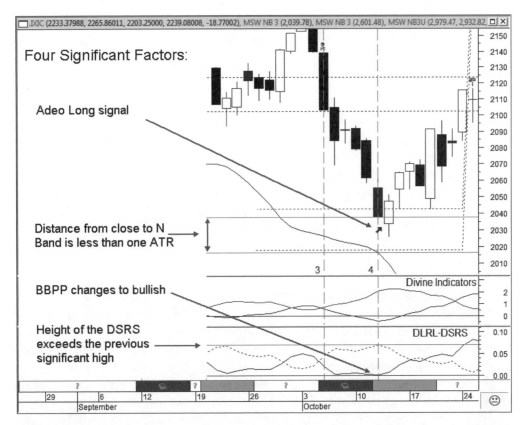

FIGURE 8.9 This chart section shows an expanded view of the circled area from the NASDAQ Composite index chart shown previously.

Chart created in MetaStock. Chart uses the MetaSwing Add-on, by Northington Trading, LLC. All rights reserved.

All of this evidence makes a good case for finding some favorable-looking long stock trade setups, using methods that you have been successful with in the past.

Based on the decision to put on long swing trades for the short term, it is then time to look for opportunities. A properly written MetaStock exploration could find trending stocks showing strength.

The MetaStock code to find this could be:

```
1 C > Trough(1, Fml("MSW NB 3 Upper"), 3) AND
2 Fml("MSW Max DLRL Delta 20") < 0 AND
3 Fml("MSW Divine Max Short") < 0 AND
4 ((Mov(V, 10, S)*100) * C) > 250000 AND
5 C > 1.50 AND
6 C < 800 AND
7 (Mov(V, 10, S) > 1500)
```

This MetaStock exploration code will find candidates that may be trending, and are possibly pulling back to a good entry point because:

- Line 1 states that the current closing price will be above the N Band S/R 3 line. This is because the S/R 3 line is actually an upper N Band trough, with the default differential parameter of 3 percent. As you can see, the formula for the upper N Band is Fml("MSW NB 3 Upper"), and is nested in the Trough function. By searching for stocks currently above the S/R 3 line, we increase the odds that they are breaking out and beginning a trend rally.
- Line 2 shows the MetaSwing formula name for the oversold Divine indicator, and requires that it currently be reading less than zero.
- Line 3 shows the MetaSwing formula name for the basic oversold DLRL indicator, and requires that it currently be reading less than zero.
- Lines 4 through 7 are for the same minimum liquidity requirements that were used previously.

Our MetaStock exploration here yields trade candidates for review. And once again Bio-Reference Laboratories (BRLI) is among them. Figure 8.9 displays a MetaSwing chart of Bio-Reference Laboratories with the exact same date range as in Figure 8.6. Because MetaSwing uses all seven important capabilities of volatility-based TA, there are additional pieces of information to consider.

Try to put your head and thought process into the state of mind that you would be experiencing on the evening of October 12, 2005. The broad market indexes have been steadily trading downward for almost two weeks. You have many signals on the intermediate-term and the short-term broad market charts, which tell you it's time for a short-term reversal. In addition to that, you are contemplating a long position in a stock that has recently seen a large increase in volatility. Anyone with a healthy respect for the markets is experiencing a degree of fear at this point. There needs to be some hard, well-grounded evidence to support this trade entry.

The MetaSwing analysis of Bio-Reference Laboratories (BRLI) in Figure 8.10 shows us at least seven key pieces of volatility mathematics. Here is the meaningful interpretation of a chart analysis with a complete set of framework components:

Circled Area 1 shows us a descending candle after the market closed on October 12, 2005. To make the view a bit more realistic, the cutout in the chart's upper left corner shows exactly what the trader would be looking at on that day without the benefit of hindsight. The lower N Band is rising rapidly. Considering the rate at which price and the N Band are closing on each other, it is conceivable that price could reach to within one ATR of the N Band during the next day's trading session. Also, the S/R 1 support line is currently at 16.33. With the current ATR at 41 in an expanding volatility environment, it is very possible that the next day's trading range could reach the S/R 1 line. That could make for a very good entry point.

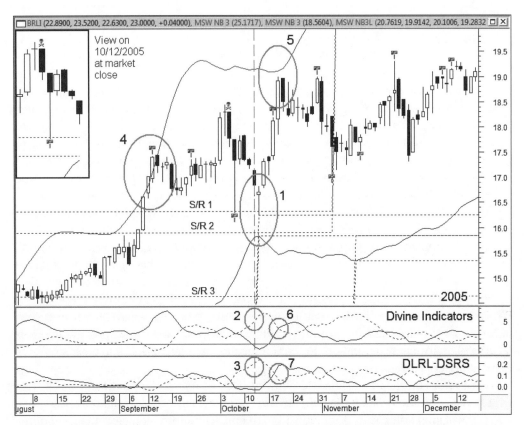

FIGURE 8.10 This daily chart of Bio-Reference Laboratories (BRLI) is the same equity and time as shown earlier. With the addition of the MetaSwing S/R lines, N Bands, and volatility-based tandem indicators, an advantage is gained at picking the entry and exit points. The entry and exit targets are effectively better defined because of support and resistance levels. High probability boundaries make trade management much less of a guessing game. The net result increased the probable profit by 3.7 percent, resulting in a 14.7 percent, five- or six-day trade.

Chart created in MetaStock. Chart uses the MetaSwing Add-on, by Northington Trading, LLC. All rights reserved.

Circled Areas 2 and 3 show us that while each of these two indicators are reading oversold levels below zero, their tandem counterparts are showing very high levels of volatility. Each tandem component has risen to levels that exceed recent significant highs. This is a sound indication that a true oversold condition exists.

Circled Area 4 shows that Bio-Reference Laboratories did indeed execute a very forceful breakthrough of resistance at the S/R 1 and S/R2 levels. It then went on to trade through and closes above the upper N Band. Two weeks later it closed at an even higher high. This recent highly volatile trading above the S/R 1 line is exactly the activity that we would look for in a stock that is breaking out into a trend rally.

Trade Entry: Based on the aforementioned three different sets of confirming data, in addition to the indications of a probable short-term broad market swing, the decision is made to put on a long trade in this stock. A limit order is placed two cents above the S/R 1 line at 16.35. If the broad market was not showing such overwhelming evidence of a reversal, it would be wiser to lower the entry point to the level of the encroaching lower N Band. An optional approach could be to wait a day or two and let the market confirm a reversal. With the upper N Band as a profit target, however, this trade entry at S/R 1 has a risk-reward ratio greater than 3 to 1.

Circled Area 5 highlights the level of the upper N Band. Significant resistance begins at one ATR below it. On October 18, three days into the trade, the upper N Band is sitting at 19.10. Also, MetaSwing has signaled an Exit Long, so any more profit is purely found money. One option is to exit upon market open the next day. It would be prudent to use the current day's low as a stop. Both sets of our over-bought and oversold indicators have yet to cross. And after all, we are trading a stock on a probable trend breakout with expanding volatility. The very fact that it fell to test support at the S/R 1 line and then reversed proves that. It is therefore best to hold on until price reaches significant resistance, closer to the upper N Band.

Circled Areas 6 and 7 show that indeed both of the tandem indicator pairs have crossed. This crossing is indicative of an increasing level of probability that price will stop rising or reverse. It is time to exit. Therefore, upon examination of the chart on October 19, after the market's close, the decision is place a stop at 18.75. The price could drop or it could just keep on going up. At this point, though, the odds are favoring an exit to protect profits. Prices do reverse in the next trading session and the trade closes at 18.75. With a long entry at 16.35, this yields a gross profit of 14.7 percent; very good eating.

The final analysis of this one particular trade gives us an opportunity to compare the charts in Figure 8.7 and Figure 8.10, and the subsequent comparative trade management. The MetaSwing chart in Figure 8.10 has the major advantage of volatility-based support and resistance detection. The result of well-defined support and resistance enables more profitable entry and exit points. High probability boundaries make trade management much less of a guessing game.

Using the chart in Figure 8.7, the entry point would likely be at market open on October 13, at 16.66. The exit would likely be at 18.50, which is the market closing price on October 20. This would yield a profit of 11 percent. With an increased level of intelligence at the point of decision, enabled by MetaSwing's complete framework, there would likely have been an increase in profit of 3.7 percent. This comes from knowing where and when to enter, and where and when to exit. That's a 33 percent profit differential. This sort of advantage can add up to a significant impact in trading performance over time. It can even make the difference in determining if the trader has a profitable brokerage account or none at all. Most important, it is what keeps the institutional players on Wall Street living high.

SEEK THE ADVANTAGE

The date was June 30, 1863. A Union cavalry officer named General John Buford Jr. was one of the first of the Army of the Potomac to arrive at the vicinity of Gettysburg, Pennsylvania. As a cavalry officer, it was not Buford's primary role to take and hold ground. As the ranking officer on the scene, he recognized the opportunity and advantage before him. Buford knew that the ability to control the high ground would give Union forces visual information and intelligence that could not otherwise be gained. He also understood that the tactical increase in artillery range was the difference between life and death. His decision to occupy and defend several key ridgelines, while greatly outnumbered, gave the Union army control of the critically important high ground for the upcoming battle. Many believe that the entire battle of Gettysburg could have taken a different course had Buford not made the decision to possess the strategic and tactical advantage.

Throughout history such deeply important decisions are what ultimately decide the outcome of events great and small. Often, as at the battle of Gettysburg, these choices are made before any major action commences. While none of us view trading the financial markets to be as morally important as war, perhaps we should. Trading is indeed mental combat, against the most intelligent and well resourced in the world, with the winner being the one who is the most capable and best prepared.

Be sure to seek every advantage you can in making your trading decisions. Accurately measuring the intermediate- and short-term market swing is likely your most important endeavor. Like Buford and his brave troops, make the sacrifice and do the work necessary in advance. By being able to confidently forecast market swings you will ensure that you are facing only one competitor and not two, the second foe being your own emotions at a time of uncertainty.

As we move forward to the coming chapters we will delve deeply into trading various volatility-based methods. All of them depend on sound market directional intelligence. It is the exception rather than the rule for a stock to reverse without any correlation to the broader market indexes. The most profitable strategy is to exploit the correlation, and multiply the payoff by carefully selecting opportunities with the highest degree of risk and reward. We explore the details and logic that point directly to short-term reversals of stocks in the next chapter. The Adeo is a condition that needs justification for its existence. If it can't be defended, then it must be exploited. Read on and you will see what I mean.

CHAPTER 9

Trading the Short-Term Reversal with Volatility-Based Technical Analysis—The Adeo

S everal generations of children were taught to put their faith in a can of spinach. A single can of it could rescue you from the direst of situations. The affable little sailor man Popeye, the underdog of the seas, was an absolute hero. No matter how well meaning the animated cartoon character seemed, he was always apt to end up with his fate, and that of his sweetie, Olive Oyl, in a perilous situation. The bully Bluto (or Brutus) was just around the corner.

In every episode, Popeye's very existence seemed to be a series of small events designed to push him, bit by bit, a little further off his path. One thing would lead to another and then another. As things got bad, it was inevitable that they would just get worse. When Popeye's situation was decided, defeated, and completely lost, he would utter the magic words: "That's all I can stands, I can't stands no more!" Out would come a can of spinach, which after being consumed, would give him the strength to defeat any foe, correct any wrong, and put him and Olive Oyl back on their original path.

If only we as traders had that incredible can of financial trading spinach! Oh, the fortunes we could make! However, careful examination of the trials and tribulations of Popeye could help us all to recognize opportunities on the chart. In fact, it would be fair to say that Popeye reached his own personal Adeo state in every episode, just like stocks often do.

Mathematically, the Adeo is reached when one after another of forms of volatility measurement are reached; generally over time, and in succession. The underlying price action that causes this is likely due to cascading human behavior–oriented events, small or large. A point is reached when interested market participants ask themselves if there is any justifiable reason for such quantity of price movement.

That point is where the Adeo lies.

THE ADEO POINT

In Latin, one definition of the word *Adeo* uses it as an adverb, meaning "to such an extent," "to such a point," or "to the boundary." In terms of technical analysis, we are using it to describe a point at which price has deviated from an established trading direction and volatility level to an extreme level of each, as measured in multiple ways. Think of the Adeo point as being the price point in time when Popeye metaphorically has reached his limit.

It occurs when price is at a place on the chart, at a specific time, when it should not be, as measured using volatility-based algorithms. This price, time, and direction relationship should be measured only by using most of the seven capabilities of volatility-based technical analysis. The instrument has extended itself in a very short period of time. Adeo situations exist when price has been pushed to a breaking point. Because price has been pushed to this boundary, it then represents either a reversal opportunity, or a trap.

With price being pushed to such an extreme, there needs to be an explanation by the normally accepted methods of fundamental data reporting, or by volatility measurement. In short, this means that price has suddenly headed in the wrong direction because something has changed with the actual business, or that it only looks as though there are underlying problems. There are three different explanations for the existence of Adeo price circumstances.

1. *The fundamental change could be good or bad for the company.* Regardless, it has prompted a dramatic change in the outlook of the stock price. It could also be related to the broad market, such as with a MetaSwing Correction event. Legally speaking, the information causing this change should be available through normal publicly distributed outlets. Regardless of how the information should be disseminated, the individual trader is usually the last to find out about it. In the case of there being a fundamentally oriented cause for the price move, then the Adeo is said to be defensible, but is difficult to trade with technical analysis.

2. *The second circumstance that produces Adeo price relationships actually occurs when there are no information-related reasons for the price-and-time imbalance.* That's right, the stock turns down and there is no bad news, market problems, or analysts' downgrade to blame for the move. This scenario can be profitable because large institutional trading involves a lot of talented market participants, with many varying time frames. These are the parties that have the volume to move prices. They also know where the invisible areas of support and resistance are, and that's the key. The volatility-based support and resistance is the can of spinach. They know where the boundary of the outer boundary exists, so to speak. Because of quantitative mathematics based on volatility, these participants know just when Popeye has had all he can "stands," and is going to open the can. This type of Adeo situation is also defensible, and can be traded profitably.

3. *The third and last type of Adeo happens within a void of fundamental data as well.* It also occurs when, try as we may, we just can't see any support or resistance

within a reasonable reach. There is no fundamental cause, or technical analysis safety net. There are only maybes. Maybe there is insider information causing massive selling and the public is not yet privy. Maybe the stock is suddenly being accumulated because of a decision to acquire the company, and the buying entity wants as much as they can get before the higher tender offer is made. Maybe it's a time when many large stakeholders decide to take profits simultaneously. Who knows? Did I say there were three explainable types of Adeo situations? This one has a reason but no explanation. Two out of three isn't bad, as the saying goes. This is an Adeo scenario to avoid. Remember you are trading, not shooting craps.

Finding the Adeo

If we are to exploit the market inefficiency of the Adeo, then we must first be able to measure it and identify it. The difficulty is that this irrationally extended price point called Adeo is normally transparent on the chart. Only the correct calculations executed inside good technical analysis software can paint the right price candles. There is a collection of volatility-based components in our framework to date, so it would make sense that combined in the right way they may be able to make an Adeo visible. Let's try using these components in a method that we have not yet tried.

The following MetaStock code creates an indicator that uses four of the components in the TTI Framework for the purpose of identifying an Adeo price point. Let's call it the TTI Composite.

```
 1 {User Inputs}
 2 pds1:= Input("LR Slope Lookback", 2, 1000, 5);
 3 pds2:= Input("Linear Regression Length", 5, 1000, 40);

 4 {Establishes linear regression slope values of oscillator
components}
 5 x1:= LinRegSlope(Fml("TTI StochEx"), pds1);
 6 x2:= LinRegSlope( Fml( "TTI RSIV"), pds1);
 7 x3:= LinRegSlope( Fml( "TTI ATR Extreme nb"), pds1);

 8 {Calculates number of ATR multiples above or below central
 9 fabric line}
10 y1:= LinearReg(C, pds2, S, 1);
11 y2:= ATR(14);
12 y3:= ((y1 - C) / y2) * -3;

13 {Adds assigned variables to create the composite value,
14 and plots it}
15 x1 + x2 + x3 + y3
```

This indicator code is meant to create a composite indicator that uses the results of four other indicators. The rationale behind it measures the direction of each individual calculation instead of the actual level of its reading. It attempts to apply the old saying of "It's not where you are at, but where you are heading that's important." It does this by converting an indicator to a straight line using linear regression, and then calculating the slope of that line. This way the indicator does not actually cross an extreme volatility threshold to be significant. It just has to be heading in that direction quickly. The slope of its trajectory is representative of its significance; the higher the slope, the greater its significance. This rationale is a departure from our earlier uses of these algorithms.

Here are the individual explanations of the TTI Composite code:

- Lines 2 and 3 establish user inputs for the parameters used in the linear regression slope statements and the TTI Fabric LR statement.
- Lines 5, 6, and 7 each individually measure the five-period (default) linear regression slope of TTI StochEx, TTI RSIV-1, and TTI ATR Extreme, respectively. The default value of five, as determined by assigning that value to the *pds1* variable in the `Input` statement in line 2, means that the linear regression line length is five periods. Thus, these lines are measuring the slope of a straight linear regression line drawn through the previous five periods of that indicator's plotted output.
- Note that the algorithm uses these indicators without actually having the individual indicator code in it. It does this by using the formula call function. By using a statement that contains `Fml("TTI StochEx")` in it, you are calling that indicator function and receiving back its default-calculated value without having to actually duplicate its code. For many reasons, this is a very concise way to write code. Note that the name of the function call looks a little strange in line 7. To receive the correct default value for the TTI ATR Extreme indicator, a separate formula was created without the upper and lower extreme boundaries, and it was named `TTI ATR Extreme nb`.
- Lines 10, 11, and 12 are bringing a value from the TTI Fabric LR indicator into this composite calculation. Line 12 simply determines how far the closing price is from the center thread of the fabric. It computes it in multiples of ATR(14), and then adds additional weight to it by multiplying it by three.
- Line 15 completes this whole process by adding together the results of the previous lines of code. Because the slopes of the indicators, and the distance of the closing price from the center fabric thread, can be positive or negative, the outcome of this summation can be positive or negative. This code, therefore, produces an oscillating value that rises and falls around a zero-centered line.

The daily chart in Figure 9.1 gives us one picture of how this TTI Composite indicator performs at isolating potential Adeo price movements. Here, Noble Corporation (NE) is shown against a backdrop of all four indicators that compose the TTI Composite indicator. In the bottom three indicator panes are the three oscillators used in the calculation. The TTI Fabric LR is shown with the price candles, as it should be. Lastly, the TTI Composite itself is plotted in the top indicator pane. It uses +25 and −25 as thresholds to demark extreme limits.

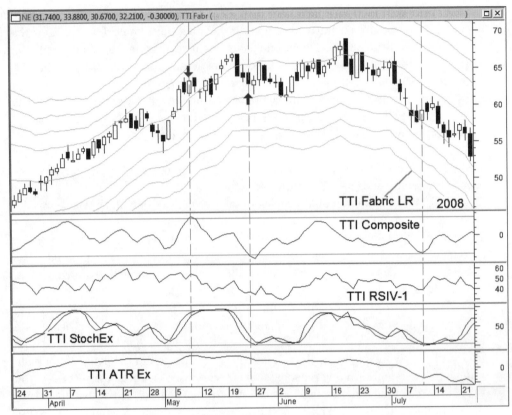

FIGURE 9.1   An initial attempt to identify Adeo price levels with the TTI Composite
component is shown in this daily chart of Noble Corporation (NE).

Chart created in MetaStock.

In Figure 9.1 the TTI Composite generates two potential Adeo signals, and one that
is close enough for horseshoes, as marked by the vertical dashed lines. With all of the
TTI Composite's inputs present and lined up, it's easier to see how this measurement
works. Examine the oscillators that provide the input and you will see that the degree
of slope of the indicators below contributes heavily to the TTI Composite reading.
Remember the look-back period for the slope measurement is five periods. These potential Adeo signals, however, are somewhat weak. Also, since there is no real measurement
of volatility-based support or resistance, it is not really possible to determine any opportunity's validity.

The TTI Composite indicator measures the intensity at which other indicators are
moving, using synergy as a basis. At a time when the broad market is experiencing
extreme volatility during a bear market, Adeo points frequently appear on individual
stock charts because of individual volatility. Support and resistance is critical when
attempting to discern if market moves are caused by the market as a whole or by
invisible levels of volatility-based support and resistance specific to the actual
underlying stock.

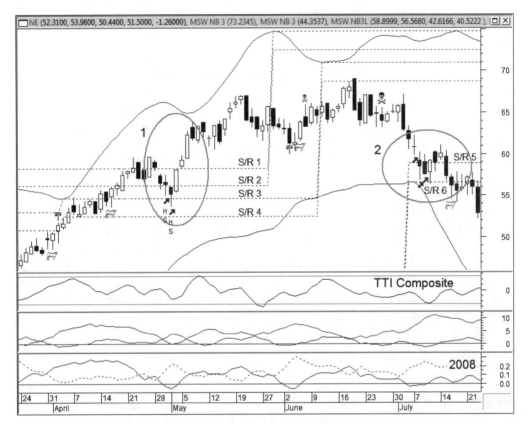

NE (52.3100, 53.9800, 50.4400, 51.5000, -1.26000), MSW NB 3 (73.2345), MSW NB 3 (44.3537), MSW NB3L (58.8999, 56.5680, 42.6166, 40.5222),

FIGURE 9.2 This MetaSwing chart shows the same stock and time frame as the previous figure. The true Adeo points occur within circled areas 1 and 2.

Really Finding the Adeo

Let's extend the analysis further by looking at the same chart in MetaSwing. The chart in Figure 9.2 has a very different look to it even though it's the exact same time frame and stock. The reason for this is the added structure that the N Bands and S/R lines give to the behavior of the price candles. The lower two indicator panes show MetaSwing's tandem indicator constructs for oversold and overbought conditions. The middle indicator pane shows the TTI Composite again.

There are two Adeo signals identified by the two circled areas. Circled area 1 shows a very typical Adeo mathematical relationship. Price is rising rapidly through levels of resistance. A sudden and dramatic shift in direction begins in the third week of April. Noble Corporation traded sideways for four days before this downturn after its earnings release on April 23, 2008. This indicates a short period of consolidation. The Adeo condition forms as price retraces to the primary support level at S/R 3. Since this Adeo can be explained, then a long entry at strong support can be justified. As price reverses strongly in the ensuing days, it illustrates the importance of support based on projected implied volatility (PIV).

Circled area 2 points out how price trades in a sideways range-bound pattern for six weeks and then takes a sudden dive. This is the same area in which the TTI Composite identifies a possible Adeo, even though it is three days late. The actual Adeo is shown for three days straight. A search of relevant news concerning Noble Corporation on July 2, 3, and 7 turns up nothing that could readily explain the recent price retracement. Noble Corporation, however, is primarily an oil drilling company. With the price of oil continuing its strong price rise during these same dates, it is troubling that Noble's stock price would be experiencing such a strong divergence. An Adeo long trade at support is therefore not recommended.

Notice, though, the price bounce that occurs when it reaches the support line at S/R 6. That's how important support and resistance actually are. Alas, our fears turn out to be correct as the stock then trades lower. It should be noted, though, that a successful long Adeo trade did exist with an entry at S/R 6 (56.57) and an exit at 58.89; a quick bounce swing trade for a 4 percent profit. Trading the ATR ranges between S/R lines typically carries a very high probability of success; you will see this in Chapter 10 (Trading the Trend with the 1-2-3).

TTI Composite Inadequacy

While the TTI Composite has its merits, with respect to identifying an Adeo price point, it was unfortunately doomed from the outset. To accurately identify when a stock price pushed to that far boundary of volatility, most capabilities of volatility-based technical analysis need to be used. Examine for a moment the updated version of the TTI Framework in Table 9.1. The seven important capabilities are listed on the left of the table from top to bottom. At the right, the columns for TTI RSIV-1 and TTI Composite have been added to this version. Take a moment and familiarize yourself with specific capabilities of these two components.

As you can see, the TTI Composite indicator still uses only three of the seven capabilities. The TTI Composite is, in effect, still only a repackaged version of the indicators that it uses as inputs. It lacks a broad enough spectrum of volatility measurement to identify Adeo points. It is also fair to say that it violates the tenet of cross-verification that we discussed in Chapter 3. Using more indicators based on the same calculations does not build a stronger technical analysis measurement.

In reality, we can say, without giving away intellectual property, that the MetaSwing Adeo signal is a neural algorithm that uses six of the seven critical capabilities. The TTI Composite did not stand a chance at Adeo measurement. This explanation, however, should give you a better understanding of the strengths needed to detect the kind of extreme volatility inefficiencies that are identified by the major institutional players on Wall Street.

On the upside, the TTI Composite works using a slightly different mathematical method. There is much to be said for the strength of slope detection that is used in its

TABLE 9.1 The TTI Framework with TTI RSIV-1 and TTI Composite Added

Capabilities Components Application	TTI ATR Extreme	TTI StochEx	TTI Fabric SD	TTI Fabric LG	TTI Fabric Ratio LR-SD	TTI Trend Strength	TTI RSIV-1	TTI Composite
1 Oversold/overbought								
Trending			x	x			x	x
Nontrending	x	x	x	x			x	x
TTI Trend Entry			x	x				
2 Trend Detection								
Trending					x	x		
Nontrending						x		
TTI Trend Entry					x	x		
3 Broad Market Integration								
Trending								
Nontrending								
TTI Trend Entry								
4 Support and Resistance								
Trending								
Nontrending								
TTI Trend Entry								
5 Historical Volatility								
Trending			x	x	x	x	x	x
Nontrending	x	x	x	x		x	x	x
TTI Trend Entry			x	x	x	x		
6 Implied Volatility								
Trending								
Nontrending								
TTI Trend Entry								
7 Multi-Time Frame Verification								
Trending				x			x	x
Nontrending	x	x	x	x			x	x
TTI Trend Entry				x				

algorithm. It's actually more capable than the chart in Figure 9.1 gives it credit for being. The TTI Composite can be very useful for trading routine swings when support and resistance is available in your framework.

Figure 9.3 is a chart of Rockwell Automation (ROC) during a very volatile market period. The TTI Composite is shown in the indicator pane with its trade signals shown using the MetaStock Expert on the price pane. The TTI Composite does accomplish the identification of routine price swings. The swings on this chart could have been traded profitably when used in conjunction with the TTI Fabric LR threads. While the TTI Composite does not identify the mathematical equivalent of an Adeo, it performs well as an oversold and overbought indicator.

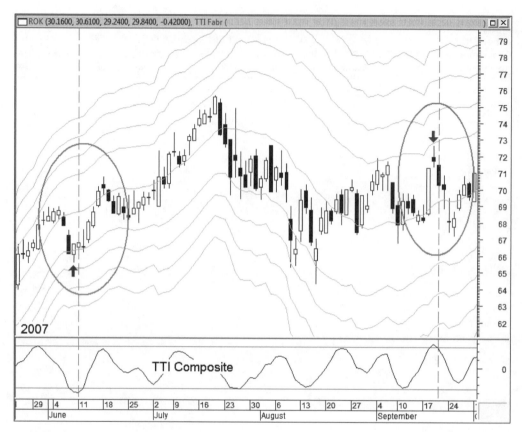

FIGURE 9.3 The TTI Composite is shown here during a high volatility broad market period. It performs very well in identifying overbought and oversold conditions.

Chart created in MetaStock.

THE ADEO TREND RALLY

There are really three circumstances in which trading short-term reversals occur. They are trend rallies, downward trends, and some other market climates that are not trending. In MetaSwing trending, stocks are defined as those trading above the S/R 3 resistance level or below the S/R 6 support level. When a stock has not recently traded above or below those levels, it is then considered nontrending. It may be range bound or just moving without a defined direction. Most stocks exist in this nontrending state at any given time.

Let's first take a good look at an Adeo rising within a significant trend. In many of the trading scenarios that we examine going forward, we will attempt to add a more significant dimension of reality by trading against that "hard right edge" of the chart, as the master swing trader Alan Farley likes to call it. Better yet, as the esteemed Dr. Alexander Elder refers to it, "trading in the middle of the chart" is simple. Hindsight is simply not in the trader's tool box. It's a practice all traders need. Using your charting and technical analysis software, manually set the chart to load only enough data to print the price candles, and calculate the indicators, because they are visible up to the point of the trade decision. This will train your mind and eyes to discern viable setups from traps. No matter how good we all think we are, each of us is susceptible to hindsight bias. It takes years of practice and experience with specific methods to be able to look at the trade setup and outcome, separately with no bias, all on the same chart.

On May 22, 2008, the daily chart of the S&P 500 Index is showing oversold conditions. The broad market is beginning to look as though it is setting up for a minor upswing. On that same day after the market closes, an exploration report that looks for Adeo signals leads us to look at a chart of Bucyrus (BUCY).

We see in Figure 9.4 a daily MetaSwing Chart of Bucyrus (BUCY). This energy sector–related company is experiencing some very good times due to the rising price of crude oil. Indeed, it has been trading steadily upward for almost 18 months. By making

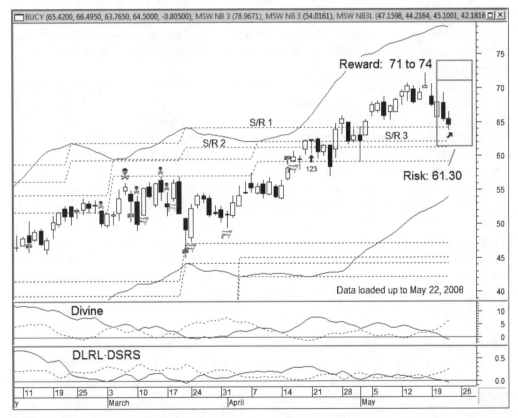

FIGURE 9.4 A daily chart of Bucyrus (BUCY) is demonstrating a trend continuation in progress. The Adeo signal at the right edge of the chart occurs at a significant level of support because of the S/R 1 line.

Chart created in MetaStock. Chart uses the MetaSwing Add-on, by Northington Trading, LLC. All rights reserved.

another push through resistance at the S/R 1 line, it shows that it is still in the game. By May 22, 2008, it retraces to test support at the S/R 1 line at 64.24. Remember that the S/R 1 line is formed by the most recent significant peak of the upper N Band. This line is a level of Projected Implied Volatility (PIV), which serves as price support by the date shown.

If you were to put on a long trade at this point, what would the risk-reward ratio look like? You need to make three decisions in advance to quantify that:

1. The price point at which to buy
2. The price point at which to sell if the trade goes against you (otherwise known as the *sell stop price*)
3. The price point at which to sell and book profits

Obviously, anything can and will happen during the trade management phase, but by knowing in advance what your decisions should be, especially the sell stop price, you are giving yourself a better fighting chance by not letting your emotions rule the decision-making process. A well thought out risk-reward calculation will keep your trade entry decision grounded in reality.

In Figure 9.4, the double level rectangle at the right side of the chart represents the probable opportunity zone of the trade. A trade entry at the S/R 1 level at 64.24 is logical at this point. The lower boundary of the rectangle sits at the S/R 2 level of 61.30. This should be a stop loss level. The top boundary of the rectangle is at 74.00, and it represents a reasonable best-case sell target. The second upper level of the rectangle is at 71.00, which is a likely worst-case profit target.

How were these profit targets derived? The upper N Band is showing signs of topping and rolling over. By examining the rate of rise and fall of the upper N Band recently, it is easy to see that it could likely converge on a rising price at 75.00, within five to seven trading days. This would present strong resistance for a several day pause, or even a downward reversal. A maximum profit target of 74.00, therefore, seems reasonable. The worst case of 71.00 represents recent highs of the previous upswing. By quantifying the answers to the three pieces of information just listed you can derive the risk-reward ratios shown in Table 9.2.

TABLE 9.2 Risk-Reward Ratio for the Daily Chart of Bucyrus (BUCY)

	Stop Loss	Lowest Profit Target	Highest Profit Target
Buy	64.24	64.24	64.24
Sell	61.30	71.00	74.00
Profit	(2.94)	6.76	9.76
Profit %	−4.58%	10.52%	15.19%
Risk = 1	Reward =	2.3	3.3
ATR(40)	2.91	2.3	3.3

With the entry point, the stop loss price, and the profit targets identified, we then have the basic numbers needed for a risk-reward analysis of the proposed trade. We can see a reward-risk ratio in Table 9.2 of 2.3:1 if we enter at 64.24 and sell at 71.00. A reward-risk ratio of 3.3:1 exists if the profit target of 74.00 is reached.

Many believe that a single target is sufficient for projecting a profit target. I like to look at the potential trade in terms of lowest to highest profit targets when possible. Doing so forces the mind to think through possible scenarios that can play out. For example, in this case it would be prudent to ask what effect time will have on the strength of the potential reversal? A price consolidation delay of a few days could cause the upper N Band to consistently get even lower, so as to reduce the likelihood of a blockbuster profit within a 5- to 10-day window. It could be best to exit at a lower profit target in a case such as this.

The following are separate cross-verifying reasons to strongly consider a long swing trade at this point:

- The broad market index (S&P 500) is showing solid oversold conditions.
- The underlying stock is in an Adeo state.
- It is just above a significant level of support.
- This stock is experiencing a solid trend rally.
- Careful analysis predicts a reward-risk ratio from 2.3:1 in the worst case to 3.4:1 in the best case.
- Also, in case you are wondering, the TTI Trend indicator, which is not shown because of chart space, is reading a positive 20-period slope with both the 10-period and 20-period look-back parameters. You can review Chapter 6 to revisit this indicator and its uses.

Figure 9.5 shows us the results of a long entry at the S/R 1 line at 64.24. The next trading day does give us the opportunity to enter at that point. Examine the inset in the middle of the chart. This rectangle shows the parallel performance of the S&P 500 Index. Its X-axis time line corresponds to the X-axis time line at the bottom of the chart. On the day of the trade entry, May 23, 2008, the broad market suffers another decline and produces an Adeo signal. This is a real treat because Bucyrus held at the S/R 1 line and had a higher close. This confirms that the decision to enter a long trade is probably a correct one at that point.

In the trading days after the long entry, the market and Bucyrus both trade a short-term reversal to the upside. The broad market has run out of steam by June 3. Bucyrus is pushing up against serious resistance because it has reached to within one ATR value below the upper N Band, which has come down to meet it. Also, the Divine oversold and overbought indicator pair at the bottom has crossed. These three pieces of information mean that it would be best to consider an exit at that time. If so, then profit taking at 73.00 produced a good trade. If, however, you had decided to raise your sell stop to the 71.00 level and put a little more time into position, then you were rewarded with price rising to the upper N Band on June 6. In this case the stock exhibited additional

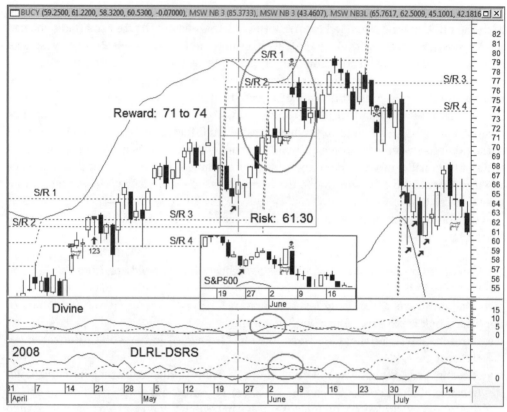

FIGURE 9.5 This chart shows us the continuation and completion of the long trade of Bucyrus (BUCY) begun in Figure 9.4. An inset of concurrent S&P 500 Index performance is shown in the middle of the chart.

Chart created in MetaStock. Chart uses the MetaSwing Add-on, by Northington Trading, LLC. All rights reserved.

strength uncorrelated to the market. This was probably due to its being in the middle of a strong trend or the underlying dynamics of the energy sector at that time.

THE MEANDERING ADEO

Imagine a situation in which you are interested in beginning a small business venture. Such endeavors require time, effort, and dedication. If you have ever started a business of your own, then you know how having even a tiny company on the side can require a lot of your attention. As most people are married, imagine attempting to have that commercial undertaking without the support of your spouse. Whether your wife or husband is either indifferent or opposed to it, you are on your own. Any time or money you sink into the venture is likely to snowball into some level of resentment.

Over time, you are not going to get the help you need in the other areas of your life that will offset what you are directing toward your business. On the other hand, having the supportive efforts of your spouse will enable you to redirect some of that special talent you possess toward the enterprise. In the end, it is obvious that the help and support you receive is what most often makes the difference between success and failure, whether our egos will admit it or not.

Just like having family support during a business endeavor, support or resistance makes every bit of the same difference in a reversal trade. The two topics do not just share the same world; they are really just alike. Support, in a reversal to the long side, is the price level at which others are going to help you. It's the price point at which there will be more buyers than sellers. By combining an Adeo condition with the buying enthusiasm of other traders at a particular support level, the reversal is usually much more powerful. It has more spring to it, and will therefore carry a more favorable reward-to-risk ratio.

When price is meandering about the chart without a well-defined trend, there is a lack of momentum. Without this energy, the price action following an Adeo signal often results in a sideways area of consolidation. For a reversal to occur, the prospect of price continuing in the previous direction needs to be removed from the minds of potential buyers. This is essentially what support and resistance does. In the case of trading a reversal to the long side, the support level serves to inform potential buyers that the odds of a continuing decline is small. With that fear lessened, enough additional buyers are added to the equation to push prices significantly in the opposite direction.

Figure 9.6 of Old Dominion (ODFL) illustrates this support and resistance and Adeo relationship well with three separate examples. Old Dominion has been trading at this point in a wandering type of range for over a year. Two of the trades have already played out on the chart. The third is just setting up at the right edge of the chart. Circled Area 1 occurs well above volatility-based support. Circled Area 2 shows a possible trade entry just at the edge of resistance. Its results are somewhat more profitable. Circled Area 3 depicts an advantageous trade setup virtually on top of N Band support.

- *Circled Area 1* shows Adeo signals for four straight days as price makes a high velocity drop. Adeo extremes don't usually go on indefinitely, however. This price move stops short of the rising lower N Band. Price and the N Band do not get close enough to each other to initiate much of a vertical bounce, and thus a sideways trading range develops for three weeks. A shift to a sideways consolidation is very common when Adeo price action does not meet up with significant support or resistance.
- *Circled Area 2* produces a situation in which price rises to within just one ATR(40) of the upper N Band. Two days after the Adeo short signals stop, the price rises to test closer proximity to the upper N Band. A brief 6 percent reversal occurs as a result, but prices subsequently continue to rise. Remember that volatility mathematics exist throughout all time frames. Two to five periods are as far forward that can

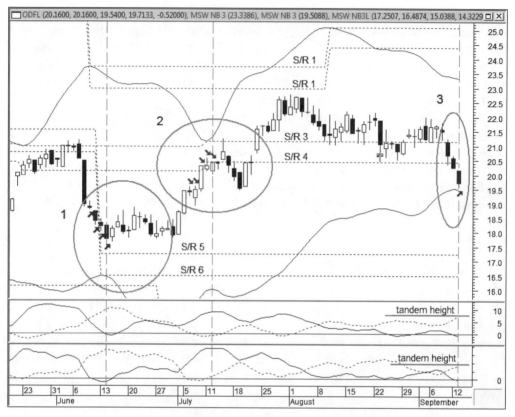

FIGURE 9.6 This daily chart of Old Dominion (ODFL) offers us an excellent example of trading short-term Adeo swings with and without support and resistance.

Chart created in MetaStock. Chart uses the MetaSwing Add-on, by Northington Trading, LLC. All rights reserved.

routinely be solidly forecasted. In this example, however, resistance made a real difference.

- *Circled Area 3* depicts an Adeo trade that is setting up nicely. Intraday price virtually reached the lower N Band. That is real support. Note that the tandem indicator pairs at the bottom of the chart each indicate oversold conditions. The opposing indicator height is not remarkable. At the same time, though, notice that the upper and lower N Bands are noticeably closer together than the recent chart history. This indicates a climate of decreasing volatility. The opposing indicator height, therefore, is not quite as important. Support is what's most significant in this case. After careful examination, this long trade should be put on at the next best entry point. Let's see how this trade pans out.

Figure 9.7 is an extended chart of Old Dominion, showing an additional month forward. The number 3 circle gives us the results of how the long Adeo trade develops

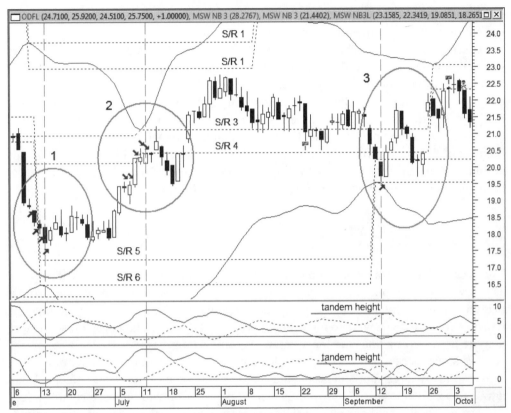

FIGURE 9.7 A further look forward from where the chart in Figure 9.6 ends shows that Old Dominion (ODFL) does indeed snap back into a short-term reversal.

Chart created in MetaStock. Chart uses the MetaSwing Add-on, by Northington Trading, LLC. All rights reserved.

after entry. It's plain to see how the addition of entering the trade with close significant support adds intensity to the reversal. As a minimum, when price hits an N Band, it will usually, not always, reverse or pause for two or three periods. If there is a pause in price movement and a trade is put on, then it gives you time to closely monitor the intraday price action to prove signs of strength.

In situations such as the trade in circle 3, market participants quickly realize that price has drifted out of bounds, so to speak. Price expands rapidly upward because the players with market-moving capacity, and with quantitative mathematics-based trading systems, see the price imbalance simultaneously. It takes buying volume of sufficient size to cause a reaction such as this.

This chart teaches us the importance of support when trading reversals without an underlying trend. It's like swimming in a lake instead of a stream. While swimming in the lake you are going to earn every foot of distance that you travel because there is no current to push you forward. If, on the other hand, you are swimming in stream with a current, it will carry you without any exertion on your part.

Don't get me wrong; trading in a nontrending market offers opportunities. This chart shows that if you are to profit from them, it is best to put support on your side. Trading scenarios 1, 2, and 3 progressively demonstrate the need for support and resistance when operating within a nontrending environment. The trade in circle 1 has no support and does not reverse. The trade in circle 2 experiences a temporary reversal and uses a moderate level of support. Finally, the trade in circle 3 experiences a strong reversal because of the close proximity of support. The behavior depicted in Figure 9.7 is not absolute; nothing in trading ever is. It is quite representative of the odds and tendencies, however, that volatility-based support will add to short-term swing reversals.

THE ADEO SHORT

Take a careful look around and you won't find nearly as much written about selling short as you will on the topic of long side trading. Here's why: it's more difficult. Oh, I know that there are many who disagree with that statement, and some disagree passionately. Indeed, there are those who do it extremely well. That does not, however, erase the fact that the preferred trading side for the vast majority is long.

The stock market has a well-known long-side bias. This is due to an environment in which so many large funds must maintain either long or cash positions. Hedge funds have had some opposing effects on this market bias, but only to increase volatility. It is still a truism, however, that a playing field where the majority of participants are demanding upside price action creates additional difficulties. As Dr. Alexander Elder states, "The one great disadvantage of selling stocks short is that the broad stock market has a centuries-old tendency to rise over time. The estimates of the angle of this so-called secular rise vary, clouded by many old stocks disappearing and new stocks being listed. Still, an average 3 percent rise per year seems like a reasonable estimate. This means that you are swimming against a gently rising tide."[1]

I believe that you will see some evidence in this section that with volatility-based technical analysis, selling short requires only slightly more attention to detail so that it may be conducted safely and profitably. The first extra detail to remember is that the short trade entry should accompany a resistance level that exists in some time frame. For instance, an Adeo short signal on the daily chart combined with a resistance level from the three-day or weekly chart can work very well. Second, be extra patient with trade entry. Use a limit order for trade entry and have the discipline to let the trade pass you by if the order does not pick up. Do not chase trade entry points. Last, and not least, trade with the trend. Let's look at an example that exemplifies these points.

In Figure 9.8 we see a daily chart of Merrill Lynch (MER), which has, over the past 10 months, exhibited a trend top. The chart shown in Figure 9.8 does not depict this entire move because of space limitations. Interestingly, on a larger chart view, the TTI Trend Strength indicator tracked the end of Merrill's trend with a rollover in advance of

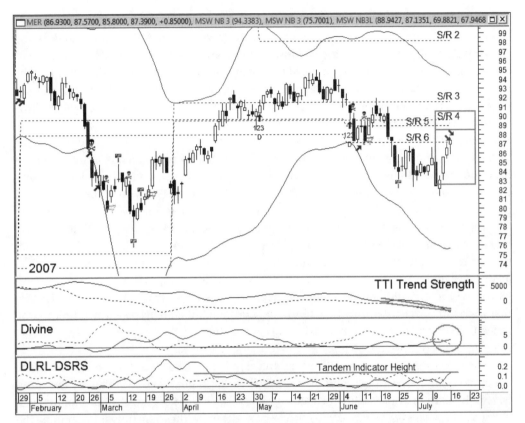

FIGURE 9.8 Because of the behavior of Merrill Lynch (MER) in the past six months, a well-balanced decision can be made to enter a potentially beginning downtrend.

Chart created in MetaStock. Chart uses the MetaSwing Add-on, by Northington Trading, LLC. All rights reserved.

its own. If you want to see the entire trend top and rollover, go to www.tradingthe invisible.com to view full-screen color versions of most of the charts in Part III of this book.

Here are the specific meaningful points of analysis for the Merrill Lynch chart with respect to the intermediate term:

- When a Zigzag indicator, with 5 percent parameters, is overlaid on the price bars, it has experienced two previous lower highs. The recent low, however, was higher than the previous one. This detail is not shown on the chart, but the rest of the points that follow are.
- Price is currently below the S/R 6 level for the second time in the past few months. This is a sign of a potential beginning downtrend.
- Examine closely the length of the price candles in June and July. Price action to the upside is much slower than price action to the down side. This is a classic sign of distribution.

- The TTI Trend Strength indicator shows a high level of price weakness. The most recent 20-period indicator lines are overlaid with a 20-period linear regression straight line so that the negative slope may be visually demonstrated.
- The price drop from February to March also produced a corresponding drop of the TTI Trend Strength indicator. The price rise from March to May, however, did not register the same rise of the TTI Trend Strength to its previous February levels. This shows a significant divergence.

So the question remains: Is it correct to derive that Merrill Lynch is at this juncture beginning to trend downward? I believe so, because the evidence for the argument outweighs the evidence against. The real tiebreaker lies with two pieces of chart-based calculations. First, the TTI Trend Strength confirms definite weakness. Second, the Adeo short signal occurs just when it reaches significant resistance at the S/R 6 line. You may remember seeing this same situation in reverse when a stock is breaking out into a trend rally; it retraces to test support at the S/R 1 or 3 lines. This is the same situation, only inverted.

Since the volatility-based evidence supports a short entry, what are the factors that should be considered so that the trade entry, exits, and risk-reward ratio may be quantified?

- The price reversal that occurred on July 11 at about 82.00 did not occur with any specific indicator or support level confirmation. Significant reversals in the intermediate time frame usually occur at overbought-and-oversold and support-and-resistance levels. The lack of existence of either of these on July 11 supports the interpretation of the price advance as a short-term counter swing.
- The DSRS component has just crossed zero. The DLRL opposing tandem component of the DLRL-DSRS pair has reached a sufficient height. It is justifiable to a degree to discount the large DLRL height in March and April because of the historical nature of the markets at that juncture. So, by discarding those events, it is plain to see that the DLRL height is significant.
- In looking at the Divine indicator overbought level, we can see that it is not quite yet below zero. It is common, however, for the Divine components to lag a day or two behind the DLRL because of the additional volatility inputs that it is based on. Based on this lagging Divine overbought signal, therefore, it would be best to use patience and place an entry limit order higher than the S/R 6 line. Somewhere between the S/R 6 and S/R 5 lines is probably best.
- Based on this information, a short entry at 88.50 by limit order is decided on. A covering stop limit order at 90.50 is planned because it is above the S/R 4 level. If price continued to that level, it would likely not stop until it met resistance at the converging upper N Band, which is at about 92.00. If the trade entry at 88.50 is wrong, allowing a loss to continue above 90.50 is just throwing money away.
- The profit target is 82.50. This is a theoretical target because the nearest support level is all the way down at the lower N Band. The actual decision to exit will need

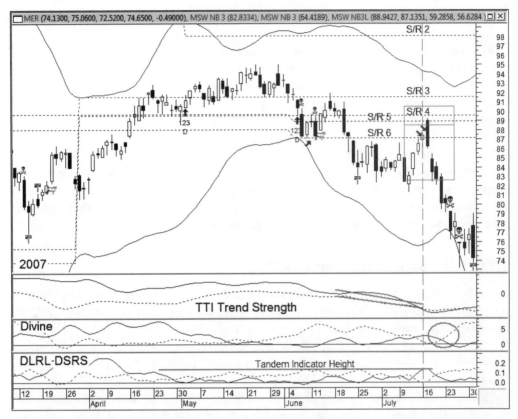

FIGURE 9.9 With an entry just below or at the S/R 5 resistance line, Merrill Lynch (MER) reverses and continues its downward trading direction, which confirms the trend.

Chart created in MetaStock. Chart uses the MetaSwing Add-on, by Northington Trading, LLC. All rights reserved.

to be determined by the indicator readings as the trade progresses. It is reasonable to assume, however, that the trade can easily reach 82.50 because it is slightly less than the recent price swing.

• Having these price levels in hand, the reward-risk ratio is approximately 3.3 : 1, which is very acceptable.

With all that said, let's see how our trade turns out. In Figure 9.9, the chart of Merrill Lynch has been moved forward by two weeks. Indeed, the limit order for a short entry at 88.50 does execute. The opening price on the day immediately after the decision to take the trade is right at the S/R 5 level. Opening gaps such as this occur because of an order imbalance before the market open. There is a mathematical tendency for these events to correspond to volatility-based S/R levels. This occurs because of the correlations between the options market and the use of quantitative trading systems.

The trade puts our short equity position in the money by the end of the first day. From that point forward, the trade does nothing but go in the right direction, down. The real decision comes on July 23. The session almost produces an inside day; both indicators have crossed and are approaching oversold conditions. The current potential profit level is exceeding our target, and cashing in the chips is looking very tempting. The option at this point is to exit, or put a buy to cover stop above that day's range near 81.00. In truth, both options are correct. There is no way to know that on the next day the U.S. major exchanges will experience a Total Correction event. Lucky you, if you went for the stop order method.

In this daily time frame, it is easy to compare the recent months of up candles to down candles and see weakness on the part of buyers. Risk can be better quantified by identifying hidden volatility-based resistance levels. This is an excellent entry setup for position traders that ride trends, as well as for swing traders.

Trade the Earnings Announcement?

There is another important topic within this trade, however, that we have not touched on. Merrill Lynch reported quarterly earnings after the market closed on July 17. They obviously had some grim things to say about the future, despite having exceeded the Street's expectations. It is a general tenet among short-term technical traders to avoid holding a position during an earnings announcement. So then why is this trade acceptable?

There is not a solid, objective answer for this question other than to say that it can depend on the trader's risk profile. Here's what I mean. By the second day of the Adeo short signal, price was at the upper third level between the two N Bands. The largest risk in this case is that a large earnings surprise occurs and price gaps far out against your position. When these types of big earnings surprises happen, price tends to gap up or down to the nearest N Band, or other significant S/R level, in either a daily or weekly periodicity.

The downside gap exposure for Merrill Lynch is around 77.00 because of the lower N Band on the daily chart, and the S/R 6 line on the weekly chart (not shown). The risk side gap is at 94.00, which is the upper N Band on the daily chart. Remember that the stock is currently *very* overbought, and because of this it probably has positive earnings expectations already reflected in the price. Indeed, the previous four days of price action were the most bullish this stock has seen in months. Therefore, let's change the risk-reward calculation to include the volatility extreme numbers of 77.00 and 94.00, and keep a short entry of 88.50. Based on these numbers, we get a reward-risk ratio of 2.6:1. This number does not include the probability that some of the risk is reduced because of the current overbought condition. Because of the subjective nature of the assumption, it's best to keep that in your back pocket as unquantifiable insurance.

This trade offers for many a risk-reward ratio that is acceptable, and for some it does not. The point is that volatility-based technical analysis exposes the invisible levels of support and resistance. Calculating risk without it would be a guess in the dark while wearing earplugs. If the trader has a high probability of projecting extreme gaps due to serious fundamental information, however, it can then be traded with an equity position or option position(s). Position sizing and other risk control measures must certainly be factored into the trade decision.

The bottom line is this: If you are going to trade earnings announcements, FDA drug trial results announcements, and the like, use volatility-based technical analysis to project where implied volatility will place the price extremes. Use it along with a proper risk-reward estimate and other risk-balancing strategies. This topic is discussed further in the chapter on options trade setups. You can also refer to the Microsoft chart example in Chapter 4.

ADEO AND FOREX

The push and pull between fundamental data and technical levels is alive and well in currency trading. A very large difference within this fundamental effect is that it is of a different nature than equities fundamentals. It is usually very broad macroeconomic and political developments that move the value of currency.

The guts of volatility-based technical analysis in the FOREX markets, however, are virtually the same as in the equity markets. It quite possibly possesses even more predictive value in currency trading than in stock analysis. This is likely due to the wide-ranging nature of applicable fundamental forces. When news is delivered about a specific company's stock, it is very clear and only applies to a finite amount of market capitalization, normally measured in millions or billions of dollars. Because of a lack of granularity of news and information, its potential effect on any one currency, and with a float measured in the trillions, there are larger voids of time and chart space for technical analysis to fill. That's one cause-and-effect possibility out of many, none of which can really be proven.

What is for certain is that Adeo levels and volatility-based support and resistance levels are extremely accurate on currency pairs charts. Figure 9.10 shows us a daily chart of the euro to the U.S. dollar. First look at each of the four smaller circled areas. Note how important the S/R lines are. Virtually all short-term swings occur at support and resistance lines. Circled areas 1, 2, and 4 show us how the S/R lines lie at reversal or pause points. In circled area 3, an S/R line from the weekly chart is manually drawn (at 1.3824) to show how that time frame dominates that area of reversal. The resistance level also holds its dominance for five weeks because it is in a weekly time frame.

Look at circled area 5 for an example of the best type of trade setup. The Adeo signal begins at the S/R 5 line. The DLRL signals oversold, and the DSRS tandem component reads excellent opposing volatility height. A limit order at the S/R 6 line makes for a great long trade entry. The significance of combining Adeo volatility mathematics and PIV level support at S/R 6 puts on a great reversal trade. This chart illustrates how an inherent nonspecific fundamental environment causes the majority of short-term trading decisions to be based on volatility measurement. The effectiveness of volatility-based technical analysis on currency trading is very high.

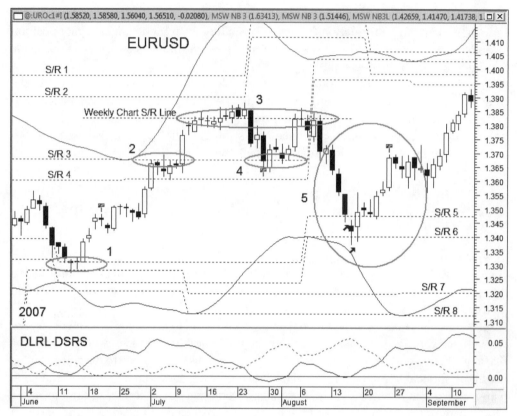

FIGURE 9.10   It is clear how Adeo signals, combined with support and resistance levels, can produce high probability swings on this daily FOREX chart of the euro trading against the U.S. dollar.

Chart created in MetaStock. Chart uses the MetaSwing Add-on, by Northington Trading, LLC. All rights reserved.

THE FRACTAL ADEO

Chart patterns occur throughout all time frames. For example, ascending triangles routinely appear on weekly, daily, and any configuration of intraday charts. It happens because there are different sets of traders that focus on each time frame. This unbiased time frame phenomenon is defined as being *fractal*. Properly designed technical analysis should also be fractal by nature. In fact, all capabilities of volatility-based TA should easily cross time frames. If you think about it for a moment, it is easy to see the simple logic of trading within its effects.

There are traders of all types: day traders, swing traders, position traders, and longer-term trend traders. Each has a preferred hold time with which he is comfortable.[2] Let's suppose that you find a good long-side swing trade entry on a daily chart. The weekly chart of that same stock simultaneously shows a proper swing entry as well. This same entry time and price point has just attracted two or more groups of traders. Look at it this way: a bunch of swing traders and position traders have combined to form a

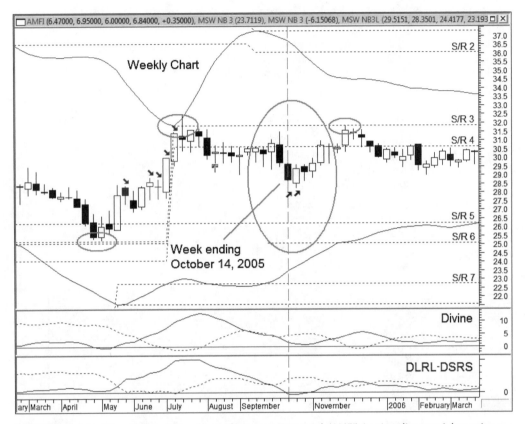

FIGURE 9.11   Here, the weekly chart of Amcore Financial (AMFI) is signaling an Adeo price condition for the week ending October 14, 2005.

Chart created in MetaStock. Chart uses the MetaSwing Add-on, by Northington Trading, LLC. All rights reserved.

larger team, albeit unknowingly. Together, they line up on the long side of the trade. This simply adds up to more buyers that outnumber sellers, and thus price advances even more quickly.

The best place to start is with a multi-time frame strategy with the longer time duration. It's a more efficient use of effort because only a subset of daily charts showing entry opportunities will also show corresponding weekly setups. Begin by searching for weekly periodicity charts that show an Adeo entry or some other signal of directional intelligence.

In Figure 9.11, a weekly MetaSwing chart of Amcore Financial (AMFI) shows an Adeo condition for the week ending October 14, 2005, and is delineated by the vertical dashed line. Examine the three smaller circled areas and it is plain to see how N Bands and S/R lines are as meaningful in this time frame as in others. In each of the three smaller circles, a sustained price move reverses at support or resistance. This shows the fractal nature of volatility-based technical analysis, and how you can leverage the trading positions of others outside your trading time frame.

FIGURE 9.12 The daily periodicity chart of Amcore Financial (AMFI) drills down into the weeks shown on the previous figure.

Chart created in MetaStock. Chart uses the MetaSwing Add-on, by Northington Trading, LLC. All rights reserved.

The larger circled area on the Amcore weekly chart shows that price has moved very decidedly downward for two weeks and is in need of seeking a more efficient balance. Longer position traders will instinctively see that it pushed hard against resistance at S/R 4 for two months before retracing some of the previous advance earlier in 2005. This means that there is a likelihood of another test of the S/R 4 level.

Switching to Figure 9.12, we can zoom in for more resolution on daily charts of Amcore Financial. The same day of October 14, 2005, is marked with a vertical dashed line. Radical price decline produced Adeo signals two days before. The decline ended at the very significant support produced by the lower N Band as well as the S/R 7 line. It's important to note at this point that if you are trading a short-term reversal time frame, it is natural to get impatient. Remember, however, that your partners, the position traders, are slower to act because they think longer term. They will likely wait a few days to ensure that the price decline is not continuing. If you are a swing trader, patience is needed because other participants may not experience the passage of time the same way you do.

As you can see in Figure 9.12, the stock reverses upward after a small amount of consolidation. Having two or more sets of traders all generating demand on the same side of the market achieves the goal of overpowering the bears. Also look closely at the daily price advance in the subsequent weeks. Note how price advances to the October S/R 5 line, and then declines to the S/R 6 line, only to reverse upward again. This is caused by the swing trade crowd that operates on daily and intraday charts, using their respective fractal levels of support and resistance. In the meantime, the longer-term position traders hold throughout their time frame until taking profits in December near the S/R 4 line. If you refer again to Figure 9.11, you can see how the weekly S/R 3 line at 31.85 is closely aligned with the November daily S/R 4 line at 31.64. At that point, the team of disparate traders is disbanding and going their separate ways.

The Amcore Financial example presented herein is not perfect. There are some flaws with the setups. For instance, the weekly chart Adeo signal does not occur anywhere near support in that time frame. Because of this, the trader would certainly not want to let her position slip much below the 28.00 price level, for fear of a lack of longer-term support. The main point here is that certainly perfect examples exist; they are the exception, however, rather than the rule.

OPEN YOUR CAN OF SPINACH

The real world of trading is not textbook neat and tidy; things don't always perfectly align. But they don't always need to. Just ensure that you are putting adequate amounts of cross-verified volatility analysis on your side. Ensure that when price looks doomed to continue up or down at an unbelievable pace, you don't just assume that your math calculations know better, because neither you nor anyone else knows anything for certain in the financial markets. It's all about the odds. The odds of a loss versus the odds of a gain are risk management on a position-by-position basis. This is what will set you free, when it is combined with a larger risk management strategy and good volatility-based technical analysis.

Profits are to be made at the extremes. The Adeo represents the extreme of extreme in regard to directional price change potential. Market inefficiency is presented to you when a void of fundamental reason for the deviation exits. The difference between the opportunities that will waste your time and those that can be profitably exploited is the can of spinach.

Either the can of spinach exists at that point or it doesn't. If it is there for you to open, you will find it in the form of volatility-based support or resistance. It will be present in the form of true overbought-oversold conditions. Spinach can be accessible to you when these factors are seen in multiple time frames too. Only when you can turn these signals from invisible to visible will you be able to say, "That's all I can stands, I can't stands no more," and thus take control of the reversal trade.

CHAPTER 10

Trading
the Trend
with the 1-2-3

Have you ever played pinball? This is not an irrelevant question if you are a trader. While you are trading, you're playing pinball but you may not know it. Right now you are probably wondering if you are the flippers or the ball.

Pinball actually dates its origins back to the fourteenth century. The most common form of pinball, the arcade game, came to its current form in the post–World War II boom era. The largest actual difference between a coin-operated pinball machine and trading stocks is that with pinball you lose only a quarter. As for the similarities, stock trading and pinball have a few significant ones.

To recognize them, begin by standing in front of a pinball machine at the controls, then turn the whole thing 90 degrees to the right. The round steel ball starts the game by rolling past you from left to right and enters the field of play. The ball rolls with a natural arc induced by momentum and gravity until it hits a reactionary boundary. Most surfaces inside a pinball machine are lined with mechanisms that sense the ball's collision and push back, kind of like Newton's law with a little electricity behind it. The ball is then sent on a different path to its next electrically powered boundary. This back-and-forth motion, ringing up points, can go on for extended periods, or only briefly.

Inevitably, the ball encounters a theoretical obstacle that allows it to pass through but still changes the ball's direction and fate. Extra points are usually rewarded for this! Whether you were aiming for the special target or not, the ball is somehow routed quickly to the void at the far left, which is guarded only by your flippers. With any luck, you can flip the ball back up into the point scoring area.

In the real world, traders are the boundaries. Their trading account sizes represent the force of the reactionary bounce that is induced onto the ball or the stock, as it were. The boundaries, manned by traders with their buying and selling power, form specific temporary lines of support and resistance. The more traders, and by default, the more trading account money, then the stronger that support line, or boundary, is. The stock is thus consistently trading back and forth between support and resistance boundaries as though it were a game of securities pinball.

But is it really that simple? Of course, it isn't. Pinball is inherently two-dimensional. At its simplest, stock trading is three-dimensional. In the previous chapter we discussed the *fractal* nature of trading and technical analysis. That time frame dimension is ever present and inescapable. Imagine for a moment that you are physically playing three-dimensional pinball. It would have to look something like a pinball game inside another, larger pinball game, with the first game sliding across the physical surface of the larger one. At certain instants, key boundaries from different dimensions line up.

And so it goes within the trend. The concept and practice of the 1-2-3 trade method, which exploits volatility-based support and resistance, plays itself out at key junctures of trends. It does so across many time frames. I examine closely in this chapter the simplicity with which this phenomenon lines up and executes right under our noses. So, crank up "Pinball Wizard" by The Who, get out your bag of quarters, and let's play.

RECTANGLES EVERYWHERE

The 1-2-3 has it origins in a simple chart pattern commonly referred to as *a rectangle*. The rectangle pattern has been examined as far back as the origination of the Dow Theory. It is commonly thought to be a temporary area of congestion, a period where price has reached an oscillating equilibrium. Rectangles usually form after a price advance or after a price decline. With the assistance of hindsight, it can be a distribution area when price rises to it and then breaks out below it. It is also termed an *accumulation area* should the opposite occur.[1]

Figure 10.1 shows a diagram of the rectangle pattern. The figure depicts the standard rectangle formation. Price is range-bound as the bulls and bears argue back and forth, letting their trading accounts do the talking. The thing about the everyday rectangle is that they occur all over the chart. You can find them in meandering chart areas as well as trending ones. This diagram is obviously very neat and tidy. The real world is seldom so perfectly organized.

We are presented in Figure 10.2 with a weekly chart of Autodesk (ADSK). Lacking the noise of a daily time frame, this weekly view shows clearly how frequently

The Rectangle Pattern

FIGURE 10.1 This shows a classic rectangle pattern.

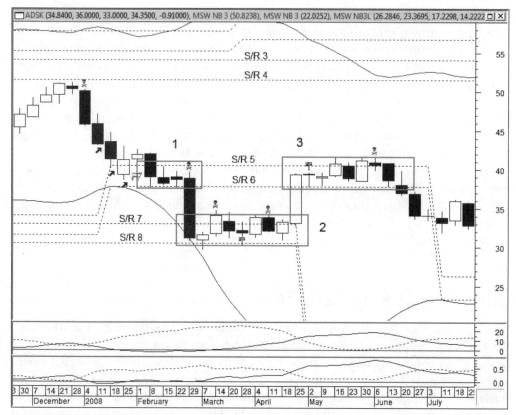

FIGURE 10.2 This weekly chart of Autodesk (ADSK) shows clearly how rectangle formations occur regularly. Bulls and bears push the pinball back and forth until it escapes to find another range in which to play.

Chart created in MetaStock. Chart uses the MetaSwing Add-on, by Northington Trading, LLC. All rights reserved.

real-world rectangle formations occur. Consider each of the rectangle-shaped patterns shown:

- In area 1, Autodesk forms a four-week rectangle continuation version of a rectangle.
- Immediately following a breakout, it begins to form rectangle 2, which turns out to be an accumulation pattern. After eight weeks of accumulation, it rises directly to yet another rectangle setup.
- Rectangle 3 lasts for another eight weeks and turns out to be a distribution formation because price falls right out of it.

Note that the price action rarely stays perfectly within a well-defined rectangle shape. A messy rectangle is very much the norm. This is what contributes to the high rate of failure for breakouts from rectangle patterns, and the tricky nature of trading them.

The most significant aspect of this MetaSwing chart is how the rectangles form around the S/R lines. Rectangle patterns 1 and 3 use S/R 5 for resistance and S/R 4 for support. Rectangle number 2 uses S/R 7 for resistance and S/R 8 for support. This is because of Projected Implied Volatility (PIV). The PIV levels for rectangles 2 and 3 were in place for months, and yet they were the building blocks for the architecture of the bull and bear battle.

These formations surrounding the S/R lines are not coincidences. They are deliberate and natural because the market-moving forces of institutional strength see these levels. To most individual traders, the levels remain invisible because they are not using the right mathematical analysis methods. So how do we make money with this knowledge?

That is the pertinent question, and yes, it is a little more complicated than pinball. But that still does not mean that we shouldn't listen to "Pinball Wizard" while trading; just make sure it's the original version by The Who.

THE TRADITIONAL APPROACH

First, let's take a moment to look at today's commonly accepted method for trading a rectangle pattern. This will only help you to appreciate the volatility-based approach. Comparing the two methods will enable you to garner greater price directional intelligence as well.

The prevailing consensus is that it's not profitable to trade the inside of the rectangle. Let me state that again: The industry's most influential technical analysts advise against trading price swings within a rectangle formation. Figure 10.3 shows the theoretical rectangle pattern with two potential price paths. Both of them are breakouts from the rectangle pattern.

It is also not recommended to trade the breakout from the rectangle. This is due to the high percentage of false breakouts. As I stated previously, price rarely rises and falls

Trading the Rectangle Pattern
(Traditional method)

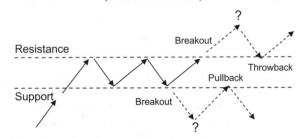

FIGURE 10.3 The classic rectangle formation is believed by most to be treacherous. Trading only the pullback and the throwback points is the prevailing opinion of those not using volatility-based technical analysis.

to the exact same levels within the formation, thus giving it a slightly messy look. This price noise fools traders into believing that a breakout is occurring. Also, the exit point for trading the breakout is fuzzy. The commonly accepted method is to use the height of the rectangle as a profit target. The minority opinion that does promote breakout trading usually uses volume increases as a telltale sign. Volume reporting by the major exchanges today, however, is highly inaccurate; and that's the kindest thing I can say about it.

Take a look at Figure 10.3 and examine the throwback and the pullback. These two points are the most commonly recommended trading opportunities for the rectangle. Once price does execute a breakout from the rectangle a retracement to the previous boundary is the potential reversal point.[2]

Actually, the pullback and throwback can be profitable trades. There is more to determining the valid pullback and throwback points, however, than most people think. Nevertheless, these prevailing practices seem to me like a waste of a lot of perfectly good rectangle opportunities. This is occurring today because of a lack of the recognition of true volatility-based support and resistance. Now let's see how we can profitably trade the inside and the outside of the best rectangle-like opportunities.

THE 1-2-3 CONSTRUCT

The 1-2-3 trade is really quite simple. It is meant to capitalize on the sustained directional movement of a trend. Some might say that it is a simple exploitation of an unremarkable price movement. These same people would use an unimpressed tone in their voice when they make that statement. They would be absolutely correct.

If the 1-2-3 is such a common and simple-looking trade, then why is it so valuable? After all, it is designed to capture only relatively small price moves. To truly understand why a 1-2-3 is so great, you have to have felt the pain of watching a broad market trend creep higher and higher, day after day, without you. Oh, the pain! As swing traders, we are taught to buy on the dips and exploit price oscillations. As position traders, we are taught to have discipline and wait for the price to correct before jumping on the trend. Well, what if there are no dips and oscillations, and also no trend end in sight?

It feels like slowly walking across a desert without water, while being forced to watch others drink iced tea. You know that many are profiting greatly from the trend, but you can find only entry points. At that point, your main problem is finding entry points with acceptable risk-reward ratios. As price creeps up slowly, it creates lower volatility. This causes indicators to flatten out and thus robs trade entries of their probability and clarity.

This is where the 1-2-3 comes to the rescue. It provides an entry point based on hidden levels of support and resistance because of PIV. The best part is that oversold levels are not necessary. The trade setup depends mainly on support and resistance lines. No significant amount of price retracement is required. The 1-2-3, therefore, provides a structured, high probability method to enter a trend for a swing or a position trade.

Another important benefit of the 1-2-3 is that it makes use of so many wasted rectangle patterns. If you recall in Figure 10.3, trading inside the rectangle is not recommended. It is the prevailing technical analysis opinion that only trades based on the exterior of the rectangle should be taken. The 1-2-3 provides a profitable use for the inside of common rectangle formations.

1-2-3 Theory

By its outward appearance, and profit target, there is nothing noteworthy about a 1-2-3 except for one characteristic. The 1-2-3 is a very high probability trade. The market dynamics that support the 1-2-3 are the following:

- Trending price action
- Intermediate market directional intelligence
- Projected Implied Volatility (PIV)
- Multi-time frame support

These market analysis dynamics should not come as a surprise to you by now. We have used each of them in virtually all of the volatility-based technical analysis shown thus far. Each individual trading method, however, has its own unique ways of capitalizing on inefficiency. So what are these unique traits that make up the 1-2-3?

In Figure 10.4, the 1-2-3 construct is outlined in three simple steps. I bet you would have been surprised if there were more than three steps. All joking aside, start with price trading in a trending direction, and the broader market in a phase that supports a trade in the direction you will be taking. After that, the trade sets up as follows:

1. In step one, price trades up through minor PIV resistance at the S/R 2 or S/R 4 level. It is best if price closes between the lines at least once. Remember that the difference between the two S/R lines is approximately one ATR(40) value. If it shoots up through both S/R lines in one trading period, it does not give market participants time to commit to their positions. Price next continues to rise and closes above the primary PIV resistance levels of S/R 1 or S/R 3. Both resistance lines can be redefined as support lines at this point. Lastly, it is important that this price rise is recent. For instance, on a daily chart, price should not have risen above these S/R lines in the previous month of trading. This reinforces a trending behavior.

2. Step two is where price retraces downward below the S/R 1 or S/R 3 levels, and closes between the major and minor PIV S/R lines. It is important that the close is between the lines; otherwise, the 1-2-3 setup is invalid. This close between the S/R lines creates an initial signal for the 1-2-3. The purpose of the signal is to alert the trader that a possible 1-2-3 trade is setting up, and to prepare for it. Step two is completed when price drops to the S/R 2 or S/R 4 level, or a lower nearby price level that represents support in the next smaller time frame. No more than five periods can have passed from the time price closes below the S/R 1 or S/R 3 line and reaches

The 1-2-3 Construct

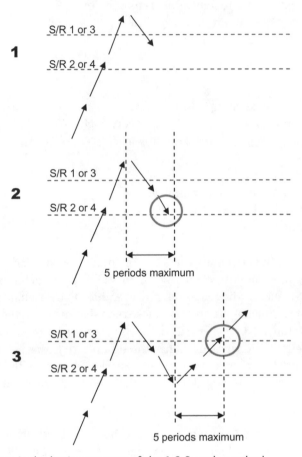

FIGURE 10.4 Here is the basic construct of the 1-2-3 trade method.

its default entry target. For instance, if on day 1, the price closes below the S/R 1 line, then the entry target price must be reached within five days; otherwise, too much time has passed and the setup is no longer valid.

3. Step three consists of entering the trade at the selected price support point. As a swing trade, the minimum profit target is the resistance line at S/R 1 or S/R 3, depending on whether you entered at the S/R 2 or S/R 4 level, respectively. Just like the trade entry time restriction of five periods, this trade's duration should be limited to five periods as well. If the profit target is not reached within five periods, then it is best to close the position because circumstances have changed, and its success probabilities are no longer valid. Profit targets can be adjusted to reach above the resistance line, depending on the technical environment. Another trade can be entered later if an appropriate pullback or throwback develops.

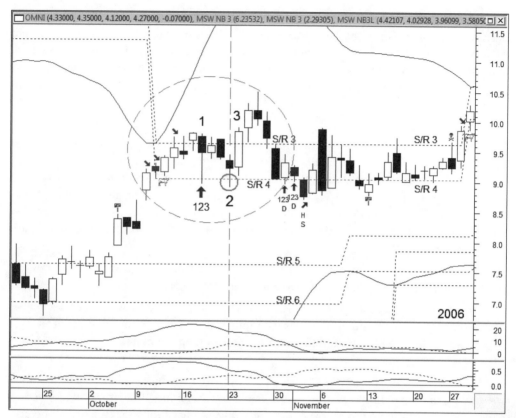

FIGURE 10.5   Omni Energy Services (OMNI) shows us a real-world example of a simple 1-2-3 setup on a daily chart.

Chart created in MetaStock. Chart uses the MetaSwing Add-on, by Northington Trading, LLC. All rights reserved.

The sequence and rules described here reflect long trade entries. The inverse of these rules applies to 1-2-3 short trades. There needs to be a greater amount of caution given to the broader market trading direction, however. Trading this specific method on the short side of the market is somewhat trickier than to the long side.

1-2-3 Reality

A 1-2-3 trade signal can very often mean the beginning of a longer area of rectangular shaped consolidation. Figure 10.5 shows a real-world example of this, as well as a typical 1-2-3 setup. It is not neat and perfect. The vast majority of profitable trades, however, aren't perfect textbook examples.

The 1-2-3 trade sets up and executes inside the dashed circled area in Figure 10.5. Price has risen in previous days to find resistance at the upper N Band and also enters an Adeo short state. By October 13, 2006, the lines at S/R 3 and S/R 4 reform and drop to 9.62 and 9.04, respectively. This is because the new N Band trough exceeds a 3 percent (default) differential. With these new S/R lines in place, the larger institutional traders have new levels of support and resistance to factor into their plans. Price closes above the S/R 3 line for one day, and has not closed above 9.62 in the past 20 days, which is a default rule. These are the three simple steps of the 1-2-3 in this real-world example:

1. The candle denoted with the number 1 is the 1-2-3 signal day because price crosses through support at the S/R 3 line to close below it and above the S/R 4 line. It is at this point that the possibility of a 1-2-3 trade comes to our attention by way of a daily exploration report. We can then review all of the 1-2-3 trade signals for that day, and the previous few days, to find the best candidates for profit. We can dispense with all of that analysis in this example and look further at this specific trade's progression.

2. Price then continues to close below S/R 3. A long trade is put on by limit order at the S/R 4 line, which is denoted by the number 2.

3. This yields a successful trade in one day when price crosses above the S/R 3 line, as denoted by the number 3. In this example, price goes on to touch each of the S/R lines at least twice more, continuing its inner rectangle movement.

There is a major difference in the 1-2-3 compared to the previous trade methods we have examined. Look at the overbought and oversold indicators in the lower panes. Neither of them is in an oversold state at the time of long entry. This is because the trade does not rely on oversold or overbought technical conditions in the 1-2-3 method's time frame.

The profit objective is also smaller when trading the 1-2-3 than it is with other trade methods. One ATR(40) measure of movement is the default minimum profit. The profit objective can be expanded by adjusting the entry and exit points based on other factors, which we explore in the pages to come. With the case of the Omni Energy Services chart, this equates to about 6 percent. Since the profit objective depends on the stock's ATR, then you can choose higher or lower volatility issues to trade, depending on your risk profile.

What the 1-2-3 lacks in profit percentages it compensates for with probability and time duration. By trading around closely related S/R lines, in a probable period of short-term consolidation, the pinball effect comes into play. Just like when the pinball is bouncing back and forth, so too does price bounce between these lines, especially when the conditions are right. Most 1-2-3 trades complete in the one- to three-day time duration. In fact, it can be best to enter and exit by limit order because the swings can happen so quickly.

There is another 1-2-3 signal that occurs a few days later. These 1-2-3 signals have a D beneath them. The 1-2-3 D is a variation of the 1-2-3, and we explore it later in this chapter.

THE DAILY 1-2-3

The best 1-2-3 opportunities generally occur because they exploit the fractal nature of technical analysis. One trader's 1-2-3 is another trader's Adeo opportunity, except that the two parties operate in different time frames. We began to explore this concept in Chapter 9, and there is ample opportunity to delve into it more deeply here. The best trading includes multi-time frame support whenever possible.

Let's begin this 1-2-3 trading opportunity with a look at a typical one. Figure 10.6 shows a daily chart of AutoNation (AN) after it has undergone a year-long decline. Bottoming in July of 2008 at 7.57, AutoNation begins a recovery rally directly into resistance at the S/R 4 level. Undeterred, however, it proceeds to close above the S/R 3 line, which is a sign of strength. Apparently a majority of longer-term players believe that this stock has been sold enough. The 1-2-3 signal sets up with a close under the S/R 3 line. The question at this point is what to do. Will price continue to retrace a little or a lot? Technical overbought and oversold levels are of no use with 1-2-3 trades; or are they?

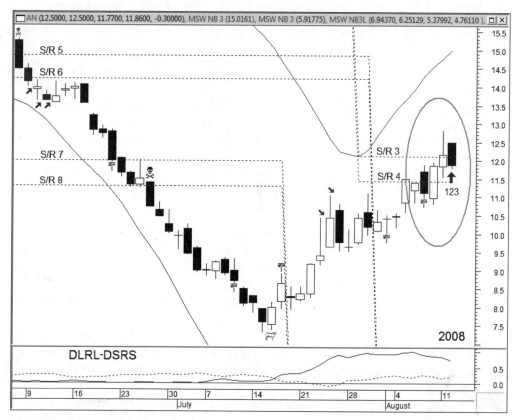

FIGURE 10.6 Here, AutoNation (AN) sets up for a 1-2-3 trade in a daily time frame.

Chart created in MetaStock. Chart uses the MetaSwing Add-on, by Northington Trading, LLC. All rights reserved.

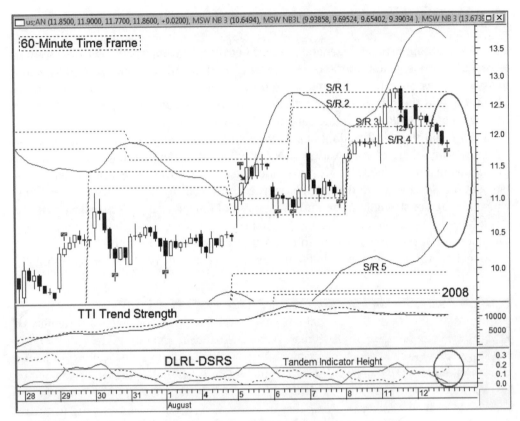

FIGURE 10.7 AutoNation demonstrates a different set of technical signals on the hourly chart.

Chart created in MetaStock. Chart uses the MetaSwing Add-on, by Northington Trading, LLC. All rights reserved.

The answers to these questions can be found in the next lower time frame. Let's switch to a 60-minute chart of AutoNation, because that's where the fun begins. Figure 10.7 adds more clarity to the current trading pattern that AutoNation has been executing in the previous days. It began playing pinball with S/R lines on August 5 and has not stopped up until the present hour. In Figure 10.7, take note of the following observations:

- Price pushed up through the upper N Band on August 5, and found resistance at the S/R 2 line (11.61) on the hourly chart, which also aligned closely with the S/R 4 line (11.42) on the daily chart.
- In the circled area, price has come to rest on the S/R 4 line seeking support, and it also prints an Exit short signal.
- Lastly, in the lower indicator pane, the DLRL-DSRS indicator pair seems to be showing an oversold condition.

Do these technical signals indicate that a price reversal is about to occur? Yes, but remember the default entry point is the S/R 4 line on the daily chart, which is at 11.42 and lower than the current close. A limit order to buy placed at 11.42 may seem prudent at this point. Despite all of this, there are also reasons on the chart to exercise some patience. They are as follows:

1. Look at the height of the DSRS (dotted line) in the lower indicator pane. It is higher than it has been in the past two weeks, but nowhere near its own level on July 28. It is also not at all above recent highs of the DLRL (solid line). Less than extreme tandem indicator height can mean that there can still be room for movement.

2. Examine the TTI Trend Strength indicator pair. They each topped a few days ago and have begun to decline. This means that the price advance in this time frame could be running a little low on steam.

3. Observe that there is a rapidly rising N Band. If price collides with it, then there will be extreme support at that point.

These three important technical clues all point to a significant enough possibility of further price retracement. For this reason, it would also be a good idea to wait for additional probability-enhancing developments. The odds, therefore, favor waiting for a long entry until a time when day traders will want to join in on the buying as well.

Figure 10.8 moves the clock forward by a mere three hours, but much happens. You can see in circled area 1 the S/R 4 line from the daily chart. This has been manually drawn so we can see the default long trade entry point. If the strategy we follow, however, is to wait for a day trader's entry, then it would be best to let price fall further. A risk of missing the trade is more than acceptable. Three important technical developments have occurred by the close of the second hour of trading on August 13.

1. Price has dropped to within almost one ATR distance from the lower N Band; see circled area 2.

2. An Adeo Long condition exists; see circled area 2.

3. The DSRS (dotted line) overbought indicator has reached a volatility height that matches that of August 28.

With these developments, it is certainly time to put on the trade. Whether you decide to enter at the daily S/R 4 level of 11.42, or somewhere lower, such as the close of the first trading hour at 11.13, each has a good case to be made as an entry point. A sell stop level should be just below the lower N Band at about 10.70. A reward-risk ratio of 2.3:1 is attained with an entry at 11.13, a sell stop at 10.70, and a profit target of 12.11, which is the daily S/R 3 price.

Figure 10.9 shows us a combined daily and 60-minute time frame view of how AutoNation completes this 1-2-3 trade. Each chart denotes the exit day with a vertical

FIGURE 10.8 By waiting until a different trade method sets up in an hourly time frame, the trader achieves the best entry for a 1-2-3 trade in a daily time frame.

Chart created in MetaStock. Chart uses the MetaSwing Add-on, by Northington Trading, LLC. All rights reserved.

dashed line. In both time frames, the S/R 3 lines are virtually identical at 12.11; the hourly S/R line is two cents higher at 12.13. The default price objective at that point has been reached on August 14, which is only the next trading day. Quick trades are a staple of the 1-2-3.

On the hourly chart, the DLRL and DSRS components have just completed a cross. This means that the highest probability portion of the potential profit has been attained. Say that fast five times. Indeed, price does rise by another 5 percent the next day, but unless you have reason to believe that a longer-term trend is in place, it is best to exit with the odds in your favor. If you recall, the TTI Trend indicator on the hourly chart in Figure 10.8 was not pointing skyward. A continuing price rise within a normal daily 1-2-3 trade duration is therefore not a high probability. This 1-2-3 trade closes with a profit ranging from 6 percent to 8.8 percent; that's not bad for a one day hold duration.

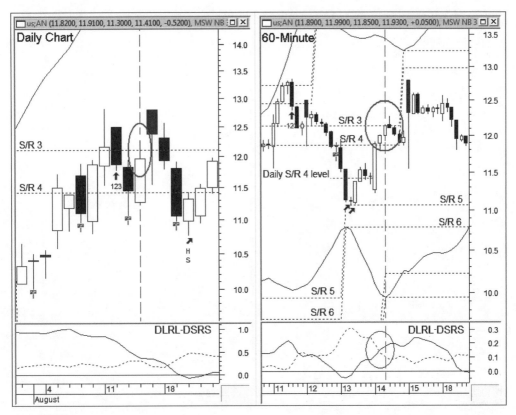

FIGURE 10.9 The daily 1-2-3 trade completes successfully with help from traders in the lesser hourly time frame.

Chart created in MetaStock. Chart uses the MetaSwing Add-on, by Northington Trading, LLC. All rights reserved.

THE WEEKLY 1-2-3

Solid trading also happens at a slower pace. This has as much to do with the dissemination of information and its analysis as it does with anything else. When method setups occur in longer time frames, so too are buyers and sellers inclined to be more careful in their decisions. As a side note, this has much to do with whether many traders succeed or fail. Each of us is mentally wired differently. Trading within a faster time frame requires a temperament that can act decisively in a way that matches the pace of that time frame. The daily schedule that many individual traders must keep prevents a significant amount of analysis time during market hours. Travel schedules and job commitments come first for many individuals.

So, if a slightly slower pace of trading market swings is more your cup of juice, then focus on trading setups that occur in a weekly periodicity. It is not uncommon to watch

FIGURE 10.10 A 1-2-3 method setup develops over three days on this weekly chart of Human Genome Sciences, Inc. (HGSI).

Chart created in MetaStock. Chart uses the MetaSwing Add-on, by Northington Trading, LLC. All rights reserved.

a setup develop across 5 to 20 days before trade entry. It certainly provides more time for the prevention of common errors due to a lack of analysis time. Remember, when it comes to trading, brain activity is much more important than brokerage account activity despite the impression that brokerage firm advertisements tend to promote the opposite.

With all this in mind, let's take a look at a 1-2-3 in a weekly time period. In Figure 10.10, Human Genome Sciences, Inc. (HGSI) signals the beginning of a possible 1-2-3 setup on a weekly chart. The chart as shown depicts the stock price as of the market close on Friday, November 10, 2006. The 1-2-3 signal was first visible two days earlier on November 8. In the previous week, it closed above the S/R 3 line at 13.18 for four days. A disappointing quarterly earnings report, however, put a stop to the optimism. It reached the S/R 4 line at 12.14 by week's end. Remember that a 1-2-3 does not usually show an oversold condition in its present time frame. With that in mind, let's switch to a lower time frame for further analysis.

Figure 10.11 shows how the negative earnings news took its toll on the stock's

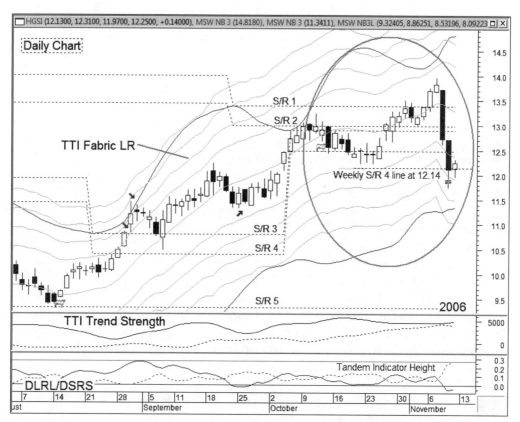

FIGURE 10.11 This same chart of Human Genome Sciences, Inc. (HGSI) shows it at week's end in a daily periodicity.

Chart created in MetaStock. Chart uses the MetaSwing Add-on, by Northington Trading, LLC. All rights reserved.

immediate value. It knocked it down, however, to an interesting technical level. By looking at the daily chart, there are six significant pieces of information that are revealed:

1. Price is now beneath the negative 2 ATR thread of the TTI Fabric LR indicator. Past price history reflects this as an oversold level for HGSI.

2. It has closed right at the weekly S/R 4 line, indicating a positive response to PIV-based support.

3. An Exit Short signal appeared on November 9, indicating definite oversold conditions. It is best, however, to discount this signal somewhat because volatility is likely to be on the rise with a negative earnings report.

4. The DLRL (solid line) indicator is oversold.

5. The DSRS has reached a definite extreme height. See the larger chart version of Figure 10.11 at www.tradingtheinvisible.com to view just how far back this height exceeds itself, and the previous reactions to that level.

6. The TTI Trend Strength is showing mixed results with respect to future trend strength. This means it's best to make this a single swing trade rather than a trend entry point.

This is all good information and points to a promising 1-2-3 trade entry. There's just that nagging problem of the negative fundamental news event. This is yet another reason why we technicians would prefer that U.S.-based corporations would report earnings only twice a year, like European companies do. Wait, why stop there? Make it so that the Federal Reserve is restricted to speaking only twice annually, as well!

Once we wake up from that dream, it is evident that more supporting technical analysis is necessary. We are not restricted to only daily and weekly charts. Two- and three-day charts are often valuable as well. Every additional time frame that confirms a trade builds probabilities in your favor. Note that the same indicators and volatility-based calculations are performed on each chart individually. All calculations, therefore, are free to reach their own individual values. This building of technical consensus just serves to add more traders to the same side of the market.

In Figure 10.12, both two-day and three-day time frames are presented, and like the previous two charts, they reflect prices as of the market close on November 10, 2006. If technical signals are positive in either of these two periods, then the trade would likely be worth entering. Here are the important volatility measurements that surface from these two charts.

- The two-day chart produces an Adeo Long signal. This is very significant because it aligns well with an Exit Short on the daily chart.
- On the two-day chart, the DLRL is showing a solidly oversold situation. The DSRS is reaching an extreme height as well.
- On the two-day chart, price has closed at the negative one thread on the TTI Fabric LR. This means that there is another measure that confirms a relatively oversold condition.
- The TTI Trend Strength indicators on both charts give conflicting readings. They all represent a price to indicator divergence, which does not support a healthy trend to continue for long.
- On the three-day chart, price is resting at the S/R 3 level, which is a more dominant level of PIV than S/R 4.
- On the three-day chart the DLRL is heading down fast and is about to cross the DSRS. The odds of a short-term reversal are much better after these tandem indicators cross.

With the majority of the volatility-based technical analysis pointing to a short-term reversal, this is a valid 1-2-3 trade setup. It is recommended, though, to watch price action for another day or so to see if the previous price decline continues. As stated previously, the weekly analysis period affords us some room for extra patience. It would also be warranted to use a tighter stop than normal for this one. Should the greater trading

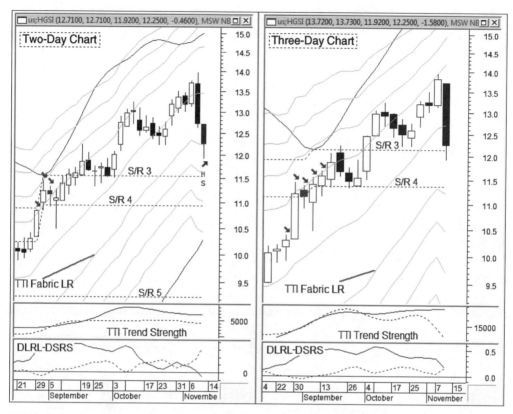

FIGURE 10.12 Two-day and three-day charts provide valid volatility-based signals to support trading the larger weekly time frame.

Chart created in MetaStock. Chart uses the MetaSwing Add-on, by Northington Trading, LLC. All rights reserved.

crowd smell a support failure, there is plenty of area in which price can fall through before the next support level.

Figure 10.13 shows us how Human Genome Sciences completed this 1-2-3 trade. The daily chart is used for additional clarity. The weekly S/R 3 and S/R 4 lines have been added and are notated. As suggested, watching the intraday price action on November 14 proves to be an added level of insurance against a downward continuation. The entry and exit days are marked with dashed lines. An entry and exit at the S/R lines yields an 8.6 percent profit. A more careful approach might enter at the close on November 14 at 12.28, yielding a 7.3 percent profit.

By week's end, the DLRL and DSRS have crossed and price has reached the weekly S/R 3 line. All of our multi-time frame analysis pointed to a short-term trade. Three individual factors derived from the analysis in Figures 10.11 and 10.12 inform us that the odds do not favor a successful longer-term position. They are:

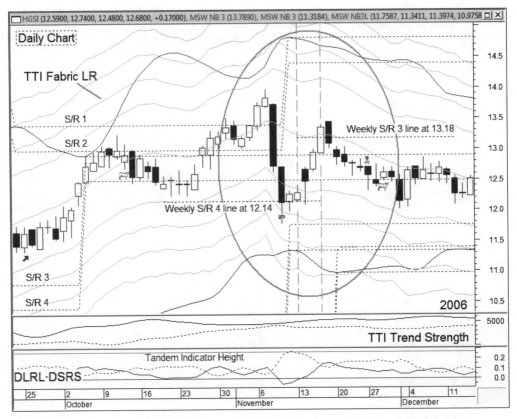

FIGURE 10.13   The weekly 1-2-3 trade is completed here on this daily chart of Human Genome Sciences, Inc. (HGSI). The weekly S/R lines are manually added for clarity.

Chart created in MetaStock. Chart uses the MetaSwing Add-on, by Northington Trading, LLC. All rights reserved.

1. The TTI Trend Strength indicator shows mixed-to-negative signals throughout the different time frames.
2. The price action on the daily charts shows a price failure below the S/R 4 line. Remember that healthy trends find support, not failure, at these levels.
3. The negative market reaction to the HGSI quarterly earnings report can have a significant impact on the end of the stock's current rally.

Our original analysis and subsequent trading plan, therefore, call for an exit at the default location on the weekly chart in Figure 10.13, which is the S/R 3 line. This trade's duration was four or five days, depending on your trade management tactics. That's a little less than most weekly 1-2-3 trades. This particular example is chosen because it is not a picture-perfect trade that sees price continuing upward with optimism and a rosy future. It is shown because it is typical. The market gives no guarantees. Indeed, a proper exit by the book in this case prevents a stop loss, and the needless time usage of capital. It profits because of the increased probabilities inherent in the 1-2-3 trade structure and because of the volatility-based trade probabilities in lower time frames.

THE 1-2-3: INSIDE AND OUTSIDE

Let's take this opportunity to think outside the box; actually, outside the rectangle. As I stated previously, trading inside of rectangles is not a commonly accepted practice among the greater population of technicians. This is mostly due to the perception that most potential rectangles experience too many pattern failures. That is to say they fail to turn into rectangles. It is further accepted that those that complete the pattern are unpredictable once the technical definition of a rectangle is met. Remember that a rectangle establishes itself by reversing up and down at least twice from the same price zone. See Figure 10.1 for a visual review of the pattern. It's the actual highs and lows of the reversals that define the upper boundary, the resistance line, and the lower boundary, the support line. I suppose you could adapt the old chicken-and-egg question to say, "Which came first, the rectangle or the rectangle?" But what if the rectangle's boundaries already exist before the price action?

That's a bit like the artist's belief that the sculpture is preexisting inside the block of marble. For most of us it is just a hunk of stone. For the artist who possesses the skill and vision, it is a masterpiece in waiting. And so the rectangle is there for us before it forms because we possess Projected Implied Volatility (PIV). PIV gives us the S/R lines that we can see days and weeks in advance. It is not necessary to wait for the rectangle formation to play out with PIV-based S/R lines.

Are we then technically correct in using the term *rectangle* when trading 1-2-3 method setups? Many experienced chartists reading this are shouting, "NO!" right now. I believe it is really just a matter of perception and success. After all, success tends to change perception, doesn't it?

To illustrate what's been described here, we will take an extended stroll down the same path that a stock price takes for a few months. Potential rectangle opportunities will be presented with options laid before you. Differing from our previous examples will be the opportunity to trade the outside of the 1-2-3.

Almost Rectangles

We begin with an examination of Figure 10.14. In it is a daily chart of Sealed Air Corporation (SEE) as it traded through the summer of 2008. In circled area 1, price declines to find support at the S/R 6 line only to experience a one-day reversal to resistance at the S/R 5 line. The trend direction stays intact when price slides down to the S/R 6 line. It is at this second crossing of the S/R 6 line that the potential rectangle pattern fails to set up. That was simple enough.

How about circled area 2; what happened there? It would appear that it is just more

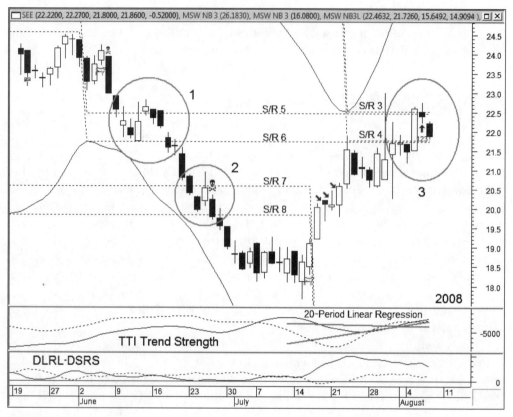

FIGURE 10.14 A series of potential rectangle patterns occur in this daily chart of Sealed Air Corporation (SEE).

Chart created in MetaStock. Chart uses the MetaSwing Add-on, by Northington Trading, LLC. All rights reserved.

of the same. Price stops its decrease just above the S/R 8 line and reverses upward to close at the S/R 7 line on June 25. The real question should be, "Is there a potential trade there?" Let's take a look.

If you drop your vantage point down to the hourly chart, an entirely different world seems to present itself. In the chart in Figure 10.15, we have zoomed in on the last week in June 2008. Manually plotted and notated on this 60-minute chart are the S/R 7 and S/R 8 lines from the daily chart in Figure 10.14. Indeed, on June 25 price does reverse and rises to an Adeo short state. The hourly Adeo signal occurs right at the S/R 8 line, which is lowest resistance line for this time frame.

The answer to the question posed two paragraphs earlier is yes. A combination of circumstances observable in Figure 10.15 has colluded to produce this yes answer. These four factors are:

1. The prevailing intermediate trend is down. In a short-term time duration, it is the desired trading direction until it ends.

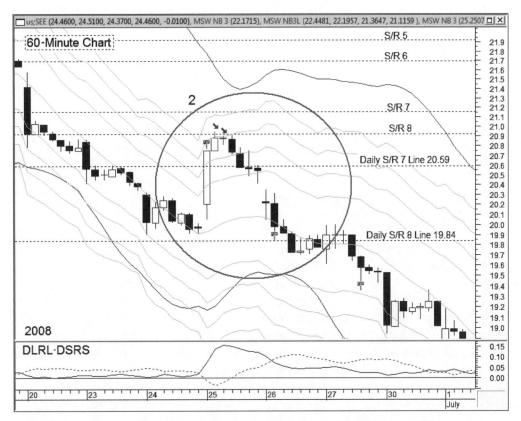

FIGURE 10.15 An hourly chart of Sealed Air Corporation (SEE) shows in detail the potential play to enter the existing trend.

Chart created in MetaStock. Chart uses the MetaSwing Add-on, by Northington Trading, LLC. All rights reserved.

2. Price has a statistical tendency to ricochet between daily S/R lines.

3. A promising Adeo short trade sets up well at the S/R 8 resistance line in the hourly time frame.

4. The height of the opposing tandem component, the DLRL (solid line), is very high.

It is important to note that this particular trade requires the attention of an active trader. By that I mean someone who watches intraday price action carefully. Also, the next trading day produced a Total Correction event for the broad market. Price gapped down at the open and did not look back for two weeks. This is really a stroke of pure luck for the short side participant. It is yet another example of why it is best to trade the broad market intermediate direction until it ends.

If the broader market had not behaved that way on the following day, however, then the situation could have been very different. Note that in Figure 10.14, Sealed Air Corporation has reached an oversold condition when it closed on June 24, right on top of the S/R 8 line. It could have reversed at that point and traded all the way up to the

S/R 6 level. The point here is to trade only intraday S/R line bounces if you have the ability to monitor intraday conditions. A quick stop order in this case might have been needed on June 26.

A 1-2-3 Inside

Referring again to Figure 10.14, let's fast forward to the right side of the chart and examine the opportunity that is before us. By this point, Sealed Air has seen its lows and risen back up to S/R 6 and then S/R 5, only to close briefly above it. Simultaneously, new S/R 3 and S/R 4 lines have formed practically right on top of the S/R 5 and S/R 6 lines. With a close above S/R 3 and then a close below it, the criteria for a 1-2-3 have been met. Also note that a 20-period linear regression analysis of the TTI Trend Strength indicator shows a mixed situation. One of the pair has a slightly negative slope while the other is strongly positive. Overall, the trend strength has been rising.

Right now you are probably wondering if there is any technical significance to the phenomenon of lines forming at or close to each other. While Northington Trading has not done formal research on it and can't say that there is, it only stands to reason that it certainly could increase the strength of support and resistance at those prices, even if only a small amount. The topic is worthy of future study, though.

Look at Figure 10.16 to delve deeper into this 1-2-3 setup. This 60-minute chart certainly gives us greater detail of the technical conditions of the lesser time frame. The two relevant daily S/R lines have been manually plotted for clarity. The larger circled area 3 corresponds to the same number and area in Figure 10.14. The question before us now is a simple one: "Will price bounce off the daily S/R 4 line and rise back up to the daily S/R 5 line?"

Upon examining the 60-minute chart in Figure 10.16, several pieces of volatility-based technical analysis suggest a long trade entry. They are:

1. In the closing hour of the trading day on August 7, MetaSwing calculates an Exit Short, at the same time closing just above the daily S/R 4 line. As you will learn in a coming chapter, that means the likelihood of reversal, or a pause in the current trading direction, has just begun to exceed 50 percent.

2. The DLRL indicator is showing an oversold condition.

3. The DSRS indicator has good height. This means that recent volatility confirms the DLRL oversold reading.

4. The low of the last price candle reversed at the negative one thread of the TTI Fabric LR indicator, which is two ATR values below the 40-period linear regression line. This is a confirming oversold condition.

These technical factors are compelling. Also significant is that the recent price trend appears strong. Based on this batch of multi-time frame analysis, the decision should be to place a limit order at the daily S/R 4 line, which is 21.76. An alternate entry point

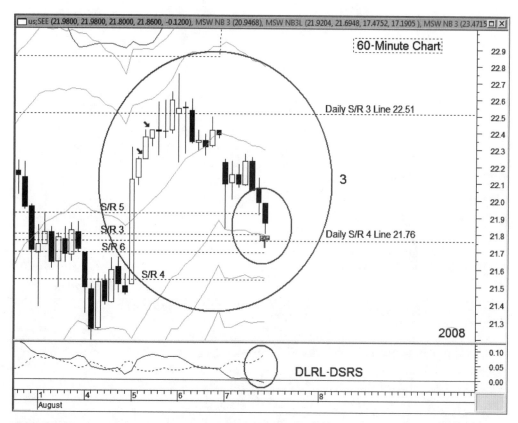

FIGURE 10.16 Another 60-minute chart of Sealed Air Corporation (SEE) gives us the important volatility characteristics needed to confirm a 1-2-3 long trade entry.

Chart created in MetaStock. Chart uses the MetaSwing Add-on, by Northington Trading, LLC. All rights reserved.

would be the hourly S/R 4 price at 21.53. It's also worth noting that I frequently add a few cents to a 1-2-3 long entry limit order. The larger players with volatility-based quantitative analysis resources often watch these levels and cause price to stop just short of the target.

So how does our trade entry decision work out? Let's continue down the path of Sealed Air's price action for a number of days. See the daily chart in Figure 10.17. It's plain to see that the short-term trend did continue. Actually, the S/R 3 and S/R 4 levels were used as resistance and support for several weeks. Sealed Air opened just beneath the 21.76 support line on August 8 and traded up rapidly. This is a very common price activity for 1-2-3 trades.

The 60-minute chart in Figure 10.18 gives us a couple of options for managing the trade. Because this is a 1-2-3, the odds favor price reaching the daily S/R 3 level. The question every trader asks at that point is, "Can I make more profit if I hold my position?" By examining circled area 1 on the chart, it is plain to see that price paused for an hour

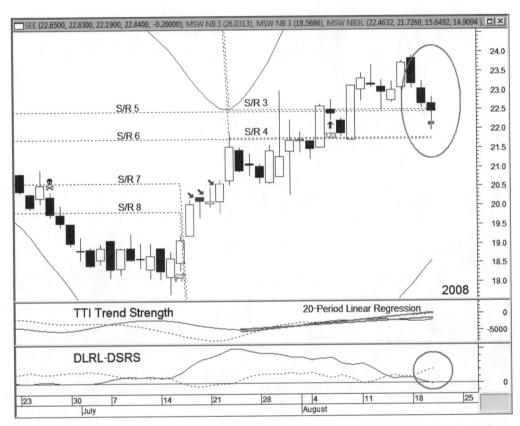

FIGURE 10.17 The chart of Sealed Air Corporation continues its short-term rally using S/R lines like steps on a staircase, leading to yet another trading opportunity.

Chart created in MetaStock. Chart uses the MetaSwing Add-on, by Northington Trading, LLC. All rights reserved.

at the daily S/R 3 line exactly. Without question, many other traders were asking themselves the same question.

By the second hour of trading on August 8, the primary oversold and overbought indicators had not yet crossed, referring to the DLRL-DSRS in the lower indicator pane. There really is no right or wrong answer at this point. In this case, price did continue to rally after the pause at resistance. As you can see in Figure 10.18, price continued to rise while pausing at the hourly S/R resistance lines. There was no truly oversold condition in the two days that followed in the hourly time frame.

The daily chart, however, tells a different story. In Figure 10.17, an overbought condition is reached on day two of the trade, which is August 11. The DSRS (dotted line) closes below the zero line. That is a signal to exit a 1-2-3. Don't try to make trading like reading tea leaves; just let the mathematical signals of the appropriate time frames point the way for you.

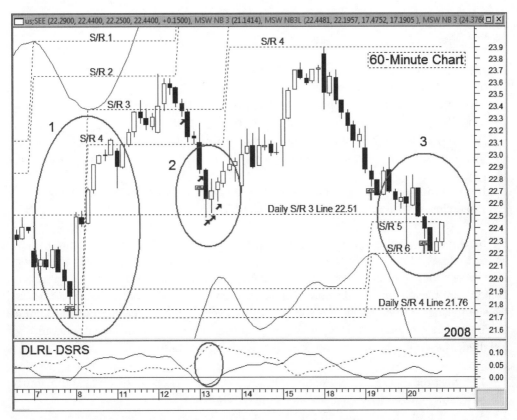

FIGURE 10.18 The 60-minute chart of Sealed Air Corporation continues to show how price plays pinball between S/R lines until a 1-2-3 outside trade reaches a point of opportunity.

Chart created in MetaStock. Chart uses the MetaSwing Add-on, by Northington Trading, LLC. All rights reserved.

A 1-2-3 Outside

With the risk of sounding like the most common of infomercials, I have to say, "But wait, there's more!" (I can just envision the legendary Ron Popeil telling you that with the Ronco Trade-O-Matic, which includes the 1-2-3 trade, you also get the 1-2-3 outside trade setup; operators are standing by!) It's true for no other reason than that rectangles just behave that way. This is also true of rectangles because of the basic nature of support and resistance.

Identifying a potentially developing trend and then entering at the point of a rectangle's exterior is the setup we should be pursuing any chance we get. The 1-2-3 method routinely offers this. Our current example with Sealed Air Corporation (SEE) leads us right to a typical one. We are naming this setup a 1-2-3 Outside because it occurs outside of the potential rectangle previously identified by the S/R lines and the 1-2-3 signal.

In Figure 10.17, the chart's right side ends with a 1-2-3 outside setup in a daily time frame. Is this opportunity worth putting on a long trade? Perhaps because of the following factors:

- An Exit Short signal is present at the close of the most recent trading day.
- The DLRL is reading oversold.
- The DSRS is at its highest point over the previous three months.
- Visually, the trend direction is up in a moderately strong rally.
- A 20-day linear regression analysis of each TTI Trend Strength indicator shows a positive slope. Also, each indicator is at its highest point since the current price rally began.
- Intraday price action on August 13 tested the S/R 3 support level and reversed.
- Price closed virtually at the support of the S/R 3 and S/R 5 lines.

Now let's put some more ammunition in the gun by looking at the next time frame lower. Figure 10.18 shows us the recent hourly price activity for Sealed Air Corporation. First, take a look at circled area 2, which highlights the intraday price reversal on August 13 at the daily S/R 3 line. What a beautiful trade, had you been looking for it. Nevertheless, the significance of the precision involved with a reversal right at the support line should not be taken for granted. That, along with these other technical signals, should be weighed when considering the 1-2-3 outside trade that is before us.

- The most recent activity on August 20 shows another precision reversal at the hourly S/R 6 line, and a close virtually at the daily S/R 3 line.
- A recent Exit Short signal on the current intraday price candles is shown.
- The DLRL (solid line) indicator shows an extended oversold condition.
- On August 19, the DSRS tandem component was at an extreme height, almost equivalent to its own reading at the most recent reversal on August 13. This extreme volatility reading, however, did not result in a reversal. Price, instead, proceeded to drop below the daily S/R 3 line. This is a potential sign of weakness.
- Intraday price action produced progressively higher highs on August 12 and 23.
- The reversal at the daily S/R 3 line on August 13 is an indication of support strength.

The questions most commonly going through the trader's mind at this point concern the location of the potential reversal. Will price reverse here? Will it decline to the daily S/R 4 line and find support there? Is the penetration of the daily S/R 3 line a failure on a larger scale?

It is completely logical at this point to have doubts about an entry point. There should be no doubt, however, as to which side of the market to be on. A long position should be taken. Virtually all of our analysis in both time frames points to a trend continuation.

Based on that decision, an entry at the lower support line and an entry above the high of August 20 are both logical. Potentially, the best alternative is to place a one-

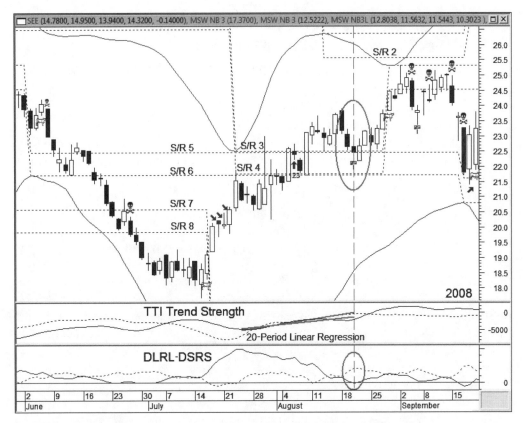

FIGURE 10.19   Here we can see the full outcome of the 1-2-3 outside trade.

Chart created in MetaStock. Chart uses the MetaSwing Add-on, by Northington Trading, LLC. All rights reserved.

cancels-all (OCA) limit order. Should price trade at or below the daily S/R 4 line, one limit order would execute. Alternatively, should price trade above the previous day's high and thus confirm a reversal, then a limit order at 22.85 would execute. The first order to execute automatically cancels the other.

In Figure 10.19, the daily chart of Sealed Air Corporation's two-month-long rally shows clearly the outcome of the 1-2-3 outside trade. Price did indeed reverse and continue the uptrend. The way it ducked under the S/R 3 line turned out to be a common fake.

An appropriate exit for a swing trade would likely be best when the DLRL-DSRS indicator pair cross on August 28. Price also rose on that day to within one ATR distance of the upper N Band, which will begin to present resistance. The upper N Band was at 25.81 and the ATR(40) value was .80. The high on August 28 was 24.51; that's exactly .80, one ATR value, beneath the upper N Band. Also note that N Band starts to rise on the next day, August 29. This means that the N Band value on August 28 is likely to be

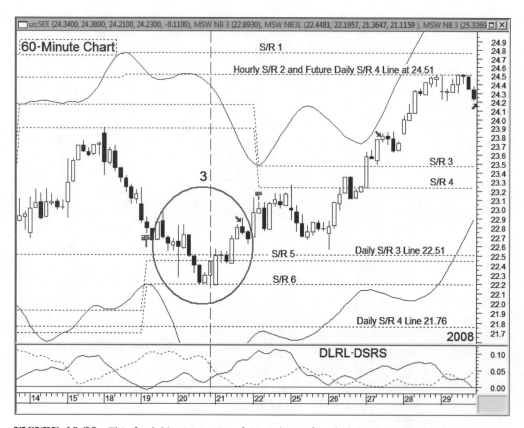

us;SEE (24.3400, 24.3800, 24.2100, 24.2300, -0.1100), MSW NB 3 (22.8930), MSW NB3L (22.4481, 22.1957, 21.3647, 21.1159), MSW NB 3 (25.3269 □|X|

FIGURE 10.20 This final 60-minute time frame chart of Sealed Air Corporation shows how price continues its trend and finds significant resistance when the hourly S/R 2 level corresponds exactly with the formation of the future daily S/R 4 line.

Chart created in MetaStock. Chart uses the MetaSwing Add-on, by Northington Trading, LLC. All rights reserved.

the trough point going forward. Once the band moves up by the default 3 percent, then the new S/R 4 will form there.

It may seem that I am splitting hairs by giving such a high level of detail and focus to how these daily and hourly resistance points are lining up so closely. These alignments, however, can be very important when you are looking for optimum entry and exit points. It also gives the analyst a degree of confirmation that the trading action is currently being dominated by technical analysis in lieu of fundamental forces.

Look closely at Figure 10.20 for a fun example of this phenomenon. Examine the price action on the last two trading days, August 28 and 29. The S/R 2 line is notated that it is also the future daily S/R 4 level. This is because of the daily N Band turning up on August 28. On these two days, price rises to this resistance and halts on both days. Indeed, the volatility-based technicians have been the driving force for this stock's movement for the previous six weeks.

AS SIMPLE AS 1-2-3

Rectangle patterns seem to establish support and resistance levels. In truth, PIV-based S/R lines preestablish the levels before the rectangle forms or fails. The 1-2-3 method exploits this projected identification of support and resistance. Imagine if you were playing an actual game of pinball with invisible mechanized boundaries and targets. That would be a very short game. Without the ability to see the support and resistance levels on the chart, rectangle formations can only exist in your rearview mirror. With the capability to project the high probability turning points, however, you are then able to trade the inside of the rectangle, or should we say, the potential rectangle.

Multi-time frame analysis based on volatility measurement greatly improves your success probabilities. If you use it consistently, the hidden levels upon which trends climb or descend become visible. Be vigilant in looking for other teams of traders within those time durations. The 1-2-3 method and PIV-based S/R lines within the different time frames can position you for the more significant stairsteps of a trend.

Should we think of S/R lines as rectangles even before the formation of the actual pattern, as it is traditionally defined? Today's pattern trader would likely say no because it is not what it is not, until it is. If a sculptor were also a trader, she would say yes because she sees the masterpiece inside the block of stone, even before her chisel touches it. In a way, this difference of opinion seems almost philosophical. Perhaps the question each trader must answer for herself should be "Which philosophy makes the most money for me?"

CHAPTER 11

Hidden Momentum with Adeo High Slope

Have you ever lost something around your home and repeatedly conducted searching expeditions to find it? Days may go by without sight of the item you are looking for. You physically lay eyes on every square inch of your house over and over again. It has vanished. Its molecules have obviously physically disintegrated into the space-time continuum. That is the only possible explanation because if it were there, you would have found it.

A short time later, once the search has stopped and the possession has been written off, it reappears. There it sits in an obvious location. Why wasn't it found before? Perhaps you just weren't looking for it. Put another way, maybe your brain did not recognize it when your eyes saw it because your brain said it should not, or could not, be in that spot.

Does momentum hide from us? Is it lurking behind random events on the price chart in cryptic ways? Or does momentum hide right out in plain sight? Do our eyes pass right over it without due recognition?

The importance of measuring price momentum can be an all-consuming activity for some traders and analysts, in that they search and search for ways to identify it. An advanced momentum indicator design can make a significant difference in many forms of trading; indeed, we have devoted a sizable amount of this book to just such advancements.

I answer these questions in this chapter by identifying one approach that differs from most forms of momentum identification. We will also make progress toward quantifying its effects. I can tell you that it does hide in plain sight and has nothing to do with the space-time continuum, although it would be really cool if it did.

WE ARE EXPERIENCING TECHNICAL DIFFICULTIES; PLEASE STAND BY

To truly appreciate the methods in this chapter, it's best to briefly revisit the concepts of *momentum*, *slope*, and *aspect ratio*. This is necessary because of all the wonderful technology advancements in the field of computerized stock charting. The computer programs that we use for charting and technical analysis have actually made part of our visual comprehension quite blind. They have advanced our capabilities technologically, but in one area they have functionally set us back. How can this be? Aren't we much better off with such monumental amounts of math crunching power at our fingertips? Mostly yes, but appearances are often misleading.

In technical analysis, *momentum* describes the rate at which prices are changing. More specifically, we are usually examining increases and decreases in the rate of price change. Think of it in terms of acceleration and deceleration. More visible momentum indicators are used on charts to make subtle amounts of change in acceleration and deceleration. The MACD, ROC (Rate-of-Change calculation), and TTI Trend Strength are all indicators capable of measuring momentum.

When mathematically describing the change between two points, it is very helpful to use the calculation of *slope*. If you recall some of your time in math class, when you were awake and paying attention, slope is the ratio of rise divided by run. In charting, the Y-axis sits at the right of the chart and usually expresses price. The X-axis sits at the bottom of the chart and expresses time. Slope, therefore, expresses the amount of rise (Y-axis) that occurs for one unit of X-axis. Mathematically, this is very simple, but visually, it is often very difficult.

At this point you might be saying that you can visually recognize a 45-degree slope angle quite accurately; therefore it is not difficult at all. Maybe you built a deck in the backyard and it turned out straight. Not so fast. Today's charting software automatically adjusts the X-axis and Y-axis of every chart to fit the physical dimension of your computer's application window. When you switch from one stock chart to the next, a change in the price grid, the Y-axis, is made automatically. Even if you make no changes to the chart's time duration, the X-axis, the visually appearing slopes of anything plotted in the chart's price pane are skewed because of the change in the price grid's span.

Now enter the problem of a consistent price range for the Y-axis. I mean by this that each dollar increment is used as the basis unit value of one for the rise part of the equation. This forces differently weighted measurements for a stock that is priced at $10 from one priced at $90. This alone makes it mathematically impossible to compute an accurate slope value based on an angle, expressed in degrees, for a stock chart. Therefore, from chart to chart, there is no consistent reference of slope.

Before computers and charting software, traders manually created charts themselves on special grid paper. That had to be somewhat grueling. At least the price slope was more static because of the fixed X-axis.

Think of the problem just described as being akin to the measurement of *aspect ratio* in the field of video and motion picture presentation. The older standard definition for video is an X:Y ratio of 4:3 or 1.33:1. The motion picture standard has always been 1.85:1, thus providing a wider screen image. When a feature film was adapted to the standard video ratio of 4:3 it was too wide, and some of each side consequently had to be lopped off. Nothing of that sort happens to your stock chart. Losing data would certainly be a disservice to you. As a trade-off, the charting program adjusts the functional aspect ratio of the chart by stretching or contracting the X-axis and Y-axis, never conforming to any fixed dimensions.

Without the consistent presentation of a fixed aspect ratio and a uniformity of the price axis in a stock chart:

- Your ability to gauge an accurate relative slope measurement is deteriorated.
- A trending stock may look strong when it is not, or may look weak when it is strong.
- The slopes of any nonhorizontal indicator lines in the price pane or indicator panes are inconsistent and distorted.

Math class in this chapter is now finished. But the effects of these challenges must be dealt with. The reason is because extreme slope recognition is the key to finding hidden momentum.

Examine Figure 11.1 casually at first. It presents two daily partial MetaSwing charts, of different listed issues. Both are experiencing a trending rally. The initial visual observation seems to indicate that each is experiencing about the same rate of price increase, or slope.

Now look at the charts in Figure 11.1 more carefully. Examine the price axis of each, and look closely at the time durations on each X-axis. In the lower indicator pane is a MetaSwing indicator that measures the slope of the closing price across a seven-trading-period lookback and returns a number expressed in degrees. This indicator compensates for Y-axis inconsistencies and provides a relatively stable, and repeatable, slope measurement. We refer to its output in degrees, although with the knowledge that these degrees are not correct with respect to trigonometry, but are repeatable. It oscillates around a zero line so that it can show positive and negative numbers for up-and-down price directions. The upper and lower threshold lines are at 45 degrees and −45 degrees, respectively. The two price plots are in reality moving at dramatically different slopes, or rates of momentum. Here's what can be observed with this chart comparison:

- The intensity of their price advances visually seems similar.
- Eaton (ETN) at right shows a low of 58.82 to a high of 68.25. This is an increase of 16 percent.
- Nvidia Corporation (NVDA) at left shows a low of 7.55 to a high of 18.66. This is an increase of 147 percent.
- For Eaton (ETN) at right, the slope indicator at the bottom has a maximum reading of 33 degrees; see the small circled area.
- For Nvidia Corporation (NVDA) at left, the slope indicator at the bottom has a maximum reading of 75 degrees; see the small circled area.

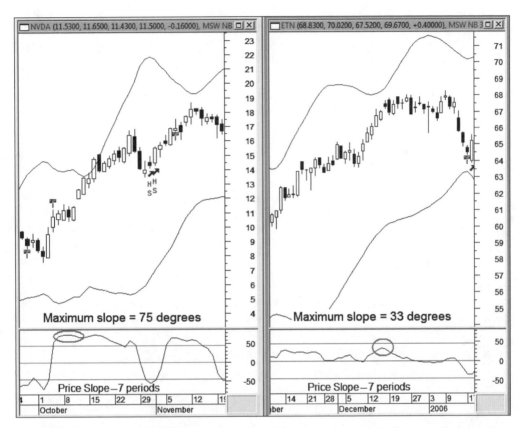

FIGURE 11.1 The visual illusion of price slope: They appear the same but actually have slopes that differ greatly.

Chart created in MetaStock. Chart uses the MetaSwing Add-on, by Northington Trading, LLC. All rights reserved.

After examining both charts carefully, I would much rather be participating in the Nvidia trend shown at the left. Even though both stocks appear to be on strong trends, their slopes are dramatically different. The 75-degree slope does not visually seem all that different from the 33-degree slope. Can momentum hide from us? You bet it can.

The point of this little exercise is to show that our eyes are easily deceived when reviewing charts. Actual slope intensity needs to be calculated, and not eyeballed. Always have the software perform slope measurement mathematics. It is best for you as a trader to stick with analysis. Lastly, never underestimate the power of the slope.

MOMENTUM HIDE AND GO SEEK

Again we ask: does price momentum hide from us? Yes it does, but not where you think. So far we've confined our discussion of momentum to the challenge of recognizing the

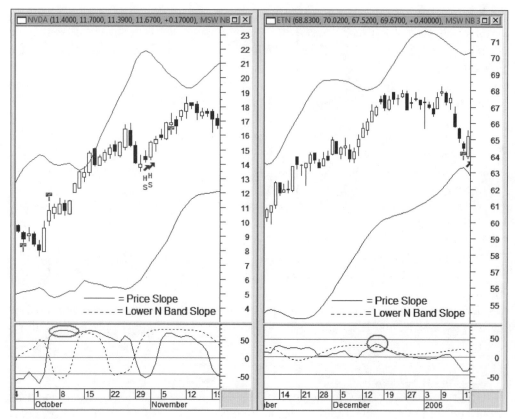

FIGURE 11.2   These charts show the addition of an indicator that measures the true slope of the lower N Band. They seem to have visually similar slopes but actually do not.

Chart created in MetaStock. Chart uses the MetaSwing Add-on, by Northington Trading, LLC. All rights reserved.

true slope of closing prices accurately. We must focus on a different aspect of price to find the most overlooked hidden momentum.

Here's the answer. Momentum hides in the movement of implied volatility. A good recent view of implied volatility is where we should measure momentum on the stock chart. The simplest direct gauge of this is to use a true slope indication of the N Band. Because implied volatility in its primary form exists as a dynamic matrix of percentages produced by option valuation models, it is difficult to identify as a single value. The N Band well represents a consolidation of its most critical levels. It does so in the immediate time frame as direct support and resistance, and in the future as Projected Implied Volatility (PIV), quantified by S/R lines. Significantly high levels of N Band slope, therefore, contain hidden price momentum. Another way to express this is that significantly high levels of N Band slope contain the energy for *potential* price movement.

We see the same chart in Figure 11.2 as shown in Figure 11.1, with one exception. The lower N Band slope measurement is added here. The chart of Nvidia (NVDA) experiences a more significant price advance because its lower N Band slope is much steeper than that of Eaton (ETN). In fact, on October 30, 2001, the lower N Band slope is almost twice as steep. This measurement is indicative of larger amounts of hidden momentum.

The following are the volatility dynamics at work, which result in hidden momentum.

- As the lower N Band *rises*, the more immediate downside volatility for a stock *decreases* in that time frame. Thus, the perceived probability of the stock's price to fall decreases, and the perceived probability for the stock's price to rise increases.
- As the lower N Band *falls*, the more immediate downside volatility for a stock *increases* in that time frame. Thus, the perceived probability of the stock's price to fall increases, and the perceived probability for the stock's price to rise decreases.
- As the lower N Band *rises*, the future potential for downside PIV for a stock *decreases* in that time frame. Thus, the perceived probability of the stock's price to decline is also decreased.
- As the lower N Band *falls*, the future potential for downside PIV for a stock *increases* in that time frame. Thus, the perceived probability of the stock's price to decline is increased.
- The same tendencies occur in an inverse manner for the upper N Band.

This theoretical stored price momentum has its roots in logic. It can be best described somewhat anecdotally. Consider that a stock's closing price is sitting evenly between the upper and lower N Bands. The upper N Band stays at the same value over the next few periods. The lower N Band rises in each of those same periods. Price declines over the same few periods. This means that price and the lower N Band are moving toward each other. Since the lower N Band represents immediate support and is rising to meet price, then a long trade entry begins to show a higher success probability because support (lower N Band) is nearer and resistance (upper N Band) is further away.

The analyst's interpretation of this situation is that upside volatility is now greater than downside volatility; and indeed, it is. With all other things being equal, as long as the downside implied volatility is being reduced at a greater rate than the upside volatility, then these conditions favor greater short-term trade success on the long side versus the short side.

Focusing too intensely on simple price movement can lull the analyst's judgment. Remember that "volatility cycles even when price does not."[1] If you are really having trouble sleeping and want to dive deeply into the reasons why this is so, then research the mathematical models of ARCH (autoregressive conditional heteroskedasticity) and GARCH (generalized autoregressive conditional heteroskedasticity). Just the names of these models can induce a yawn.

So how can we be more secure in believing that a rapidly rising N Band improves the probabilities for a rising price? Certainly a handful of examples can be found that support virtually any theory, good or bad. How can we feel confident that these slope measurements will identify additional hidden momentum?

You may recall that in Chapter 7 we conducted some primary research to identify the effectiveness of some traditional Japanese candlestick reversal patterns; see Table 7.1. We have conducted the exact same number crunching to quantify this slope-based hidden price momentum, but have adapted it to detect a different technical signal. We focused in Chapter 9 on the art of the Adeo. We are exploring in this chapter the Adeo under high slope conditions. By *high slope*, I am referring to the slope of the lower N Band.

For the designation of a high slope condition, MetaSwing uses the arbitrary level of 45 degrees. The technical description of the Adeo high slope, therefore, is an Adeo condition that occurs while the lower N Band's slope is greater than 45 degrees. The combination of these two volatility-based measurements is the minimum beginning requirement that can flag the technician to examine the chart for hidden momentum.

The objectives of our analysis are to answer these questions:

1. For the Adeo signal, how do the potential profits weigh against the potential losses, within a given trading time window, in a high slope environment compared to when a high slope does not exist?

2. How does the existence of the high slope condition perform relative to the broader market within the same given trading time window? In other words, does the high slope condition outperform the broader market?

3. How frequently does the high slope requirement occur with Adeo signals?

For the study featured in Chapter 7, Table 7.1 showed a nine-point list explaining the method used as well as the market and time duration details. This study uses the exact same method and time duration. The periodicity is daily, with the duration being for 2,000 trading days, beginning on June 29, 2000, and ending on June 13, 2008—approximately eight years.

The only thing that has changed is the signal selection criteria. We are focusing in this study on the effects of the high N Band slope factor while an Adeo condition exists. Two sets of data are consequently presented, with each containing an Adeo long signal present. The differentiating technical measurement is that the high slope set occurs when the lower N Band slope is equal to or greater than 45 degrees, and the no-high-slope set occurs when the lower N Band slope is less than 45 degrees. Based on these criteria, the two data sets are mutually exclusive.

The MetaStock code used in the Exploration feature for this data finding is available at the companion web site for this book, www.tradingtheinvisible.com. There, among the support content for this chapter, you will find an Excel spreadsheet file for each signal tested. Each has all of the code and the full numerical contents of the exploration results.

The results of our high slope research can be found in Figure 11.3. The outcome of

Test Event	Total Instances	Profit Potential	Loss Potential	Forward Duration
1 With High Slope				
Adeo	2316	9.0%	−6.3%	10 Days
S&P 500	2316	2.9%	1.6%	10 Days
Adeo	2316	6.1%	−4.4%	5 Days
S&P 500	2316	2.1%	0.6%	5 Days
2 Without High Slope				
Adeo	21632	5.3%	−4.9%	10 Days
S&P 500	21632	2.5%	1.2%	10 Days
Adeo	21632	3.9%	−3.3%	5 Days
S&P 500	21632	1.8%	0.4%	5 Days
3 Effective Comparison				
Adeo: greater increase in profit than loss		69.5%	28.7%	10 Days
S&P: profitability improves overall		18.2%	34.3%	10 Days
Adeo: greater increase in profit than loss		56.9%	32.5%	5 Days
S&P: profitability improves overall		15.6%	48.6%	5 Days

FIGURE 11.3 Analysis results for the comparison of the Adeo in a high slope condition and the Adeo without a high slope reading.

this study is very revealing with respect to the effects of hidden momentum within slope intensity. In area one of Figure 11.3, the profit potential and loss potential for high slope conditions are shown. Once again, this study uses the trade durations of 5 and 10 days. In section two, the same performances are measured when the lower N Band slope is less than 45 degrees.

Section three lists the performance percentage changes between the different data sets, based on the presence of the high slope criteria. To add clarity to the numerical relationship of each section, the top lines are boxed and connected with lines. The same relationship exists for each data line, respectively. Note that the results in area three are calculated from the actual study results, which are real numbers accurate to 12 floating digits. The results listed in areas two and three have been rounded.

What do these results really mean? In plain English, here's how they affect trading:

- When the lower N Band has a high slope condition, the average Adeo potential trade profit increases from 5.3 percent to 9.0 percent. That's a 69.5 percent increase. During the same trades the average potential trade loss experiences only a 28.7 percent increase.
- The largest implication of this study is that the potential profit increases two and a half times more than the potential loss: 69.5 percent versus 28.7 percent. That means that the increase in profit is not just due to volatility magnification. It strongly supports that there is genuine value to the high slope measurement.
- A similar relationship occurs during the Adeo five-day duration as shown on line 3 of area three.
- Overall, the positive change in profit potential to loss potential is greater when the time duration moves further out from 5 days to 10 days. This means that the hidden momentum is more than simply short-term fluctuations.
- The second most important implication is that the overall change of the broad market during high slope Adeo signals becomes even more favorable. The profit potential increases by 15.6 percent and 18.2 percent for 5-day and 10-day durations, respectively. Meanwhile, the loss potential of the entire body of S&P 500 stocks actually decreases.

The bottom line here points to a win-win proposition of volatility analysis. The change in performance between the two groups is due to high N Band slope because:

- The disproportionate increase in profit to loss improves the successful trade probability.
- The broad market conditions improve because the potential profit increases and the potential loss decreases. This, therefore, improves the risk profile of any individual trade.

I challenge you to find a section of text in some other body of work that compels you to read the words *increase* and *decrease* as often as you see them in this chapter. If you are going to do trading methodology and system development, this is the thought process you will experience. Every change you make to a trading decision process has positive and negative implications. Weighing the positives and negatives against each other is a never-ending trek.

There is one other important numerical finding in this study's results, which we discussed in Chapter 7. The size of the sample for a high slope condition is much smaller than the sample without a high slope. At 2,316, the high slope condition is 11 percent, and the size of the non-high-slope sample is 21,613. It is a reality that as markets become more efficient, then strategies that exploit inefficiencies are less numerous. The question then becomes one of practicality; does the inefficient condition happen frequently enough to be realistically exploited?

In this case, it does. The high slope condition is a derivative of price movement. It is a component that can be applied to many different technical trading methods. It is not confined to Adeo trades only. For instance, it could be combined with an extreme reading on the TTI Composite indicator, while price is at a support level, to make a long trade setup. In this way, the high slope measurement is not restricted to a small quantity of trade setups and methods. Think of it as an ingredient in a soup recipe such as cayenne pepper. We look at more on that thought a bit later in this chapter. For now, let's descend from the orderly world of the theoretical to the messy, noisy conditions found in the real world.

MOMENTUM FOUND

Illuminating the invisible and exploiting it with volatility measurement is a central theme of this book. As a general rule, you can accomplish this by using the component framework to build technical structure into the chart. In same way a master builder lays a foundation and constructs the frame of a house, you can create mathematical measurements with predictive value. Using N Band slope embodies this practical application. It adds meaning to a mathematical form of physical structure plotted on the chart. It is messier, as always, when applying the techniques to an actual trade.

When you are picking out those beautiful new tires in the showroom, they look perfect. But as the saying goes, "when the rubber meets the road," those tires get dirty. In the case of slope measurement, there are tools and techniques that we will rely on to make slope recognition more obvious and more profitable. We will incorporate them as this chapter progresses.

Figure 11.4 shows a daily MetaSwing chart of Powerwave Technologies (PWAV) during the spring of 2007. This chart's components are displayed to assist us in accurately recognizing the slope of each N Band. The two N Band slope indicators are plotted in the middle indicator pane. The solid line represents the lower N Band slope, and the dotted line is for the upper N Band slope. The upper and lower thresholds are set at the positive and negative 45-degree marks. Overlaying each N Band for seven days in April is a linear regression line plot, which appears as a thick solid line. The N Band slope indicators base their calculations on a seven-period linear regression line. This seven-day look-back duration is bordered on each side with vertical dashed lines. Lastly, the Adeo HS (high slope) signal is shown for four consecutive days inside the circled area.

The chart of Powerwave Technologies in Figure 11.4 clearly shows us that:

- The rapidly rising lower N Band registers a slope intensity of 58 degrees on April 23, well above the 45-degree threshold. This means that downside implied volatility is decreasing quickly. It also means that immediate support is rising quickly.

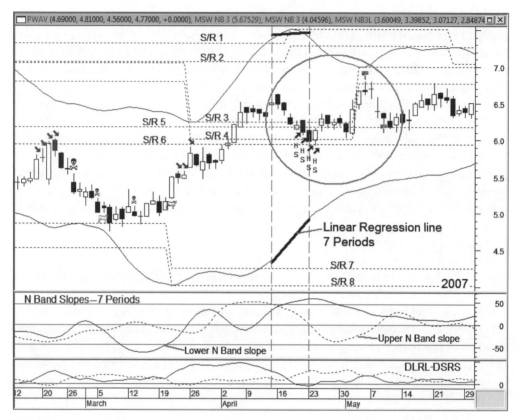

FIGURE 11.4 This chart of an Adeo with high N Band slope shows the effects of hidden momentum.

Chart created in MetaStock. Chart uses the MetaSwing Add-on, by Northington Trading, LLC. All rights reserved.

- On April 23, an Adeo long trade sets up nicely. It has good DLRL-DSRS indicator levels. It has retraced some of its advance to find support at the S/R 4 and S/R 6 lines.
- You can examine the full color long-term version of this chart at www.tradingthe invisible.com and see that Powerwave Technologies is not in the middle of a nice, safely rising trend, pushing it higher. In truth, this trade setup is part of a downward trend break.
- With a trade entry on April 24 and an exit nine days later on May 4, when the lower indicators cross and the Exit Long signal appears, this trade produces an 11 percent profit. This makes it very representative of the 10-day sample population described in Figure 11.3.

Volatility Shift

Over this seven-day period ending on April 23, 2007, it is obvious that Powerwave Technologies underwent a *volatility shift*. That is to say, its downside volatility decreased while its upside volatility remained virtually static. Stock traders are accustomed to thinking of volatility as a single measurement with equal implications for the long and short side potential of the market. They could benefit from looking at volatility the way their option trading cousins do. The option trader understands that implied volatility percentage values for calls and puts are separate from each other for a reason. They are separate because each represents a probability of movement in a specific direction.

Let's look at Figure 11.4 again from the standpoint of its volatility shift. Our analysis so far has focused only on the lower N Band slope value. Powerwave Technologies presents a different picture of upside volatility across the same seven-day time window. The upper N Band slope is dropping daily, but is still a positive three degrees. These two slope measurements imply that resistance is remaining the same distance away while support is rising fast. For trading on the long side of the market, this logically translates to the following:

- The risk of loss is decreasing.
- The probability of profit has not yet decreased. Also, if it does, it is likely to decrease at a lower rate than the risk of loss.
- This stock is therefore undergoing a short-term upward volatility shift.
- The probable short-term trading range is rising because of the upward volatility shift. This is the objective we are seeking.
- Logically then, the current price is likely positioned beneath the future mean of that new short-term trading range, especially if price has been falling during the slope measurement time window.

Figure 11.5 takes us in for a closer look at Powerwave Technologies to apply some central tendency analysis by plotting the TTI Fabric LR indicator. On April 23, it shows that price closed one penny beneath the negative one thread, which is two ATR(14) units beneath its 40-period linear regression line. Logically then, if price is well below the current line of central tendency, it will have an even higher likelihood of being below it in the coming periods when the trading range rises. Also important is that this is another framework component to increase the odds of success for a long position here.

One Slope or Two?

This is very interesting so far, isn't it? Is it not solely the lower N Band slope, however, that's in charge? Perhaps the upper N Band slope should be considered as well. These two slopes could be somewhat like the yin and yang of consolidated implied volatility. But how can we understand this potential relationship better? How can we come closer to knowing the effects of the upper N Band slope on trading probabilities?

Since this is an important part of exploiting a stock's short-term volatility shift, it would be prudent to crunch some more numbers. Let's run another analysis that incorporates an upper N Band slope value as an additional qualifier for the trade signal. We compare in this study potential profit and potential loss calculations from our Adeo with high slope to the same signal enhanced to include an upper N Band slope measurement

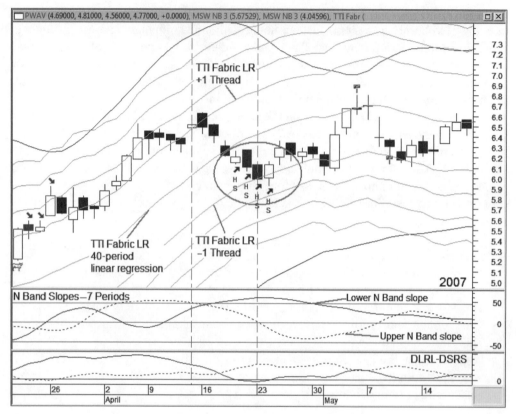

FIGURE 11.5 A closer look at Powerwave Technologies (PWAV) with the TTI Fabric LR shows that it is well beneath its central tendency.

Chart created in MetaStock. Chart uses the MetaSwing Add-on, by Northington Trading, LLC. All rights reserved.

qualifier. We add a criterion in this case that the upper N Band seven-period slope be greater than –5 degrees. This reading means that the slope is positive or relatively flat. All other analysis details and methodology are the same.

Figure 11.6 shows us the results of this new comparison. We are attempting to quantify the potential effects of adding a positive, or almost flat, slope requirement for the upper N Band in addition to the previous high slope requirements. Plainly put, we need to see if the slope of the upper N Band is a significant factor.

The numbers are once again supportive of the upward volatility shift effect. The previous results have been moved to area two of the table. The performance results for the Adeo HS with an upper N Band slope of greater than –5 degrees are listed in area one of the table. The percentage increase or decrease of the respective group performances are listed in area three. Note that the results in area three are calculated from the actual study results, which are real numbers accurate to 12 floating digits. The results listed in areas two and three have been rounded.

Test Event	Total Instances	Profit Potential	Loss Potential	Forward Duration
1 **With High Slope**				
and Upper Band Qualifier				
Adeo	860	10.7%	−7.1%	10 Days
S&P 500	860	3.0%	1.7%	10 Days
Adeo	860	7.1%	−4.9%	5 Days
S&P 500	860	2.1%	0.6%	5 Days
2 **With High Slope**				
Adeo	2316	9.0%	−6.3%	10 Days
S&P 500	2316	2.9%	1.6%	10 Days
Adeo	2316	6.1%	−4.4%	5 Days
S&P 500	2316	2.1%	0.6%	5 Days
3 **Effective Comparison**				
Adeo: greater increase in profit than loss		18.7%	12.4%	10 Days
S&P: profitability improvement marginal		4.5%	4.5%	10 Days
Adeo: greater increase in profit than loss		16.7%	11.0%	5 Days
S&P: profitability improvement negligible		1.3%	−2.9%	5 Days

FIGURE 11.6 This shows the analysis results for the comparison of the Adeo HS (high slope) and the Adeo HS with the upper N Band slope criterion.

Based on the results in area three we can see that:

- The addition of the upper N Band criteria improves the 10-day profit potential by 18.7 percent, but increases the loss potential by only 12.4 percent over that of a lower high slope only. Once again, the profit potential increases more than the loss potential, about 50 percent greater.
- Proportionally, the five-day results are virtually the same.
- The S&P 500 Index performance results showed little significant change.
- The new sample size in area one has been reduced to 860 from 2,316. That's a 63 percent reduction.

Based on the interpretation of these results we can conclude that:

- Using the upper N Band slope requirement is a positive component addition to an Adeo long trade setup. Its positive effect supports an understanding of the volatility shift, and an increased probability of a rising trading range.
- The addition of the upper N Band slope requirement does not present such a dramatic improvement in profit to loss potential that it would preclude us from using the lower N Band slope component alone, which is the method presented in area two.
- The instances of opportunity represented by the sample size are shrinking to a point that forces us to consider if this criterion occurs frequently enough to be of practical use to a trader.

Often Enough?

If we trade the Adeo long method and combine it with the previously mentioned N Band slope measurement qualifiers, then our total instance quantity for the S&P 500 population of stocks is down to 860, spread over an eight-year period. That's getting kind of thin, yes? Well, yes and no. It is if you only use it with Adeo signals, but that need not be a limitation. Actually, a volatility shift analysis with N Band slopes can be used with many long trading methods. High slope readings occur quite frequently. Let's quantify that statement, though.

By running another analysis study to detect the total quantity of occurrences, we can determine what the true frequency of this technical qualifier is. To maintain consistency, this study was conducted during the same time as that in Chapter 7 and the previous two in this chapter. The periodicity is daily, with the duration being 2,000 trading days, beginning on June 29, 2000, and ending on June 13, 2008.

Collecting these data is really very simple. For example, let's suppose you want to find out how many instances of days occur when the lower N Band slope is greater than 45 degrees, which is the slope qualifier we used in Figure 11.3. MetaSwing users would open a new Exploration and enter this function code into one of the Exploration Editor tabs:

```
x1:= Fml("MSW Slope NB3L - 7") > 45;
Cum(x1)
```

The first statement establishes a condition. It requires that the value of the custom indicator named "MSW Slope NB3L - 7" be greater than 45. If that resolves to true, then a value of 1 will be assigned to the variable $x1$; otherwise $x1$ will be assigned a value of 0. The second statement performs a summation of the $x1$ variable values for each of the periods in the exploration.

You will set two options in order to repeat the exact same analysis that is presented herein. Set the specific option for exploration date to June 13, 2008, and the exploration

	Slope Criteria Degrees	Total Instances For All S&P 500 Stocks	Average Instances Per S&P 500 Stock	Quantity of Days Between Instances Per S&P 500 Stock	Trade Direction
1					
Lower N Band	> 45				
Upper N Band	n/a	55,194	110	18	Long
2					
Lower N Band	> 45				
Upper N Band	> –10	14,471	29	69	Long
3					
Lower N Band	> 45				
Upper N Band	> –5	12,520	25	80	Long
4					
Lower N Band	n/a				
Upper N Band	< –45	29,096	58	34	Short
5					
Lower N Band	< 10				
Upper N Band	< –45	6,800	14	147	Short
6					
Lower N Band	< 5				
Upper N Band	< –45	6,382	13	157	Short

FIGURE 11.7 Study results that quantify instance frequencies of different high and low N Band slope configurations.

periodicity to daily. Then set the Explorer application, data loading option, to 2,000 records. Lastly, run the exploration on the S&P 500 population of stocks. The exploration will return the total quantity of days on which the lower N Band experienced a high slope condition.

Figure 11.7 shows us how often key high and low slope conditions occur. It is divided into six different rows. Row one is the lower N Band slope condition used in the study contained in Figure 11.3. Row three is the slope configuration used in the study shown in Figure 11.6. As you recall, Figure 11.6 adds the requirement that the upper N Band slope be greater than –5 degrees. Row two is the same as row three except it allows the upper N Band slope to be slightly more negative. Rows one through three are slope configurations conducive to long side trading. Rows four through six measure slope conditions exactly opposite to the first three, and are used for short side trading. These are referred to as low slope conditions.

As it turns out, when a high N Band slope instance is not required to coincide with an Adeo signal, it happens often enough to be a great tactic in our arsenal. Row one tells us that a high lower N Band slope occurs frequently. Each stock in the S&P 500 experienced an average of 110 instances during the eight-year time span. These data indicate to us that the condition happens often enough to be used as a qualifier with many other long trading methods. Consider also that the frequency numbers in Figure 11.7 are based on an extreme slope definition of plus-or-minus 45. This is a nice round arbitrary number.

Many less volatile stocks respond well to an extreme threshold of 40 or less. The broadening of acceptable values can increase the quantity of instances significantly. The topic of marginal sensitivity to high slope thresholds is worthy of further research, but is outside the scope of this book.

More important, this technical measurement is in fact a valuable component and application in the MetaSwing framework. The best way to think of it is that the framework table has two more columns listing the components for upper and lower N Band slope. Then, in the application rows, the term *Volatility Shift* would represent a new trading method. For a visual reference and review of the framework, refer back to Table 9.1. This demonstrates one of the major strengths of a component-based framework and methodology. It can give the analyst the ability to isolate a specific component and use its application when it can do the most good.

Discovering a probable volatility shift has real predictive value and directional intelligence. When searching for the best-of-the-best trade setups, we need to be mindful not to use several framework components that are based on the same data. This error is most often committed by stacking up several momentum oscillators that all agree. The truth is that each additional oscillator adds little incremental value because its calculations typically overlap the others. Volatility shift analysis through N Band slope measurement is unique. It identifies hidden price momentum in a different way. You can therefore experience a genuine probability increase by adding its findings to the component mix.

Dueling Slopes

Did you ever play chicken as a child? Riding a bicycle directly toward one of your buddies, and not wanting to be the first to swerve away, is a defining moment that's hard to forget. It usually happened after some sort of disagreement or debate. Neither youngster dominated the contest quickly or decisively. The disagreement stretched on without a winner. In the end, both parties seemed equally right and tough. One kid must win, so there had to be some activity to break the tie of egos. Chicken seemed like a logical idea, especially to the bystanders rooting for it. The game of chicken in many forms follows us all into adulthood. What if volatility levels played chicken?

It is probably so, since the financial markets are a never-ending contest between buyers and sellers. It would appear that if a high slope environment is affected by its upper N Band counterpart, then there could also be some sort of opposing force at play. Time is the culprit. Early and decisive price movement in one direction creates the opportunity, and lack thereof can erase it.

Figure 11.8 is a daily chart of Electronic Data Systems (EDS) during a time when the upper and lower N Band slopes are opposing. The time span is outlined by the two vertical dashed lines. The vertical line on the right is aligned with an Adeo HS signal. Seven-period linear regression lines are plotted to overlay the upper and lower N Bands so that their slopes are visually referenced. The middle indicator pane contains the seven-period N Band slope indicators.

Price breaks through resistance at the S/R 3 and S/R 4 levels without pause in October. It trades atop support at the S/R 3 line for three weeks, however, in a narrow

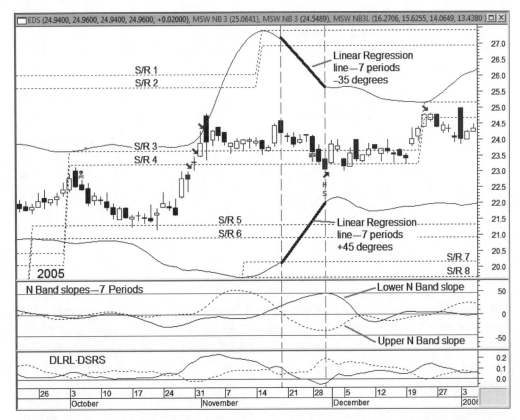

FIGURE 11.8 A trading range can be forced into a lack of movement when faced with the circumstance of opposing extreme slopes.

Chart created in MetaStock. Chart uses the MetaSwing Add-on, by Northington Trading, LLC. All rights reserved.

range straight line. This price action is a telltale sign that efficiency exists in the market for this stock. Efficiency is the last thing a trader wants to see. We want our employees, our home, and even our car to be efficient; we want to see inefficient stock prices. Inefficient markets are where we make money.

This efficient price action also creates a contraction of short-term implied volatility. Both upside and downside volatility decreases and are heading right for each other, not unlike a game of chicken. The upper N Band slope is at –35 degrees while the lower one is at +45 degrees. This is a very different technical setup from our Powerwave Technologies chart. Had price not stopped where it did in late October and pushed up to the S/R 1 line, the slope measurements would look very different. Here's what we can deduce from the volatility measurements in Figure 11.8.

1. Excessive price malaise in the first half of November, which is in effect price efficiency, causes the upper N Band peak and the lower N Band trough to form at the

same time. The lower N Band slope, therefore, cannot reach a high level prior to the upper N Band slope reaching a low reading.

2. On the Adeo HS signal day, both bands are approaching price rapidly. This translates to a rapid and simultaneous decrease in upside and downside volatility.

3. With upside and downside implied volatility converging rapidly on price, a volatility shift is not likely to develop immediately following the signal day.

The bottom line in situations like this need not be that the trade is doomed to failure. It is simply not taking advantage of the best odds for success. Anything can and does happen in trading. If you are going to put on a long trade in this situation, it is best to know your odds of participating in an upward volatility shift before entering the position. With the N Band slopes being what they were at the time of the trade signal, an upward volatility shift was not likely to happen.

Momentum Found

So far in this chapter we've been studying the middle of the chart. But things aren't always as clear at the time of decision. High and low N Band slope conditions are often created when sudden moves or changes occur. Getting caught on the wrong side of the market in an extended price retracement, while expecting a reversal, is always something we fear.

The chart in Figure 11.9 gives us an opportunity to stare into the abyss of the right side of the chart, and all of the glory and failure it could possess. This daily chart of Nektar Therapeutics (NKTR) shows us a potentially scary trade setup. Actually, with the look of the price candles over the most recent two weeks, it would be a bit risky to take a long position without a favorable volatility shift analysis. This chart has the same seven-day slope measurements plotted as our previous examples had.

At this point on the chart, the analysis factors that we can identify are:

• The N Band slope measurements are great, with upper and lower at +4 and +55 degrees, respectfully. This is a signal of a probable upward volatility shift about to occur.

• The TTI Trend Strength indicator has looked positive for the past two months. Its previous 20 days are blocked off by two dotted lines for clarity. The 20-day level changes are favorable as well.

• The Adeo long signal has set up well with indicator readings that are positive for an Adeo trade.

• The price action in the beginning of January blasted up and through all four upper S/R lines quite forcefully. Support at the S/R 1 line has held firm for almost three weeks.

• A negative sign is that price has not closed far above the S/R 1 line but for two sessions. This is not favorable behavior.

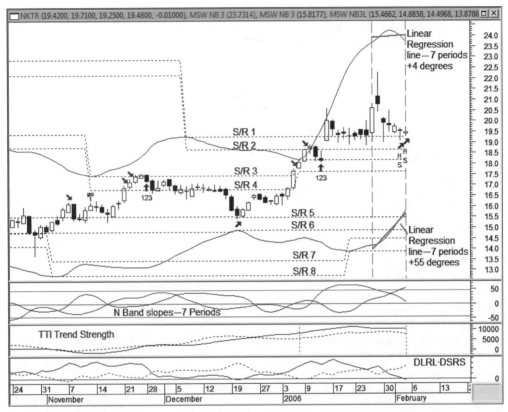

FIGURE 11.9 A tempting Adeo HS trade setup on this chart of Nektar Therapeutics (NKTR) shows how volatility shift analysis provides the additional directional intelligence needed for the trade entry.

Chart created in MetaStock. Chart uses the MetaSwing Add-on, by Northington Trading, LLC. All rights reserved.

- The opposing tandem indicator height (DSRS) is acceptable, but not at an absolute high. There were instances over the past seven months when the DSRS indicator was higher. This is not a major problem, but it never hurts to have the opposing height at an extreme.

With all of the factors lining up to make this a very profitable trade, there are a couple of them that are also detractors. The recent choppy price action settling for such an extended period on the S/R 1 line is one of them. That's a long time to be at one support level. Also, the lack of an extreme height on the DSRS is the other. Together, they point to the possibility of some further price retracement.

On the flip side of the coin are the good overall indicator readings combined with an Adeo signal. In reality, the tiebreaker has to be the N Band slope readings. The odds of an upward volatility shift make this trade too hard to pass up. It decreases the risk

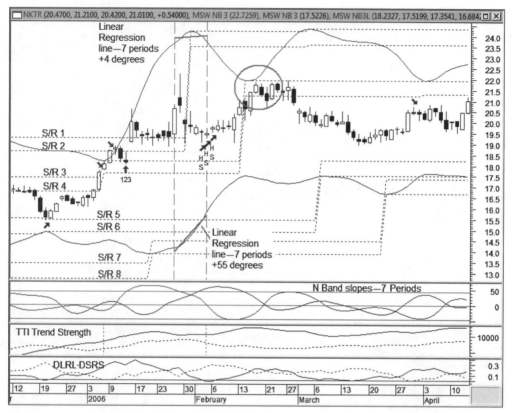

FIGURE 11.10 The effects of volatility shift analysis are clear as Nektar Therapeutics establishes its higher trading range.

of a long position stopping out. It would be best, however, to keep a tight stop on this one. A good level would be just below the S/R 2 line.

In Figure 11.10, we move the right side of the chart forward by two months. This makes it clear that Nektar Therapeutics did indeed carve out a new and higher trading range. This is the effect of a volatility shift. A high slope trade should be managed with that expectation. If price does not behave as though it is finding a new range, then it is time to exit.

If the trade proceeds as planned, then find your exit at the next level of resistance. Do not get greedy. The top of the next trading range is your target. In this case, it would be as price approaches the upper N Band on February 15 or 16. Whether price stops there or continues on to infinity, you have done your job as a trader. You have entered with the odds in your favor, and you have also exited with the odds in your favor.

Looking forward through March, it is easy to see that price found a neutral position between the previously established N Bands. Perhaps the fundamentals presented on

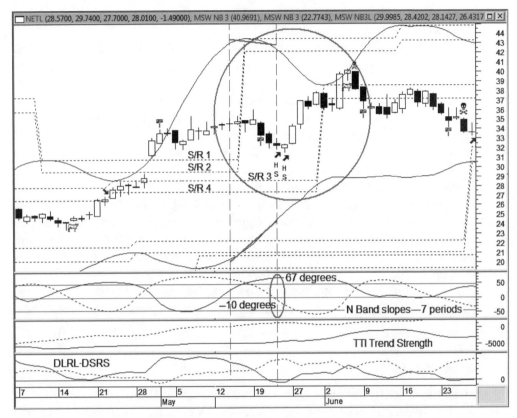

FIGURE 11.11 This chart of Netlogic Microsystems (NETL) shows how the effects of N Band slope and the resulting volatility shift can apply equally well with small cap stocks.

Chart created in MetaStock. Chart uses the MetaSwing Add-on, by Northington Trading, LLC. All rights reserved.

February 28 at its earnings announcement did not help to push prices any higher. Those are fundamental factors you cannot calculate, so as a general rule, remember to stay clear of their effects.

Irrelevance of Size

When it comes to a corporation's market capitalization, liquidity issues notwithstanding, the predictive qualities of volatility shift are agnostic. We see a daily chart in Figure 11.11 of Netlogic Microsystems (NETL), which is small cap stock with sufficient liquidity. The chart has vertical dashed lines, which delineate a seven-day lookback for linear regression N Band slope analysis. The first Adeo HS signal occurs on May 22, 2008.

At that point, the chart clearly shows favorable N Band slope conditions. The upper slope is at an acceptable –10 degrees, and the lower slope is at a very strong 67-degree reading. All other Adeo method component contributions were positive. Northington Trading did well with this long swing trade.

There was only one component that was not ready at the point where the reversal occurred. The price retracement did not drop fully to the S/R 1 level at 30.79. Remember that the S/R 1 line would have still been in place at that price on May 22. It is normally best to enter the trade at an appropriate support line. An entry on May 27, however, just after the opening, was acceptable because the opening price action was indicative of a reversal. Also, despite no further retracement to a support level, the risk-reward ratio was still favorable. The exit occurred at 37.55 on May 30, while price reached a point of less than one ATR from the upper N Band. Also, since this was a long trade during a bear market, a brief trade duration was prudent.

The buyers at 37.55 were not likely aware of volatility-based resistance. A common TA tactic is to buy as price breaks above a recent trading range anticipating a breakout. If you look closely at the price candles without the N Bands and S/R lines, the pattern does appear to be a price breakout through a horizontal resistance area. This trading practice often works but it often stalls or fails when volatility-based resistance is in its way, which is what happened with this stock on and after May 30. If more traders could see the normally invisible volatility-based resistance, then they could avoid many false breakouts.

On the Short Side

Volatility shifts obviously occur on both sides of the market. Figure 11.7 clearly shows how the same N Band slope conditions exist as inverse configurations. As is generally the case, a short trade is not as simple as executing a long trading method that's been flipped over. Downside price action and the downside volatility it creates come from a different set of market dynamics. This is evidenced by the large difference of instances found for the Figure 11.7 low slope configurations. To be exact, only half as many were found. Because these low slope configurations are truly just flipped over, they don't possess the same level of predictive value. When shorting with volatility shift, be careful to use the same safeguards that are normally prudent in any short trade. Be patient and use a higher degree of price confirmation.

In Figure 11.12 we see a daily chart of Unisys Corporation (UIS). In this example of using volatility shift for a short trade, there is a different set of technical tools plotted than those previously used. The S/R lines are not shown so that the TTI Fabric LR can be more easily visible. Also, the TTI Composite oscillator is plotted in lieu of the DLRL-DSRS indicators in the bottom pane. The last of the Adeo LS signal days is aligned with a vertical dashed line.

This trade works well because it lines up as a good short trade in general. The low slope readings that forecast a downward volatility shift provide a degree of extra probability. The TTI Composite is solidly overbought. Also, with price above the TTI Fabric LR positive one thread, the trader can probably count on some reversion to its central tendency line. In the end, a new trading range was defined going forward. Indeed, the

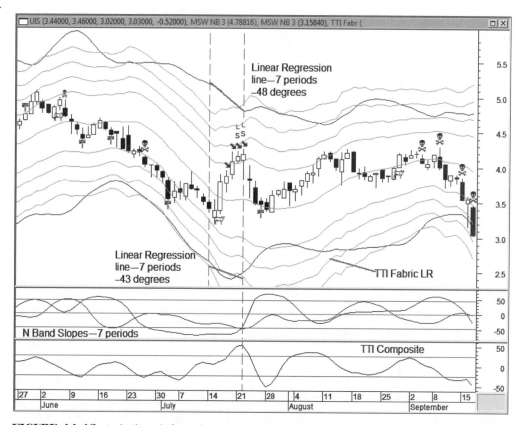

FIGURE 11.12   Volatility shift analysis is not as common for short trade setups, but works well when the technical circumstances correctly come together.

Chart created in MetaStock. Chart uses the MetaSwing Add-on, by Northington Trading, LLC. All rights reserved.

two Adeo LS signal days defined the range high until September's broad market turmoil dragged it into the basement for a beating.

On the whole, you can expect to find far fewer short trade candidates with volatility shift analysis. However, don't hesitate to search for, find, and use the favorable setups that exist. Short trading benefits from any valid analysis-based probabilities that you can use. When it is present, volatility shift analysis works well.

THE QUICK AND THE BROKE

Detecting a volatility shift quickly enough alerts us that the short-term trading range is likely to be changing. Institutional market participants with quantitative resources and megacomputing ~ TQF power will detect these probable shifts as well. It is their size that moves trading ranges. Note that the numerical studies performed in this chapter have been on S&P 500 components, which are generally mid cap and large cap stocks. Significant moves of a highly liquid stock require the strength of large players.

It is also their size that limits their timeliness. It's okay to be a middleweight fighting in the heavyweight division if you are faster and have better timing. Just don't let your opponent hit you. As individual traders, we must work in much the same way. Our size means we can enter and exit trades in seconds. We have to recognize, however, the market's hidden momentum and inefficiencies before other market players grab them.

Early detection gives us the opportunity to enter a position before the move happens. This means it can be less often that we utter the words, "Darn—I missed that one!" Instead, you can more frequently yell, "Score!"

CHAPTER 12

Designing the Exit

Three people were sitting in a passenger train heading east one afternoon. The first passenger, a man sitting next to the window, smiled as he gazed out the window. The second passenger, a woman who fidgeted nervously, routinely surveyed the compartment. The third person, an elderly gentleman, sat there reading the newspaper intently. The train clacked along with a steady rhythm as it moved through the countryside.

The woman said to the first passenger, "So where are you heading to?"

The smiling man at the window replied, "Seattle. I'm getting off in Seattle."

The woman looked puzzled. She thought for a second and then said to him, "Are you sure about that? Because we just passed through St. Louis and we are heading east. It would seem that Seattle is at least 1,200 miles the other way."

The first passenger smiled and said confidently, "Well, what you're saying is simply not possible. My destination is Seattle. Therefore, this train will be passing through Seattle before long. I'm sure it's just up the track a ways."

The woman kept looking around routinely. The older passenger continued reading the newspaper. The man by the window said to the woman, "Where are you going?"

She replied, "Well, my mother's house is in Nashville and I might go there. My cousin lives in Louisville and it's nice there this time of year. But I'm supposed to be on a business trip to Cleveland. I'm…I'm just not quite sure. I can't really decide. Can anyone tell me what time it is?" She looked around nervously.

"That's nice," said the man by the window, still smiling confidently. "How about you, sir?" he said to the older gentleman. "What's your destination?"

The gentleman rested the paper on his lap and looked at the other two passengers. He replied in an emotionless tone devoid of voice inflection, "I'm not sure, really. But I'll definitely let you know when I get there. That part will be clear."

The next logical development of this story is for Rod Serling to walk into the scene and explain that trains go many places, including…the Twilight Zone. In this story, however, these three passengers are *you*—every time you hold an active position in a security.

That's right; passenger one, two, and three sit inside each of us when we trade. You could call them our schizophrenic exit subconscious. To some degree, each one is influencing our decision-making process in managing the trade. We can't get rid of them; we are who we are. The best we can hope to accomplish is to recognize each one for what they are, and manage them accordingly.

Selecting a security to trade is a critical function requiring all of our talents, but it is still not nearly as important as choosing when and at what price to close the position. That is where the money is made or lost. It is the most overlooked and misunderstood facet of trading by individuals. It is also, by far, the second most profitable skill to have if you can master it. So let's explore the right time for each passenger to access a brokerage screen and close the position.

THE OBJECTIVE: OPTIMIZE THE PROFIT TARGET

As a minor curiosity, do you suppose that exit is considered a four-letter word in trading circles? I think it may be. Why else does it seem so ignored? Actually, I don't think it is so much ignored as it is hidden. I believe that successful traders do not disclose their exit tactics because of how critical those tactics are. It is much easier to find accounts of traders describing their setups and stop loss tactics than how they extract the maximum profit from an exit.

The exit is, after all, the very thing we set out to achieve: to get out of the trade with more money than we entered it. Is that really a formal description of the term *exit* as it pertains to trading? We can define it, at least preliminarily, as:

Closing an existing trade position to achieve the maximum gain, or to suffer the minimum loss.

This chapter focuses on the "maximum gain" part of this definition. We do this because the stop loss tends to be a function of the same methods that should be used in choosing optimum profit targets. We need every bit of profit we can get to make up for the stop losses we do incur. When the trade produces a profit, but money is left on the table, it represents somewhat of a hollow victory.

Let's start, however, by identifying what we should *not* do while choosing exit points. There are three common traps that traders fall into. Each of us exhibits at least one of them. We discuss two of them now, and the third trap is covered later in this chapter. The exit snares are:

1. One size fits all: using static percentages as exit targets

2. Feelings- and intuition-based exit decisions

3. Overdependence on rules and mathematical calculations

The First Trap: One Size Fits All

We look first at the mindset, or strategy, that leads a trader to choose a single fixed value to apply to the exit. For instance, the practice of back-testing trading strategies and tactics has come into particular favor in recent years. This is likely because the technology, in the form of powerful hardware and software, is finally able to perform the tasks well. While back-testing is a good thing, it must be approached correctly.

The exit in the algorithm is too often executed as a fixed percentage profit target. In other words, the trader sets the exit to occur when a specific profit target has been reached, such as 8 percent or 25 percent. This is an illogical practice since it completely ignores an individual stock's volatility. Eight percent may work fine with a stock that has an ATR(14) of 3 percent. For an equity with an ATR(14) of 6.5 percent, however, the same 8 percent profit target will likely leave money on the table needlessly.

Look at Figure 12.1 to better understand the impact of using a fixed percentage profit

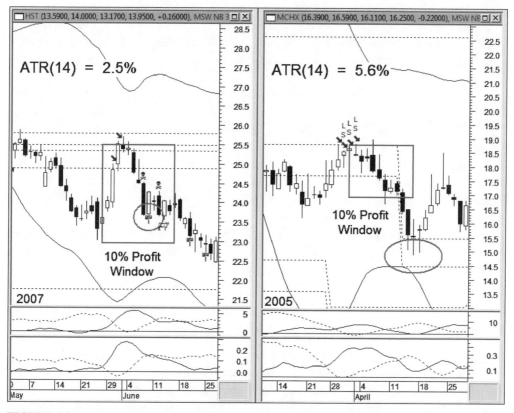

FIGURE 12.1 This side-by-side comparison of two charts with different daily volatility levels illustrates how a fixed percentage price target fails to capture the profits available to the astute trader.

Chart created in MetaStock. Chart uses the MetaSwing Add-on, by Northington Trading, LLC. All rights reserved.

target. This dual-chart comparison shows Host Hotels and Resorts (HST) with an ATR(14) of 2.5 percent, and Marchex Inc. (MCHX) with an ATR(14) of 5.6 percent. Obviously Marchex has the greater capacity for movement. Both charts have a proper Adeo short trade setup at the S/R 5 line. A rectangle is drawn from that point depicting a 10 percent profit window. The smaller circle drawn on each chart shows the obvious and best exit area.

The Host Hotels and Resorts short trade would have taken three weeks to reach a 10 percent target. In only seven days, however, a profit of 7 percent could have been attained. The shorter seven-day trade is much more efficient and exposes your capital to far less market risk. The Marchex short trade did achieve its 10 percent target. However, it would have left an additional 10 percent profit on the table, if the 10 percent profit target were used.

Returning to the rail travelers analogy from the beginning of the chapter, which passenger do you think would commit this particular error? If you think it's the first passenger, next to the window, you would be correct. In his blind single-mindedness, he thought of only one outcome and considered only direction. As far as he was concerned, he was traveling west and therefore Seattle must be in front of him. His mind was closed to considering any other action. It is a simple way of thinking and being, but very far removed from reality. There are times to keep your thoughts rigid and simple, but contemplating the processes of exiting a position is usually not one of those times.

Fixed percentage decision-making also ignores opportunities created by time. This is because volatility is a function of time and price movement. The solution to this tactical pitfall is very simple. Resist thinking of price movement in terms of currency units or percentages. Relate to it instead in terms of units of volatility. Specifically, use average true range instead of percentages. For instance, conduct your back-testing using exits that execute three units of ATR away from the trade entry. Further optimize the strategy by varying the exact quantity of ATR units to find the best setting. You will find that the strategy will actually perform much more reliably when you normalize for volatility.

Back-testing is very useful and beneficial to finding good trading methods. No matter what the optimal ATR setting ends up being, though, you would still do best not to execute exits based on test results parameters only. Use the test results as a general guide. Each trade should be exited based on its applicable volatility measurements.

The Second Trap: Feelings, Lies, and Ticker Tape

If it is problematic to be too rigid with profit targets, then should we swing the other way and wing it? Suppose we just rely on our intuition. That would certainly give a trader the position of being flexible. But will he end up with the results needed?

Allowing the pendulum to swing toward a more anarchistic process of position exiting is a recipe for a short trading career. Some traders can pull it off, though. Remember our little feathered friend the sanderling, and how they can instinctively predict just how far out they can go into the waves for food. These traders are that rare breed who have volatility subprocessors in their brains, which makes them part sandpiper. The vast majority of us don't fit that profile.

For many people, the formula of buy low and sell high equates to a thought process where high is some price level that will make them feel good. How do you define *high*, though? For traders without solid methods, high is too often where they theorize it is based on a nonrepeating logic. You can disagree by listing any number of possible tactics that are related to a judgment call, but it still boils down to a feeling.

Here is how you can tell if your exiting behavior falls into this category. If you experience a single decision to enter the trade, but it feels like you execute 100 decisions pertaining to the exit, then you likely have much more in common with passenger number two on the Twilight Zone Express. This exit process is the opposite of being too rigid because it has a lack of rules or well-defined tactics.

To the trader, it seems that like a constant stream of junctures asking, "How about here; should I exit here?" The question repeats itself as if it is a steady state. This constant reasoning and attempt at feeling-oriented logic will wear out anyone. It will also produce results most often attributable to chance. These traders tend to make some money when they are trading in the market's direction, and lose even more when the market goes against them. In the end, the losses outnumber the gains.

In the area of profit target selection, the short-term pattern trader can also fall into this category. We discussed in Chapter 7 some of the positives and pitfalls of trading short-term price patterns. Those who work very hard at trading patterns can do well. The price target calculations and methodologies can vary, depending on the research and rules you subscribe to. The entry tactics are not often based on feelings. The profit target, however, is usually a ratio or percentage of a portion of the chart's pattern in question. The ratios and percentages were derived by statistical research.

Here's where the inaccuracy occurs. The pattern's original measuring area of basis is specific to the chart; for example, the flagpole portion of a flag pattern. Next, the price target is a specific percentage of this measuring area. The percentage or ratio applied to that measuring area is statistically derived from the population in the original research. This is another way of saying that one target percentage formula fits any given chart regardless of the stock's current volatility level. Lastly, this percentage is supposed to be used as a guideline. Because it is a guideline, it is then subject to uncertainty.

Look again at the visual references of precision chart pattern profit targets using volatility analysis. We explored them in depth in Figures 7.8, 7.9, and 7.10. Figure 7.10 is repeated here in Figure 12.2. This chart of Union Pacific (UNP) shows the benefits of being chart specific with profit targets. Two profit targets are shown, one for the breakout exit, and another for the pullback trade. As you can see, making decisions based on the chart's specific volatility signals produces a higher level of precision and conviction.

Why not apply measures of volatility to the actual chart and exit based on them? Why not be exact, instead of hoping that the pattern you are trading ultimately fits within the population distribution of a batch of research? Would you accept your surgeon's decision to perform a heart bypass on you if she was only basing her action on statistics? I'm certain that you would insist upon her testing and diagnosing your specific arteries before opening up your chest.

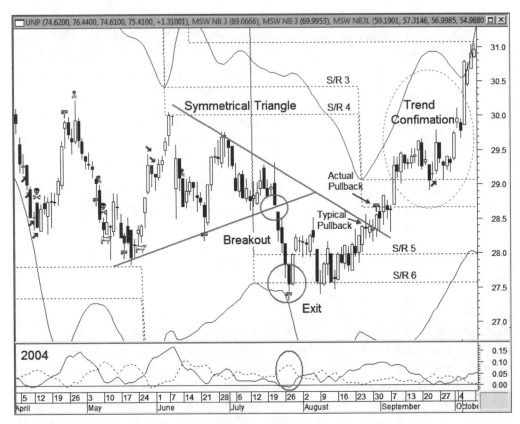

FIGURE 12.2 The chart of Union Pacific (UNP) shows a breakout and a throwback trade with specific volatility-based profit targets.

Chart created in MetaStock. Chart uses the MetaSwing Add-on, by Northington Trading, LLC. All rights reserved.

USING TIME SLICING TO UNDERSTAND YOUR TIME FRAME

To this point, our discussion of profit targets has been missing one major area of clarification: time. Virtually every trade has a potentially optimum execution within it. It's our duty to find it and make that execution a reality. This sort of profit nirvana can be achieved consistently only within one set time span. Individuals who repeatedly get closest to executing perfect trades have behavior in common. One of these top common traits is that they know their personal trading time frame and stick with it.

Within the scope of the exit, the trade duration is paramount. Time frame issues are one of the most underlying reasons for lackluster performance. Obvious drawbacks of not having, or misunderstanding, consistent position durations are:

- Late exit: increased risk through exposure to the market
- Late exit: missed trading opportunities because capital is tied up on position(s) too long

- Late exit: small losses turn into large losses
- Premature exit: missed profit opportunities
- Premature exit: accepting stop losses needlessly

By knowing your trade duration, you can find the proper exit signals. The periodicity of the chart must match your personal trading time frame. This is why the technical methods an analyst uses need to be fractal. Your selection of chart periodicity holds a real key to your success. The emphasis of time is so important that it now compels us to properly restate the definition of the *trade exit* as:

Closing an existing trade position to achieve the maximum gain, or to suffer the minimum loss, within a given time duration that matches the primary trade strategy.

Let's consider an example using three different trading time frames. They are:

1. Swing trader: 2 to 10 market days
2. Position trader 1: 10 to 20 market days
3. Position trader 2: 15 to 40 market days

We are presented in Figure 12.3 with a dual MetaSwing chart of the PowerShares QQQ Trust (QQQQ), which represent two different chart periodicities. The chart at left is a daily time frame, and the chart at right is a three-day time frame. The three-day chart fully includes the date range of the daily chart. In this comparison, all three traders enter on the day after the daily Adeo long signal on October 12, 2005, which is denoted with a rectangle on both charts.

Here's what we can observe about the exit strategies for each of the three time frames:

- The swing trader will want to manage the position using daily and hourly charts, similar to examples in previous chapters. In circle area 1 the DLRL-DSRS indicator has crossed. On an hourly chart (not shown), price hits the upper N Band. This makes for a good profit target on day 6 or 7. If, however, he had chosen to hold out longer and gets greedy, he is forced to needlessly sit through a three-day retracement.
- The 10- to 20-day position trader manages her trade using the daily and the two-day chart. The two-day chart is shown in Figure 12.4, and is shown as seen after the market closes on October 8, 2005. Adeo short signals have formed at the resistance of the S/R 3 line. The daily chart has already signaled an exit. The DSRS and Divine indicators are both reading overbought levels on both charts. This is an obvious point to take profits and exit at the S/R 3 line of the two-day chart. As a side note, price pauses on the daily chart from October 4 until October 9. On the two-day chart, however, it is clear that Adeo short signals and the S/R 3 line are responsible. Unexplained price stalls in one periodicity are often explained in a different one.

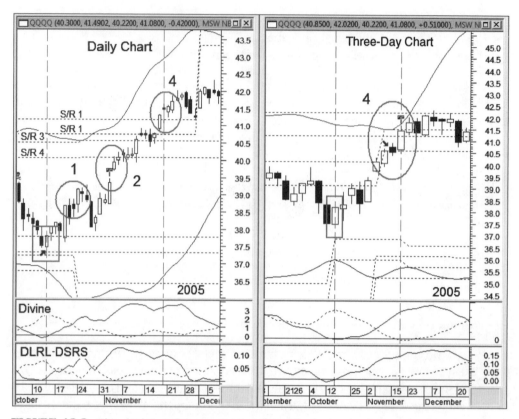

FIGURE 12.3 This dual time frame example of the Q's shows clearly how important it is to choose exit points within the appropriate chart periodicity.

Chart created in MetaStock. Chart uses the MetaSwing Add-on, by Northington Trading, LLC. All rights reserved.

- The 15- to 40-day position trader manages his trade using the daily, the three-day, and the weekly chart. If this trader had put too much credence in the two-day chart, he might have been scared out of his position and exited too soon. He knows, however, to stick with his time frame. In circled area 4 on the three-day chart, the exit is clear because of indicator readings, an Exit Long signal, and very close proximity to the upper N Band.

The lesson here is to know your trade duration. Stick with it time and again. Use the applicable combination of charts with the correct periodicities for your trading time frame. Consistency is the key to maintaining objectivity in your decisions.

FIFTH-GRADE ARITHMETIC

It's not sufficient to make money on a trade and feel good about it; you must make the most money on a trade and choose that to feel good about. This needs to be your cause and your quest. It's all in the arithmetic.

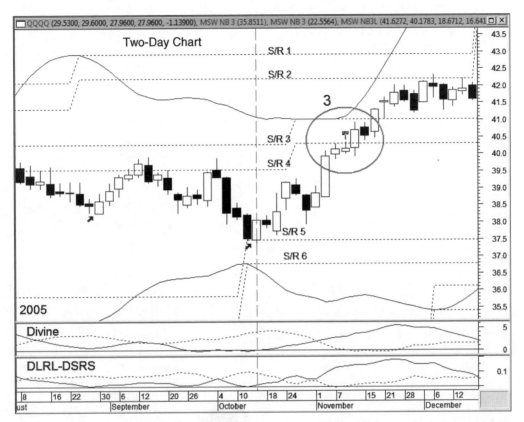

FIGURE 12.4 Two-day charts are very valuable for the swing trader and the shorter-term position trader.

Chart created in MetaStock. Chart uses the MetaSwing Add-on, by Northington Trading, LLC. All rights reserved.

Table 12.1 illustrates the importance of optimizing profit targets. The purpose of this simple math exercise is to quantify the impact of a relatively small increase in profit target. This is an example showing three different traders, all making the same series of six different trades. The trades include three losses and three wins. Instead of defining the amount of profit or loss as percentages, Table 12.1 expresses the amount in units of ATR(14). When the three traders lose, they each lose the same amount per trade. The only performance difference in the table is in the three trades that win. Specifically, Bill achieves ½ ATR(14) more profit than Jane. This is because Jane tends to cash out too soon or too late. Wanda achieves ½ ATR(14) more profit than Bill. Therefore, the difference between Wanda's profit per trade and Jane's profit per trade is one unit of ATR(14) of the stock's price. All three start with $10,000.

There is only one unit of ATR(14) difference between Jane, who finishes with a 2.9 percent loss, and Wanda, who achieves a 10.5 percent profit: a 13.4 percent differential. Just one day's trading range on three trades can make a huge difference. Remember that this is within a 50-50 win-loss ratio. Beyond their trading accounts, how do you think

| TABLE 12.1 | The difference that better profit targets can make. Each trader incrementally achieves a difference of only ½ day's true range, and experiences very different results |

	Jane	Bill	Wanda	
Winning ATR delta	−0.5	0.0	0.5	
Losing ATR delta	0.0	0.0	0.0	
Trading Account	10,000	10,000	10,000	
1				
Stock's ATR(14)	4%	4%	4%	
Exit ATRs	2.5	3.0	3.5	Win
Trading Account	11,000	11,200	11,400	
2				
Stock's ATR(14)	3.5%	3.5%	3.5%	
Exit ATRs	2.5	3.0	3.5	Win
Trading Account	11,963	12,376	12,797	
3				
Stock's ATR(14)	6%	6%	6%	
Exit ATRs	−1.2	−1.2	−1.2	Loss
Trading Account	11,101	11,485	11,875	
4				
Stock's ATR(14)	6%	6%	6%	
Exit ATRs	−2.5	−2.5	−2.5	Loss
Trading Account	9,436	9,762	10,094	
5				
Stock's ATR(14)	3.5%	4.0%	4.5%	
Exit ATRs	2.5	3.0	3.5	Win
Trading Account	10,262	10,934	11,684	
6				
Stock's ATR(14)	4.5%	4.5%	4.5%	
Exit ATRs	−1.2	−1.2	−1.2	Loss
Trading Account	9,708	10,343	11,053	
Net Performance	**−2.9%**	**3.4%**	**10.5%**	

this affects Jane and Wanda from a confidence standpoint? If these results are typical for the two traders, then going forward, Wanda is more likely to make the more objective and effective decisions. The lesson here is to trade like Wanda. It makes one wonder if Wanda likes the beach; she could be part sandpiper.

It's simple, really. Marginal returns generated by better profit targets are the source of your resilience. By increasing your ATR units of winning profit, you can more easily afford to take reasonable stop losses. Too often, those who cannot afford to lose money in the form of a stop loss hesitate to do so, only to watch the loss grow. Your logical self needs to be free of encumbrances. A better net sum profit position, achieved by positive marginal profit targets, will permit your logical self to do its job. It enables a trader to make more money on winners, and lose less on losers.

EXIT TACTICS

So far, this chapter should help you to appreciate the importance of optimizing profit targets, and doing so within the trade method's applicable time frame. We explore the primary volatility-based methods of selecting the best points to close the trade in the sections to come. There are five different tactics presented, most of which draw strength from disparate areas of the framework. They are:

1. Relative Exit
2. Volatility Band Exit
3. PIV Exit
4. Entry Exit
5. Broad Market Exit

The first thing to understand is that exiting is not a simple objective decision. The decision uses components from our volatility-based framework in much the same way that trade entries do. Analysis is applied and probabilities are estimated. You have already witnessed most of these tactics in previous chapter examples. We are about to go into greater detail, though.

Great exits carry huge benefits. Understanding when, and in which periodicity, to apply them is empowering. Booking your profits and then watching price stall or reverse is downright fun. Best of all, I believe these tactics will help to keep those Twilight Zone passengers from causing problems on your train.

The Relative Exit

Alas, this tactic is not about ejecting your brother-in-law from your home because he's worn out his welcome. Rather, it is a way of measuring the relative volatility height of a qualifying overbought and oversold indicator. When looking at a MetaSwing chart, the small exit symbols are directly calculated using this method.

First, let's explain what's meant by *qualifying overbought and oversold indicator*. It is an indicator that:

- Measures overbought and oversold conditions
- Is based on volatility measurement
- Is not bound by high or low numerical limits
- Returns a nonlinear value
- Is trend compensated

For example, the TTI StochEx indicator would not qualify because its value will always fall between 0 and 100. Even though it has no numerical boundaries, the traditional MACD would not qualify because it is not based on volatility measurement; nor is it an overbought and oversold indicator. A traditional Stochastic oscillator would not qualify for both volatility and numerical limitation reasons.

Examples of indicators that do qualify are:

- TTI Composite
- TTI ATR extreme
- MetaSwing DLRL-DSRS

All three of these indicators have no numerical boundaries, are based on volatility measurement, and do perform overbought and oversold functions. The degree to which a qualifying indicator performs as a Relative Exit component is subject to other parameters. The DLRL-DSRS performs somewhat better than the other two because of its tandem construct principle: each of its two components focuses on a specific side of the market.

The Relative Exit is derived from a series of peaks or troughs of a qualifying indicator. A quantity of peaks is averaged to produce an extreme level. When the indicator itself crosses the extreme level, then the probability of price pausing or reversing is high; it is thus time to consider exiting the trade. The best way to understand those parameters is visually.

Figure 12.5 shows a daily chart of Aracruz Celulose (ARA). The bottom indicator pane has the MetaSwing DLRL oversold indicator plotted. Overlaid on it as a dotted line is a standard Zigzag indicator configured with a 90 percent reversal parameter. Theoretically, this means that a value of .2 must fall to .018 before a trough can form. A trough must form before another peak can form, and so on. The horizontal line plotted is another indicator named DLRL Peaks and it performs the job of identifying the extreme level. An Exit Long signal is displayed on the price pane above the candle that causes the DLRL oversold indicator to cross above the DLRL Peaks indicator line.

Figure 12.5 shows this process in action. When the DLRL indicator goes to the zero line, it is indicative of an oversold condition. When it rises enough, however, the odds of exiting with having captured the majority of the long-side price movement is high.

- In circled area 1, two exits are signaled. If you look closely at the lower pane you can see how the DLRL went above the DLRL Peaks twice in three days.
- In circled area 2, the exit is an optical illusion that I discuss later.
- In circled area 3, the exit works well again and allows the trader to book the majority of the total price move as profit.

The tactic is not a stand-alone signal to be obeyed in a mechanical way. It is information for the trader to consider. It is one component of the framework. With multiple components combining their probabilities, the analyst can make a very informed exit decision.

The MetaStock code to create the Relative Exit is very simple. Here is the code for the DLRL Peaks indicator:

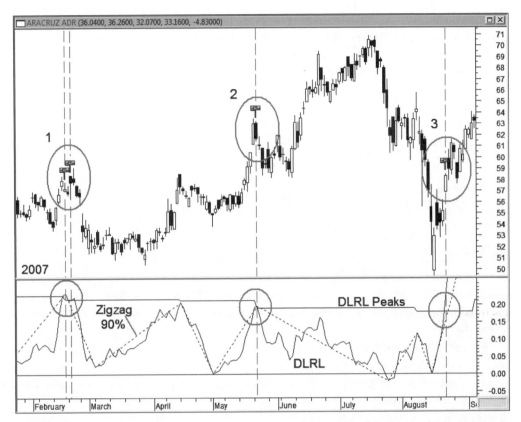

FIGURE 12.5 This daily chart of Aracruz Celulose (ARA) graphically portrays the Relative Exit construct.

Chart created in MetaStock. Chart uses the MetaSwing Add-on, by Northington Trading, LLC. All rights reserved.

```
 1 {Assigns the Metaswing DLRL indicator value to the x variable}
 2 x:= Fml("MSW Max DLRL Delta 20");
 3 {Identifies and adds the most recent 7 peak values}
 4 {Then divides by 7 to return an average}
 5 (Peak(1, x, 90) +
 6 Peak(2, x, 90) +
 7 Peak(3, x, 90) +
 8 Peak(4, x, 90) +
 9 Peak(5, x, 90) +
10 Peak(6, x, 90) +
11 Peak(7, x, 90)) / 7
```

Here is an explanation of the code:

- Line 2 establishes the variable x. It then invokes the external formula call to the MetaSwing DLRL indicator.

- Lines 5 through 11 each use the Peak function to identify individual highs of the DLRL indicator. Each Peak statement takes three arguments.

  1. The first number defines which of the most recent peak instances is being measured.
  2. The second argument specifies what time series data are being measured for a peak. In this case, it is the variable x, which is actually the DLRL indicator.
  3. The last argument is the number that specifies the Peak percent change parameter.

As you can see, there are two central parameters that can be changed in this formula code.

1. The first is the Peak percent change parameter. It is currently at 90, by default. Decreasing this setting would increase the sensitivity to more recent volatility levels.
2. The second is to increase or decrease the actual quantity of peaks used in the calculation. The code shown here uses a total of seven recent peaks. Of course, decreasing the quantity focuses on more recent peak activity, and increasing it would create a longer look-back basis.

The Exit Long symbol on the price chart is turned on by using the following code in the MetaStock Expert system.

```
Cross(Fml("MSW Max DLRL Delta 20"),Fml("MSW Max DLRL Delta 20 Peaks"))
```

This is actually one single statement. It nests two external formula calls inside of a Cross function. The Cross statement has two arguments, which are in this case the two external formula calls. It looks for the first argument value to rise above the second argument value. When the cross occurs, the formula returns a value of 1 for that period.

Figure 12.6 gives another look at the same chart of Aracruz Celulose so that we can see how more components can contribute to more confident exit decisions. N Bands, S/R lines, Adeo signals, and the DSRS indicator have been added back in. The Zigzag overlay has been removed. With more areas of our framework represented, we can use cross-verification in the decision process. In looking at the chart again, we can recognize the following factors:

- In circled area 1, there is an Adeo Short signaling with price getting to within one ATR of the N Band. This means that it is time to exit, especially if the intermediate trend is down.
- In circled area 2, there is another Adeo Short signal with price close to the N Band. The DLRL does not yet have the height to reach the DLRL Peaks line, however. With

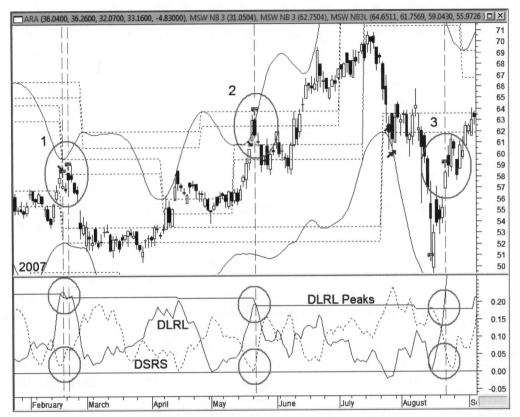

FIGURE 12.6 Another look at the chart of Aracruz Celulose (ARA) is shown here with more exit tactic components present.

Chart created in MetaStock. Chart uses the MetaSwing Add-on, by Northington Trading, LLC. All rights reserved.

price rallying in recent weeks, a trailing stop is called for here. But stay tuned for the optical illusion explanation.

- In circled area 3, the explosive upward price behavior foretells of an expanding volatility environment. Also, the DSRS has not descended close enough to zero to indicate an overbought situation. This means that price has a tendency to rise to resistance, and so looking to exit at the S/R line would be prudent.

As you can see, adding more components to the chart helps with the decision process. The Relative Exit tactic is very reliable. It is not meant, however, to be used as a stand-alone mechanical process.

Peak and Trough Illusions A word of caution about Peaks and Troughs in programming code. The Peak and Trough functions are very useful. They use a standard technical analysis Zigzag algorithm. This function defines a peak when there has been a set percentage change in the measured value from its most recent high. As such, the following trough cannot begin to be defined until there has been a given percentage drop in the measured value from its most recent high, or peak.

It's important to understand, however, that until a sufficient percentage move is made from the previous peak or trough, a new one can't be formed, that is, made permanent. This means that the most recently forming peak or trough, whichever is the case, is only temporary. For example, the most recent peak is not permanent until there is a trough forming right after it. If the most recent one forming is a peak, however, then all previous peaks are permanent; they will not change. Only the most recent one forming can be in question.

Why is this important, you may ask? Well, look at the code for the DLRL Peaks again. With Peak number one being only temporary in the calculation, then the resulting formula value can change when a new trough is finally formed. A good example of this is shown in Figures 12.5 and 12.6, in circled area 2. This chart was deliberately chosen to illustrate this phenomenon. If you will look closely at the DLRL line, it does not reach the DLRL Peaks line. In fact, the DLRL Peaks line drops to meet the DLRL, thus creating the cross of the two lines. On that date, however, there was no cross. The Exit signal was not plotted on the screen until after the DLRL had fallen by 90 percent to create a trough. That did not happen until weeks later. Therefore, this Exit Long signal did not occur in reality in real time. This situation is quite infrequent, but it can happen.

This may seem misleading or even dangerous. On the one hand, it could be if the trader does not know about the limitation and is not on guard for it. To make sure that this does not occur, the formula could be changed to use Peaks two through eight, and ignore the most recent one altogether. This would fix the problem. But wait, there is a flip side.

By using the most recent Peak value in the formula you are seeing the level of peaks that are more representative of the current market conditions. It's similar to avoiding a simple moving average calculation in favor of using an exponential moving average because it removes much of the lag. By getting a better measurement of the more current peaks, you are seeing a better volatility representation and can thus make more accurate decisions in real time. It is my personal preference to always view the most current volatility measurement possible.

This is a limitation to consider and understand. It is also why other components are added to the profit target selection process. In circled area 2 on the chart in Figure 12.6, there is an Adeo Short and close N Band proximity. Both are important exit tactics on their own, and will be shown in detail on the pages to come.

The Volatility Band Exit

Have you ever taken a very large dog for a walk? During this process of fresh air and answering nature's call, which one of you is in charge? Is the dog pulling you around, or are you directing it? This relationship is similar to the volatility band and price. In this analogy, you are the band, and the dog is price.

A good volatility band should possess these characteristics:

- When price comes in close proximity, it should reverse, change the trend direction, or pause. Price should not continue in the same direction as if unaffected by the band.
- The band should not simply follow price around with no effect on it.
- The slope of the band should have an effect on the direction that price takes after they come into close proximity.

The bands need to display these behavior characteristics to have a good Volatility Band Exit tactic. The more the bands reflect consolidated implied volatility, the better they will work. Implied volatility is what convinces large hedge funds to change position sizes or exit altogether. In other words, the owner should walk the dog.

A daily chart of Level 3 Communications (LVLT) is in Figure 12.7. The N Band slope

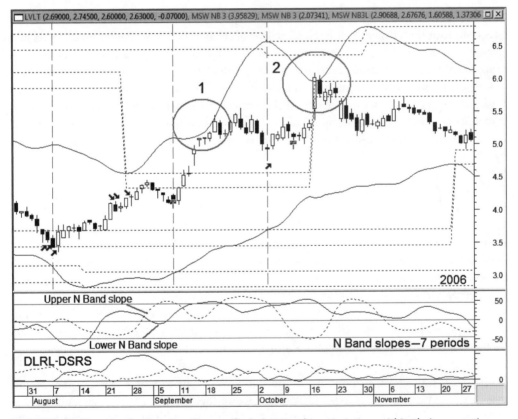

FIGURE 12.7 Volatility bands with specific behavior characteristics, within their respective chart periodicities, make for good profit target points.

Chart created in MetaStock. Chart uses the MetaSwing Add-on, by Northington Trading, LLC. All rights reserved.

indicators are plotted in the middle indicator pane, the same ones used in the previous chapter. There are three vertical dashed lines plotted. These represent potential trade entry points. The circled areas show profit target areas. Here's what the price and band behavior tells us.

- In circled area 1, price pauses for two days when it first encounters the upper N Band. It then rises slightly and consolidates for a month. The upper N Band slope is +6 degrees on September 15. If the slope were heading in the opposing direction to price on that date, the results would have likely been different.
- In circled area 2, a very different set of circumstances develops. Price again rises to touch the upper N Band. On October 27, the upper N Band slope value is –47 degrees. The band's momentum is opposing the price direction; price then subsequently reverses. As we discovered in the previous chapter, when the upper N Band is at that level, it indicates a low slope reading and a potential downward volatility shift. A hedge fund manager, sitting on a sizable position, sees this falling implied volatility and reduces her holdings by selling.

While the Volatility Band Exit does not always provide as high a degree of granularity as other profit target tactics, it excels in different ways. Consider the two examples just discussed in Figure 12.7. By adding the band slope measurement, we gain some valuable probability about the strength of the band's effect on price, and its more immediate direction. If you know that the encroaching band's slope is positive, then you may want to use a trailing stop, as price may continue onward a short distance. If the band slope is steeply opposing the direction of price, however, you may want to take profits right away. We see that it's not just a matter of proximity, then, but also one of implied volatility momentum.

The PIV Exit

The predominant form of support and resistance in the markets today shows up as Projected Implied Volatility (PIV). The classic, and still current, definition of *support* being a place where buyers overpower sellers is alive and well.[1] *Resistance* is defined the same way, only it is a price level where sellers overpower buyers. With equities, support and resistance are driven primarily by the options marketplace. They are expressed in the peaks and troughs of implied volatility. Since N Bands are a consolidated representation of implied volatility, its peaks and troughs form horizontal levels (S/R lines) of support and resistance. For more information on PIV, review its section in Chapter 5.

The PIV Exit in MetaSwing is a tactic that sells a long position when price rises to meet an S/R line. This is because as price rises into the S/R line, its average gain per day will likely decrease to less than an amount worth risking capital for. Likewise, when price descends to an S/R line, it encounters support, and thus the PIV Exit tactic is to cover the position. Selling at resistance and covering at support is a basic trading practice that is older than most people reading this book. The PIV Exit adapts this practice for today's volatility-driven markets. It updates the strategy by enabling equities traders to exit at support or resistance, as it is created by the more dominant options trading marketplace.

We saw in Chapter 10 how PIV can produce profitable trading around volatility-based levels of price consolidation. The PIV Exit tactic enables a trader to book profits and spend less time in positions. There are some important guidelines to its use:

- The inner S/R lines are numbers 3, 4, 5, and 6. The outer S/R lines are numbers 1, 2, 7, and 8.
- The inner S/R lines should be used more often when trading range conditions exist, that is, when there is no predominant strong trend in place.
- The inner S/R lines should generally be combined with other signals for greater predictive value.
- The outer S/R lines do not need as much cross-verification with other technical measurements for their predictive value.
- The strength that an S/R line carries as a support or resistance level is directly relative to the amount of time price has been away from it. The longer price has not existed at a particular S/R line, the greater the line's strength is. If price has traded at or through a particular S/R line recently, then the line's strength is lower.

These guidelines are very common to classic forms of technical support and resistance. Let's look more closely at how we can apply them for effective profit targets. In Figure 12.8 is a daily MetaSwing chart of Symantec Corporation (SYMC), with three examples of PIV Exits. Here are the analysis points we can derive from each:

- In circled area 1, price pauses an upward move at the S/R 3 line. The S/R line is manually extended forward until the day that the upper N Band causes it to reset to a new and higher trough level. This is so that we can see the line as it exists on the day the analyst would be looking at the chart and making a decision. It is accompanied by an Adeo short signal. Price had been at that level twice in the previous two weeks, though. Therefore, a reversal does not occur. Actually, price consolidates there for seven days, until finally rolling over a bit.
- In circled area 2, traders come to recognize that resistance based on short-term PIV has risen. Price then trades up to it at the new S/R 4 line. Since the stock's trading price had not been there in over a month, the level holds firm and produces a shallow reversal. This instance is accompanied by a slightly oversold DSRS reading.
- In circled area 3, we can witness how the outer S/R lines behave when price becomes more volatile. Once again, the S/R lines are manually extended to the date when it still exists before resetting. As you can see, Symantec gaps up out of its trading range into a strong rally. Remember that it is a sign of real strength when price jumps over resistance. The first Exit Long signal should be considered, therefore, with that in mind. Price proceeds on to pause at the S/R 2 line for 10 days. It then rises to the S/R 1 line and reverses. Taking profits at either of these levels would have been a

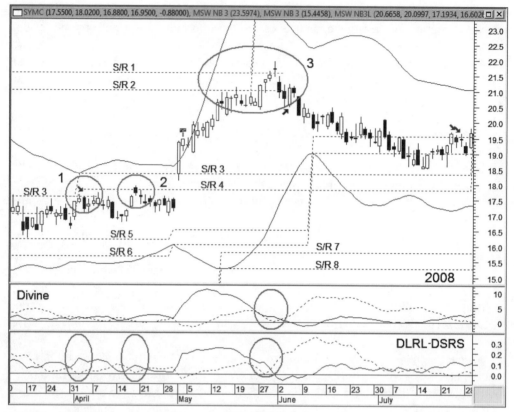

FIGURE 12.8 This daily chart of Symantec Corporation (SYMC) illustrates well the general guidelines of taking profits at resistance.

Chart created in MetaStock. Chart uses the MetaSwing Add-on, by Northington Trading, LLC. All rights reserved.

success. Note, however, that overbought readings only confirm when price reaches the S/R 1 line.

It is easy in the Symantec Corporation example to observe the correlation between recent price level and time since the resistance level has been traded. In each of the three instances, price approaches the resistance line from further away, and in each instance, resistance is proportionately stronger. In fact, the circled area 3 example could also be examined on the larger weekly periodicity chart (not shown) to see the resistance forces at play there.

In circled area 3, the position trader actually makes a good decision to take profits at the S/R 2 line. The swing trader may wish to hold out, however, for the extra ATR offered by the combination of the oversold DSRS and S/R 1. This is the extra day's trading range referred to in Table 12.1.

Levels of PIV are created on stock charts because of stock options trading. In the

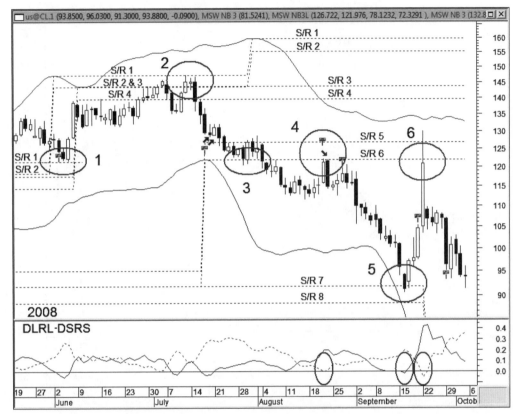

FIGURE 12.9 Using PIV support and resistance works very well on most commodity and FOREX charts, as is show here on this chart of NYMEX Crude Oil.

Chart created in MetaStock. Chart uses the MetaSwing Add-on, by Northington Trading, LLC. All rights reserved.

world of commodities and FOREX they are traded only as futures. The very nature of futures trading is based on volatility. It should be no surprise, therefore, that commodities and FOREX respond very well to support and resistance levels created by implied volatility extremes.

The daily chart in Figure 12.9 is of Light Sweet Crude Oil as traded on the NYMEX. In 2008, the volatility level of oil expanded as commodities began to peak and break down. In an environment such as that, PIV levels become outstanding profit targets. The circled areas on this chart show just how intensely commodities traders depended on PIV price targets.

- In circled area 1, the S/R 1 line is extended until it resets, as in the previous examples. Profit taking of a short position would be the right thing to do for many reasons. Oversold reading on the DLRL, Exit Short signal, and the S/R 1 line all converge. Also look at Figure 12.10, the weekly chart of Crude Oil. It shows that the S/R 1 line

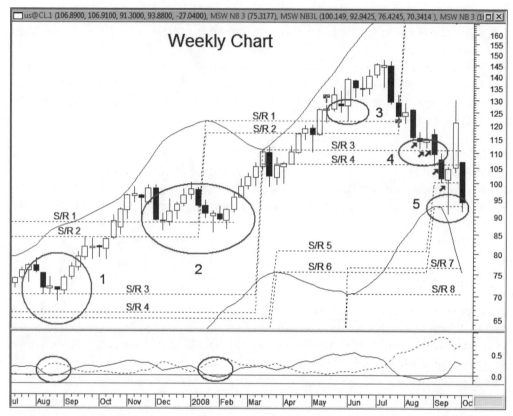

FIGURE 12.10 The weekly charts can be extremely important for short-term and position trading. Here, weekly S/R lines align frequently with those on the daily chart, producing stronger levels of support and resistance.

Chart created in MetaStock. Chart uses the MetaSwing Add-on, by Northington Trading, LLC. All rights reserved.

is only a .06 difference from the S/R 1 line on the daily chart. This kind of alignment adds strength to PIV-based support.

- In circled area 2, price experiences its final pause at resistance by using the S/R 1 line as its high. For the short-term trader, this is a natural spot to take profits. For the position trader, the oversold confirmation days earlier, combined with the current price stall, means that it is a signal to reduce position size.
- Circled area 3 shows a seven-day pause and consolidation between the S/R 5 and S/R 6 lines. Also, this daily S/R 6 line is roughly equal to the weekly S/R 1 at that date (Figure 12.10), thus producing higher support significance.
- Circled area 4 shows a rise to resistance at the S/R 6 line. Combined with an Exit Long and Adeo Short combination, price begins its reversal. A trader may not have had a long position on here, but look at the respect for the resistance line.
- In circled area 5, the long deliberate downtrend finds support at S/R 7 accompanied by an oversold DLRL signal. This means it's time to take profits. After large volatility

moves like these, the outer S/R lines become very significant. Also note that the daily S/R 7 line is virtually equal to the weekly S/R 6 line in circled area 5, in Figure 12.10: more strength.

- Finally, an amazing, high-volatility, four-day reversal brings price all the way back to the S/R 6 line. In such turbulent times, the forces of supply and demand are in great turmoil. The volatility-based support and resistance lines are the only things that the large fund traders can quantify and count on.

The same chart of Crude Oil in Figure 12.9 is presented in a weekly periodicity in Figure 12.10. It is easy to see visually how the rising trend finds support at the S/R lines shown in circled areas 1, 2, and 3. The sell-off uses the PIV-based support in circled areas 4 and 5. It is extremely significant when the S/R lines of a daily chart virtually match the S/R lines found on the weekly chart. The significance is greater because you are joining forces on the same side of a market with traders from other time frames.

The Entry Exit

Here's a question that most people can answer if they have been in the workforce for about 10 years or more. When is the second-best time to quit your job? Inarguably, the best time is after you've won the lottery. Setting that situation aside, the next best time to leave your present employment is when your current position offers little growth and you have a much better opportunity to jump to. This situation describes the Entry Exit perfectly.

Certainly, if you won $100,000,000 in the lottery, you would likely exit all current equity or option positions in order to rethink the balance of your life. If that's not what you have won, however, then you should generally heed the signals of the Entry Exit. This type of exit seems as if it should not require definition, explanation, or, for that matter, space in this book. But when a trader is confused about her time frame, or is unaware of her greed factor, she often holds her position right through this signal needlessly.

The Entry Exit is one you encounter after your trade has gone well. In fact, it's gone so well that price has moved in the desired direction far enough to set up a good trade entry for a reversal. It's not complicated, but it does require that you temporarily change your mindset. You must set your existing trade aside and look at the signal independently. This is sometimes the only way to recognize that a trade has set up in the opposite direction. You may not want to reverse your position, but you should certainly see reason and take profits.

In Figure 12.11 is a daily chart of PPL Corporation (PPL), with some of the original technical indicators that we created in this book. The TTI Fabric LR is plotted across the price pane. The TTI ATR Extreme is plotted in the middle indicator pane. And the TTI Composite is plotted in the lower indicator pane.

Circled areas 1, 2, and 3 all qualify as good trade entry points. Assuming you are a swing trader, let's say you've entered a long position in area 1. The −1 thread on the TTI Fabric LR is a good entry point. Your trade then works out perfectly. In eight days you

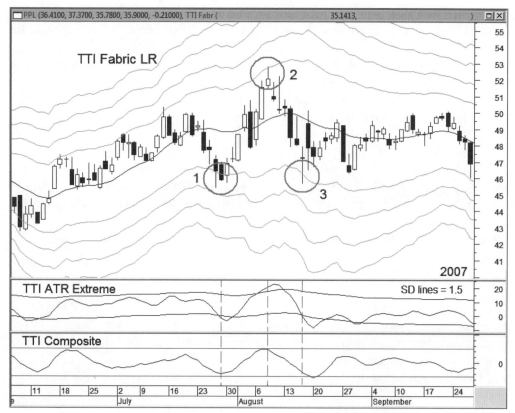

FIGURE 12.11 This daily chart of PPL Corporation (PPL) illustrates well how a good entry is a sure sign of a good exit.

Chart created in MetaStock.

reach the +1 thread on the Fabric as well as overbought conditions on both indicators. These three criteria were most of the basis of your long entry decision. Is there any technical reason to stay in this trade?

The answer to that is a simple no. You may not choose to take the short trade, for any number of possible reasons. It is undeniable, however, that the probabilities of further profit in the short term are low. It is therefore time to take profits and do the victory dance.

This same profit-taking tactic works well for longer trading time frames. The ever-patient position trader frequently sees entry points as his exit. Examine the weekly chart in Figure 12.12. This is a weekly periodicity MetaSwing chart. Areas 1, 2, and 3 each represent good entry points. Each have excellent indicator cross-verification. Look at the DLRL-DSRS tandem indicator height in the lower pane. These relative levels indicate qualified, extreme conditions. See the extended chart version of this figure online at www.tradingtheinvisible.com so that you may compare the past tandem heights to these.

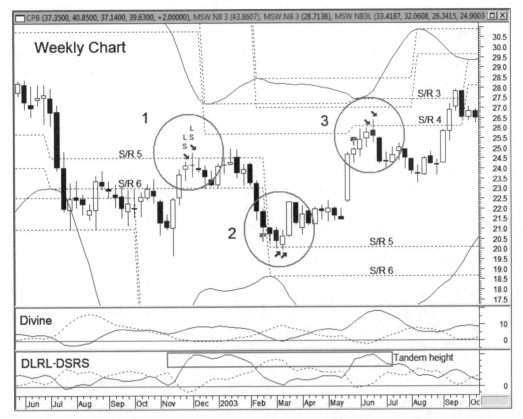

FIGURE 12.12 Position traders face similar Entry Exit profit targets on weekly time frame charts.

Chart created in MetaStock. Chart uses the MetaSwing Add-on, by Northington Trading, LLC. All rights reserved.

Remember that when clear entry signals appear that are counter to your current position, you are fighting the forces of supply and demand if you stand pat. Other traders don't care about how proud you are of your position. Nor do they care about your pride as your profits slip away because you did not exit. The bottom line is to see it for what it is.

The Broad Market Exit

Suppose that 30 minutes before you and your spouse are to go out for dinner and a movie you discover that your three-year-old child has a fever of 104 degrees. Cancel the baby sitter, right? Or, consider that you break your ankle the day before you are scheduled for that great weekend of hiking in the mountains. Looks like it's going to be another stay-at-home weekend, doesn't it?

Now consider that you have a long position in place in one of your favorite stocks.

The market and all the technical signals had set up perfectly for this trade. Things have been going well with it, and it is halfway to its profit target. Suddenly, the major indexes start to turn down. The selling continues into the afternoon session. All indexes end up drastically down. Even worse is that virtually every sector sold off and ended the day with negative breadth. The vast majority of traded issues on the major exchanges finished the day lower. Even your position has retraced downward to within 1 percent of your entry point. What do you do?

None of these three nasty turns were anticipated. None were a part of your plan. Each must be dealt with, however. There is no doubt that you would stay home and care for your child. You would certainly not hop around on one leg on a mountain trail with a broken ankle. These two changes of plans are obvious.

Why then would you hold on to a long position, when in the next few days the majority of stocks in the market will be racking up further losses? Why would you delude yourself into thinking that your long position will be different from the rest of the market? Right now as you read this, you are probably thinking that you would not react that way. It's likely that you believe that you would be rational about the situation and close your position.

An unbelievable percentage of individual traders sit on their long positions, grit their teeth, and squirm for days as they watch their trade lose money. All the while, they create justifications for the incorrect decision. This is a problem that plagues most individual, nonprofessional traders. It is unfortunate, but it is true.

The Broad Market Exit follows the following principle: One of the best ways to make money is by not losing it. This exit tactic is a simple knee-jerk reaction to an extreme market-breadth event. This occurs when the number of stocks that finish lower greatly outnumber those that finish higher, or vice versa. When the ratio of gainers to losers is so one-sided, it foretells the broader market action for days to come. Your action to exit your position is a simple decision to keep yourself on the right side of the market.

At this point, I'm not going to describe the event detection method or details any further. The MetaSwing Correction and Surge method, complete with code and parameters, is explained in the next chapter. At this point, it is sufficient to understand that when a Correction event occurs, you should probably exit all long positions. Furthermore, when a Surge event occurs, you should strongly consider exiting short positions. The tactical methods for using the MetaSwing Correction and Surge system are also discussed in the next chapter.

As an illustration of a typical stock's reaction, Figure 12.13 shows us a chart of Oracle Corporation (ORCL) when a Total Correction signal occurs. In the circled area at left, Oracle has been experiencing a mild trend rally when in mid-July the broad market gets a swift kick where it hurts. On July 24, 2007, a Total Correction event takes place. It appears on the chart as a skull and crossbones symbol. Immediately following this day, Oracle experiences a rapid price decline over the next four weeks, along with most of the market. When the initial signal becomes visible, the odds of a further price increase are against you. It is best to exit and accept any profit or loss you currently find yourself with.

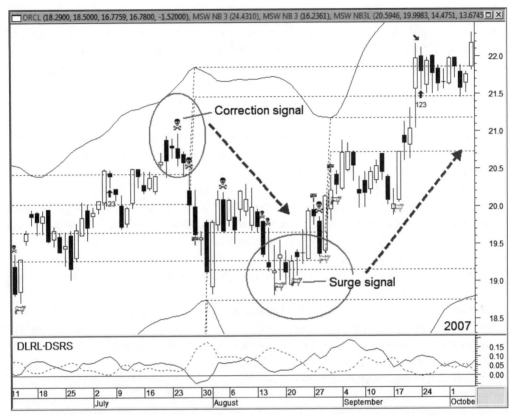

FIGURE 12.13 This chart of Oracle Corporation (ORCL) shows clearly how extreme market breadth events affect the immediate trading direction of individual stocks.

Chart created in MetaStock. Chart uses the MetaSwing Add-on, by Northington Trading, LLC. All rights reserved.

Several MetaSwing Surge signals form in the circled area at right. They appear on the chart as bull symbols. When these positive market breadth signals begin to appear in sequence, it is best to exit short positions. On August 22, 2007, the second Surge signal shows the market's intent for a temporary bottoming action. Further gains to the downside, therefore, are not likely in the short term, and probably not so for the intermediate term, either. At that point, it is time to exit. It's really as simple as that. This is what is meant by "go with the flow."

ACHIEVING THE OBJECTIVE

To return to our train passengers, you may be wondering right now where passenger number three got off the train, and how was he so sure it would be the right place? The older fellow with the newspaper probably took his exit at an advantageous stop, though he did not know where that would be until he got there. Volatility-based tools work that way. Fixed target points aren't possible when volatility measurements are a function of movement and time. What is to come is a function of what has happened, which does not fully occur until you get there. But when the exit is right, volatility-based exit tactics will tell you.

The elder gentleman does not represent the ideal mindset for choosing profit targets, but he is close. He puts total faith in mathematical calculations, which is the third trap that traders can fall into. The flaw is the *total* aspect. If it were not, then people would not trade; computer programs would do it all for us. If we behave too mechanically, then we fail to take advantage of our ability to use creativity. The human element cannot be discounted.

The confidence of passenger number one is a trait we all need, or else we could not stomach the risk of which the markets are composed. Passenger number two was far too open-minded and indecisive. Sometimes, though, each of us needs to step back and reconsider the desired outcome. We therefore each need some of the traits of all three Twilight Zone Express passengers. The challenge is to use them in the right way and to the correct degree. That is a human challenge.

If we can harness these traits, then we can improve our trading and achieve the objective. Make it your personal goal to increase your profitable trades by one unit of ATR. Maximizing profit targets with volatility-based exit tactics can happen only if you know and live your trading time frame consistently. The methods we just explored will serve you well within that envelope.

CHAPTER 13

Correction and Surge

An Early Warning System

There once was a small, elderly man named Sam, who was known as the best fisherman in the entire county. No one understood how Sam could catch so many fish throughout the region's many vast lakes with just a rowboat. You see, Sam always fished alone, forever refusing requests to join him for a fishing trip.

For years, Sam longed for a slick, new, high-powered fishing boat, but could not quite afford one. He finally went to a bank to get a boat loan. Sam's longtime friend and bank manager, Roy, informed him that he lacked the collateral necessary for the loan, but said if Sam would take him along on his next fishing trip he might be able to find a way to get the loan approved. Sam did not want to do this, but he so longed for a new boat. After several weeks of weighing the pros and cons, Sam agreed to Roy's terms and got the loan.

Two weeks later Sam and Roy went fishing in the fantastic new boat. After dropping anchor in a suitable but private cove, Roy took out his fishing pole and began to choose his bait. Sam reached into a brown canvas satchel and pulled out a hand grenade. He then proceeded to pull the pin. Roy's eyes became as large as grapefruit and his jaw dropped. Sam then let the striker lever fly and tossed the grenade overboard about 20 feet from the boat. A huge *whomp* sound vibrated the boat and water shot up into the air. Thirty seconds later, there were six large fish floating on the surface of the water.

Roy quickly recovered from his shock and exclaimed that Sam could not do this. He yelled that such a thing was highly dangerous and illegal. Sam calmly reached into his bag and pulled out another hand grenade. He extracted the pin, tossed the grenade into Roy's lap, and said to Roy, "Are you going to sit there and argue, or are you going to fish?"

The stock market does not ask our permission or approval before it makes unexpected and outrageous price movements. Neither does it care what we think about the move after it occurs. We do have two choices, though. The first is to sit on our hands and complain how this move is irrational and makes no sense. This quickly leads to additional losses in our trading accounts because of inaction. The other option is to fish.

We began using the MetaSwing Correction and Surge signals in Chapter 8. There they were used to predict market direction in the intermediate time frame. Then we just saw in Chapter 12 how important they can be as a quick exit signal. We examine them more closely in this chapter. We will focus specifically on the short-term market direction, and the trading opportunities that these two signals present. This will include a discussion of how these signals are calculated, and why they differ from other market breadth measurements. You will also be presented in these pages with the MetaSwing proprietary source code. This is the first time that this code has ever been released.

The point of this chapter is twofold. It is first to correct a mistake that most individual traders make, which is to ignore valuable signals of directional intelligence. The second purpose is to show you how to take advantage of the largest gift the stock market has to offer. Actually, these two things are one and the same; it just depends on your mindset for how you want to view them. You can consider it a mistake to ignore a loud siren that announces the market's intention to change its trend. It can also be viewed as a fantastic opportunity to enter new positions that are in agreement with the broad market's intentions.

You can purchase any one of hundreds of market timing and expert newsletter services. Some are very expensive; most are neither timely nor accurate. In fact, the professional technical analysis community considers paid advisory services, as an aggregate, to be a contrary sentiment indicator.[1] On the whole, these market guru services are wrong consistently enough that if you took the opposite side of the market you would be decidedly profitable over time. Now there is a dish of irony!

I don't mean to condemn market advisory services as a whole. Should you choose not to do market directional analysis for yourself there are some very good advisory services to choose from. Just beware that competence in this area is not the majority.

The truth is that there is a very simple method to forecast short-term market direction. Purchasing advice for this directional intelligence is quite unnecessary. The daily data values for manual calculations may be obtained from many web site sources for free. Allow yourself a moment to feel good about this topic. You can do this well, without anyone's expert commentary.

Now sit back and enjoy yourself because we're going fishing.

MARKET BREADTH

Every day the major stock exchanges in the United States report data regarding stocks that close above or below their previous session's closing price. They also report the number of stocks that close at the exact same price as the previous session's close. Many sources report the quantities of stocks making 52-week new high or new low closings. *Market breadth* is the analysis of these data, and their derivations, to predict turning points and market direction.

Classic technical analysis offers many different ways to measure and analyze market breadth. No matter how you slice it and dice it, the real objective is to measure internal market strength. As the major exchanges and their procedures have changed over the decades, market breadth measurement methods have had to adapt. For example, the move to decimalization, and away from fractional stock pricing, has forced less reliance on calculations, which focus heavily on the unchanged issues total. This leads us to realize that we need to understand the nature of the data themselves.

Devils and Details

The first important thing to focus on is that once again there is money to be made at the extremes. Where market breadth is concerned, we are referring then to an extreme event. Extreme events by nature mean that they must be a high level of deviation from the norm.

Think of the normal distribution diagram shown in Figure 4.1. The further out from the center, the higher the quantity of standard deviations. Once you get far enough out, the incremental measurement change is small compared to the change in standard deviation. This implies that a small change in numbers makes the difference between a threshold being crossed and not being crossed. Therefore, at the extreme point of market breadth, a few additional stocks advancing or declining can make all the difference.

There are three pieces of market data used as reported by the exchange in calculating a Correction or Surge event:

1. Advancing Issues

2. Declining Issues

3. Unchanged Issues

These three numbers seem relatively simple and objective, yes? Not really, because each is a constantly moving target. Obviously, they change because the closing price changes daily. Just as important, though, is the process of listing and delisting at each stock exchange.

Each of the major U.S. exchanges has specific rules and procedures for listing a stock for active trading. The same goes for the delisting process. Existing stocks are delisted from the exchange every day, just as others are listed or delisted. Therefore, every day there exists a total quantity of listed stocks actively traded. Figure 13.1 shows a highly compressed daily chart view of these totals for the NYSE and the NASDAQ exchanges. The first thing you might notice is how greatly the NASDAQ total decreased after the technology bubble popped. Almost 2,000 stocks lost their listed status in a few short years. What a gigantic transfer of wealth!

Suppose you were trying to measure market breadth using finite numbers as a basis. If you are looking for some fixed number of advancing or declining stocks as a measure, this rising and falling total of actively listed stocks would make that difficult. The equation and thresholds would need periodic adjustments. Also, the results could be inconsistent.

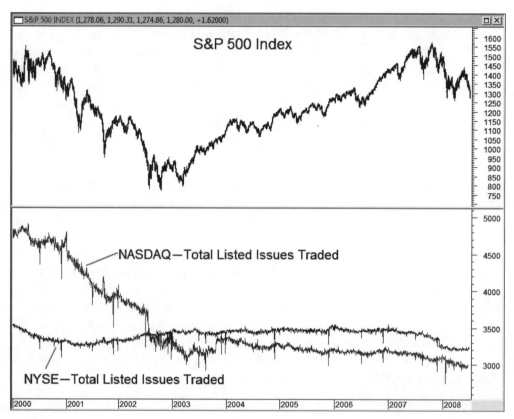

FIGURE 13.1   This chart shows a sum of the total listed stocks on the NASDAQ and NYSE. Chart created in MetaStock.

This quantity of total listed stocks rises and falls daily, with a wider range than you might think. Figure 13.2 zooms into the same chart showing the total listed securities for a smaller time. This gives a more accurate view of the daily fluctuations. The circled example shows how the NASDAQ fluctuated by 99 listed issues over a two-trading-session time frame. The total decreased by 3.1 percent, and then snapped back upward to a higher quantity. In fact, from January 3, 2000, to June 30, 2008, the average positive or negative daily percentage fluctuation for each exchange was:

- NYSE: .53 percent
- NASDAQ: .9 percent

This level of daily and weekly change in the quantity of listed stocks makes measuring highly granular market breadth very tricky. This is especially true when you look at the additional delisting activity that occurs when a sudden market downturn forces weak stocks into an unlisted status. The impact is that a sudden increase of delisting occurs right at a time when you most need to measure a Correction event. All of this means

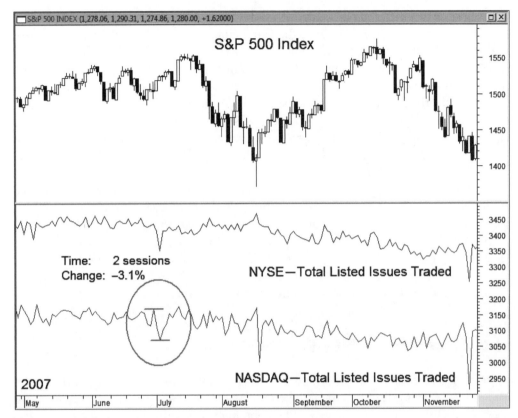

FIGURE 13.2 A closer view of the daily fluctuations of listed issues shows that the quantity can vary significantly.

Chart created in MetaStock.

that the best measurement method for market breadth is that of a ratio. A ratio is the method that the MetaSwing Correction and Surge signals are based on.

Data Consistency

I made mention in earlier chapters of the questionable reliability of market price and volume data. Errant trade execution can overstate high and low price values for a day's session. Accurate reporting of volume data, if it ever existed, is certainly a thing of the past. From what I've experienced, however, data vendors do everything within their control to deliver a clean and accurate product. But unfortunately, many things are out of their control.

With respect to market breadth data, it isn't as simple as accurate or inaccurate. There are multiple sources for the aggregate data regarding advancing, declining, and unchanged issues. The MetaSwing system was designed using the Reuters DataLink service from Reuters, which is the end-of-day feed. Reuters also had, when this chapter was written, a different data feed, named QuoteCenter, for real-time analysis. One would expect that these two services from the same company would report the exact same market breadth data at the end of each day.

This is not the case, however. When compared side by side, they render different values for the exact same data. To be fair, some investigation into the matter uncovered the reason for this. As it turns out, the data come from two different collection sources. As of this writing, one source reports only NYSE trades, which execute in New York. The other source adds the Boston exchange activity. One source includes rights and warrants, and the other does not. Therefore, neither source is more correct than the other; they are just different.

The important thing is that your data source be consistent. Also, if you replicate the calculations and code shown in this chapter, understand that different sources can produce different data, and the results you get could consequently show differences from what is presented here. As a result, you may need to adjust your thresholds accordingly. There is an Excel spreadsheet at this book's companion web site, www.tradingthe invisible.com, that contains the data used in these examples. By downloading it, you can compare the base data used here with that from your own source.

THE CORRECTION EVENT

We've all seen the nature shows where the herds of herbivores are drinking at the watering hole. As soon as the first one of them detects the nearby stalking lion they all move together, and they do it very quickly. Each one knows that the slowest of them gets to be dinner for the lion. This is classic herd mentality at times of danger. In all likelihood, only a few of the herd know it's a lion they are running from. The rest don't care. They are just trying to run faster than their peers.

This is a loose description of nature's pure herd behavior at a time of danger. It is also the type of behavior that describes a wide-breadth market sell-off day. The vast bodies of experts in the market have decided to exit long positions, or to at least reduce position sizes. An exceptionally high percentage of them have independently decided to take the same action. The best and brightest in the world cannot hide their actions or intentions on a day such as this. This is an advisory service worth listening to.

The MetaSwing Correction event is designed to detect this type of trading day. It is, in essence, a measurement of immediate fear. It is also a harbinger of follow-through selling that occurs in the immediate subsequent trading sessions.

The Correction Ratio

The Correction event is created when a ratio measurement exceeds a fixed threshold value. The Correction ratio is composed of declining issues, advancing issues, and unchanged issues. Although some other methods incorporate volume, the MetaSwing method does not use volume in any way.

The ratio is as follows:

$$\frac{\text{Declining Issues}}{\text{Moving Average (Advancing Issues} + \text{Declining Issues} + \text{Unchanged Issues)}}$$

The divisor in this equation is shown as a moving average of the sum of its parts. It's shown this way because the data are usually reported individually and must be summed. The advancing, declining, and unchanged issues combined compose the total issues traded. Therefore, we can also express it as:

$$\frac{\text{Declining Issues}}{\text{Moving Average (Total Issues Traded)}}$$

The Correction Code

Our next task, obviously, should be to express this equation in a computer code that technical analysis software can use. The ratio is the NYSE declining issues traded, divided by a five-period simple moving average of the total issues traded. The following is the MetaStock function language code to create the MetaSwing (version 3.2) Correction ratio for the New York Stock Exchange (NYSE):

```
1 {Declining issues}
2 Security("C:\MetaStock Data\BM Data\X.NYSE-D", C) /
3 {Divided by}
4 {A Moving Average of the Sum of Advancing + Declining + Unchanged
5 listed issues}
6 Mov(Security("C:\MetaStock Data\BM Data\X.NYSE-A", C) +
7 Security("C:\MetaStock Data\BM Data\X.NYSE-D", C) +
8 Security("C:\MetaStock Data\BM Data\X.NYSE-U", C), 5, S)
```

This code may at first appear to be a repeat of the same statements in lines 2, 6, 7, and 8. This is not the case though. Each of these lines uses the Security function. This is a function that retrieves a security or data value that is not part of the time series data already fed into the existing chart. By that, I mean that a chart of the S&P 500 Index automatically has the S&P 500 high, low, open, close, and volume data fed into it. If you want other time series security data in the chart, you will need to instruct the system to go and get them. That's what the Security function does.

We use the Security function for this because the broad market breadth data are delivered to you as though they are a stock price, that is, a time series with a high, low, open, and close value for each period. If you look closely at these statements, you see that there is a hard drive file location and a security name in each one. The only difference is the final letter in the security name. In this case, the A delineates that the symbol is that of the advancing issues, and so forth. The C argument specifies the closing value for that security. Also note that code shown here uses the Reuters DataLink service symbol names as they exist at the time this book is published.

Suppose we want a symbol to be plotted by the MetaStock Expert, above or below the day's price bar. In that case, we would need to add a qualifier to the aforementioned code so that it rendered a true or false (Boolean) value in lieu of a real number value. The new code would look like this:

```
1 (Security("C:\MetaStock Data\BM Data\X.NYSE-D", C) /
2 Mov(Security("C:\MetaStock Data\BM Data\X.NYSE-A", C) +
3 Security("C:\MetaStock Data\BM Data\X.NYSE-D", C) +
4 Security("C:\MetaStock Data\BM Data\X.NYSE-U", C), 5, S))
5 > .805
```

What you see here is essentially the MetaSwing (version 3.2) source code for the NYSE Correction event. The changes are:

- The comment statements have been deleted.
- Lines 1 through 4 are now enclosed in an additional set of parentheses so that they collectively render one ratio value.
- Line 5 is added as a threshold qualifier, thus producing a true or false output.

You can see the results of the MetaSwing code samples in Figure 13.3. The individual Correction events for the NYSE are plotted as skull-and-crossbones symbols above the price candles. In the lower indicator pane is a day-by-day plot of the actual Correction ratio. The upper value of .805 has been plotted to represent the extreme threshold. It is clear that when the ratio crosses the threshold line, the Correction symbol is visible above.

The following is the MetaSwing (version 3.2) code for the NASDAQ Correction ratio and signal.

Ratio

```
1 {Declining issues}
2 Security("C:\MetaStock Data\BM Data\X.NASD-D", C) /
3 {Divided by}
4 {A Moving Average of the Sum of Advancing + Declining + Unchanged
5 listed issues}
6 Mov(Security("C:\MetaStock Data\BM Data\X.NASD-A", C) +
7 Security("C:\MetaStock Data\BM Data\X.NASD-D", C) +
8 Security("C:\MetaStock Data\BM Data\X.NASD-U", C), 5, S)
```

Expert Symbol Code

```
1 (Security("C:\MetaStock Data\BM Data\X.NASD-D", C) /
2 Mov(Security("C:\MetaStock Data\BM Data\X.NASD-A", C) +
3 Security("C:\MetaStock Data\BM Data\X.NASD-D", C) +
4 Security("C:\MetaStock Data\BM Data\X.NASD-U", C), 5, S))
5 > .76
```

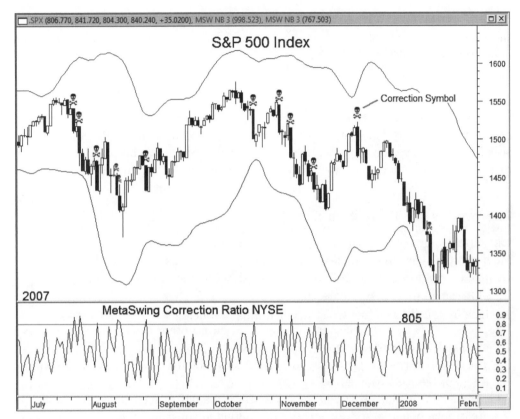

FIGURE 13.3 This chart of the S&P 500 Index is shows individual MetaSwing Correction signals for the NYSE, along with the Correction ratio plotted below.

Chart created in MetaStock. Chart uses the MetaSwing Add-on, by Northington Trading, LLC. All rights reserved.

Suppose the trading day experiences a really broad-breadth selling event. Fear is running rampant on Wall Street in both major stock exchanges. This would mean that the NYSE and the NASDAQ both experienced a Correction event. There are skulls and crossbones lying all over the place! When this occurs, it is known as a MetaSwing Total Correction event, and has an even greater impact.

The following is the MetaSwing (version 3.2) Expert symbol code for measuring and signaling a Total Correction event.

```
1 ((Security("C:\MetaStock Data\BM Data\X.NYSE-D", C) /
2 Mov(Security("C:\MetaStock Data\BM Data\X.NYSE-A", C) +
3 Security("C:\MetaStock Data\BM Data\X.NYSE-D", C) +
4 Security("C:\MetaStock Data\BM Data\X.NYSE-U", C), 5, S))
5 > .805)
6 And
```

```
7  ((Security("C:\MetaStock Data\BM Data\X.NASD-D", C)  /
8  Mov(Security("C:\MetaStock Data\BM Data\X.NASD-A", C)  +
9  Security("C:\MetaStock Data\BM Data\X.NASD-D", C)  +
10 Security("C:\MetaStock Data\BM Data\X.NASD-U", C),  5,  S))
11 >  .76)
```

As you can see, this is a combination of the previous two code sets. The only difference is that each has had an extra set of parentheses added to ensure that the program sees it as a single yes or no value. In line 6, the And operator has been added to qualify that if each condition is true, then the entire function returns a value of true.

Interpreting the Correction Signal

Like virtually all technical analysis signals, human interpretation is required. In general, the better the signal, then the less judgment is required to use it profitably. In this case, we take care not to overlap the content covered in Chapter 8. Here are some best practices for using Correction signals.

- The signal is most significant and potent when no other Correction signals have occurred for at least 15 days.
- The Total Correction event has much greater predictive value than the individual NYSE or NASDAQ Correction events.
- The higher the close between the N Bands on the day of the Correction event, the greater the potential for downward price action in subsequent days.
- When a Surge signal appears immediately after a Correction signal, the short-term market direction is unclear.

Figure 13.4 shows us a daily chart of the S&P 500 Index with Correction and Surge signals plotted above and below the price candles, respectively. Vertical lines have been drawn to show the Correction events that meet the first in-15-days criterion. Each signal has a letter plotted above or below it. The T represents a Total event, the N is for a NYSE specific signal, and the Q is for a NASDAQ specific signal. Note that chart shows a largely rising market.

Circled areas 1 and 3 show new Correction events with no immediate Surge signals following them. The market direction is decidedly negative in those cases. Circled area 2 presents a circumstance where a Surge signal occurs on the next trading day. This means that the market likely overreacted to some information or catalyst, and quickly recovers.

In the seven instances on the chart that meet the first in-15-days criterion, it is easy to notice the increased level of significance compared to those signals, which are one in a series. Also, the initial signal occurs higher between the N Bands in circles 1 and 3. This means that volatility-based support is further away, and thus the market's reaction is to sell somewhat more intensely.

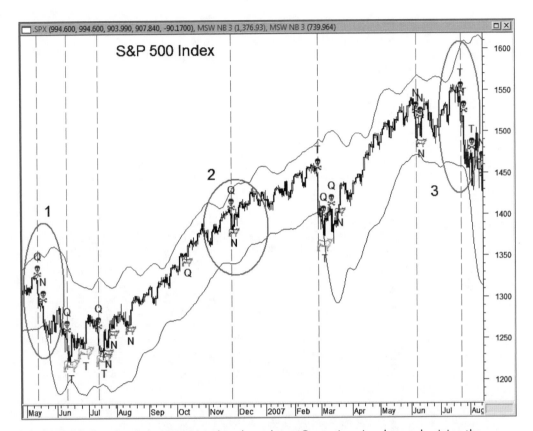

FIGURE 13.4 This daily S&P 500 Index chart shows Correction signals, emphasizing the importance of those that are the first Correction signals within at least 15 days.

Chart created in MetaStock. Chart uses the MetaSwing Add-on, by Northington Trading, LLC. All rights reserved.

In looking at these signals, there are many ways that we could quantify their performance. There are three different signal types as well as different market conditions. But our objective is to avoid unnecessary losses, after all, and turn adversity into opportunity. Based on that statement, maybe we should look at the stocks that make up the index, in lieu of the actual index movement.

To that end, the data in Table 13.1 were collected. Let's use this summary of stock performance characteristics to better understand how to exploit Correction signals. But first, here is an explanation of what these data represent.

- The performance results measured are based on 15 Correction signals between January 3, 2004, and June 30, 2008. This time period represents a mostly rising market. Even though this research was conducted after the October 2008 market crash, the June 30, 2008, date was used as a cutoff so that the performance results would better represent normal market conditions.

TABLE 13.1 New Correction Event Performance

	Correction Type	Correction Date	Time Frame Average	2-Day < S/R 5	2-Day > S/R 5	5-Day < S/R 5	5-Day > S/R 5	7-Day < S/R 5	7-Day > S/R 5	10-Day < S/R 5	10-Day > S/R 5
							Time Frames				
1	Total	13-Apr-04	0.0%	-0.4%	-0.3%	-1.5%	-1.1%	0.9%	1.3%	0.6%	0.7%
2	NYSE	14-Jun-04	1.8%	1.1%	1.0%	1.0%	0.9%	3.1%	2.6%	2.6%	2.1%
3	NASDAQ	5-Oct-05	-0.7%	0.2%	-0.2%	-1.3%	-2.1%	-0.2%	-1.5%	0.1%	-0.9%
4	NASDAQ	11-May-06	-1.7%	0.1%	-0.9%	-1.2%	-3.2%	-1.2%	-3.5%	-1.1%	-2.7%
5	NASDAQ	12-Jun-06	0.7%	-0.1%	-1.0%	1.0%	0.1%	2.2%	0.7%	2.1%	0.8%
6	NASDAQ	13-Jul-06	0.3%	-0.7%	-0.4%	0.1%	0.0%	1.0%	0.8%	0.9%	0.7%
7	NASDAQ	27-Nov-06	2.1%	0.8%	1.0%	2.1%	2.2%	3.4%	2.5%	2.3%	2.3%
8	Total	27-Feb-07	-0.4%	0.2%	0.1%	-0.3%	-0.4%	0.0%	0.1%	-2.0%	-1.1%
9	NYSE	7-Jun-07	2.1%	1.3%	1.3%	2.0%	2.1%	2.5%	2.7%	1.9%	2.6%
10	Total	24-Jul-07	-2.6%	-1.5%	-2.2%	-3.0%	-3.4%	-2.5%	-2.6%	-2.7%	-3.1%
11	Total	19-Oct-07	1.2%	0.8%	1.2%	1.8%	1.8%	1.8%	1.8%	-0.7%	0.8%
12	Total	11-Dec-07	-0.9%	-0.5%	0.3%	-2.2%	-1.6%	-2.2%	-1.4%	-0.5%	0.6%
13	NYSE	29-Feb-08	-1.4%	0.1%	-0.4%	-1.7%	-2.7%	-0.6%	-1.3%	-2.4%	-2.3%
14	NASDAQ	6-Jun-08	-2.0%	-1.2%	-0.6%	-2.2%	-0.1%	-2.9%	-0.7%	-6.1%	-2.4%
15	Total	26-Jun-08	-2.0%	-1.5%	-0.2%	-3.1%	-1.5%	-1.1%	-0.7%	-5.6%	-2.5%
	All	Average	-0.25%	-0.09%	-0.07%	-0.56%	-0.61%	0.28%	0.06%	-0.71%	-0.29%
	Total	Average	-0.81%	-0.48%	-0.20%	-1.40%	-1.06%	-0.51%	-0.25%	-1.82%	-0.75%
	N and Q	Average	0.12%	0.17%	0.01%	0.00%	-0.31%	0.81%	0.26%	0.02%	0.01%

- Each of the 15 Correction events conform to being the first new signal for at least 15 market days without Correction signals occurring. There were actually a total of 39 individual Correction signals during this time frame.
- The stocks in the sample are the 500 member stocks of the S&P 500 Index.
- Each stock's post-Correction signal performance was measured individually for a 2-day, 5-day, 7-day, and 10-day trading window. The performance measurement is from the closing price on the signal day to the closing price of the particular time window.
- Furthermore, each of the trading windows was divided into two groups of stocks based on a support and resistance profile. The purpose of this segregation was to find out if weaker stocks performed with greater losses than stocks that were less likely to be on a downtrend.
  1. The first profile is for stocks whose closing price on the signal day was less than the MetaSwing S/R 5 level.
  2. The second profile is for stocks whose closing price on the signal day was greater than the MetaSwing S/R 5 level.
- Each of the 15 Correction signal events is labeled in the first column to denote the specific stock exchange(s) that the signal pertains to.

There are a lot of numbers presented in Table 13.1. But it is important to note that there are only 15 sample events analyzed in these data. The data set for each event measures the individual performance of 500 stocks. That's 7,500 trade entries, with four trading time frames each, for a total of 30,000 individual trades. If performing statistical distribution analysis is your favorite pastime, the Excel file containing all of these data is available for download at www.tradingtheinvisible.com. The MetaStock exploration code used for this study is also included in the file.

When these results are carefully examined, we can derive the guidance needed to achieve our next goal. That goal is to exploit the conditions that immediately follow an isolated Correction signal event. Here is the unique performance intelligence that we can extract from these data.

- Look at the columns with a heading of <S/R 5. These represent any stock that closed below its S/R 5 level on the Correction signal day. The columns with a heading of >S/R 5 denote the opposite. The rationale here is that stocks below the S/R 5 line are exhibiting weaker performance, and are more likely to be in a downtrend. Therefore, the lion will probably catch them first. Indeed, the <S/R 5 column performance numbers tend to be more negative, and thus should make better short trades.
- The Total Correction signals produce a greater level of price declines than do the individual NYSE or NASDAQ Correction signals. Look at the average performances listed at the bottom of the table.
- The 2-day, 5-day, and 10-day time frames tend to perform best. The 7-day trade duration does not perform as well. This tends to suggest that between day 5 and day 7, stocks experience an upward price retracement before turning back down until at

least day 10. It is therefore possible to look at this signal as two trading opportunities. The first is day 1 through 5. The second is day 7 through 10.

- The performance for the individual NYSE or NASDAQ Correction signals does not appear to be very good. Perhaps without excessive negative breadth on both exchanges, fear does not pervade enough to garner much follow-through. Based on experience, however, this author knows that there are indeed significant opportunities following the individual exchange signals.

Become the Lion

When the lion attacks at the watering hole the lucky gazelles get away, but even after they are far from the predator, they are still defenseless. This is where a trader's life differs. In the stock market, if you're smart about it, you can transform yourself from the hunted into the hunter.

When the Correction event happens, you do need to first think like a defenseless gazelle. Exiting your vulnerable long positions will keep you alive. By acting simultaneously, you can find the right short positions and take advantage of the probable short-term negative market environment. There is a good likelihood that you were in long positions, and so the Correction event probably cost you some money. Now it is time to take that money back. Be aware, though, that time is of the essence.

When a Correction event occurs, a vast base of expertise is giving you a gift of directional intelligence. There are two very good ways to use this information and go on the offensive. Both require immediate analysis and action.

The first method for trading the day after a new Correction signal is to look for those stocks showing weakness by having closed below the S/R 5 level. Small cap and mid cap stocks usually provide the best returns for this type of opportunity. Figure 13.5 shows a daily MetaSwing chart of Abiomed Incorporated (ABMD). The Correction and Surge signals are once again notated to show the exchanges upon which the signal occurred. This correction event date is shown on line eight in Table 13.1, on February 27, 2007. The signal day is denoted with a vertical dashed line. The succeeding days are labeled to coincide with the time frames measured in Table 13.1.

One of the first things you might notice is the oversold reading on the DLRL indicator, in the lower indicator pane. Abiomed is quite oversold by the close of the signal day. Is this a stock we should trade short?

The answer is yes, but only because of the Correction event. In this circumstance, we can disregard oversold indications. Instead of oversold conditions, we are actually looking for weakness. The TTI Trend Strength indicator works well for this type of trade. It is plotted in the middle indicator pane. As you can see, both the 20-period and the 10-period look-back configurations show negative sloping linear regression lines. This is a sign of price momentum weakness. Remember that the failure of PIV support, and the indication of trend weakness, are framework components with completely separate origins. There is a higher probability of success when multiple framework capabilities are used to provide cross-verification.

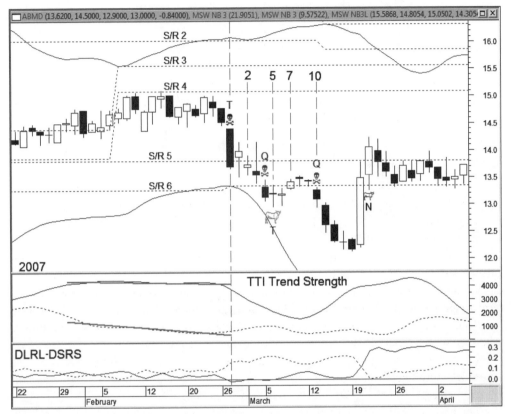

FIGURE 13.5 When a new Correction event happens, those stocks that are below the lower levels of PIV support provide a higher probability for short trade successes.

Chart created in MetaStock. Chart uses the MetaSwing Add-on, by Northington Trading, LLC. All rights reserved.

Another interesting characteristic is the way that price stages a retracement from day 5 through day 8. This price action plays out very similar to what is summarized in Table 13.1. This trade works out well, and enables the trader to recoup long-side losses incurred on the Correction day. It feels good to be the lion and roar a little.

Another good method for trading the Correction event is to choose a stock that has been on a solid price rally. At the time of the Correction signal, however, it is overbought and is also showing signs of trend weakness. In other words, it presents as a credible short-term countertrend trade.

Figure 13.6 depicts just such a setup very well. Unlike the chart in Figure 13.5, this one has been consistently moving through and above PIV resistance, at the S/R 4 and S/R 3 levels. Also different is the recent overbought readings of the DSRS indicator. It was overbought two days before the Correction signal, with a very high tandem volatility indicator (DLRL) reading.

The similarities for these to chart are in the area of trend strength. Once again the TTI Trend Strength indicators show negatively sloping linear regression lines using a

FIGURE 13.6 This daily chart of Air Transport Services Group (ABXA) shows how another method for profiting in the face of a Correction event is to short stocks that are overbought and showing trend weakness.

Chart created in MetaStock. Chart uses the MetaSwing Add-on, by Northington Trading, LLC. All rights reserved.

20-period linear regression line analysis. Since Air Transport Services Group has been on an aggressive rally, and is now exhibiting price to trend strength divergence, it is likely to be ripe for a short trade.

The broad breadth–based Correction event creates widespread fear in the markets. When a stock has had a significant price rally stakeholders are eager to protect their profits. Selling ensues therefore as stocks with this profile very quickly get hit hard. But remember that stock price declines generally happen much faster than price increases. Therefore, don't sit around holding the hand grenade when you should be fishing.

THE SURGE EVENT

After the gazelles have run at full stride for a safe distance from the hungry pack of lions they stop, rest, and settle back into their routine. Upon sensing the presence of the predator, they went from eating to running for their lives in a matter of a few seconds or less. Once the event is over, however, they don't kick back and relax in nearly such a short period of time. Becoming comfortable and feeling safe in a new setting takes comparatively much longer.

Nature has coded humans the same way. The fight-or-flight response is quick and universal. The recovery to normal process is also universal, but not so quick. As we saw in Chapter 8, intermediate market downtrends tend to begin with Correction events. Once prices have collectively overshot their equilibrium points, buyers step in to try and profit from the perceived inefficiency. At the height of this perception of inefficiency is when Surge events occur.

The Surge Ratio

A Surge event is an extreme market reaction of broad breadth buying. Its ratio construction uses the same method as the Correction. The trading tactics and interpretation required, however, are very different.

The ratio is as follows:

$$\frac{\text{Advancing Issues}}{\text{Moving Average (Advancing Issues} + \text{Declining Issues} + \text{Unchanged Issues})}$$

Thus the ratio can be restated as:

$$\frac{\text{Advancing Issues}}{\text{Moving Average (Total Issues Traded)}}$$

The Surge Code

Given that the Surge ratio uses the same equation as the Correction ratio, with the exception of the numerator, the code is virtually identical. The following is the MetaStock function language code to create the MetaSwing (version 3.2) Surge ratio for the New York Stock Exchange (NYSE):

```
1 {Advancing issues}
2 Security("C:\MetaStock Data\BM Data\X.NYSE-A", C) /
3 {Divided by}
4 {A Moving Average of the Sum of Advancing + Declining + Unchanged
5 listed issues}
6 Mov(Security("C:\MetaStock Data\BM Data\X.NYSE-A", C) +
7 Security("C:\MetaStock Data\BM Data\X.NYSE-D", C) +
8 Security("C:\MetaStock Data\BM Data\X.NYSE-U", C), 5, S)
```

In this Surge code, the only difference is in line 2. The security value for the numerator has been changed from the declining issues to the advancing issues. To plot the Surge symbol with the MetaStock Expert, above or below the day's price bar, that code would look like this:

```
1 (Security("C:\MetaStock Data\BM Data\X.NYSE-A", C) /
2 Mov(Security("C:\MetaStock Data\BM Data\X.NYSE-A", C) +
3 Security("C:\MetaStock Data\BM Data\X.NYSE-D", C) +
4 Security("C:\MetaStock Data\BM Data\X.NYSE-U", C), 5, S))
5 > .77
```

An additional difference in the NYSE Surge signal is the adjustment of the threshold value to. 77. The threshold value for each type of signal is specific to that exchange. Here is the MetaSwing (version 3.2) code for the NASDAQ Surge ratio and signal.

Ratio

```
1 {Advancing issues}
2 Security("C:\MetaStock Data\BM Data\X.NASD-A", C) /
3 {Divided by}
4 {A Moving Average of the Sum of Advancing + Declining + Unchanged
5 listed issues}
6 Mov(Security("C:\MetaStock Data\BM Data\X.NASD-A", C) +
7 Security("C:\MetaStock Data\BM Data\X.NASD-D", C) +
8 Security("C:\MetaStock Data\BM Data\X.NASD-U", C), 5, S)
```

Expert Symbol Code

```
1 (Security("C:\MetaStock Data\BM Data\X.NASD-A", C) /
2 Mov(Security("C:\MetaStock Data\BM Data\X.NASD-A", C) +
3 Security("C:\MetaStock Data\BM Data\X.NASD-D", C) +
4 Security("C:\MetaStock Data\BM Data\X.NASD-U", C), 5, S))
5 > .73
```

Here is the MetaSwing (version 3.2) Expert symbol code for measuring and signaling a Total Surge event.

```
 1 ((Security("C:\MetaStock Data\BM Data\X.NYSE-A", C) /
 2 Mov(Security("C:\MetaStock Data\BM Data\X.NYSE-A", C) +
 3 Security("C:\MetaStock Data\BM Data\X.NYSE-D", C) +
 4 Security("C:\MetaStock Data\BM Data\X.NYSE-U", C), 5, S))
 5 > .77)
 6 And
 7 ((Security("C:\MetaStock Data\BM Data\X.NASD-A", C) /
 8 Mov(Security("C:\MetaStock Data\BM Data\X.NASD-A", C) +
 9 Security("C:\MetaStock Data\BM Data\X.NASD-D", C) +
10 Security("C:\MetaStock Data\BM Data\X.NASD-U", C), 5, S))
11 > .73)
```

Interpreting the Surge Signal

The presence of a Surge event does not carry the same implications or opportunity as that of a Correction event. Think of a Surge day as an emotional equivalent to a warm and fuzzy stuffed animal. It could be a little soft bull with floppy horns. This type of broad-based buying event serves to make potential buyers feel good, or more aptly put, safe. In reality, it tends to mean one of two very different things, depending on market conditions. They are:

1. It is an important part of an intermediate-term price bottom, or base of support, when it occurs after a market decline.
2. When a Surge signals during a market rally, it serves as a continuation confirmation.

When Surge events begin to happen there are opportunities that you can seize. Just as important, you have a little more time to consider your actions than you do with Correction events. Here is a list of best practices that should be followed for short-term trading.

- If the Surge event occurs after an intermediate market downtrend then strongly consider finding exit points for any short positions you currently hold.
- After a downtrend, wait for a second surge event to confirm that a current intermediate-term bottom may be forming. Make sure that the recent Surge signals outnumber recent Correction signals. In other words, wait for there to be two Surge signals that are more recent than the most recent Correction signal. They also need to be relatively close together.
- The Surge signal is more predictive of higher prices to come, the lower its position between the N Bands. This is because PIV and volatility-based support is closer, and thus resistance is further away.
- Consider trend strength to be the most important technical measurement once two successive Surge events have occurred; use a three-day periodicity for this.
- Unlike Correction signals, a stock's oversold technical reading can be important for short-term trading.
- Unlike Correction signals, time is not of the essence for Surge signals. Carefully choose a stock that has been showing signs of strength during the previous downtrend.
- During a bull market, if the Surge signal occurs while the market has been experiencing an intermediate-term uptrend, then consider it a continuation signal.

Figure 13.7 once again presents a daily chart of the S&P 500 Index, but this time it shows MetaSwing Surge signals. Just as in Figure 13.3, the ratio is graphically plotted in the lower indicator pane, along with a threshold line of .77. We learned in Chapter 8 how Surge signals form at intermediate-term bottoms. This chart makes that clear as well.

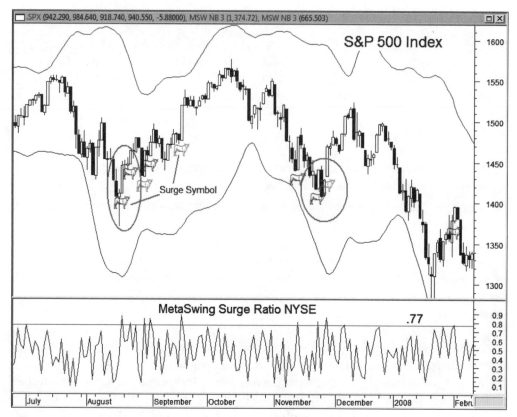

FIGURE 13.7 This daily chart of the S&P 500 Index shows how the Surge event is an important part of an intermediate-term bottom.

Chart created in MetaStock. Chart uses the MetaSwing Add-on, by Northington Trading, LLC. All rights reserved.

There are two Surge events in the two circled areas of this chart that occur within five days of each other. Also, they happen in series such that there is no Correction event between them. This type of market behavior means that it is best to buy instead of sell.

Patience and the Surge

It's okay to be the lion when the right Surge conditions arise, but you must remember that they are also patient. Big cats are known for their ability to stalk their prey for hours. This is the aspect of the cat that we need to emulate when beginning short-term trading after Surge signals.

After an intermediate-term downtrend, time is needed for fear and uncertainty to subside. Bottoms are usually tested. This is why it is best to wait for a second Surge event to signal. During this waiting and observing period, however, you are provided with time to begin a selection process. Specifically, you are looking for a stock that exhibited trend strength while the broad market was in decline.

One of the best ways to find strength is to search for it in a larger periodicity. Try using an analysis time frame that a position trader would normally look at. I find that the three-day periodicity chart to works well for this. Many aspects of strength become visible that would otherwise go unnoticed.

The chart of Digital River (DRIV) is shown in a three-day periodicity in Figure 13.8. This chart is loaded with data ending on July 24, 2006, the day of a second successive Surge signal on the daily chart. This gives you a view of the chart just as it would have been seen at the time of decision. Once again, we can rely on the TTI Trend Strength indicator to identify underlying price strength. It is plotted with overlaid 20-period linear regression line analyses. Here are the important signs of strength that this chart shows us.

- The first obvious sign is that both TTI Trend Strength measurements are very positive.

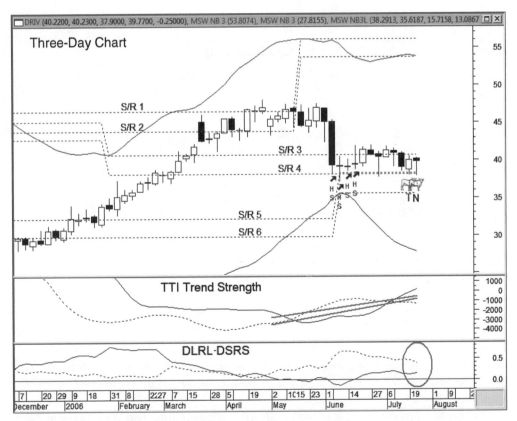

FIGURE 13.8 This chart of Digital River (DRIV) shows how a three-day chart time frame works well for identifying strength during a recent intermediate-term downtrend.

Chart created in MetaStock. Chart uses the MetaSwing Add-on, by Northington Trading, LLC. All rights reserved.

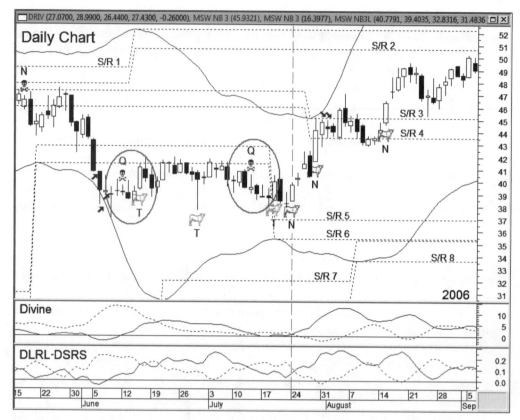

FIGURE 13.9   On the daily chart of Digital River (DRIV), it is clear how there are signs of strength when price does not react negatively to recent Correction signals in addition to its positive TTI Trend Strength readings.

Chart created in MetaStock. Chart uses the MetaSwing Add-on, by Northington Trading, LLC. All rights reserved.

- During June of 2006, price sold off and found high slope support at the lower N Band. It then held there for six weeks while the rest of the broad market continued on its decline. The summer decline of 2006 was particularly harsh for technology stocks, and yet this one held at PIV support.
- The DLRL indicator is still low enough that there is plenty of room for rise. This means that price can easily increase without violating volatility measurements.

Figure 13.9 gives us a view of Digital River in a daily chart. The vertical dashed line denotes the second Surge signal day on July 24, 2006. The Divine indicator gives a relatively low reading for each of its components. This is because of a lack of cyclical volatility. The DLRL, however, reads somewhat oversold. When price opens the next day at a higher level, additional strength is indicated, making this a good entry point.

It should be noted that price has traded in a narrow range for many days. This means that waiting for some retracement is not very logical. Any price movement is more indicative of a minor breakout, up or down. Nor would any trader be wrong in this case, however, to wait for some retracement and for a perfect setup for entry. There are always many opportunities to choose from. That choice is part of the human element of trading.

THE BEST FREE ADVICE

Winners in the stock market are the ones who collectively succeed in pushing prices in the direction that they themselves want them to go. Let those experts help you by listening when they speak loudly. These experts are shouting at the top of their lungs on days when Correction or Surge events take place. A simple ratio is the key to deciphering what they are saying.

New Correction events require swiftness. When they happen, the hand grenade is sitting in your lap. If you act within the best practices described previously, your odds favor success; meanwhile, many others watch their long positions decline. These are nights to burn some midnight oil and be prepared when the market opens the next morning.

On the other hand, Surge signals demand patience. This is because market participants are bombarded with every possible scenario projection by information sources that surround us all. The herd needs time to regain confidence. Once that happens, buying strength is very important.

Following extreme breadth events, directional intelligence oriented in trend strength or weakness can be the key for short-term trading. For many traders, the option of going flat and watching the market is also a profitable move. Whatever your reaction to this free advice the market gives you might be, just make sure that at first you're listening for it.

CHAPTER 14

Trading System Design

Detecting the Invisible

What do a trading system and the sixteenth-century portrait of the Mona Lisa have in common? From a concrete standpoint, nothing, really. But from an abstract point of view, they share much.

The person in the painting has no facial hair. She is believed to be a woman, but she has no eyebrows or eyelashes. Her hands are slightly enlarged and she wears a very thin veil, two clues that suggest she is possibly with child. Leonardo da Vinci even posed her in front of an imaginary landscape, which was relatively new at that time. These attributes, and many others, make the subject ambiguous. Or was it simply a grand effort by the artist to create something that could serve as a unique experience for each person? This would have also been quite new for the time. Whatever the reality, it certainly embodied great creativity.

Designing a trading system or its components is in many ways just as individual an experience as viewing the Mona Lisa. Trading is such a personal endeavor that the tools you use need to feel like they are your own. Whether you use the same technical framework components as a controlled quantity of other traders or you create your own, it is important that you gain from them what you uniquely need.

If you decide to construct or customize your own framework components, I believe you will find it to be a growth experience. The inner feeling derived is not unlike that of an artistic creation. It will certainly be an endeavor you will not forget.

There is an important difference to point out as well, however. Trading systems or individual components do not need to be ambiguous to be useful. They can be very specific. There is no need to design a tool that will serve everyone. You are the only patron that matters.

As we discussed in Chapters 1, 2, and 3, a few of this book's objectives are:

- To help you realize how well equipped and prepared your opponents are.
- To immerse you in volatility-based technical analysis so that you know how to use the correct framework and components for your trading style.

- To show you how to build your own personal framework components, or to license them from a credible source.

This chapter, indeed this book, is not about developing or implementing mechanical trading systems. The components and framework that we are working with are for discretionary trading use only. The Merriam-Webster dictionary defines a *system* as a set of regularly interacting or interdependent group of items forming a unified whole. As the term *trading system* is used here, the majority of this definition holds accurately. The only exception could be the "unified whole" aspect. Some analysts in the trading community would prefer that the word *system* be used only when referring to mechanical trading, which is 100 percent not discretionary. Indeed, we are designing trading systems, but it is with the intent that the system can be used in part or in total, and that it is traded only in a discretionary way.

This chapter ties together the component development content presented in Chapters 4 through 12 with development procedures, tactics, and techniques implemented within a basic scientific process. This topic is worthy of an entire book unto itself, but we focus here only on the meatier endeavor of producing highly focused components.

SEEING THROUGH THE FOG OF WAR

One of the reasons why volatility-based technical analysis works well is that it executes on the understanding that money is to be made at the extremes. It is at the inflection point of supply or demand domination that the extremes are usually found. These extremes take the form of:

- Doubt
- Uncertainty
- Compressed communication
- Price volatility
- Underlying or hidden volatility

The best word to describe the effect of these extreme point attributes is *ambiguity*. In his book *On War*, Carl von Clausewitz, the famous Prussian military theorist, described this effect as the *Fog of War*.[1] During a military campaign, commanders and leaders at all levels experience a distorted view of their situational awareness. A great level of uncertainty is present, and metaphorically speaking, it's as though one is standing in a fog bank, so by default, visibility is limited.

It occurs at the strategic, operational, and tactical levels. As the intensity level of the military action increases, leaders also are inflicted with greater levels of communication delays and inaccuracies. Information and the intelligence upon which it is based become less reliable. Finally, at the tactical level, these effects result in less than perfectly planned actions, which are carried out at the unit level. The platoon leader experiences his own levels of the fog even while being hurled forward within an often ill-planned larger initiative. With the direct consequences of life and death at his feet his own troops suffer degraded levels of communication and coordination.

It is at the height of all this chaos that a winning initiative can be obtained. Simply put, a smaller and lesser-equipped force can prevail if it executes with a level of discipline greater than its opponents. Thus the emotionless can defeat the emotional.

Your personal and professional degree of situational awareness will also determine the outcome of your trades. While the analysis will usually be made during calmer periods of preparation, the instant of decision, whatever your trading time frame, is generally executed during some form of the fog. This is because the extremes are where the money is to be made, and it is also where you need to be prepared to execute with calm emotional control.

This chapter is not about trading psychology, although you wouldn't know that based on its content so far. The point here is that the volatility-based trading components you create need to be effective during the fog of trading, which mainly occurs when price is at extremes. This cannot be stressed enough. The analytical tools you rely upon while trading at the extremes need to be good enough to extinguish doubt during those times. They need to communicate specific market conditions clearly so that you are confident enough to hand over to them the appropriate degree of control over your actions. The bottom line is that they need to work well enough so that you can remain objective and emotionless.

NAIL IT DOWN: RECOGNIZE THE SPECIFICS

It's time to be specific and honest with the client; and the client is you. The first step of the development process is to state your time frame. For instance, "I want my hold time to normally be at least two days, but no more than five days." Or you may choose a three-week hold duration. Whatever you choose is up to you. You must not begin development, however, until you have decided and stated it accurately. Do yourself a favor and write it clearly on a note. Tape the note to the front of your computer monitor. Keep this time frame statement at the forefront of your mind consistently throughout the development process.

Don't get distracted with other time frames and experiment with offshoots or tangents. If you do, you will likely end up committing a very serious error. It is too easy to end up with mediocre component performance in several time frames, rather than good performance in one. Remember that a good component is fractal and thus works well in different periodicities. However, each trading time span has optimal numerical parameters. With consistency of time frame during the development process, you learn what those optimum settings are.

The second step of component or system development is to objectively state what you want. Be very specific about the exact trade you want to develop a method for. This is actually the fun part. It's kind of like sitting on Santa's lap. You get to say, "I want to capture two ATR(14) swings that immediately follow a trading range breakout." Imagine the look on Santa's face when eight-year-old little Janie says that to him, with her mom and dad looking on proudly.

This is an extremely critical step. It's important to develop component(s) to accomplish specific tasks. Stay on target and do not stray. By stating this goal clearly, your intent is solid. Write it down and tape it to your monitor right beside your time frame statement. Once you are deep into the process of development, and feeling lost in a potentially endless sea of correlations, you will appreciate this level of specificity. It will keep you from investigating every visually tempting peak or trough, like an undisciplined hound dog chasing every critter but the rabbit it should be focused on.

The third step in this specification process is to consider what you just wrote down. It's the point at which to think seriously about your compatibility with the goals you just set. Ask yourself:

- Does this time frame match my lifestyle and typical routine?
- Does my emotional psyche fit with the tricky nature of this particular type of trade?
- Is my risk profile right for this type of trade?
- What is the win-loss ratio that I need to remain emotionally objective? Can this trade method sustain that ratio?
- Do you get the gist?

Keep these types of questions in mind throughout the development process. It's important to create trading methods that you are compatible with.

THE IMPORTANCE OF BELIEVING

When you engage in the process of creating an original technical analysis component you are committing to navigating a potentially frustrating path. For each 100 hypotheses that you think are responsible for an observation, perhaps one will be proven true with a viable correlation. It can be a tough process. For this reason, you should follow these four beliefs:

1. Deep inside you, you must believe that there is a definable, logical, and predictable way to quantify the technical condition that accurately forecasts the price movement phenomenon of your observation. In short, you must have total confidence that you will be able to find and code the signal. Why else would you put yourself through the arduous process? Also, you will need this as motivation to keep you going. There will likely be extended periods when everything you try seems to hit a dry hole. You must believe you can do it.

2. Every change in price movement, either reversal or pause, has a logical reason. The underlying cause may be fundamental, technical, or a combination of both, in origin. There is a reason for the change.

3. Trust in responsible technical analysis and not media pundit opinions. Listening to outside sources of explanation about market or security price movement will only serve to make your task more difficult. Discipline your access to online and broadcast media opinions. They are paid to have an opinion and deliver it to your brain. The media does not need to be correct in order to profit. Their grasping-at-straws explanations will only serve to throw your development process off course.

4. Original technical analysis components and methods will serve you better than those available in the public domain. Most existing technical analysis indicators and methods were developed before program algorithmic trading. These institution-based trade execution methods have altered price action and patterns past the reach of traditional TA math. Well-developed volatility-based calculations and algorithms exploit current market inefficiencies with higher degrees of accuracy and for the right reasons.

SYSTEM DESIGN STRUCTURE

The Framework is your structure. When you build anything, a structure is important. In this case, the structure is built on a strong foundation of its seven capabilities. It is also flexible so that it can be expanded to accommodate the trading methods you choose to pursue. A quick review of the Framework is probably in order at this point.

Table 14.1 shows the most recent Framework iteration from Chapter 9. The Framework has three dimensions. The capabilities dimension is the foundation upon which the structure resides. The application dimension is the second column with the identical list beneath each capability. Think of this dimension as the specific trade method you are designing for. It is the name you assigned to the trade objective that you just stated in the previous section. Table 14.1 shows that the most recent application is a trade method named TTI Trend Entry.

The third dimension is composed of the components. These are the individual mathematical calculations that you develop. They are your custom indicators. They are applied individually to an appropriate trade method so that a trade's success probability is increased with cross-verification. If a component has value for a particular trade method, it shows an x in that component's column.

The Framework presented should be more than adequate for most technical trading activities. If you feel that the capabilities dimension can be expanded to better suit the trading of a particular market or instrument, then I say go for it. Make it your own. Create the structure you need for the times when the fog of trading is thick.

There are other important design aspects that pertain more to structure than anything else. Think of them as the materials and workmanship aspects of what you build. If you were building your dream home for life you certainly would want to use only the highest quality materials. You would also settle only for the best craftsmen working on the project. The abstract practices in the following sections, in a way, represent those interests.

TABLE 14.1 The TTI Framework with TTI RSIV-1 and TTI Composite Added

Capabilities Components Application	TTI ATR Extreme	TTI StochEx	TTI Fabric SD	TTI Fabric LG	TTI Fabric Ratio LR-SD	TTI Trend Strength	TTI RSIV-1	TTI Composite
1 Oversold/overbought								
Trending			x	x			x	x
Nontrending	x	x	x	x			x	x
TTI Trend Entry			x	x				
2 Trend Detection								
Trending					x	x		
Nontrending						x		
TTI Trend Entry					x	x		
3 Broad Market Integration								
Trending								
Nontrending								
TTI Trend Entry								
4 Support and Resistance								
Trending								
Nontrending								
TTI Trend Entry								
5 Historical Volatility								
Trending			x	x	x	x	x	x
Nontrending	x	x	x	x		x	x	x
TTI Trend Entry			x	x	x	x		
6 Implied Volatility								
Trending								
Nontrending								
TTI Trend Entry								
7 Multi–Time Frame Verification								
Trending				x			x	x
Nontrending	x	x	x	x			x	x
TTI Trend Entry				x				

Specific Use

Some components work well for many different trade methods; they're like the Tylenol or duct tape of volatility-based technical analysis. Relying on one of them per method can be a common basis of decision for trading. When you are deep in an overbought or oversold market condition, however, and pulling the trigger on a trade seems too scary, a special purpose indicator can be what you need. It's best to have a special purpose indicator for as many of your methods as possible.

One very specialized component is TTI Trend Strength. This indicator is used when there is steep trending price action. At these times, it confirms the beginning, continuation, or ending of a trend. The TTI Trend Strength is of little to no value when there is no strong trending price behavior. Its readings at that time are insignificant. But that's okay, because we don't need it then. A wrench is helpful while you are fixing the plumbing, but not so much when water skiing.

Figure 14.1 shows clearly how a specific use component behaves. This daily MetaSwing chart of Radio Shack (RSH) is of an expanded time period just before the chart in Figure 6.17. The two charts overlap during January to February of 2007. Both charts feature the TTI Trend Strength indicator, and show how it was able to confirm the beginning of a trend rally in February 2007.

In Figure 14.1, it is also very important to show a weakness in the downtrend, first visible during April 2006. By signaling a divergence, it served as an early warning that this trend was beginning to run out of steam. The lower indicator pane displays rectangles that point out the times when it was useful as a confirmation.

From July to December of 2006, however, as denoted by the center rectangle, it was not especially helpful. There were no significant signs of a strong trend in either direction, and the TTI Trend Strength indicator is therefore not needed. If you examine this chart closely, you can see other price inflection points where it was helpful in trend-following decisions. It's really great to have the right component at the right time to take advantage of good trade setups.

Take Aim

Regardless of your trading time frame, remember that your opportunity for profit is embedded inside market inefficiency. Price travels too far in one direction and you are going to ride it back in the other direction. You are going to take your side of the market before the majority does. You must endeavor to see relationships and correlations before the major trading crowd seeing them to achieve it. This is why volatility-based technical components must contain predictive capabilities.

Finding inefficiency is a mindset. You can find it within multiple time frames. Inefficiency in a larger time frame can be great in your smaller time frame. It's as if crumbs are falling from the giant's dinner table. They are insignificant to him, but to you one of his crumbs represents and entire meal.

Scientific Process

Yes, we all learned the scientific method in the fifth grade. Likewise, this seems like common sense. Well, if it's such common sense, then why do so many traders lose large amounts of money chasing hunches and feelings with their trading accounts? I know many people who have lost the majority of a sizable trading account because they didn't use a simple process that we all learned in grade school. What astounds me, even to this day, is the number of individuals I've met who have lost six-figure sums of money because they did not force themselves to prove their trading method with a simple logical process. If a restaurant blatantly overcharges you for a dinner, it is grounds to be upset.

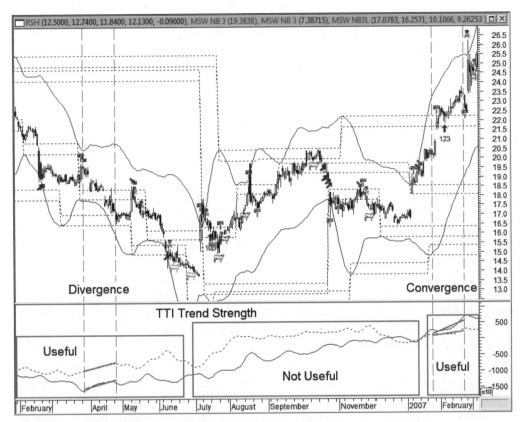

FIGURE 14.1 This daily chart of Radio Shack (RSH) shows how the TTI Trend Strength component works well when it is needed, but is insignificant when it is not; it is thus a specific-use indicator.

Chart created in MetaStock. Chart uses the MetaSwing Add-on, by Northington Trading, LLC. All rights reserved.

Why allow your own ignorance to steal so much more from you? Therefore, be thorough and get back to basics. Anyone can do it.

The process of developing a technical component works best when some form of the scientific process is followed. Figure 14.2 displays the scientific method in one of its most basic forms. This process differs when used in various disciplines of logic, philosophy, or science. It would be a good use of your time to read up on the subject. A simple Internet search will present you with sufficient content about its history, variations, and applications. Don't feel the need to get too immersed in its more abstract and advanced methodologies; stick to the basics.

Chart Discipline

Training your brain to view the chart as an analyst should is easier said than done. I am referring specifically to the ability to view the middle of a chart up to a specific date or event, without seeing or considering anything on the chart past that date or event. It

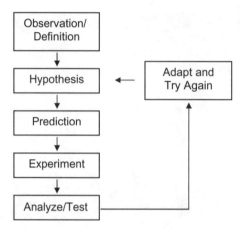

FIGURE 14.2 This is a basic form of the scientific method.

means to be able to recognize the chart activity to a point in the time series, but absolutely no further.

Everyone is afflicted with the problem of *hindsight bias*, which was discussed in Chapter 4. The path to overcome it is to rely heavily on manual and visual chart analysis as the primary method for disproving a hypothesis. Use computer-based study or back-testing as a confirming process once manual chart analysis fails to disprove the hypothesis. Visual analysis of charts is therefore the primary method of hypothesis analysis. It forces you to look at a lot of charts. You begin through this repetitive discipline to gain the ability to look at data and price activity in a sequentially objective manner. Only in this way can you actually see the hidden characteristics of your hypothesis. Your brain will also learn to think more like a microprocessor.

This process of manually testing a hypothesis, which in reality is a trading method algorithm, directly conflicts with methodology and benefits being pitched to us all today. In advertisements of online brokers and software vendors, the ease of software-based back-testing is promoted as the solution to successful trading. We are led to believe that we need only think up an effective solution and the back-testing software will tell you just how successful you will be. Also, I can play football better than any NFL quarterback but I just don't want to show off. It just isn't so.

Remember the Fog of War aspect of trading. You will experience times of high tension and uncertainty. During these moments, hours, or days you will need to know the intricacies of your trading components and methods. Software-based back-testing does not allow you become intimate with your own creation. It does not provide you with hundreds, or thousands, of instances in which you have visually seen the component perform in numerous market circumstances. Your brain does not get to absorb these nuances and form that important sixth sense about the indicator you are now using. If you perform a thousand chart viewings, then you'll likely gain this necessary insight, which back-testing can never provide.

Then there is the flip side. When we look at an original trade setup, which we've just created, and watch it succeed, we see dollar signs. Those mental dollar signs feel really good. The more we see our trade signal work, the more we want to. Then before you can say, "Cha-ching" you are shouting, "Hallelujah! I'm going to be rich." Not so fast.

Because we are human, we see what we want to see, and we avoid seeing that which we do not want to see. It's how our brains are wired. It's widely believed to be responsible for part of our survival as a species. I have personally discovered numerous billion-dollar trading methods, burning midnight oil in the process. After a good night's sleep, the unbelievable trade setup or component is in reality just an elegant way to break even.

This is the point at which we all need the cold hard objectivity of a computer program. At this stage, we can rely on back-testing software to step in and deliver a dish of truthful humility. At a minimum, you should use the exploration study method that we have applied in previous chapters. Producing an arithmetic mean that relies on the law of large numbers is important to understand the component's or method's tendency for positive or negative profit potential.

The main thing is to remember that chart viewing and analysis during the development process cannot be replaced with software-based back-testing. Likewise, back-testing will keep you honest if it is used correctly. Keep the horse in front of the cart. Do the work and put in the required time: view the charts first, and back-test second.

SYSTEM DESIGN TACTICS

Visibility is now the key. A stock's price action moves all over the chart. Its movement, in so many possible ways, needs to be visible on your development screen. The mathematical relationships of price and volatility measurements also need to be visually expressed throughout the development process. A rare few individuals can truly see complex mathematical relationships in their mind's eye. The rest of us need to see them with our actual eyes.

Development Layout

You may recall in Chapter 9 when the TTI Composite indicator was introduced in Figure 9.1. It is a compound derivative indicator based on four of the indicators we created previous to it. Figure 14.3 is a recreation of that chart. As you can see, there are four different indicator panes plotted beneath the price pane. This is necessary so that we may develop the TTI Composite. It's essential to visually see each part of the new indicator within a vertically aligned chart so that we can visually comprehend their correlations. In Chapter 9, the development process for this indicator was skipped to save space and remain focused on that chapter's scope. As you will see in the coming pages, routine development requires that more indicator panes be used on a single screen.

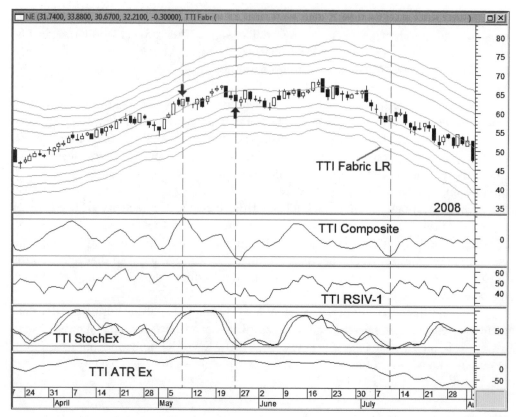

FIGURE 14.3 A stock chart using a single monitor provides very limited space for price and indicator panes, and thus makes for a deficient development environment.
Chart created in MetaStock.

This chart actually shows a very poor development environment. It's all about visual recognition. Each pane of the screen requires a certain amount of vertical space to accurately represent the change of value from candle to candle, regardless of chart periodicity.

The indicator panes in Figure 14.3 that contain the various components are sized well for clarity of movement. The price pane, however, is compressed to a poorly recognizable aspect. It is difficult to quickly appreciate the effect of price movement compared to component correlation. Remember that you will be consistently changing formula code and then visually reviewing charts to observe the effects of the tweaked code. This process must be able to be executed quickly. A single monitor screen, therefore, will not suffice in a development environment.

Most traders use at least two monitors, usually in a side-by-side configuration. A proper development environment also requires at least two monitors but in a vertical configuration. After you have physically mounted your monitors vertically you will need

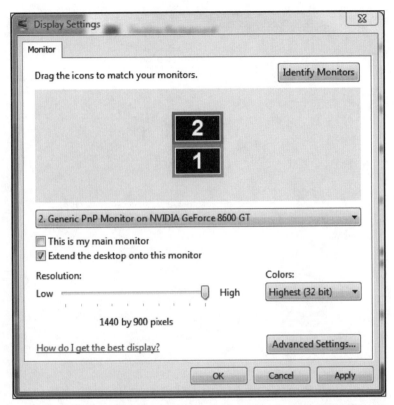

FIGURE 14.4 A typical Microsoft Windows screen for configuring dual monitors in a vertical fashion.

to configure them within the display settings of the operating system. Figure 14.4 shows a typical Microsoft Windows monitor configuration window.

Once your monitors are physically and virtually configured as dual vertical displays, your software development environment can change to match it. MetaStock, TradeStation, and most other technical analysis software packages allow for a single application window to be stretched across multiple monitors.

Figure 14.5 shows the result of stretching a MetaStock chart window across two monitor screens. This is the best way to develop components and trade methods. The price candles are allowed enough vertical space to show real movement. There are four components plotted. A configuration like this can simultaneously display price and up to eight individual indicator plots. Remember this is a screen for development, not analysis. You can see how this layout is important in the pages to come.

Guided Introspection

In this exercise, we look closely at the process taken to develop the TTI Composite indicator in Chapter 9. It involves an element of imagination that can be fun. A word of

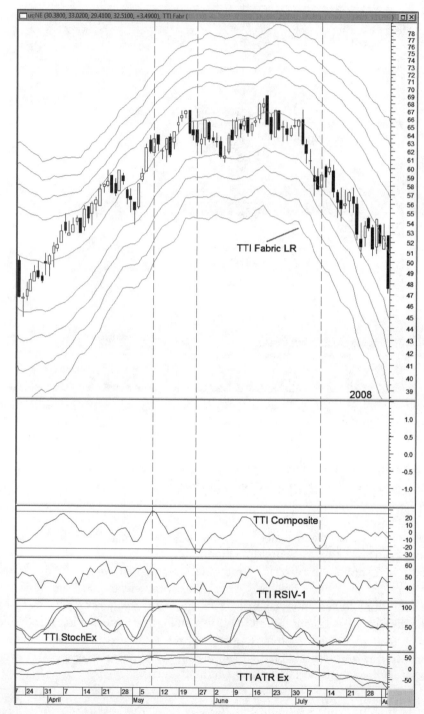

FIGURE 14.5 The best component development environment uses a vertically stretched, dual monitor application window.

Chart created in MetaStock.

caution, though: patience is a requirement. For reference purposes let's reexamine the following finished TTI Composite component code.

```
 1 {User Inputs}
 2 pds1:= Input("LR Slope Lookback", 2, 1000, 5);
 3 pds2:= Input("Linear Regression Length", 5, 1000, 40);

 4 {Establishes linear regression slope values of oscillator
components}
 5 x1:= LinRegSlope(Fml("TTI StochEx"), pds1);
 6 x2:= LinRegSlope( Fml( "TTI RSIV"), pds1);
 7 x3:= LinRegSlope( Fml( "TTI ATR Extreme nb"), pds1);

 8 {Calculates number of ATR multiples above or below central
 9 fabric line}
10 y1:= LinearReg(C, pds2, S, 1);
11 y2:= ATR(14);
12 y3:= ((y1 - C) / y2) * -3;

13 {Adds assigned variables to create the composite value,
14 and plots it}
15 x1 + x2 + x3 + y3
```

Let's marry it to the scientific process to get inside the thought process that went into the development of this indicator. Thinking and developing in the sequence of the scientific process will keep you grounded and focused. The first three steps of the process are:

1. *Observation and Definition:* The objective of the TTI Composite is to design a component to find Adeo conditions. Key oversold and overbought levels are visually identified through chart observation. A characteristic of the key points are those with quick and multiple ATR reversals.

2. *Hypothesis:* The primary strategy that is to rely on the strength of the four previous volatility-based components that were developed. The primary tactic, which exploits their strength, is to detect the individual component's momentum. The hypothesis is that a summation of the momentum of each indicator would measure extreme levels.

3. *Prediction:* The prediction is that these extreme momentum levels would be consistent and repetitive at key overbought and oversold levels.

The next step involves refining a method for measuring each component's momentum. In looking at the chart in Figure 14.5 again, it is easier to observe instances where the components agree and disagree. Of key interest to the developer should be the rate of response each component displays. Equally important, but different, is the actual measured level that each indicator produces.

Momentum is a rate; it is not a destination. It is therefore appropriate to use a mathematical method for measuring a rate. Typical rate measurements are a rate of change (ROC) calculation, or a slope measurement. Other methods would take us into more compound derivations, like those used in actual TA indicators such as a momentum oscillator or a stochastic oscillator, and so forth. A good practice is to first try simple methods before resorting to those that are more complex.

The measurement of a significant extreme level is different for each of the four indicators. Finding a non-weighted calculation, therefore, to sum their outputs could prove messy. Furthermore, a Boolean value is returned when one of them reaches a desired point. There is an inadequate sum of indicators to simply take a vote from each and determine an output by consensus.

It would seem one way to commonly measure their momentum would be to examine the linear regression slope of each. This could work well. Understand that at this point of the process you could go in many directions. There could easily be five or more additional ways to measure the component's momentum. If, after some analysis, the linear regression slope method does not pan out, you could return to this point in the process and go forward with a different measuring method. We can now proceed to the next step of the scientific process.

4. *Experiment:* To proceed with trying a linear regression slope we will need to use the development environment to express the measurement as function language code. Then it's a process of visually inspecting charts to find a suitable mathematic expression.

Make It Visual

What do our thoughts look like during this hypothesis process? What values do individual pieces of the hypothesis measure out to? During the experiment stage, it's time to begin answering these questions. Simply put, you've got to quantify the different parts of your hypothesis, code them, and plot them as a part of the time series. This is the point at which to use some of the power of your technical analysis software.

In Figure 14.6, we again see the daily chart of Noble Corporation (NE). There are seven individual indicator panes in this development layout. We have created four temporary indicators to express a piece of the hypothesis that we are experimenting with. In panes 3, 5, and 7, each of the three components that we are using are plotted individually. Right above each in panes 2, 4, and 6 are temporary indicators that express the component's five-period linear regression slope.

The code for these slope measurements are as follows:

Pane 2 – TTI StochEx linear regression slope

```
pds1:= Input("LR Slope Lookback", 2, 1000, 5);
LinRegSlope(Fml("TTI StochEx"), pds1)
```

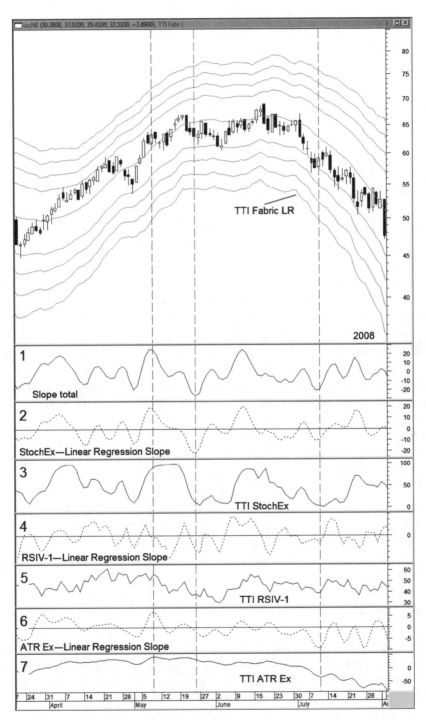

FIGURE 14.6 In a good development environment, you can define and quantify portions of your hypothesis to visually understand how they behave as a part of the time series, and directly observe their responses to price movement.

Chart created in MetaStock.

Pane 4 – TTI RSIV-1 linear regression slope

```
pds1:= Input("LR Slope Lookback", 2, 1000, 5);
LinRegSlope(Fml("TTI RSIV"), pds1)
```

Pane 6 – TTI ATR Extreme linear regression slope

```
pds1:= Input("LR Slope Lookback", 2, 1000, 5);
LinRegSlope(Fml("TTI ATR Extreme nb"), pds1)
```

Pane number 1 is a temporary indicator that sums the three values presented in panes 2, 4, and 6. This gives an initial view of the hypothesis development. The code for the summation is as follows:

Slope total:

```
pds1:= Input("LR Slope Lookback", 2, 1000, 5);
x1:= LinRegSlope(Fml("TTI StochEx"), pds1);
x2:= LinRegSlope(Fml("TTI RSIV"), pds1);
x3:= LinRegSlope(Fml("TTI ATR Extreme nb"), pds1);
x1 + x2 + x3
```

With the actual values of our thoughts presented in front of our eyes we can see the hypothesis begin to take shape. In this case, the alignment of slope peaks and troughs will create some extremes. When creating a compound derivative such as this, the goal is the draw from the strengths of the different components while keeping the weaknesses at bay.

There's no real way to judge the effectiveness of your creation until you look at some charts. At a step such as this, you should, at a minimum, look at 20 large cap stock charts, and a mixture of 20 small and mid cap stocks. The old saying of "one thing leads to another" is kind of what this part of the process is about. The visual process spurs even more ways to exploit volatility measurement. As alternative ideas come to you, write them down. Then refer to them later in the *Adapt and Try Again* step.

You would likely want to examine different period lengths for the regression lookback period during the chart observation process. You may want to also explore different periods for each component. Approach this as a creative process.

There is another volatility-based component in our arsenal that we've yet to tap. The TTI Fabric LR is plotted on the chart in Figure 14.6 as well. How could it be used? We already know that when price strays past the positive and negative one-thread point, it will have a tendency to temporarily pause or reverse. Let's investigate a way to incorporate this measurement.

The same Noble Corporation (NE) chart is plotted in Figure 14.7, with some additions. An indicator pane number eight is added to the bottom of the chart environment. This temporary indicator expresses the distance of the closing price to the center 40-period linear regression line, in units of ATR(14). This value quantifies the threads of the TTI Fabric LR. The MetaStock code for this is:

```
pds2:= Input("Linear Regression Length", 5, 1000, 40);
y1:= LinearReg(C, pds2, S, 1);
y2:= ATR(14);
y3:= ((y1 - C) / y2) * -3;
y3
```

This code establishes four variables. You have seen all of this code before in the TTI Fabric LR and some of it in the TTI Composite. The `y1` and `y2` variables establish the units of measurement necessary to create the TTI Fabric LR indicator. `y3` performs a difference calculation and then divides it by the current ATR(14) value to express the distance from the center line.

The last part of the `y3` calculation multiplies it by –3. This is done for a couple of reasons. Through the process of observation, the initial measurement of ATR(14) units would not provide enough incremental value to the slope summation. It is therefore necessary to give it more weight by using a multiplier. By trial and error, a multiplier of 3 seems to bring it closest to the individual weight of the other three component slopes. You did not observe this, because that chart iteration is not shown for space reasons. Also, the value is reversed by using a negative multiplier so that its directional effect matches those of the other slopes. Smaller changes of the overall development process are obviously not shown here for the purpose of being concise.

What this produces is a value of units that can be added to the slope summation with a roughly equal weighting as each of the other slopes. In Figure 14.7, the added original slope total is expressed as a dotted line plot in pane 1. Added to it is a solid line plot, which adds the additional value of the TTI Fabric LR that is expressed as `y3`. With both plotted next to each other, it is easy to see the effect of incorporating the TTI Fabric LR component to the prospective new indicator. Examine the circled areas on the chart. At three different points of the time series, circles in pane 1, 8, and the price pane show the additional effect.

The code for all of these four components combines to create the current version of the TTI Composite. Once again, it is stated as:

```
1 {User Inputs}
2 pds1:= Input("LR Slope Lookback", 2, 1000, 5);
3 pds2:= Input("Linear Regression Length", 5, 1000, 40);

4 {Establishes linear regression slope values of oscillator
components}
5 x1:= LinRegSlope(Fml("TTI StochEx"), pds1);
6 x2:= LinRegSlope( Fml( "TTI RSIV"), pds1);
7 x3:= LinRegSlope( Fml( "TTI ATR Extreme nb"), pds1);

8 {Calculates number of ATR multiples above or below central
9 fabric line}
10 y1:= LinearReg(C, pds2, S, 1);
```

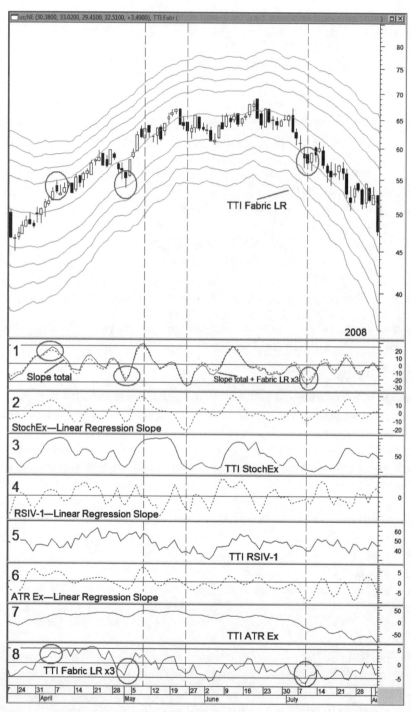

FIGURE 14.7 An additional indicator pane explores the incremental effect of the TTI Fabric LR component.

Chart created in MetaStock.

```
11 y2:= ATR(14);
12 y3:= ((y1 - C) / y2) * -3;

13 {Adds assigned variables to create the composite value,
14 and plots it}
15 x1 + x2 + x3 + y3
```

Can you see how the whole indicator was broken down and plotted visually in the development environment? You should be able to better understand how it was developed. Now, can you better imagine ways to change it to be more responsive? Perhaps giving greater weight to the Fabric component might help. Changing the look-back period for the linear regression slopes could have positive effects. Other components could potentially be added to produce better performance. After all, this is a compound derivative. Almost any development is possible.

Just be sure to examine an abundance of charts after each change. That step will imprint the nuances of the final component's performance right onto your brain. You will understand the how, when, and why the component performs the way it does. When the Fog of Trading occurs, you will have much less doubt, and far greater certainty, because of your intimate knowledge of your tools.

Simple Testing

Now that we have a component developed that seems to work effectively, at least visually, it is appropriate to dig a little bit deeper into its profit or loss potential. This is the correct point at which to use the cold and emotionless objectivity of the microprocessor. This is the *Analyze and Test* step of the scientific process. Sometimes it's hard to define the difference between the experiment and the analyze-and-test steps, but that's okay. Focus on visual chart examination before any software-based study or data analysis.

The process of a simple analysis of potential profit to potential loss has been performed previously in Chapters 7 and 11. As you may recall, it performs a study over a specific time span to quantify the following:

- The total quantity of trades signaled for each stock in the S&P 500 Index, based on a specific Boolean signal.
- It separately sums the total profit potential and total loss potential for each stock in the S&P 500 Index.
- It separately sums the total profit potential and total loss potential for the S&P 500 Index.

This process of mining trade signal and performance data produces two essential values: a sum of trades, and a sum of the performance attributed to those trade signals. This enables an easy and accurate collection of the following five values:

1. The total quantity of trades for the S&P 500 Index of stocks during the study time span
2. Average potential profit per trade for each stock in the S&P 500 Index
3. Average potential loss per trade for each stock in the S&P 500 Index
4. Average potential profit per trade for the S&P 500 Index, which occurs simultaneously with each stock trade signal
5. Average potential loss per trade for the S&P 500 Index, which occurs simultaneously with each stock trade signal

Most good technical analysis software programs, such as TradeStation and MetaStock, have the ability to produce this type of data. The MetaStock function language code that performs this study runs within the MetaStock Explorer application. The version of the code to study long side trades using the TTI Composite component is as follows:

Column A: x Cum

```
Cum(
Ref(
Cross(-25,Fml("TTI Composite"))
, -9) = 1
)
```

Column B: x+Prof%

```
Cum(If(Ref(
Cross(-25,Fml("TTI Composite"))
, -9) = 1, (HHV(H, 10) - Ref(C, -9)) / Ref(C, -9), 0) )
```

Column C: x-Prof%

```
Cum(If(Ref(
Cross(-25,Fml("TTI Composite"))
, -9) = 1,
(LLV(L, 10) - Ref(C, -9)) / Ref(C, -9), 0) )
```

Column D: SP +Prof%

```
y1:= Security("c:\MetaStock Data\Indices &
Indicators\US & Canadian Indices\.spx",C);

y2:= Security("c:\MetaStock Data\Indices &
Indicators\US & Canadian Indices\.spx",H);

x1:= Ref(
Cross(-25,Fml("TTI Composite"))
, -9) = 1;
Cum(If(x1 = 1,(HHV(y2, 10) - Ref(y1, -9)) / Ref(y1, -9), 0))
```

Column E: SP-Prof%

```
y1:= Security("c:\MetaStock Data\Indices &
Indicators\US & Canadian Indices\.spx",C);

y2:= Security("c:\MetaStock Data\Indices &
Indicators\US & Canadian Indices\.spx",L);

x1:= Ref(
Cross(-25,Fml("TTI Composite"))
, -9) = 1;
(Cum(If(x1 = 1,
(HHV(y2, 10) - Ref(y1, -9)) / Ref(y1, -9), 0)))
```

This exploration code produces a five-column flat file of significant data, in addition to columns for the stock ticker, the company name, and the location of the security source data file. The five columns of raw data are the truly valuable content. The software will perform many thousands of arithmetic and logic calculations in a few minutes or less. It will do so according to your exact instructions. This is a process that the human brain is unable to perform reliably. It's as though the data and conditions viewed by our eyes travel through our emotion filter, and are then changed to fit what we want. Thus, we see what we want to see.

The program will not make a single error, whether you disagree with its results or not. If you do disagree with the resulting data, then either you have made a mistake in the code, or you just don't like the disappointing results. Both of these things happen often and are a part of the challenging process of finding actionable inefficiencies in the market.

To explain each and every line of the function code would likely be tedious and dull. Instead, here is a list of pertinent explanations for different sections of the study code:

- A 10-day trade time frame is measured.
- Each section of code runs within a column of the MetaStock Explorer. In Figure 14.8, the Explorer window is shown and contains the code for column A. It's pretty simple.
- The code is actually a collection of function statements nested within each other. Their order of execution is controlled by the parentheses, much like in basic algebra. The innermost parentheses execute first. The order of execution then works its way outward.
- To illustrate this nested order, the code for column A has been segmented for more detail. The center line, which reads `Cross(-25, Fml("TTI Composite"))` is the Boolean signal for the trade. It returns a value of true when the TTI Composite drops below a value of 25. The other parts of the code sum the total quantity of true readings that occur over the time span of the study.
- The seven different functions used are relatively simple. For an explanation of each, the resource section of the Equis web site, www.equis.com, has a formula reference primer that's easy to follow.

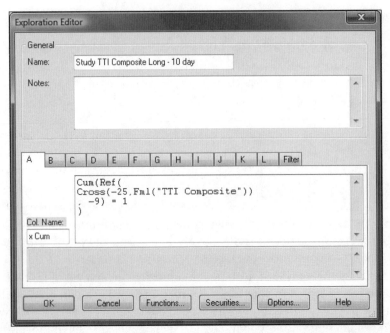

FIGURE 14.8 The MetaStock Explorer application is easily configured, and is used to find daily trade candidates as well as perform valuable component performance research.

Created in MetaStock.

- Column B calculates the total amount of individual stock trade profit potential, in percent, that occurred over the time span of the study, as a result of the trade signals.
- Column C calculates the total amount of individual stock trade loss potential, in percent, that occurred over the time span of the study, as a result of the trade signals.
- Column D calculates the total comparative amount of profit potential for the S&P 500 Index, in percent, that occurred over the time span of the study, as a result of the trade signals.
- Column E calculates the total comparative amount of loss potential for the S&P 500 Index, in percent, that occurred over the time span of the study, as a result of the trade signals.
- This same code can be used to test any trade signal. All that is required is to replace the code line, `Cross(-25, Fml("TTI Composite"))`, with a proper Boolean statement that describes your desired trade signal.
- If you wish to study a different trade time span, then adjust the `Ref()` bar arguments accordingly.
- This code uses a rather unscientific fudge factor. The HHV() function identifies the greatest value during the trade time span and is therefore the limiting number for profit. The HHV(H, 10) function represents the highest high value on the day before the signal day. In the case of most profitable trades, it does not increase the profit.

In the case of signal failures, however, it does increase the loss levels. Thus, using an argument of 10 in lieu of 9 biases the average more toward loss than profit. It is your option to use either number. I like some cushion built in to my trading strategies. Note that in terms of the function's look-back argument, the most current day is stated as zero, and therefore 10 days before is expressed as nine. It uses a zero-based counting scheme.

As stated in previous chapters, it is important to point out that this study produces a raw average only. It demonstrates a nonstatistical potential for profit and loss. It measures only the population you choose. It does not use any formal inferential statistics. Just as important, it does not produce a statistically valid back-test, such as the type produced by a Monte Carlo simulation. It should be used for comparative performance measurement. It should also be applied to a sizable population, and therefore draw some strength from the law of large numbers.

With all that said, you are likely wondering about the results of this study when applied to the TTI Composite component. Remember that we are striving for performance improvements over that of the different components that make up the TTI Composite. To facilitate some comparison, the following results also list the performance data for the TTI RSIV-1. As in the previous studies in Chapters 7 and 11, the periodicity is daily, with the duration being for 2,000 trading days, beginning on June 29, 2000, and ending on June 13, 2008. This equates to approximately eight years of data, which occur during bear and bull markets.

Table 14.2 lists the results of the MetaStock exploration code for testing the TTI Composite component. This test assumes a long trade signal for 10-day and 5-day time spans. The exact same study was conducted previously for the TTI RSIV-1, and its results are listed in section two.

As you can see, the TTI Composite trades tend to produce signals in times of greater market volatility than does the TTI RSIV-1. These numbers suggest that the TTI Composite produces a slightly better profit outlook. In terms of change from the TTI RSIV-1, its profit potential increased by 39.3 percent, while its loss potential increased by 30.8 percent. Its profit-to-loss change delta is therefore a positive 8.5 percent. This confirms a measured improvement, which is what the development process is all about. The analyze-and-test step of the scientific process is to provide proof of results.

Another very important piece of information is that the TTI Composite component produced 48 percent more test events. Increased performance usually comes at a cost of fewer signals. This metric comparison points favorably to further performance improvements if changes are made to the component's parameters or to the signal threshold value.

The performance measurements in Table 14.2 tell us that we are on the right track, and that there is likely to be further opportunity for improvement. If you consult the Basic Scientific Method presented in Figure 14.2, you can see that we have just completed the *Analyze and Test* step, and can now proceed to the *Adapt and Try Again* step. Component development is a cycle. Some may say that it is a never-ending cycle.

TABLE 14.2 Exploration study results for the TTI Composite and the TTI RSIV-1

Test Event	Sample Size	Profit Potential	Loss Potential	Duration
1 Long Trade				
TTI Composite	15,656	7.8%	−6.8%	10 Days
S&P 500	15,656	2.7%	1.3%	10 Days
TTI Composite	15,656	5.7%	−4.9%	5 Days
S&P 500	15,656	2.0%	0.5%	5 Days
2 Long Trade				
RSIV-1	10,572	5.6%	−5.2%	10 Days
S&P 500	10,572	2.3%	1.1%	10 Days
RSIV-1	10,572	4.1%	−3.6%	5 Days
S&P 500	10,572	1.7%	0.4%	5 Days

Perhaps, but it is a necessary part of finding the markets' inefficiencies so that you can trade ahead of your competitors.

Software-Based Statistical Back-Testing

The simple testing that we just reviewed is sufficient for the process of component development. An important point to stress here is that this is component development within a trading system framework. When it comes time to test the performance of a specific method, one that relies on multiple components, and is to be used as a part of an overall trading plan, then a more intensive and statistically valid testing method should be used.

Today, this is commonly, and very loosely, referred to as back-testing. There are many products that perform back-testing, which is useful, but not statistically valid. Take great care when relying on this type of software. There's a lot more to back-testing than you might think. First, consider that all trading decisions are 100 percent defined as software algorithm-based rules with no exceptions. Discretionary trading goes out the window at this point.

The whole purpose of back-testing is to use a trading system's previous theoretical performance to predict that trading system's performance in the future. Given the endless possible differences of future circumstances, this is no small task. Trading methods that have worked well in the past cease to do so at given points; this is a real-world market consistency. There are valid statistical methods for measuring the potential for this effect.

Another challenge that traders face is that two people can trade the same rule-based method perfectly and achieve very different results. No one can trade all of the tradable securities that a method can be applied to. Each of us will therefore select different stocks, commodities, or markets at varying times. This means that the actual sequence of trades in which the method is applied will vary. Consider that two individuals each trade three stocks, but only one at a time. They do so, however, in a different sequence, and therefore on different days. This will produce varying results. They could each follow the same method rules without error, and one could be profitable while the other loses money. A system's potential for this type of performance can be statistically measured.

There are two pervasive methods for software to back-test trading systems in a statistically valid way. The first is the bootstrap method. The second and more commercially used method is the Monte Carlo permutation. Both methods use a random sampling of the original sample population of possible trades. The instances of the resample number in the thousands. The results of so many possibilities are then combined to form a very large distribution of the sample statistic. This renders such a large distribution of possible outcomes that statistical analysis can then be performed to give a much better probability of a trading system's variability.[2]

The mathematical science of statistical back-testing is worthy of your time investment if you want to be successful as a technical trader. It is a discipline of thought process that technical analysts are embracing ever more intensely as markets become more efficient. *Evidence-Based Technical Analysis*, by David Aronson, is an excellent source of knowledge for this topic, as well as many other aspects of trading system design. His book is also required reading for the Market Technicians Association (www.mta.org) certification exams.

The Math

In Part II of this book we focused heavily on the practical integration of simple volatility measurements into component design. These techniques are a significant part of what makes volatility-based technical analysis come alive. It's what gives indicators the ability to be responsive to actual market moving forces and to possess predictive value. Here is a brief review of the ones that were used.

- *Standard Deviation:* This simple step magnifies the value that is most deviant to an even greater value than it already is. It gives the most weight to values that are the farthest from an average. It identifies the extreme by doing so; it makes visible the fringes.
- *Average True Range:* An excellent method for measuring the short-term volatility of daily price movement. ATR gives calculations and algorithms a better method for normalizing price movement.
- *Linear Regression:* Is possibly the best statistical measure of time series data because of how it represents the most efficient pathway for the specified period of time. It is highly responsive to price direction, and is more representative of central tendency for a specified time period. Its use results in greater levels of accuracy when prices are trending. Algorithms that use it properly can experience the ability to project or forecast.
- *R Squared:* Gives a value that measures the degree of efficiency to which a linear regression line represents the series of data points. The official explanation is that

it gauges what percentage of the data point movement in the series can be explained by the linear regression statistical method. It provides a quantifiable means to predict, or forecast, the likelihood that coming data values will continue in the same direction with the same slope. Its use can add predictive value to components.

- *Peaks and Troughs:* These are special software functions that, through the benefit of hindsight, identify qualified highs and lows, respectively. Using these functions to identify significant highs and lows can assist you greatly when the task at hand is to quantify significant extreme levels. Special care should be taken when using them to avoid their illusory nature, as pointed out in Chapter 12.

This list of volatility and volatility-related measurements is by no means comprehensive. There are more ways to skin the volatility cat. Here are a few more that will broaden your creative potential should you choose to study them.

- Standard error
- Variance
- Correlation
- Geometric mean
- Median
- Mode
- Skew

As markets become increasingly efficient, the opportunities for profit become increasingly invisible. Removing the cloak that hides the profit of inefficiency relies on using the mathematics of volatility measurement and statistics. If you are practicing technical analysis, personally or professionally, you should improve your understanding of basic statistics as it is applied to trading and finance. *Technical Analysis: The Complete Resource for Financial Market Technicians*, by Charles D. Kirkpatrick, CMT, and Julie R. Dahlquist, Ph.D., is a book that should be on any trader's bookshelf. Appendix A, written by Dr. Richard J. Bauer Jr., provides an excellent primer in basic statistics as applied to financial and trading applications.

ASK THE QUESTIONS AND USE THE ADVANTAGES

Pablo Picasso famously said, "Computers are useless. They can only give you answers." He was right because all those masses of silicon only execute the instructions that came from human brains in the first place. It's the questions that are meaningful. If we broaden our ability to ask the right questions, then our ability to see what others do not will broaden as well. At its foundation, trading system and component design depend on that.

It is equally important for today's traders to remember the 3B rule as it applies to trading methods:

Build *or* Buy, *but do not* Borrow

Trading ahead of other market participants requires you to equip yourself with an advantage. Borrowing indicators and trading methods from the tool chest of the public domain will seldom give you any advantage. The vast arrays of classic technical analysis components available at web sites, and as standard features in TA software packages, seldom hold the predictive qualities of the tools that the winning market competitors are using.

If you want to compete with a realistic probability of success, then you must use a volatility-based framework of original components and methods that are not available to the masses. Building your own methods and measurements requires dedication, effort, and time, but is a most worthwhile endeavor. Should you choose to do so then you will benefit greatly from the experience. There are also credible sources from which to acquire volatility-based systems. The content of this book provides you with an excellent knowledge baseline for choosing a system to meet your goals.

A very successful person I once disliked said, "I don't mind competition, so long as I am the only one who can possibly win." He won consistently. There are no extra points awarded for playing fair when trading. Whether you Build it or Buy it, make sure that the probabilities are always in your favor with volatility-based technical analysis.

TradeStation Examples and EasyLanguage Code

This appendix is written for readers who use TradeStation as their technical analysis platform. It presents all of the previously written code in a TradeStation EasyLanguage code equivalent, along with new TradeStation charts. Also included are a few useful bonus functions for added value.

Obtaining the EasyLanguage code presented in this appendix is easy. It is all listed at this book's companion web site, www.tradingtheinvisible.com. Once at the site, you can download it as an EasyLanguage Document (ELD) file. The discussion that follows assumes that you have a journeyman's understanding of TradeStation and EasyLanguage programming. I focus on specific code portions that pertain to unique volatility measurement techniques.

The EL code presented herein is written with an emphasis on clarity. There are likely ways that it can be written to better optimize processor usage, which is up to the reader to pursue. The EL code for indicators and ShowMe studies is written in its simplest format for the initial examples. I then gradually add more complexity for user input control. Emphasis, however, is consistently placed on readability.

AVERAGE TRUE RANGE

The EasyLanguage (EL) code to call the Average True Range function is:

```
AvgTrueRange(length)
```

The EL code for AverageTrueRange() is:

```
inputs:
Length( numericsimple ) ;
AvgTrueRange = Average( TrueRange, Length ) ;
```

This will compute a simple moving average of True Range. It will not output the ATR value using the original Wilder's smoothing method. An EL function to return Average True Range using the original Wilder's smoothing method, previously used throughout this book, is as follows:

```
{ATR_WS}
Inputs:
  PDS(numericsimple);

If CurrentBar <= PDS then
  Value1 = Summation(TrueRange,CurrentBar) / CurrentBar
else
  Value1 = ((Value1 * (PDS - 1)) + TrueRange) / PDS;
ATR_WS = Value1;
```

TradeStation uses a software architecture that separates a function from an indicator. This makes the EL structure very flexible when you want to create functions that can be called from many different applications, using different numerical parameters. The EL code for an indicator to call the Average True Range function just presented, using a 14-period lookback and plotting it to an indicator pane, is written like this:

```
Value1 = ATR_WS(14) ;

Plot1( Value1, "ATR" ) ;
```

When it's desired to normalize the Average True Range function by the closing price and express it in percentage units greater than zero, the function call could be the code that follows. Note that the only difference is in the additional math in the last line. The indicator code that holds a function call would be the same, except that the function name has changed to ATR_WS_NormC.

```
{ATR WS NormC}
Inputs:
  PDS(numericsimple);

If CurrentBar <= PDS then
  Value1 = Summation(TrueRange,CurrentBar) / CurrentBar
else
  Value1 = ((Value1 * (PDS - 1)) + TrueRange) / PDS;

ATR_WS_NormC = (Value1 / Close) * 100;
```

THE TTI ATR EXTREME

In Chapter 4, we created the TTI ATR Extreme. The first complete version of it adjusted for upper and lower extremes by incorporating High and Low values, in lieu of Close values. It also established an upper and lower extreme boundary based on one standard deviation above the indicator value. Here is the EL function code for TTI ATR Extreme:

```
{TTI_ATREx_1}
inputs:
  PDS1(numericsimple), {moving average periods}
  PDS2(numericsimple), {ATR periods}
  PDS3(numericsimple), {standard deviation periods}
  PDS4(numericsimple), {smoothing periods}
  uExtreme(numericref), {upper extreme - by reference}
  lExtreme(numericref); {lower extreme - by reference}

if Close < XAverage(Close, PDS1) then
  Value1 = (((Low - XAverage(Low, PDS1)) / Close) * 100) * ATR_WS_NormC(PDS2)
else
  Value1 = (((High - XAverage(High, PDS1)) / Close) * 100) * ATR_WS_NormC(PDS2);
  uExtreme = XAverage(Value1, PDS1) + StandardDev(Value1, PDS3, 1);
  Value2 = Average(Value1, PDS4);
  lExtreme = XAverage(Value1, PDS1) - StandardDev(Value1, PDS3, 1);

TTI_ATREx_1 = Value2;
```

Here is the EL indicator code, which calls the preceding function and plots it on the chart.

```
{TTI ATREx 1}
variables:
 uExtreme(0),
 lExtreme(0);

Value2 = TTI_ATREx_1(40, 14, 200, 3, uExtreme, lExtreme) ;
Value1 = uExtreme;
Value3 = lExtreme;

Plot1( Value1, "ATR Ex" ) ;
Plot2( Value2, "uExtreme" ) ;
Plot3( Value3, "lExtreme" ) ;
```

A key difference in the `TTI_ATREx_1` function and the indicator that is calling it is the use of multiple values being passed to the function. The function code does not

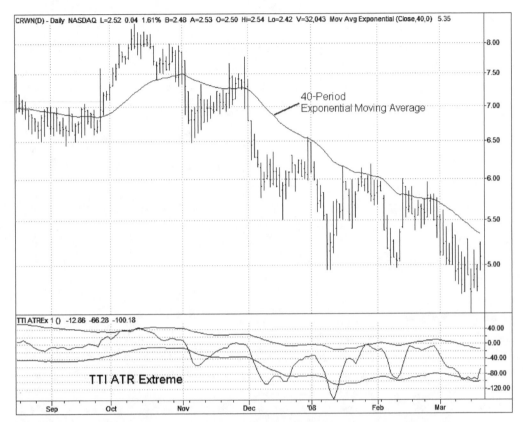

FIGURE A.1 This chart of Crown Media Holdings (CRWN) shows the TTI ATR Extreme.
Created with TradeStation. ©TradeStation Technologies, Inc. All rights reserved.

include any specific numerical values. It receives all of its specific numeric parameters
from the function call in the form of arguments as follows:

```
Value2 = TTI_ATREx_1(40, 14, 200, 3, uExtreme, lExtreme) ;
```

The values expressed as arguments in the preceding statements are passed to the
function as defined by the input definitions in the function. The last two are defined in the
function as reference variables; that's what the (numericref) is defining in the function. This is a way that a function, which normally returns only one value, can return more
than one. In this way, the function is directly writing values to the variables uExtreme
and lExtreme, which are established in the indicator code calling the function.

The TradeStation equivalent to Figure 4.14 is shown in Figure A.1. You may note
that the TradeStation charts will be shown with OHLC style bars. While TradeStation
normally displays high-resolution candlestick charts, its bar charts give the best clarity
when images are reproduced in a black-and-white format for this book.

Let's take things forward by generating some onscreen prompts to show possible

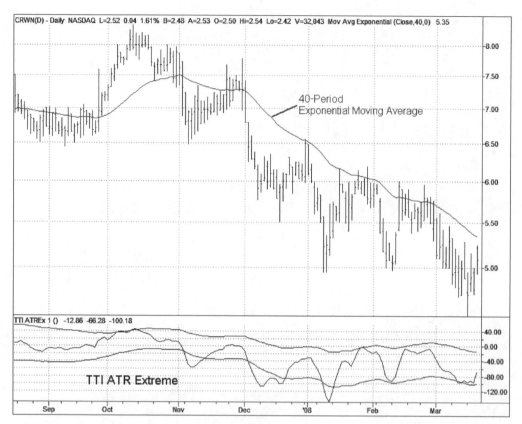

FIGURE A.2 This chart of Crown Media Holdings (CRWN) shows the TTI ATR Extreme with a ShowMe study.

Created with TradeStation. ©TradeStation Technologies, Inc. All rights reserved.

trade entry signals based on the TTI_ATREx_1 function. This is accomplished in TradeStation with ShowMe and PaintBar studies. The PaintBar study manipulates the price bar color, based on your coded strategy. Since this book is printed in black and white, it would be of little use to feature charts depicting PaintBar studies. We will therefore focus on the EL code as written for ShowMe studies.

In Figure A.2 is the same chart of Crown Media Holdings (CRWN) that features a ShowMe strategy based on the TTI_ATR_Ex_1 function code. This chart is an equivalent to Figure 4.15. You may note that the onscreen symbol is a dot accompanied by the text "ATREx."

The following is the EL code that is used to create the ShowMe study.

```
{TTI ATREx 1 shme}
variables:
 uExtreme(0),
 lExtreme(0);
```

```
Value1 = TTI_ATREx_1(40, 14, 200, 3, uExtreme, lExtreme) ;

Condition1 = Value1 Crosses Above uExtreme ;
Condition2 = Value1 Crosses Below lExtreme ;
If Condition1 then
  begin
  Plot1( High ) ;
  Value4 = Text_New(Date, Time, High, "ATREx") ;
  Value5 = Text_SetLocation(Value4, Date, Time, High * 1.03) ;
  Value5 = Text_SetStyle(Value4, 2, 0) ;
  Value5 = Text_SetColor(Value4, Black) ;
  end ;

If Condition2 then
  begin
  Plot2( Low ) ;
  Value4 = Text_New(Date, Time, Low, "ATREx") ;
  Value5 = Text_SetLocation(Value4, Date, Time, Low - (Low *. 03)) ;
  Value5 = Text_SetStyle(Value4, 2, 1) ;
  Value5 = Text_SetColor(Value4, Black) ;
  end ;
```

In Chapter 5, we examined the effects of enhancing the upper and lower extreme thresholds. To do this, we used R-Squared as an additive measure to the existing extreme. If we make the same change to the TTI_ATREx_1 function code, it would look like this:

```
{TTI_ATREx_2}
inputs:
  PDS1(numericsimple), {moving average periods}
  PDS2(numericsimple), {ATR periods}
  PDS3(numericsimple), {standard deviation periods}
  PDS4(numericsimple), {smoothing periods}
  PDS5(numericsimple), {R squared periods}
  uExtremeR(numericref), {upper extreme - by reference}
  lExtremeR(numericref); {lower extreme - by reference}

If Close < XAverage(Close, PDS1) then
  Value1 = (((Low - XAverage(Low, PDS1)) / Close) * 100) * ATR_WS_NormC(PDS2)
else
  Value1 = (((High - XAverage(High, PDS1)) / Close) * 100) * ATR_WS_NormC(PDS2);

  uExtremeR = XAverage(Value1, PDS1) +
  ((1 + RSquare(BarNumber, Close, PDS5)) * StandardDev(Value1, PDS3, 1));
  Value2 = Average(Value1, PDS4);
```

```
  lExtremeR = XAverage(Value1, PDS1) -
  ((1 + RSquare(BarNumber, Close, PDS5)) * StandardDev(Value1, PDS3, 1));

TTI_ATREx_2 = Value2;
```

To call this new TTI_ATREx_2 function from an indicator, which we will name TTI ATREx 2, the code can be written as follows:

```
{TTI ATREx 2}
variables:
 uExtremeR(0),
 lExtremeR(0);

Value2 = TTI_ATREx_2(40, 14, 200, 3, 20, uExtremeR, lExtremeR) ;
Value1 = uExtremeR;
Value3 = lExtremeR;

Plot1( Value1, "ATR Ex" ) ;
Plot2( Value2, "uExtremeR" ) ;
Plot3( Value3, "lExtremeR" ) ;
```

The first difference of note between iterations 1 and 2 is the addition of an argument passed to the function. When TTI_ATREx_2 is called, the fifth argument is now the look-back period for the R-Squared measurement. In the preceding indicator code, it is 20. Likewise, the function now has the additional variable PDS5 added. Looking further into the TTI_ATREx_2 function, you can see where the RSquare() function is called, and how it uses PDS5 as an argument.

Both versions of our TTI ATR Extreme indicator are featured for comparison in Figure A.3. (This is the same chart as shown in Figure 5.14.) Also on the price chart of Figure A.3 is a ShowMe study that labels potential trade entries. Here's what the letters beneath the dots mean:

- Those labeled "D" are triggered by TTI_ATREx_1.
- Those labeled "R" are triggered by TTI_ATREx_2.
- Those labeled "RD" are triggered by TTI_ATREx_1 and TTI_ATREx_2 concurrently.

What follows is the EL code for the ShowMe study in Figure A.3.

```
{TTI ATREx 2 shme}
variables:
 uExtreme(0),
 lExtreme(0),
 uExtremeR(0),
 lExtremeR(0);
```

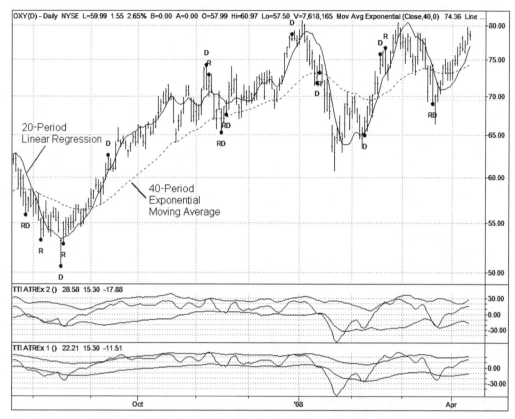

FIGURE A.3 This daily chart of Occidental (OXY) compares the TTI ATREx 1 and TTI ATREx 2 indicators.

Created with TradeStation. ©TradeStation Technologies, Inc. All rights reserved.

```
Value1 = TTI_ATREx_1(40, 14, 200, 3, uExtreme, lExtreme) ;
Value2 = TTI_ATREx_2(40, 14, 200, 3, 20, uExtremeR, lExtremeR) ;

Condition1 = Value1 Crosses Above uExtreme ;
Condition2 = Value1 Crosses Below lExtreme ;
Condition3 = Value2 Crosses Above uExtremeR ;
Condition4 = Value2 Crosses Below lExtremeR ;

If Condition1 and Condition3 then begin
  Plot1( High ) ;
  Value4 = Text_New(Date, Time, High, "RD") ;
  Value5 = Text_SetLocation(Value4, Date, Time, High * 1.03) ;
  Value5 = Text_SetStyle(Value4, 2, 0) ;
  Value5 = Text_SetColor(Value4, Black) ;
  end
  else begin
```

```
   If Condition1 then
     begin
     Plot1( High ) ;
     Value4 = Text_New(Date, Time, High, "D") ;
     Value5 = Text_SetLocation(Value4, Date, Time, High * 1.03) ;
     Value5 = Text_SetStyle(Value4, 2, 0) ;
     Value5 = Text_SetColor(Value4, Black) ;
     end ;
   If Condition3 then
     begin
     Plot1( High ) ;
     Value4 = Text_New(Date, Time, High, "R") ;
     Value5 = Text_SetLocation(Value4, Date, Time, High * 1.03) ;
     Value5 = Text_SetStyle(Value4, 2, 0) ;
     Value5 = Text_SetColor(Value4, Black) ;
     end ;
     end ;


If Condition2 and Condition4 then begin
   Plot2( Low ) ;
   Value4 = Text_New(Date, Time, Low, "RD") ;
   Value5 = Text_SetLocation(Value4, Date, Time, Low - (Low *. 03)) ;
   Value5 = Text_SetStyle(Value4, 2, 1) ;
   Value5 = Text_SetColor(Value4, Black) ;
   end
   else begin
   If Condition2 then
     begin
     Plot2( Low ) ;
     Value4 = Text_New(Date, Time, Low, "D") ;
     Value5 = Text_SetLocation(Value4, Date, Time, Low - (Low *. 03));
     Value5 = Text_SetStyle(Value4, 2, 1) ;
     Value5 = Text_SetColor(Value4, Black) ;
     end ;
   If Condition4 then
     begin
     Plot2( Low ) ;
     Value4 = Text_New(Date, Time, Low, "R") ;
     Value5 = Text_SetLocation(Value4, Date, Time, Low - (Low *. 03));
     Value5 = Text_SetStyle(Value4, 2, 1) ;
     Value5 = Text_SetColor(Value4, Black) ;
     end ;
     end ;
```

THE TTI STOCHASTIC EXTREME

In Chapter 5, we examined the classic Stochastic Oscillator. After understanding its structure, we attempt some modifications so that it will become more effective through volatility sensitivity. The first iteration adjusts the classic algorithm to measure volatility with standard deviation. Presented next is the EL code that creates the TTI Stochastic Extreme 1 (TTI StochEx 1) function for the TradeStation platform.

```
{TTI_StochEx_1}
Inputs:
   PDS1(numericsimple), {standard deviation periods}
   PDS2 (numericsimple), {%K}
   PDS3 (numericsimple), {%D}
   PDS4 (numericsimple); {additional smoothing}

Value1 = StandardDev(Close, PDS1, 1);

Value2 = (Summation(Value1 - Lowest(Value1, PDS2), PDS3) /
   Summation(Highest(Value1, PDS2) - Lowest(Value1, PDS2), PDS3)) * 100;

Value3 = XAverage(Value2, PDS4);

TTI_StochEx_1 = Value3;
```

To call the TTI_StochEx_1 function, the following EL code creates the TTI StochEx 1 indicator.

```
{TTI StochEx 1}
Value1 = 100;
Value2 = 95;
Value3 = TTI_StochEx_1(14, 5, 3, 3);
Value4 = 0;

Plot1( Value1, "Upper Range" );
Plot2( Value2, "Extreme" );
Plot3( Value3, "StochEx 1" );
Plot4( Value4, "Lower Range" );
```

You can see in Figure A.4 how the TTI_StochEx_1 function performs. In the preceding function code you may have noticed one characteristic of this version that is different from the same indicator presented in Chapter 5 (see Figure 5.16). In this version, all of the possible time duration parameters are built into the function as inputs. They are therefore passed to the function by the function call itself. This is visible in the indicator code line, which reads: `Value3 = TTI_StochEx_1(14, 5, 3, 3);`. When written this way, there is flexibility built into the function. It can thus be used with different time parameters without recoding.

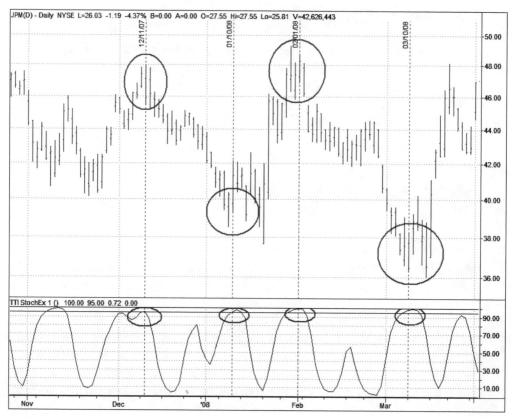

FIGURE A.4 This daily chart of JP Morgan (JPM) displays the TTI StochEx 1 performance with an upper extreme of 95.

Created with TradeStation. ©TradeStation Technologies, Inc. All rights reserved.

The second version of TTI Stochastic Extreme fine-tunes overbought and oversold detection by using an ATR accelerator. In this way, it reduces the quantity of signals generated so that the quality of them can be improved. We will call this function the TTI_StochEx_2. What follows is the EL code for it.

```
{TTI_StochEx_2}
Inputs:
  PDS1(numericsimple), {standard deviation periods}
  PDS2 (numericsimple), {%K}
  PDS3 (numericsimple), {%D}
  PDS4 (numericsimple), {ATR periods}
  PDS5 (numericsimple), {additional smoothing}
  StochExSD (numericref), {StochEx utilizing standard deviation only}
  StochExATR (numericref); {StochEx with added ATR acceleration}
```

```
Value1 = StandardDev(Close, PDS1, 1);

If Close > Average(Close, PDS1) then
   Value1 = Value1 else Value1 = (Value1 * -1);

Value2 = (Summation(Value1 - Lowest(Value1, PDS2), PDS3) /
   Summation(Highest(Value1, PDS2) - Lowest(Value1, PDS2), PDS3)) * 100;

Value3 = Value1 * ATR_WS(PDS4);

Value4 = (Summation(Value3 - Lowest(Value3, PDS2), PDS3) /
   Summation(Highest(Value3, PDS2) - Lowest(Value3, PDS2), PDS3)) * 100;

StochExSD = XAverage(Value2, PDS5);
StochExATR = XAverage(Value4, PDS5);

TTI_StochEx_2 = 1;
```

Just as in Chapter 5, this code actually computes the previous and the new version. This is done for comparative analysis reasons. In this EL code version, there are two inputs used to pass the TTI_StochEx_1 and TTI_StochEx_2 values back by variable reference to whatever code calls the function. The inputs are `StochExSD` and `StochExATR`, respectively. This version also fixes the issue of having both extreme levels at the top of the indicator. This is accomplished with the `If` statement, which determines if the close is above or below an input defined exponential moving average. Now the value of 95 represents overbought, and the value of 5 represents oversold. Indicator code to call this new function could look like this:

```
{TTI StochEx 2}
Inputs:
   UpperRange(100),
   UpperExtreme(95),
   LowerExtreme(5),
   LowerRange(100),
   GuideColor(Black),
   StochExSDColor(Black),
   StochExATRColor(Black),
   StDevPeriods(14),
   PctKPeriods(5),
   PctDPeriods(3),
   ATRPeriods(5),
   AddlSmoothPeriods(3);

Variables:
   StochExSD(0),
   StochExATR(0),
   StochEx(0);
```

```
StochEx = TTI_StochEx_2(StDevPeriods, PctKPeriods,
PctDPeriods, ATRPeriods, AddlSmoothPeriods,
   StochExSD, StochExATR);

Plot1(UpperRange, "Upper Range", GuideColor);
Plot2(UpperExtreme, "Up Extreme", GuideColor);
Plot3(StochExSD, "StochEx SD", StochExSDColor);
Plot4(StochExATR, "StochEx ATR", StochExATRColor);
Plot5(LowerExtreme, "Low Extreme", GuideColor);
Plot6(LowerRange, "Lower Range", GuideColor);
```

As you can see, the function call statement has grown to a considerable length. These values could easily be hard-coded into the function, as it was originally written in Chapter 5. Should you wish to pursue optimization testing, however, passing input parameters to the function is a much more efficient, and less error prone, method than editing code. Also at this point and going forward, indicators are written to enable user input control over parameters. The indicator code takes additional length, and a small degree of complexity, but the user gains the ability to change parameter settings for his specific needs.

Should you want to see the effectiveness of these changes, then it is best to first plot them on the chart as visual signals. A TradeStation ShowMe study can do this well. The following is EL code that we will name TTI ATREx 2 shme. It is very similar to the previous section's ShowMe code.

```
{TTI ATREx 2 shme}
Variables:
 StochExSD(0),
 StochExATR(0);

Value1 = TTI_StochEx_2(14, 5, 3, 5, 3, StochExSD, StochExATR);

Condition1 = StochExSD Crosses Above 95 and
   Close is > XAverage(Close, 20) ;
Condition2 = StochExSD Crosses Below 5 and
   Close is < XAverage(Close, 20) ;
Condition3 = StochExATR Crosses Above 95 and
   Close is > XAverage(Close, 20) ;
Condition4 = StochExATR Crosses Below 5 and
   Close is < XAverage(Close, 20) ;

If Condition1 and Condition3 then begin
   Plot1( High ) ;
   Value4 = Text_New(Date, Time, High, "C") ;
   Value5 = Text_SetLocation(Value4, Date, Time, High * 1.02) ;
   Value5 = Text_SetStyle(Value4, 2, 0) ;
   Value5 = Text_SetColor(Value4, Black) ;
   end
```

```
    else begin
    If Condition1 then
      begin
      Plot1( High ) ;
      Value4 = Text_New(Date, Time, High, "SD") ;
      Value5 = Text_SetLocation(Value4, Date, Time, High * 1.02) ;
      Value5 = Text_SetStyle(Value4, 2, 0) ;
      Value5 = Text_SetColor(Value4, Black) ;
      end ;
    If Condition3 then
      begin
      Plot1( High ) ;
      Value4 = Text_New(Date, Time, High, "ATR") ;
      Value5 = Text_SetLocation(Value4, Date, Time, High * 1.02) ;
      Value5 = Text_SetStyle(Value4, 2, 0) ;
      Value5 = Text_SetColor(Value4, Black) ;
      end ;
      end ;


If Condition2 and Condition4 then begin
    Plot2( Low ) ;
    Value4 = Text_New(Date, Time, Low, "C") ;
    Value5 = Text_SetLocation(Value4, Date, Time, Low - (Low *. 02)) ;
    Value5 = Text_SetStyle(Value4, 2, 1) ;
    Value5 = Text_SetColor(Value4, Black) ;
    end
    else begin
    If Condition2 then
      begin
      Plot2( Low ) ;
      Value4 = Text_New(Date, Time, Low, "SD") ;
      Value5 = Text_SetLocation(Value4, Date, Time, Low - (Low *. 02)) ;
      Value5 = Text_SetStyle(Value4, 2, 1) ;
      Value5 = Text_SetColor(Value4, Black) ;
      end ;
    If Condition4 then
      begin
      Plot2( Low ) ;
      Value4 = Text_New(Date, Time, Low, "ATR") ;
      Value5 = Text_SetLocation(Value4, Date, Time, Low - (Low *. 02)) ;
      Value5 = Text_SetStyle(Value4, 2, 1) ;
      Value5 = Text_SetColor(Value4, Black) ;
      end ;
      end ;
```

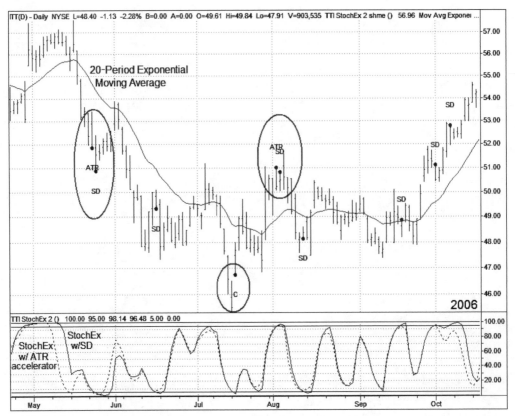

FIGURE A.5 This daily chart of ITT Industries (ITT) directly compares the TTI_StochEx_1 and the TTI_StochEx_2 functions.

Created with TradeStation. ©TradeStation Technologies, Inc. All rights reserved.

You can see in Figure A.5 how this ShowMe plots the potential trade signals. This chart is the TradeStation equivalent to Figure 5.18. Trade signals to buy or short are determined when the signal crosses 5 and 95, respectively. On the chart *SD* represents the TTI_StochEx_1 signals, *ATR* represents the TTI_StochEx_2 signals, and *C* represents a concurrent signal from each. The dotted line in the indicator pane displays the new TTI_StochEx_2 value. Any interpretation of the chart is identical to that written in Chapter 5.

Continuing our look at the TTI_StochEx_2, we find that an inherent weakness still exists. The current configuration fails to adjust for trend direction. In Figure A.6 (the same as Figure 5.19), an example of a strong and low oscillating trend is present in this daily chart of Thomas & Betts (TNB). Of the ten signals generated, six of them trade against the trend, and would likely result in losing trades. Note that in Figure A6 only the ATR version of the StochEx is plotted. By inserting a double slash in front of the Plot3 statement, a comment line is created. This change is accomplished by changing the code to read as follows:

FIGURE A.6 This chart compares the TTI_StochEx_2 indicator when it is used in a trending environment.

Created with TradeStation. ©TradeStation Technologies, Inc. All rights reserved.

```
//Plot3(StochExSD, "StochEx SD", StochExSDColor);
```

By contrast, when methods and frameworks use calculations that implement trend compensation, many of the poor signals can be eliminated. Figure A.7 (a duplicate of Figure 5.20), shows the same chart of Thomas & Betts plotted within MetaSwing. Only two potential trading signals remain; they both work out well, however. Fewer trades and greater profits is the goal. In this first look at the TradeStation version of MetaSwing, it is important to note that Adeo signals appear as dots with the letter *A* beneath them. Also, the letter *E* denotes an exit signal. Additionally, S/R lines reform only after the N band has confirmed with adequate movement.

THE TTI FABRIC LR

In Chapter 6, we created the TTI Fabric components. These simple indicators better enable the trader to recognize a more accurate central tendency, and to measure

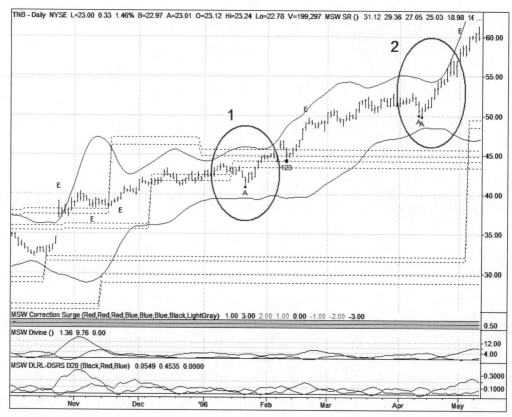

FIGURE A.7 This chart shows the same security as Figure A.6 but plotted within MetaSwing. Created with TradeStation. ©TradeStation Technologies, Inc. All rights reserved.

deviation from that central tendency. Part of the choice an analyst must make, however, is what establishes central tendency.

The first version we created used an exponential moving average to accomplish this. The second version, however, is a center line based on a 40-period linear regression line, and I much prefer its performance. We called this component the TTI Fabric LR. Here is the EL code to produce it.

```
{TTI_Fabric_LR}
Variables: FCL(0), ATR(0);

Inputs:
  PDS1(numericsimple), {linear regression periods}
  PDS2(numericsimple), {ATR periods}
  LT2(numericref), {first lower thread: 2 ATR's below centerline}
  LT3(numericref), {second lower thread: 3 ATR's below centerline}
```

```
    LT4(numericref),  {third lower thread: 4 ATR's below centerline}
    LT5(numericref),  {fourth lower thread: 5 ATR's below centerline}
    UT2(numericref),  {first upper thread: 2 ATR's above centerline}
    UT3(numericref),  {second upper thread: 3 ATR's above centerline}
    UT4(numericref),  {third upper thread: 4 ATR's above centerline}
    UT5(numericref);  {fourth upper thread: 5 ATR's above centerline}
FCL = LinearRegValue(Close, PDS1, 0);
ATR = ATR_WS(PDS2);
LT2 = FCL - (2 * ATR);
LT3 = FCL - (3 * ATR);
LT4 = FCL - (4 * ATR);
LT5 = FCL - (5 * ATR);
UT2 = FCL + (2 * ATR);
UT3 = FCL + (3 * ATR);
UT4 = FCL + (4 * ATR);
UT5 = FCL + (5 * ATR);

TTI_Fabric_LR = FCL;
```

The structure of this component is simple and so is the code, too. The function itself returns the centerline value, which is the linear regression line. All of the thread values are returned by variable reference. The following is the ShowMe code, which displays the TTI Fabric LR component on the stock chart.

```
{TTI Fabric LR}
Inputs:
    LinRegPeriods(40),
    ATRPeriods(14),
    ThreadColor(LightGray),
    CLColor(Black);

Variables:
    Centerline(0),
    LT2(0), LT3(0), LT4(0), LT5(0),
    UT2(0), UT3(0), UT4(0), UT5(0);

Centerline = TTI_Fabric_LR(LinRegPeriods,  ATRPeriods,
      LT2, LT3, LT4, LT5, UT2, UT3, UT4, UT5);

Plot1(UT5, "UT5", ThreadColor);
Plot2(UT4, "UT4", ThreadColor);
Plot3(UT3, "UT3", ThreadColor);
Plot4(UT2, "UT2", ThreadColor);

Plot5(Centerline, "Centerline", CLColor);
```

```
Plot6(LT2, "LT2", ThreadColor);
Plot7(LT3, "LT3", ThreadColor);
Plot8(LT4, "LT4", ThreadColor);
Plot9(LT5, "LT5", ThreadColor);
```

As you can see, the function call for the TTI_Fabric_LR is lengthy because of all the values that are received back. The first two values passed to the function are the linear regression periods and the ATR periods, respectively. This is very helpful when it comes time to test various trading methods. This degree of granularity in the function call will also add great flexibility should you choose to create an automated trading strategy, and optimize it with back testing. The line colors are stipulated as light gray in the ShowMe code. You may wish to adjust this for clarity. By eliminating the exact color designation from the plot statement, the color control is returned to the user for manual adjustment.

In Figure A.8, the TTI Fabric LR is plotted across a daily chart of Motorola (MOT). This kind of onscreen reminder of central tendency can be a very enlightening tool for short-term traders. (This was previously shown in Figure 6.3.)

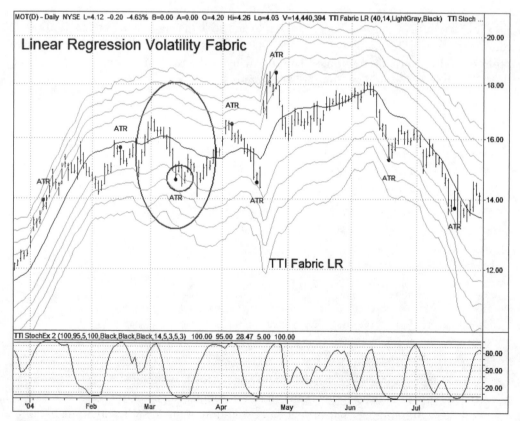

FIGURE A.8 Here is the TTI Fabric LR shown on a daily bar chart of Motorola (MOT).
Created with TradeStation. ©TradeStation Technologies, Inc. All rights reserved.

THE TTI TREND STRENGTH

In Chapter 6, we recognized the value of detecting the presence and strength of a price trend. Certainly, there are great benefits to improving overbought and oversold indicators with volatility measurement, but they tend to be subject to weakness during trending environments. We therefore introduced the TTI Trend Strength component as an example of a compound derivative. The TTI Trend Strength is a unique combination of the TTI StochEx and the TTI Fabric LR components.

The actual TTI Trend Strength algorithm and function code are proprietary, and currently exist only as the MSW Trend Strength component of MetaSwing. I can share with you, however, the indicator code that calls the function. The following code calls the MSW Trend Strength function and passes two parameters to it. The first is the overall look-back period, and the second is the strength comparison period.

```
{MSW TS Slope}
Inputs:
  TS2Color(Black),
  TS2LookBack(100),
  TS2rsPeriods(20),
  TS2SlopePeriods(20),
  TS1Color(Black),
  TS1LookBack(100),
  TS1rsPeriods(10),
  TS1SlopePeriods(20),
  CenterlineColor(Black);

Variables:
  TS2(0),
  TS1(0);

TS2 = MSW_Slope(MSW_Trend_Strength(TS2LookBack, TS2rsPeriods)
  + 50000, TS2SlopePeriods);
TS1 = MSW_Slope(MSW_Trend_Strength(TS1LookBack, TS1rsPeriods)
  + 50000, TS1SlopePeriods);
Value3 = 0;

Plot1( TS2, "TS 20 Slope", TS2Color );
Plot2( TS1, "TS 10 Slope", TS2Color );
Plot3( Value3, "Centerline", CenterlineColor );
```

Figure A.9 displays a daily chart of Radio Shack (RSH) with the MSW Trend Strength plotted in the upper indicator pane. This chart is a rough equivalent to Figure 6.17. There are a few key differences, however. The interpretation of the MSW Trend Strength component involves an analysis of the previous 20-period linear regression line and its relative slope. You can see in the lower indicator pane that the MSW TS Slope component

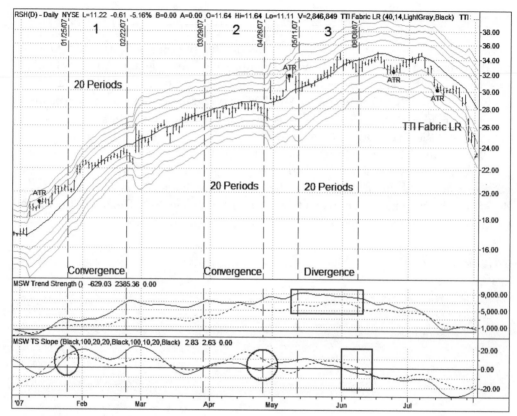

FIGURE A.9 This daily chart of Radio Shack (RSH) displays the MSW Trend Strength component, along with its analysis partner the MSW TS Slope component.

Created with TradeStation. ©TradeStation Technologies, Inc. All rights reserved.

is plotted. This indicator pair measures and displays the relative slope of the MSW Trend Strength. This negates the need for manual line study analysis. It can also be incorporated directly into back testing and Trading Strategies. The EL code that calls the MSW_Slope function is as follows. You may note that the MSW_Slope function call adds a 50000 number to the value returned by MSW_Trend_Strength. This is done so that only a positive value is passed as an argument, which is a requirement.

```
{MSW TS Slope}
Value1 = MSW_Slope(MSW_Trend_Strength(100, 20) + 50000, 20);
Value2 = MSW_Slope(MSW_Trend_Strength(100, 10) + 50000, 20);
Value3 = 0;

Plot1( Value1, "TS 20 Slope", Black );
Plot2( Value2, "TS 10 Slope", Black );
Plot3( Value3, "Centerline", Black );
```

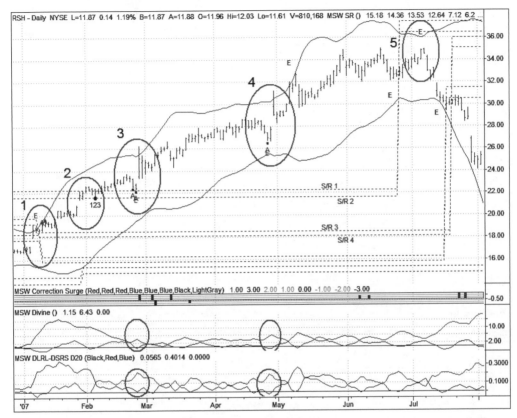

FIGURE A.10 The same view of Radio Shack (RSH) in MetaSwing reveals trend compensated and trend entry signals in circles 3 and 4.

Created with TradeStation. ©TradeStation Technologies, Inc. All rights reserved.

Figure A.10 shows us the standard MetaSwing chart analysis view of Radio Shack over the same time span. This chart is a TradeStation equivalent to Figure 6.18. In it, the trend-compensated components are better able to identify trend entry points such as the Adeo long signals in circled areas 3 and 4. The MSW Trend Strength and slope indicators are not plotted on this chart because of space limitations, but they have a firm place in the decision framework.

THE TTI RSIV

In Chapter 6, the need to adapt an overbought and oversold component for trend-compensated performance became evident. As a result, we continued our work with linear regression in Chapter 7. Specifically, we adapted the structure of classic Relative Strength Index (RSI) to utilize changes in the linear regression of price. The goal was to produce a trend-compensated indicator of overbought and oversold price levels.

The component we created for this task is named the TTI RSIV 1. The EL code for the TTI_RSIV_1 function follows. It is fully commented so that you can follow the calculations and logic flow of the algorithm.

```
{TTI_RSIV_1}
inputs:
  PDS1(numericsimple), {Linear Regression periods}
  PDS2(numericsimple); {Look back periods}

{Defines the difference between the day's closing price and the
linear regression line, and assigns the value to the variable x1}
Value1 = (Close - LinearRegValue(Close, PDS1, 0));

{Conditional logic to define an Up day for Value1}
If Value1 > Value1[1] then Value2 = 1 else Value2 = 0;

{Conditional logic to measure an increase in Value1 on an Up day}
If Value1 > Value1[1] then Value3 = Value1 - Value1[1] else Value3 = 0;

{Conditional logic to define a Down day for Value1}
If Value1 < Value1[1] then Value4 = 1 else Value4 = 0;

{Conditional logic to measure a decrease in Value1 on a Down day}
If Value1 < Value1[1] then Value5 = Value1[1] - Value1 else Value5 = 0;

{Multiplies the sum of the increases on Up days by the number of Up days}
Value6 = Summation(Value3, PDS2) * Summation(Value2, PDS2);

{Multiplies the sum of the decreases on Down days by the number of Down days}
Value7 = Summation(Value5, PDS2) * Summation(Value4, PDS2);

{Calculates the ratio of trend adjusted increases to trend adjusted
decreases, and then converts it to a value between 0 and 100}
Value8 = 100 - (100 / (1 + (Value6 / (Value7 +. 00001))));

TTI_RSIV_1 = Value8;
```

The EL code for an indicator to call the TTI RSIV 1 and plot it below a chart is as follows.

```
{TTI RSIV 1}
Inputs:
  LinRegPeriods(40),
  LookBackPeriods(30),
  UpperRange(100),
  UpperExtreme(75),
  LowerExtreme(25),
```

```
  LowerRange(100),
  GuideColors(Black),
  RSIVColor(Black);

Variables:
    RSIV(0);
RSIV = TTI_RSIV_1(LinRegPeriods, LookBackPeriods);

Plot1( UpperRange, "Upper Range", GuideColors );
Plot2( UpperExtreme, "Up Extreme", GuideColors );
Plot3( RSIV, "TTI RSIV 1", RSIVColor );
Plot4( LowerExtreme, "Low Extreme", GuideColors );
Plot5( LowerRange, "Lower Range", GuideColors );
```

As you can see, the TTI_RSIV_1 function requires two arguments. The first is to specify the number of linear regression periods. The second is to quantify the look-back period for the relative strength self-comparison. The parameters of a 40-period linear regression combined with a 30-period look-back time span works well when the upper and lower extremes are set to 75 and 25, respectively. To make visual observations of these settings, the following EL code produces a ShowMe study that plots signals on the charts.

```
{TTI RSIV 1 shme}
Value1 = TTI_RSIV_1(40, 30);

Condition1 = Value1 Crosses Above 75;
Condition2 = Value1 Crosses Below 25;

If Condition1 then
  begin
  Plot1( High ) ;
  Value4 = Text_New(Date, Time, High, "RSIV1") ;
  Value5 = Text_SetLocation(Value4, Date, Time, High * 1.05) ;
  Value5 = Text_SetStyle(Value4, 2, 0) ;
  Value5 = Text_SetColor(Value4, Black) ;
  end ;

If Condition2 then
  begin
  Plot2( Low ) ;
  Value4 = Text_New(Date, Time, Low, "RSIV1") ;
  Value5 = Text_SetLocation(Value4, Date, Time, Low - (Low *. 05)) ;
  Value5 = Text_SetStyle(Value4, 2, 1) ;
  Value5 = Text_SetColor(Value4, Black) ;
  end ;
```

FIGURE A.11 This daily chart of Stryker Corporation (SYK) displays the performance of the TTI RSIV 1 component compared to the classic RSI indicator.

Created with TradeStation. ©TradeStation Technologies, Inc. All rights reserved.

In Figure A.11, there is a daily chart of Stryker Corporation (SYK) which concurrently displays the performance characteristics of the TTI RSIV 1 (40,30) and the classic RSI(14) indicators. Also, the preceding ShowMe is plotted in the price pane. This chart is a TradeStation equivalent to Figure 7.14.

The RSI is well known for remaining high during trend rallies, and remaining low during downward trends. By utilizing linear regression mathematics, the TTI RSIV 1 is better able to maintain a sense of balance during trending price action. Indicator signals alone are never a reason to place a trade. Figure A.11, however, shows good performance in the area of overbought and oversold indication.

For the purposes of comparison, Figure A.12 shows much of the same Stryker Corporation trend. Specifically, it isolates the October 2007 to March 2008 time span when the MSW Trend Strength was decidedly positive. The two vertical dashed lines denote this time span. At the first vertical line, both slopes turn positive. During these conditions, it would make sense to utilize the two Adeo long signals to enter the trend;

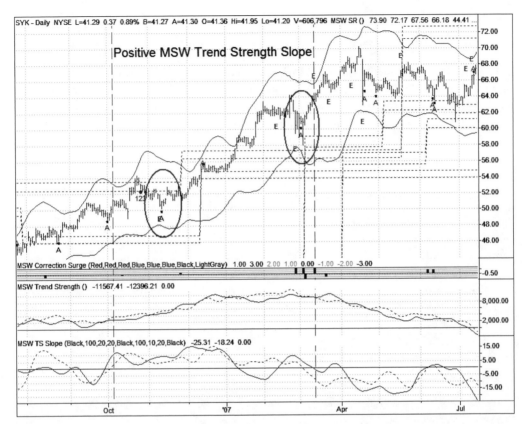

FIGURE A.12 Part of Stryker Corporation's trend is isolated as positive for trend entry by the MSW Trend Strength components.

Created with TradeStation. ©TradeStation Technologies, Inc. All rights reserved.

both of them are circled. On March 13, 2008, both slope signals become negative. This means it is time to consider finding an exit point and closing the position.

THE TTI COMPOSITE

To exploit the volatility-based components that have been constructed thus far, it is a natural progression to try to fuse them together. As a practice, this can work well under the correct circumstances. Adding more components, however, and thus multiplying the total number of potential parameters, can make the development process more complex. An initial attempt at this is the TTI Composite. It is composed of the following functions:

- TTI ATRExtreme
- TTI Stoch Extreme

- TTI RSIV 1
- TTI Fabric LR

This new component is slightly different in that it attempts to capture the momentum of three components through a linear regression slope measurement of each. It also uses deviation from a central linear regression as a fourth ingredient. The following is the EL code that creates the TTI_Composite function.

```
{TTI_Composite}
Inputs:
   LinRegSlopePeriods(numericsimple);

Variables:
   StDevPeriods(14),
   PctKPeriods(5),
   PctDPeriods(3),
   ATRPeriods(5),
   AddlSmoothPeriods(3),
   StochExSD(0),
   StochExATR(0),
   uExtremeR(0),
   lExtremeR(0);

{Establishes linear regression slope values of 3 oscillator components}
Value1 = TTI_StochEx_2(StDevPeriods, PctKPeriods,
   PctDPeriods, ATRPeriods, AddlSmoothPeriods,
   StochExSD, StochExATR);
Value2 = LinearRegSlope(StochExATR, LinRegSlopePeriods);

Value3 = TTI_RSIV_1(40, 30);
Value4 = LinearRegSlope(Value3, LinRegSlopePeriods);

Value5 = TTI_ATREx_2(40, 14, 200, 3, 20, uExtremeR, lExtremeR);
Value6 = LinearRegSlope(Value5, LinRegSlopePeriods);

{Calculates number of ATR multiples above or below central fabric line}
Value7 = (LinearRegValue(Close, 40, 0) - Close);
Value8 = (Value7 / ATR_WS(14)) * -3;

{Sums values to create the composite indicator}
TTI_Composite = Value2 + Value4 + Value6 + Value8;
```

The following is the TTI Composite indicator code that calls and plots the TTI_Composite function.

```
{TTI Composite}
Inputs:
```

```
   UpperExtreme(25),
   LowerExtreme(-25),
   GuideColors(Black),
   CompColor(Black);

Variables:
     Composite(0);

Composite = TTI_Composite(5);

Plot1( UpperExtreme, "Up Extreme", GuideColors );
Plot2( Composite, "Composite", CompColor );
Plot3( LowerExtreme, "Low Extreme", GuideColors );
```

This indicator code is obviously relatively simple. The actual core function calls are in the TTI_Composite function itself. Any amount of optimization through individual parameter changes will therefore need to be done there. This version of the TTI_Composite uses the default parameters demonstrated in the components as they were constructed previously in this appendix. Only one user input is passed as an argument to the preceding function. It is the quantity of periods for the linear regression slope measurement, and is passed as the `LinRegSlopePeriods` input.

Lastly, the ShowMe study that plots signals when the extreme thresholds are crossed is as follows:

```
{TTI Composite shme}
Value1 = TTI_Composite(5);

Condition1 = Value1 Crosses Above 25;
Condition2 = Value1 Crosses Below -25;

If Condition1 then
   begin
   Plot1( High ) ;
   Value4 = Text_New(Date, Time, High, "Comp") ;
   Value5 = Text_SetLocation(Value4, Date, Time, High * 1.05) ;
   Value5 = Text_SetStyle(Value4, 2, 0) ;
   Value5 = Text_SetColor(Value4, Black) ;
   end ;

If Condition2 then
   begin
   Plot2( Low ) ;
   Value4 = Text_New(Date, Time, Low, "Comp") ;
   Value5 = Text_SetLocation(Value4, Date, Time, Low - (Low *. 05)) ;
   Value5 = Text_SetStyle(Value4, 2, 1) ;
   Value5 = Text_SetColor(Value4, Black) ;
   end ;
```

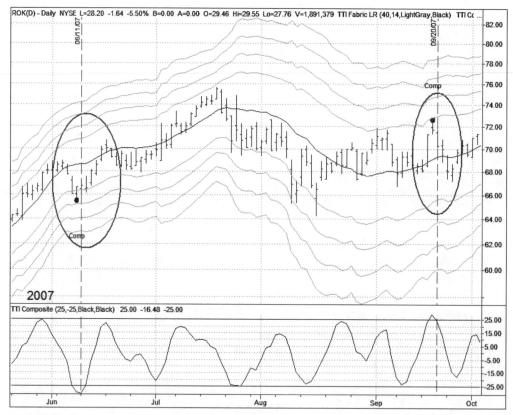

FIGURE A.13   This daily chart of Rockwell International shows us some visual performance cues of the TTI Composite indicator.

Created with TradeStation. ©TradeStation Technologies, Inc. All rights reserved.

Figure A.13 shows us a daily chart of Rockwell International (ROK) with the TTI Composite in the lower indicator pane. (This chart is an equivalent to Figure 9.3.) The preceding ShowMe EL code plots two extreme signals, based on TTI Composite component.

THE RELATIVE EXIT

One of the most profitable activities a trader can perform is to close the position at the correct time and price, regardless of the target she envisioned at the outset. We explored in Chapter 12 the art of the exit, and some of the mathematical methods that can be used to execute it. The Relative Exit is a method of measuring the relative extremes of a qualifying indicator, establishing a proper threshold value, and then projecting it forward. When this upper threshold is next crossed, it is likely a good time to consider an exit.

This is the method that MetaSwing uses for its onscreen exit signals. They appear as an *E* above or below the price bars.

The key to the success of this method is to use an indicator with the right characteristics. It needs to be a component that:

- Measures overbought and oversold conditions.
- Is based on volatility measurement.
- Is not bound by high or low numerical limits.
- Returns a nonlinear value.
- Is trend compensated.

In MetaSwing, the functions used are the DLRL and DSRS Delta 20 components. The following is the MetaSwing function code, which determines the threshold value used for exiting a long trade.

```
{MSW_DLRL_Peaks}
Value1 = MSW_DLRL_fnc(20);
Value2 = (MSW_Peak(Value1, 90,0) +
  MSW_Peak(Value1, 90,1) +
  MSW_Peak(Value1, 90,2) +
  MSW_Peak(Value1, 90,3) +
  MSW_Peak(Value1, 90,4) +
  MSW_Peak(Value1, 90,5) +
  MSW_Peak(Value1, 90,6)) / 7;

MSW_DLRL_Peaks = Value2 * 1.1;
```

The MSW DLRL-DSRS D20 indicator plots this exit system as it happens. The following is its EL indicator code with comment lines that disable the display of the overbought measurements. As written in the following, it will plot the chart that you see in Figure A.14. I normally only comment out the code lines that display the peaks unless I want to see them. The *E* exit prompts on the chart are normally all that I use.

```
{MSW DLRL-DSRS D20}
Inputs:
  BaselineColor(Black),
  OBColor(Red),
  OSColor(Blue);
Value1 = MSW_DLRL_fnc(20);
Value2 = MSW_DLRL_Peaks;
//Value3 = MSW_DSRS_fnc(20);
//Value4 = MSW_DSRS_Peaks;
Value5 = 0;
```

FIGURE A.14 This daily chart of Aracruz Celulose (ARA) demonstrates the mechanics of the Relative Exit.

Created with TradeStation. ©TradeStation Technologies, Inc. All rights reserved.

```
Plot1( Value1, "Oversold", OSColor );
Plot2( Value2, "OS Peaks", OSColor);
//Plot3( Value3, "Overbought", OBColor );
//Plot4( Value4, "OB Peaks", OBColor );
Plot5( Value5, "Baseline", BaselineColor );
```

You can see in Figure A.14 how the relative exit functions. In the two exit examples shown, each is triggered when the MSW_DLRL_fnc(20) crosses above the MSW_DLRL_Peaks line. The letter *E* is plotted on the chart above the bar on which the cross occurs.

Figure A.15 shows an expanded view of the same chart. In the first half of 2006, Aracruz Celulose (ARA) experiences a period of higher-than-normal volatility, as denoted by the rectangles on the chart. As a consequence of this, the MSW_DLRL_Peaks line rises. In this way, the exit signals become more relative to appropriate volatility levels.

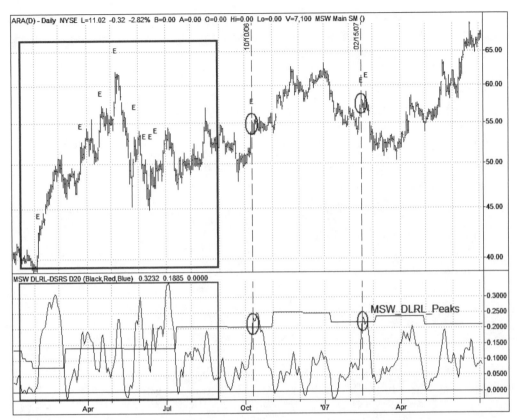

FIGURE A.15 A longer-term view of the Relative Exit component demonstrates how the exit-determining threshold rises in response to price volatility.

Peaks and Troughs

The Relative Exit technique depends on being able to accurately detect a peak and a trough occurrence in time series data. TradeStation did not provide functions to accomplish this when this chapter was written. Northington Trading, therefore, had some developed. They work the same as those shown in previous chapters with one exception. These functions return a peak or a trough value on the bar, which confirms that the peak or trough has formed, using the percentage parameter argument. Unlike the peak and trough functions in previous chapters, these do not retreat to the actual bar where the peak or trough forms, and thus restate.

There are three functions necessary to perform peak and trough identification:

- MSW_Trough
- MSW_Peak
- MSW_PT_PCT

As you can see in the MSW_DLRL_Peaks function earlier, the MSW_Peak function is called. Then from within the MSW_Peak function, the MSW_PT_PCT function is called. The EL code for the MSW_Peak function is as follows:

```
{MSW_Peak}
{EL Programming code written by Richard Saidenberg¹}
input:Data_Array(numericseries),PCT_Min_Change(numericsimple),Nth(numericsim
  ple);

var:PTline(-999999),lookforlow(true),bsT(0),bsP(0),
 holdT(0),holdP(0),lasth(false),z(0),znth(0);

array:TroughA[9](-999999),PeakA[9](-999999),TroughbarA[9](0),PeakbarA[9](0);

PTline=MSW_PT_PCT(Data_Array,PCT_Min_Change);
if PTline=Data_Array AND PTline<PTline[1] then bsT=0 else bsT=bsT+1;
if PTline=PTline[1] and Data_Array=Data_Array[1] and Data_Array=PTline then
  bsT=0;
if PTline=Data_Array AND PTline>PTline[1] then bsP=0 else bsP=bsP+1;
if PTline=PTline[1] and Data_Array=Data_Array[1] and Data_Array=PTline then
  bsP=0;

for z=9 downto 1 begin
 PeakbarA[z]=PeakbarA[z]+1;
 TroughbarA[z]=TroughbarA[z]+1;
end;

if lookforlow[1] then begin
 if PTline=Data_Array AND PTline<PTline[1] then begin
  for z=9 downto 2 begin
   PeakA[z]=PeakA[z-1];
   PeakbarA[z]=PeakbarA[z-1];
  end;
  PeakA[1]=PTline[1];
  PeakbarA[1]=bsP;
  lookforlow=false;
 end;
end;

if lookforlow[1]=false then begin
 if PTline=Data_Array AND PTline>PTline[1] then begin
  for z=9 downto 2 begin
   TroughA[z]=TroughA[z-1];
   TroughbarA[z]=TroughbarA[z-1];
  end;
  TroughA[1]=PTline[1];
```

```
  TroughbarA[1]=bsT;
  lookforlow=true;
 end;
end;

if Data_Array=TroughA[1] AND TroughBARA[1]<PeakBarA[1] then TroughbarA[1]=0;
if Data_Array=PeakA[1] AND TroughBARA[1]>PeakBarA[1] then PeakbarA[1]=0;

znth=intportion(Nth);
if znth<1 then znth=1;
if znth>9 then znth=9;

MSW_Peak=PeakA[znth];
```

The EL code for the MSW_Trough function is as follows.

```
{MSW_Trough}
{EL Programming code written by Richard Saidenberg¹}
input:Data_Array(numericseries),PCT_Min_Change(numericsimple),
  Nth(numericsimple);

var:PTline(-999999),lookforlow(true),bsT(0),bsP(0),
 holdT(0),holdP(0),lasth(false),z(0),znth(0);

array:TroughA[9](-999999),PeakA[9](-999999),TroughbarA[9](0),PeakbarA[9](0);

PTline=MSW_PT_PCT(Data_Array,PCT_Min_Change);
if PTline=Data_Array AND PTline<PTline[1] then bsT=0 else bsT=bsT+1;
if PTline=PTline[1] and Data_Array=Data_Array[1] and Data_Array=PTline then
  bsT=0;
if PTline=Data_Array AND PTline>PTline[1] then bsP=0 else bsP=bsP+1;
if PTline=PTline[1] and Data_Array=Data_Array[1] and Data_Array=PTline then
  bsP=0;

for z=9 downto 1 begin
 PeakbarA[z]=PeakbarA[z]+1;
 TroughbarA[z]=TroughbarA[z]+1;
end;

if lookforlow[1] then begin
 if PTline=Data_Array AND PTline<PTline[1] then begin
  for z=9 downto 2 begin
   PeakA[z]=PeakA[z-1];
   PeakbarA[z]=PeakbarA[z-1];
  end;
  PeakA[1]=PTline[1];
  PeakbarA[1]=bsP;
```

```
  lookforlow=false;
 end;
end;
if lookforlow[1]=false then begin
 if PTline=Data_Array AND PTline>PTline[1] then begin
  for z=9 downto 2 begin
   TroughA[z]=TroughA[z-1];
   TroughbarA[z]=TroughbarA[z-1];
  end;
  TroughA[1]=PTline[1];
  TroughbarA[1]=bsT;
  lookforlow=true;
 end;
end;

if Data_Array=TroughA[1] AND TroughBARA[1]<PeakBarA[1] then TroughbarA[1]=0;
if Data_Array=PeakA[1] AND TroughBARA[1]>PeakBarA[1] then PeakbarA[1]=0;

znth=intportion(Nth);
if znth<1 then znth=1;
if znth>9 then znth=9;

MSW_Trough=TroughA[znth];
```

The EL code for the MSW_PT_PCT function is as follows.

```
{MSW_PT_PCT}
{EL Programming code written by Richard Saidenberg[1]}
input:Data_Array(numericseries),PCT_Min_Change(numericsimple);

var:PTline(-999999),go(false),up(false),lpnt(-999999),hpnt(999999);

if go then begin
 if up[1] then begin
  if Data_Array>PTline then begin
   PTline=Data_Array;
   {up=true;}
  end else begin;
   if PTline>=0 then begin
    if Data_Array<PTline*(1-(PCT_Min_Change/100)) or Data_Array<lpnt then begin
     PTline=Data_Array;
     up=false;
    end;
   end else begin {PTline<0}
    if Data_Array<PTline*(1+(PCT_Min_Change/100)) or Data_Array<lpnt then begin
```

```
   PTline=Data_Array;
    up=false;
   end;
  end;
 end;
end;
if up[1]=false then begin
 if Data_Array<PTline then begin
  PTline=Data_Array;
  {up=false;}
 end else begin;
  if PTline>=0 then begin
   if Data_Array>PTline*(1+(PCT_Min_Change/100)) or Data_Array>hpnt then begin
    PTline=Data_Array;
    up=true;
   end;
  end else begin {PTline<0}
   if Data_Array>PTline*(1-(PCT_Min_Change/100)) or Data_Array>hpnt then begin
    PTline=Data_Array;
    up=true;
   end;
  end;
 end;
end;
end else begin {go=false}
 if Data_Array>Data_Array[1] then begin
  PTline=Data_Array;
  go=true;
  up=true;
  lpnt=Data_Array[1];
 end;
 if Data_Array<Data_Array[1] then begin
  PTline=Data_Array;
  go=true;
  up=false;
  hpnt=Data_Array[1];
 end;
end;

if up and up[1]=false and PTline[1]>-999999 and go[1] then lpnt=PTline[1];
if up=false and up[1] and PTline[1]>-999999 and go[1] then hpnt=PTline[1];

if Data_Array<lpnt then lpnt=-999999;
if Data_Array>hpnt then hpnt=999999;
```

```
MSW_PT_PCT=PTline;
IF PTline=-999999 THEN MSW_PT_PCT=Data_Array;
```

CORRECTION AND SURGE

The MetaSwing Correction Surge system is a collection of market breadth–based ratios. These ratios are used to generate the Correction, or Surge, signals. The signals are an important part of forecasting the intermediate broad market direction, and the short-term market swing. The ratio formulas, logic, and application are the same for the TradeStation version of MetaSwing as those presented in Chapter 13.

The internal method that TradeStation software uses to access the market breadth data, however, is somewhat different. Six additional historical data streams must be assigned to the chart for the correction and surge function code to return a value. While they remain hidden from view, they are active in that they can be referenced by EL code, historically and in real time.

You can see in Figure A.16 the Format Symbols application window, which shows the exact data assignments that match the MSW_Correction_Surge function code. The added symbols must be assigned to the matching data numbers as shown in the window so that the logic flow of the function is correct. Any symbol can occupy the Data1 assignment, but Data2 through Data7 must be assigned the exact symbols as shown. Also, each of the Data2 through Data7 symbols must be formatted as *Hidden* in the subgraph drop-down selection of its specific Format Symbol application window so as not to occupy visual chart space. Obviously, you would want to save these settings as a specific Workspace file so that the manual part of the setup need be performed only once.

Once the Data# requirements are in place, the MSW_Correction_Surge function and the MSW Correction Surge indicator will be able to display on the chart. If you implement the MSW Correction Surge indicator, you will need to perform some manual

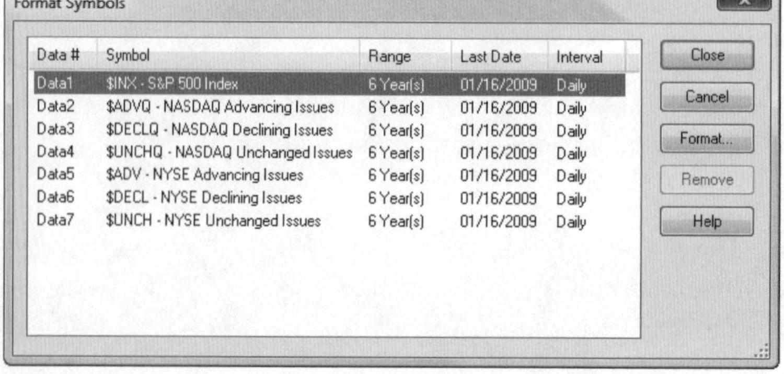

FIGURE A.16 This shows the Format Symbols application window.

Created with TradeStation. ©TradeStation Technologies, Inc. All rights reserved.

formatting commands for it to achieve the desired presentation. An alternative is to download the TTI VBTA.tsw file from this book's companion web site, www.tradingtheinvisible.com. By using the. tsw file, you will not have to perform the manual formatting. You will, however, still need to manually configure the data assignments described previously.

The following is the MSW_Correction_Surge EL function code.

```
{MSW_Correction_Surge}

{Assignment of market breadth data streams}
Value2 = Close of Data2 ; {$ADVQ}
Value3 = Close of Data3 ; {$DECLQ}
Value4 = Close of Data4 ; {$UNCHQ}
Value5 = Close of Data5 ; {$ADV}
Value6 = Close of Data6 ; {$DECL}
Value7 = Close of Data7 ; {$UNCH}

{Correction NASDAQ}
If Value3 / Average(Value2 + Value3 + Value4, 5) >. 76
    then Value8 = 1 Else Value8 = 0;

{Correction NYSE}
If Value6 / Average(Value5 + Value6 + Value7, 5) >. 805
    then Value9 = 2 else Value9 = 0;

{Surge NASDAQ}
If Value2 / Average(Value2 + Value3 + Value4, 5) >. 73
    then Value11 = -1 else Value11 = 0;

{Surge NYSE}
If Value5 / Average(Value5 + Value6 + Value7, 5) >. 77
    then Value12 = -2 else Value12 = 0;

{Correction/Surge determination}
MSW_Correction_Surge = Value8 + Value9 + Value11 + Value12;
```

In this function code, it is clear how the added Data# assignments are made. What's next is the MSW Correction Surge indicator code.

```
{MSW Correction Surge}
Inputs:
    NASDAQCorrectionColor(Red),
    NYSECorrectionColor(Red),
    TotalCorrectionColor(Red),
    NASDAQSurgeColor(Blue),
    NYSESurgeColor(Blue),
```

```
    TotalSurgeColor(Blue),
    PrimaryLineColor(Black),
    SecondaryLineColor(LightGray);

Value1 = MSW_Correction_Surge;

If Value1 = 1 then Plot1( Value1, "NASDAQ Corr", Red);
If Value1 = 2 then Plot2( Value1, "NYSE Corr", Red);
If Value1 = 3 then Plot3( Value1, "Total Corr", Red);
If Value1 = -1 then Plot4( Value1, "NASDAQ Surge", Blue);
If Value1 = -2 then Plot5( Value1, "NYSE Surge", Blue);
If Value1 = -3 then Plot6( Value1, "Total Surge", Blue);

Plot7(3, "Total C", PrimaryLineColor);
Plot8(2, "NYSE", SecondaryLineColor);
Plot9(1, "NASDAQ", SecondaryLineColor);
Plot10(0, "Baseline", PrimaryLineColor);
Plot11(-1, "NASDAQ", SecondaryLineColor);
Plot12(-2, "NYSE", SecondaryLineColor);
Plot13(-3, "Total S",PrimaryLineColor);
```

The TradeStation version of the MSW Correction Surge signals is visually different from that which was presented in Chapter 13. There, the signals that designated the index specific correction or surge event were graphically plotted on the price chart. In this version, the signal is numeric and in the form of a thinly plotted indicator. At your discretion, it can appear as small as a ribbon below the price chart. Figure A.17 shows us a key to understanding the value presented by the indicator. It is also color coded when viewed on your computer screen.

3 : Total Correction
2 : NYSE Correction
1 : NASDAQ Correction

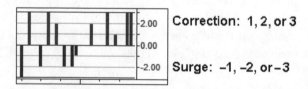

–1 : NASDAQ Surge
–2 : NYSE Surge
–3 : Total Surge

FIGURE A.17 The Correction Surge indicator returns a simple histogram value, which corresponds to the specific index-related signal.

Created with TradeStation. ©TradeStation Technologies, Inc. All rights reserved.

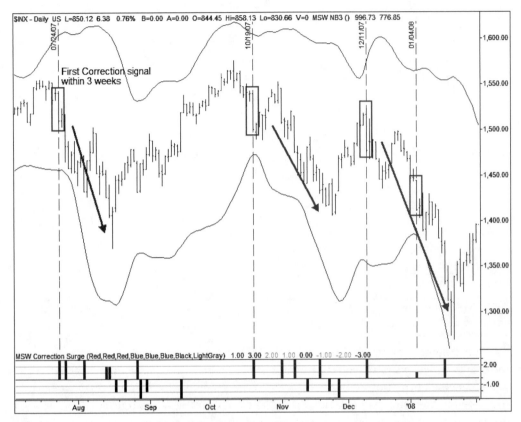

FIGURE A.18 This daily chart of the S&P 500 Index shows newly occurring correction signals warning of lower trading to come.

Created with TradeStation. ©TradeStation Technologies, Inc. All rights reserved.

We see in Figure A.18 a daily chart of the S&P 500 Index with the Correction Surge indicator plotted beneath it. This chart is functionally the same as Figure 13.3. There are four vertical lines plotted, which align with each instance of a correction signal occurrence when it is the first after three weeks without one. Time since a previous correction signal, and the closing height between the N Bands, are the two most important factors when interpreting correction signals.

METASWING FOR TRADESTATION

In Chapter 3, I presented a tutorial on MetaSwing. So that you can familiarize yourself with the workings of MetaSwing in TradeStation, I perform here a couple of chart analyses. Both versions work virtually the same, and are only subject to the differences introduced by their respective underlying platforms. For the fun of it, focus on two

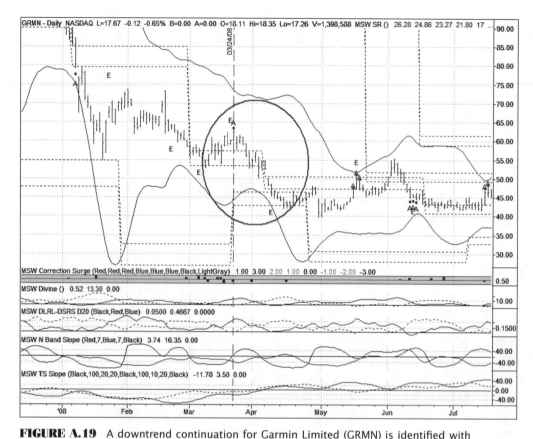

FIGURE A.19 A downtrend continuation for Garmin Limited (GRMN) is identified with MetaSwing MSW Trend Strength and volatility shift measurement.

volatility shift setups during volatile markets. Hidden momentum with volatility shift was introduced in Chapter 11.

We see in Figure A.19 a daily MetaSwing chart for Garmin Limited (GRMN). In this chart, the default Divine and DLRL-DSRS indicators are plotted. The slope measuring indicators for the N Bands and the Trend Strengths are also plotted.

On March 24, 2008, an Adeo short signal arrives, which is denoted with a circled area and a vertical dashed line. Here are the relevant technical factors for this short position:

- The Divine and the DSRS are both showing extreme overbought readings, with a good confirming DLRL tandem component height.
- The 7-period lower N Band slope is decidedly negative. The 7-period upper N Band slope is relatively flat. This sets up a probable lower short-term trading range due to volatility shift.

- The 20-period slope for each Trend Strength indicator is negative. This supports an opinion that a new trend rally is unlikely to begin at this point.
- You can see in the circled area that an Exit long and an Adeo short signal have just occurred.
- The current close, at which the Adeo short signal appears, is lower than previous successive lower highs.

The combination of these factors tell us that Garmin is ready for a short position, with an acceptable risk-to-reward ratio. For short-term trading, volatility shift adds a strong probability to the framework. This setup is also counter to the two surge signals that occurred in the previous few days. Volatility shift is a very strong mathematical scenario, and can telegraph a stock's intention to trade independently from the broader market. Also of note is that on April 7, 2008, less than two weeks later, both trend strength slopes turned positive, thus forecasting a transition from a downtrend to a trading range.

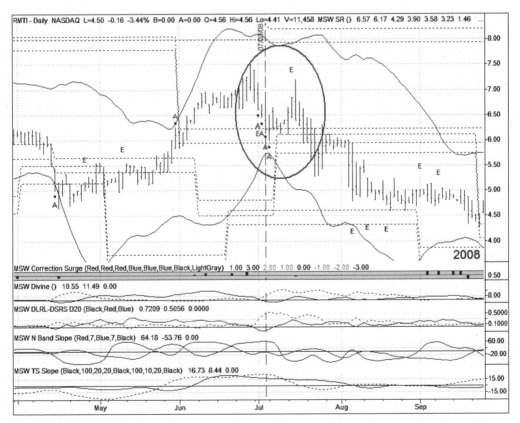

FIGURE A.20 A daily MetaSwing chart of Rockwell Medical Technologies (RMTI) uncovers a quick swing trading opportunity with confirming volatility shift analysis.

Created with TradeStation. ©TradeStation Technologies, Inc. All rights reserved.

For our second MetaSwing example, we can view another stock that bucks the market direction for the short term. In Figure A.20, there is a daily chart of MetaSwing showing Rockwell Medical Technologies (RMTI). An Adeo Long signal first appears on July 1, 2008. The technical measurements for this trade set up oppositely mirror the previous example. Here are the technical factors to consider for a long trade setup:

- The oversold readings on the Divine and DLRL are at extremes. The DSRS has sufficient height to confirm the extreme oversold condition.
- The upper N Band slope is close to zero. The lower N Band Slope is at 64. This signals strong hidden upside momentum for the short term.
- Both trend strength indicator slopes are completely positive.
- In recent days, Correction events have signaled, putting negative pressure on the broad market.
- On July seventh, an Adeo condition persists and the intraday price bounces off of the lower N Band resistance area, and support at S/R 4.

Price succumbs to downward market pressure but not without first trading higher by 10 percent. The market is the ultimate master. For individual issues, however, quantitative programmed trading based on volatility calculations rule in the short term.

The PIV Options Advantage

Using Projected Implied Volatility to Trade the Butterfly, Condor, Strangle, and Straddle

The purpose of this appendix is to show how Projected Implied Volatility (PIV) can improve on traditional technical analysis methods to find high probability options spread trades. Support and resistance is the classic method for finding option spread trade candidates, and then selecting strike prices. This appendix does not propose to change that. I do believe, however, that the basis of determining support and resistance can be greatly improved when it incorporates volatility. We will use MetaSwing N Bands and S/R lines to define volatility-based support and resistance.

A more intensive use of chart-based technical analysis could certainly benefit many private and professional options traders. We will explore here how volatility-based support and resistance should be a primary selection criterion for Butterfly and Condor trade selection. The method will be described in detail, and then back-tested to show its statistical performance. We present also statistical proof that PIV-based support and resistance can accurately forecast a substantial reduction in short-term volatility.

Then, in the second part of this appendix, I focus on using N Bands and S/R lines in multiple time frames to best trade corporate earning releases with strangle and straddle option spreads. Also included will be MetaStock exploration code for finding historically high movement stocks within any specific month of the year.

PIV FOR THE BUTTERFLY AND CONDOR

When searching for good Butterfly and Condor trade candidates, the objective is to select an option-capable security that you believe will trade within a low volatility range for three to four weeks. It is desirable to find a stock that has been on the move, but going forward, it will experience a pause in its movement. This previous movement creates greater levels of implied volatility, and thus a better profit-making environment for the trade. In short, everyone else thinks it will continue its trading direction, but you know that it is less likely to do so.

A traditional technical analysis method for butterfly and condor trade selections involves identifying a stock that has established a trading range. It would have preferably experienced a minimum of two clear highs and two clear lows, with each high and low pair at the same level. The highs are used to identify resistance and the lows are used to identify support. A trading range is thus formed. This sounds a lot like the formation of a rectangle pattern, doesn't it?

You may recall that we explored trading rectangle patterns in Chapter 10. There we stated that the majority of the technical analysis community believes that the only rectangle pattern–related price activity that has shown predictability are throwback and pullback retracement patterns, which occur outside of the rectangle; movement inside the rectangle is unpredictable (refer to Figure 10.3). This hardly seems desirable for a butterfly or condor. This contradiction of methodology shows how classic technical analysis has not always been helpful to option traders.

It would be much more advantageous to identify the trading range prior to its formation. In reality, it is more necessary than advantageous. The technology and activity of programmed trading by large institutions has significantly nullified the predictability of visually recognizable price patterns.

The MetaSwing Compression

The MetaSwing method for Butterfly and Condor trade candidates is called a *Compression*. There are four different types of Compression setups. We explore one of them in this appendix.

The goal of the Compression method is to identify a narrow zone of extreme resistance and support in a weekly periodicity. The more narrow the zone of support and resistance the better, because the ultimate profitability of the trade will be greater. This zone should increase the probability of price behavior that subsequently results in a temporary trading range for four weeks. Furthermore, this method should produce a trade candidate that is exhibiting sufficient implied volatility levels to make a Butterfly or Condor trade profitable.

We see in Figure B.1 a weekly MetaSwing chart of Thomas & Betts Corporation (TNB). Only N Bands and S/R lines are plotted on the chart. Note how price rallies through the first half of 2007 and begins to encounter resistance around S/R 4. This larger view of the price activity shows plenty of movement, and that can be a dangerous environment for a low-volatility option spread trade.

Now let's take a closer look at the anatomy of the Compression. Figure B.2 shows another look at the Thomas & Betts weekly chart, which zooms in on the trade setup. The week in which the trigger occurs is denoted by the vertical dashed line. The

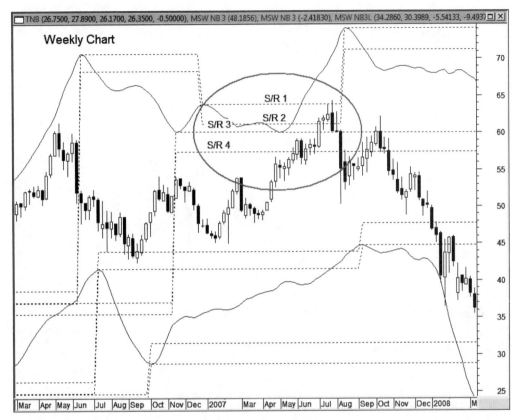

FIGURE B.1 This weekly chart of Thomas & Betts (TNB) shows an absence of well-defined trading ranges. Chart created in MetaStock.

Chart created in MetaStock. Chart uses the MetaSwing Add-on, by Northington Trading, LLC. All rights reserved.

Compression signal appears as a right-facing arrow with the letter *C* above it. On further inspection, the daily chart (not shown) indicates that price closed above the S/R 3 line on Tuesday, July 3, 2007.

The criteria that define a Compression setup are listed here. Figure B.2 is notated to identify these criteria.

- The Compression setup is found on a weekly chart.
- Price rises up through the S/R 4 line and closes above the S/R 3 line.
- Price has not closed above the S/R 3 line in the past three weeks.
- The price high has not crossed above the S/R 1 line in the past three weeks.
- The distance between S/R 2 and S/R 3 is less than one unit of ATR(40).
- This means that the distance between S/R 1 and S/R 4 is less than three units of ATR(40).

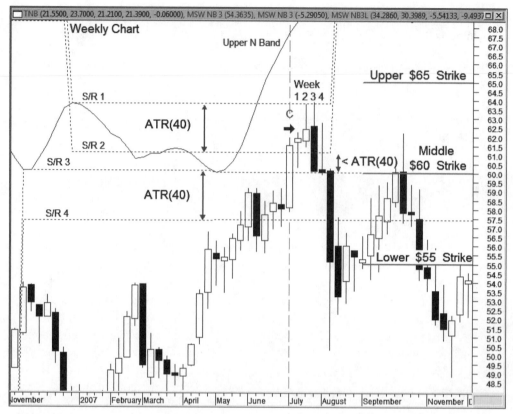

FIGURE B.2 A closer look at Thomas & Betts gives us a detailed view of the Compression setup and characteristics.

Chart created in MetaStock. Chart uses the MetaSwing Add-on, by Northington Trading, LLC. All rights reserved.

Figure B.2 clearly shows how the distance between S/R 2 and S/R 3 is less than 1 ATR (40). The weeks that follow the Compression signal are labeled one through four, just above S/R 1. It is obvious to see how price is rising aggressively until it hits resistance at the S/R 1 level. The Upper N Band is on a continuous rise in the weeks preceding the Compression signal, and also after the signal. This helps profit potential of the Butterfly trade because implied volatility readings are rising.

The effectiveness of the Compression signal is derived from the unusually tight configuration of S/R lines. Once price rises to cross S/R 3, it is well into the center of a compressed area of support and resistance. The result is price movement that pauses at S/R 1 resistance, and often oscillates between that level and S/R 4.

At the right of Figure B.2 are the three option strike prices that would be logical choices for a narrow Butterfly trade. During weeks three and four, price goes on to close at the sweet spot for this example, which is the $60 option strike price. This is a teaching example that works out very well, but, of course, not all do. The question any trader asks at the outset of the trade is, "What is my probability of success?" That's the topic of the next section.

A Study of Compression Performance

When we attempt to conduct a study of option trading strategies, a very real problem presents itself. Historical option premium prices are not as readily available as stock prices. Capturing and storing the multiple matrixes of prices, which represent an option chain, for even a single stock, is a daunting task. Historical option premium price data are available, but it is prohibitively expensive for all but very large institutions.

Because of this dilemma back-testing an option strategy with results based on actual option premium prices is simply not an option to most of us. This forces us to be more resourceful. Instead of using the option premium price, we will use the underlying stock price movement as a correlation to option profitability. To further ensure a positive correlation, we will overachieve by setting the trading range goal to be typically narrower than the actual option spread strike prices.

Compression Testing Method For this backtest, the primary measure of trade success is determined by analyzing how well price remains between the S/R 1 and S/R 4 lines during the period of a typical Butterfly or Condor trade. Through observation, the zone existing between these to price levels is significantly narrower than commonly available option strike prices. Figure B.3 shows a diagram that outlines how we will measure movement, which is, in effect, performance. Since the goal of the trade is for price to remain within a narrow trading zone, the optimum underlying stock price is identified as the Center Line.

The Center Line is exactly half way between S/R 1 and S/R 4. Therefore, from the Center Line to S/R 1 is equal to +1 Unit of Movement. Consequently, when the underlying stock price changes by that amount, we state that it has moved a +1 Unit of Movement. If the underlying price decreases from the Center Line to S/R 4, then it has changed −1 Unit of Movement. The actual changes in prices are reported as positive or negative Units of Movement. It is very important to understand that the numbers shown in the

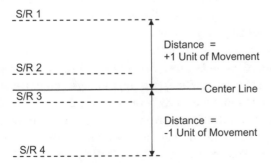

FIGURE B.3 This is a diagram of Compression movement measurement.

TABLE B.1 MetaSwing Compression Performance Results

	2.5 Weeks	3.5 Weeks	4.5 Weeks
Distribution of Unit Movement Distance from Center Line:			
Close Between 1 and −1	79.9%	70.6%	64.5%
Close > 1	13.2%	18.8%	22.4%
Close < 1	6.9%	10.6%	13.0%
Arithmetic Mean of Close	0.14	0.15	0.20
Median Close	0.123	0.123	0.159
Arithmetic Mean Distance from Center Line	0.65	0.79	0.90
Geometric Mean Relative from Center Line	0.419	0.521	0.595
Standard Deviation from Center Line	0.542	0.643	0.751

Trades were conducted on the S&P 500 stock population from July 2000 to June 2008. Total Quantity of Trades = 851. (Represents one of four types of MetaSwing Compression methods.)

study results are expressed in Units of Movement. Examine Figure B.3 closely before reading the performance results.

The testing period is the same as the studies conducted in previous chapters, which is July 2000 through June 2008. All trades occurred in the S&P 500 population of stocks. One of the four MetaSwing Compression setup methods produced 851 trades during the test period. Results from all 851 trades were analyzed, thus no random sampling was needed.

In the example shown in Figure B.2, the signal day can be any day of the week. If the signal week is considered week zero, then the average trade duration for that week can be assumed to be ½ week. Therefore the close of week two signifies an average trade duration of 2.5 weeks.

Compression Test Performance Results The performance results of 851 Compression signal trades is listed in Table B.1. These results are given for three distinct hold periods: 2.5 weeks, 3.5 weeks, and 4.5 weeks. The most common trade duration for a Butterfly or Condor seems to be three to four weeks. Therefore, the middle column showing 3.5 week data is likely the sweet spot for performance. To reiterate, the results are presented mainly to demonstrate the likelihood of price to remain between the S/R 1 and S/R 4 price levels. Consequently, any result of less than one unit of movement achieves that.

The top three rows of results in Table B.1 describe the distribution of performance for the three different periods. The top row lists the percentage of trades that close within the S/R 1 to S/R 4 boundary; that is, less than one unit of movement away from the Center Line. As we would expect, each successive week away from the Compression signal shows a higher percentage of closes outside the boundaries. At 3.5 weeks, 70.6 percent represents favorable odds. Figures B.4, B.5, and B.6 show the unit of movement distribution histograms for weeks 2.5, 3.5, and 4.5 respectfully.

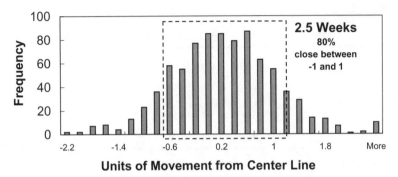

FIGURE B.4   This shows Compression 2.5-week performance distribution.

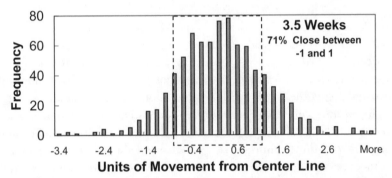

FIGURE B.5   This is an illustration of Compression 3.5-week performance distribution.

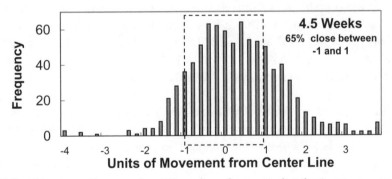

FIGURE B.6   This shows Compression 4.5-week performance distribution.

Row four of Table B.1 shows the arithmetic mean of all the movement data. At week 3.5, the average price closes .15 Unit of Movement above the Center Line. The positive progression of data for higher prices at each successive week, for the arithmetic mean and median, suggests that upward price momentum carries it higher after the period of reduced volatility. The progressing right translation of the histograms support the same implication.

TABLE B.2 MetaSwing Compression Cumulative Performance Results

	2.5 Weeks	3.5 Weeks	4.5 Weeks
Cumulative Measure of Unit Movement:			
Below S/R 1 and Above S/R 4	452	327	287
Above S/R 1 and Below S/R 4	82	147	205
% Unit Distance Below S/R 1 and Above S/R 4	85%	69%	58%
Above S/R 1	55	97	144
Below S/R 4	27	50	60

Trades were conducted on the S&P 500 stock population from July 2000 to June 2008. Total Quantity of Trades = 851. (Represents one of four types of MetaSwing Compression methods.)

The middle section of Table B.1 shows the key descriptive statistics. These values were derived from the absolute value of the movement data. All of these measurements imply that for the majority of trades, price remains within the narrow trading zone.

Suppose we measure the raw data in a different way. We know how many were inside, above and below the S/R 1-to-S/R 4 zone. Another important piece of information would be to know how far above 1 or below –1 the trade failures reached. Knowing this would help us to quantify the severity of the outliers. Likewise, it would be good to know how far inward from the support or resistance level the winners reached. Table B.2 shows the Compression signal's cumulative performance. This serves as another correlation to profitability.

In other words, this table shows movement away from the S/R 1 line for values closing above the center line and movement away from the S/R 4 line for values closing below the center line. Unlike Table B.1, it is using the S/R 1 and S/R 4 lines as the points where measurement begins. For example, if a trade closes at +.25, which is above the center line, Table B.2 reports it as a .75 Unit of Movement away from the S/R 1 line, in the first row. If a trade closes at +1.45, Table B.2 reports it as .45 away from the S/R 1 line in row 2.

What Table B.2 tells us is that the sweet spot is indeed week 3.5. In row 3, we see that 69 percent of the movement away from the theoretical breakeven points is profitable. I say that this is a theoretical breakeven because the S/R boundaries are known. The actual option strike prices should form the real breakeven price points for the trade, but those aren't known in this study.

After my own observation of many Compression chart signals, I can state that the functional option strike prices are normally spread much wider than the distance between the S/R 1 and S/R4 lines. Therefore, the typical Compression trade zone represented in these performance figures would be considered very narrow. Also this S/R trade zone is by nature self-adjusting to the underlying stock's volatility level, due to the characteristics of N Bands. N Bands themselves rise and fall with the underlying volatility. Also, the S/R lines are separated by a unit of ATR(40), which is another measurement of volatility.

TABLE B.3 MetaSwing Compression Performance Relative to Random Market

Definitions:
Unit of Movement = (S/R 1 − S/R 4) / 2
Center Line = S/R 4 + Unit of Movement
Unit of Movement = Distance from Center Line
Mean Unit of Movement: Compression   12.4% of Price
Mean Unit of Movement: Random Market   23.6% of Price

	2.5 Weeks	3.5 Weeks	4.5 Weeks
Mean Unit of Movement: Compression[1]	0.65	0.79	0.90
Mean Unit of Movement: Random Market[2]	0.53	0.65	0.75
Mean Coefficient of Movement: Compression[3]	0.080	0.098	0.112
Mean Coefficient of Movement: Random Market[3]	0.124	0.153	0.177
Volatility Reduction of Compression vs Random	35.5%	36.3%	37.0%

[1]Unit of Movement Relative to 12.4 percent of Price.
[2]Unit of Movement Relative to 23.6 percent of Price.
[3] Mean Unit of Movement multiplied by its associated percent of price.
Trades were conducted on the S&P 500 stock population from July 2000 to June 2008.

Compression Relative to Random Another method for determining a trade signal's performance is to compare it to random market movement. In this case, we compared the movement of price during the Compression trade period to the weekly movement that each stock exhibited. To avoid sampling discrepancies, we measured the same 2.5, 3.5, and 4.5 week price movement for each trading week during the test period. This was done for each stock in the S&P 500. Therefore we were measuring the entire population, not a sample of the population.

The same unit of movement shown in Figure B.3 was used in all of these calculations. Table B.3 shows the Compression Unit of Movement performance relative to random market movement. However, one difference surfaces during this process. Specifically, we are measuring all market trading weeks, which includes many more weeks when price is not sitting between S/R 1 and S/R4. For most of the weeks, price is sitting at a level far lower than S/R 4. To compensate for this, we measure the mean price percentage between the S/R 1 and S/R 4 lines during a Compression signal, and the same mean for times when price is not in that zone. As you can see in the second section of Table B.3, the S/R zone is a much wider percentage of price during random market days; it is almost double. This makes the random price movement percentage more relevant than the actual price movement expressed in dollars.

After adjusting for this unit of movement disparity, each condition is expressed as a mean coefficient of movement. In the middle section of Table B.3 are the results showing the results of decreased volatility subsequent to a Compression signal. At the end of the 3.5-week trade duration, the Compression method shows a 36.3 percent decrease in price movement, that is, a decrease in short-term volatility, when compared with normal weekly price behavior. This also serves as empirical proof that N Band S/R lines function as price support and resistance, which is to say that volatility-based support and resistance works well.

Additional Factors Affecting Compression Performance   The study just presented does not consider two normal and important market occurrences. Anyone trading Butterfly or Condor option spreads would avoid holding such positions during a corporate earnings announcement of the underlying stock. The data collected for this study did not filter out hold periods when earnings announcements happened. Since earnings releases generally cause increases in volatility, it is safe to assume that the results were negatively affected by some quantity of those events. Therefore, the Compression performance just stated would likely be improved by implementing the avoidance of corporate earnings releases.

Also, when a MetaSwing Correction signal occurs there is a higher likelihood that overall market downside volatility will happen in the short term. This study does not include exiting positions when Correction signals happen. Incorporating the proper response to those events would also be likely to improve the Compression method performance. See Chapter 13 for a complete understanding of the Correction signal and its market breadth ratio calculation.

PIV FOR THE STRANGLE AND STRADDLE

We explore in this section how PIV supports trading spreads that rely on an increase in volatility. Fundamentally based catalysts create immediate reactions in underlying stock price movements. Different sectors experience information releases that are unique to their specific industry. The most common catalyst is a corporate earnings report. You may recall the Microsoft (MSFT) chart examples in Chapter 4. We focus in this section on another earnings release scenario.

If an option trader has reason to believe that the underlying stock price will move in response to an earnings release, she may choose to put on a straddle spread trade. If she thinks that price will make a large move, then a strangle may be the best choice. The more difficult part of the technical analysis is forecasting the extremes that price will reach. This is the task that PIV and N Bands can help you solve. Predicting the market's reaction, however, is not a scientific process because of the subjective nature of the severity of the news release, which is the largest contributing factor.

Reaction: Immediate and Projected

The N Band represents immediate support or resistance, while the S/R line represents future support and resistance. When a surprise earning release occurs, there is usually an immediate reaction: a price move up or down to a different level. In the days or weeks that follow, price will often continue on to an even more extreme level.

Specifically, N Bands tend to identify the limits of the immediate reaction. S/R lines are usually better at forecasting price movement to its highs or lows, before any significant retracement. The part of the analysis that requires the most judgment is in choosing the proper chart periodicity. As a general rule a daily chart is best for looking at an immediate reaction, and the three-day and weekly charts are best for short- to intermediate-term targets.

Figure B.7 shows us a daily and a weekly chart just before an earnings report by Google (GOOG) on April 17, 2008. Let's now assume that we are looking at the Google opportunity as a strangle option spread. Our decision for the strangle selection could be based on Google's history of making large moves after earnings release days. This daily and weekly chart combination is what's known to us at the close of April 17th. Your task now is to predict where price will jump to, and ultimately reach, before your particular choice of option expiration date.

On the daily chart at left are two small circles. Upon a significant earnings surprise, these are usually where price will jump to just after the earnings release, often in after

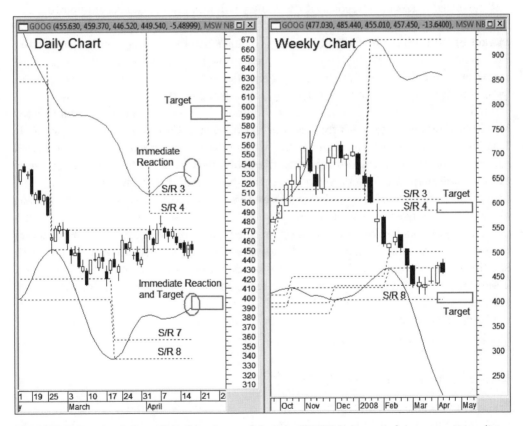

FIGURE B.7 The daily and weekly charts of Google (GOOG) help us to forecast an immediate and intermediate-term reaction to a scheduled earnings announcement.

Chart created in MetaStock. Chart uses the MetaSwing Add-on, by Northington Trading, LLC. All rights reserved.

hours or premarket trading. Going forward for a few days, or weeks, the next level of support or resistance is frequently where price will trade to. The weekly chart is usually the best place to find the intermediate-term support and resistance. In this case resistance is S/R 4, which is at 584.42. Weekly support is at S/R 8, which is 408.51. These two levels are marked with rectangles on both charts.

You may be wondering why I am choosing a support level that is so much closer to price than the resistance level. In this case, that's happening for two reasons. First, support is just plain closer, so as they say, "It is what it is." The second reason is that price had undergone a serious decline in recent months. Negative price moves tend to be less severe when a stock has already been recently beaten down.

On the daily chart, the strike price target for the call leg of the spread looks quite high. It is important to never underestimate the weekly time frame for projected implied volatility. Based on this analysis, your job is to buy a call and a put further out of the money than most other market participants think price will reach. What will work in your favor is that you know it can reach a given extreme while most others believe it will not. This makes the deep out of the money call and put much less expensive.

We can see in Figure B.8 the outcome of the strangle trade. Google does indeed issue an earnings surprise. Price actually gaps up to close just above the upper N Band on the daily chart, landing at the high end of a typical immediate reaction area. Closing above the upper N Band is a very bullish sign; it signifies the market's longer-term interest in owning the stock. Price then continues to rise to just past the weekly S/R 4 line.

While this is a teaching example, it is very typical. The single most important factor for a strangle option spread is the strength of the earnings surprise or disappointment. That can be difficult prediction to make. Those that follow fundamental news events closely can develop a sense for getting the probability correct. Studying stock chart histories will help to find underlying issues that have a history of movement.

Finding stocks with a tendency toward excessive sudden movement could mean that many of those movement events are probably due to earnings announcements. Mining through large quantities of charts looking for this type of high price movement event can be very time consuming. Another way to approach it is to let your software do the work for you. The following MetaStock code is written to run inside the MetaStock Explorer. It searches through a large stock database and identifies the largest moving issues in a particular month.

Here is the code:

Column A: Jan %

```
x1:= Abs(H - Ref(L, -2)) / Ref(L, -2);
y1:= If(Ref(Month(), -2) = 10,
If(Year() = 2008, x1, 0), 0);
y2:= If(Ref(Month(), -2) = 10,
If(Year() = 2007, x1, 0), 0);
y3:= If(Ref(Month(), -2) = 10,
If(Year() = 2006, x1, 0), 0);
```

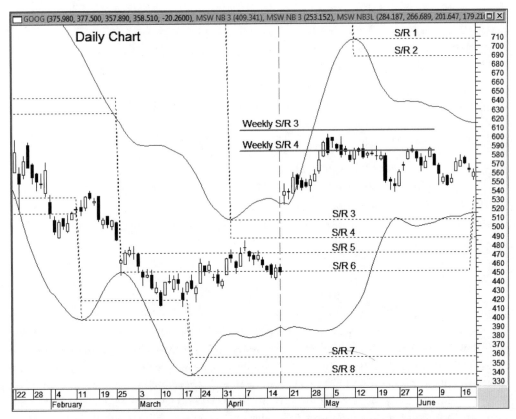

GOOG (375.980, 377.500, 357.890, 358.510, -20.2600), MSW NB 3 (409.341), MSW NB 3 (253.152), MSW NB3L (284.187, 266.689, 201.647, 179.21)

FIGURE B.8 After an earnings surprise, Google (GOOG) displays price movement that conforms to daily extreme resistance and weekly PIV levels (S/R lines).

Chart created in MetaStock. Chart uses the MetaSwing Add-on, by Northington Trading, LLC. All rights reserved.

```
y4:= If(Ref(Month(), -2) = 10,
If(Year() = 2005, x1, 0), 0);

(HHV(y1, 1900) + HHV(y2, 1900) +
HHV(y3, 1900) + HHV(y4, 1900)) / 4
```

Column B: Jan ATR

```
x1:= Abs(H - Ref(L, -2));

y1:= ValueWhen(1, Year() = 2008 AND
Month() = 12 AND BarsSince(Month() <> 12) > 0, ATR(40));
z1:= If(Ref(Month(), -2) = 1,
If(Year() = 2008, x1, 0), 0);
```

```
y2:= ValueWhen(1, Year() = 2007 AND
Month() = 12 AND BarsSince(Month() <> 12) > 0, ATR(40));
z2:= If(Ref(Month(), -2) = 1,
If(Year() = 2007, x1, 0), 0);

y3:= ValueWhen(1, Year() = 2006 AND
Month() = 12 AND BarsSince(Month() <> 12) > 0, ATR(40));
z3:= If(Ref(Month(), -2) = 1,
If(Year() = 2006, x1, 0), 0);

y4:= ValueWhen(1, Year() = 2005 AND
Month() = 12 AND BarsSince(Month() <> 12) > 0, ATR(40));
z4:= If(Ref(Month(), -2) = 1,
If(Year() = 2005, x1, 0), 0);

((HHV(z1, 1900) / y1) +
(HHV(z2, 1900) / y2) +
(HHV(z3, 1900) / y3) +
(HHV(z4, 1900) / y4));
```

The code in column A quantifies the largest three-period percentage price change, on a daily periodicity, for the month of January. It then averages this change for the years of 2005 through 2008 to produce a single price change percentage. The code in column B does the same thing, but instead of using a percentage of price, it returns a value in units of ATR(40). This column is probably more useful because the ATR measurement adjusts the measurement for volatility. You can change the code to return results for any month by changing the desired month number in the code. When you run this exploration, be sure to load at least 300 records per year of history desired.

PIV FOR OPTION SPREADS

The market will always reward options traders that act on knowledge that other traders don't possess. As I write this, volatility-based support and resistance levels are generally known only to larger, resource-rich organizations. We have explored two important applications of PIV in this appendix, but there are many more. Options trading and PIV go together like salt and pepper.

The significance of Projected Implied Volatility will consequently only grow. You need not fit the profile of a large institutional investment firm to exploit it, though. If you can trade with a greater ability to accurately forecast support and resistance, then the nonlinear relationships between underlying price movement, risk, and reward found in the option markets will be your ally.

About
the Companion
Web Site

Because markets and the opportunities within them are ever changing, the development of technical analysis must endeavor to be in front of those dynamics. With that goal in mind, we offer you the use of this book's companion web site, which can be found at: tradingtheinvisible.com.

It has been created in lockstep with this book to enrich your learning experience. There you will find:

- Content and resources for each chapter
- MetaStock and TradeStation indicator pack downloads for the components created in this book, open and unprotected
- Author's blog
- Updates and variations of the indicators within this book as they become available
- A monthly update of volatility-based technical analysis techniques and applications
- Complete details and links for the MetaStock and MetaSwing special offer extended to this book's readers

Table C.1 shows the additional subject matter resources by chapter available to you.

Thank you for choosing to add *Volatility-Based Technical Analysis* to your resource library. I hope that it actually puts money into your trading account. The companion web site should help to continue that trend.

TABLE C.1 Additional Content and Resources at tradingtheinvisible.com

	Expanded Charts	Additional Chart Examples	Excel File Study Results
Chapter 1			
Chapter 2	X		
Chapter 3	X		
Chapter 4	X	X	
Chapter 5	X	X	
Chapter 6	X	X	
Chapter 7	X	X	X
Chapter 8	X		
Chapter 9	X		
Chapter 10	X	X	
Chapter 11	X	X	X
Chapter 12	X		X
Chapter 13	X		X
Chapter 14	X		X
Appendix A	X	X	
Appendix B	X	X	X

Notes

PART ONE ARE YOU PREPARED?

1. Gillian Holloway, *The Complete Dream Book: Discover What Your Dreams Reveal About You and Your Life*, 2nd ed. (Naperville, IL: Sourcebooks, Inc., 2006), 16–17.

CHAPTER 1 THE CHALLENGES

1. Richard Bookstaber, *A Demon of Our Own Design: Markets, Hedge Funds, and the Perils of Financial Innovation* (Hoboken, NJ: John Wiley & Sons, 2007), 5.
2. Volker Knapp, "Equity Range Trader–Trading System Lab," *Active Trader* (September 2007). This well-conducted study analyzes a short-duration trading system that uses the Average Directional Movement (ADX) indicator to enter nontrending stocks and capitalize on a consolidation breakout. This study was conducted from June 1997 to May 2007. It was, on the whole, a very volatile but profitable period in the stock market. The system produced positive results, but was only half as profitable as a buy-and-hold method.

CHAPTER 2 THE OPPORTUNITIES

1. Richard Bookstaber, *A Demon of Our Own Design: Markets, Hedge Funds, and the Perils of Financial Innovation* (Hoboken, NJ: John Wiley & Sons, 2007), 1–6, 255–260.
2. Charles D. Kirkpatrick, CMT, and Julie R. Dahlquist, Ph.D., *Technical Analysis* (Upper Saddle River, NJ: Pearson Education, Inc., 2007), 216.
3. Terrance Odean, "Do Investors Trade Too Much?" *The American Economic Review*, December 1999, 1279–1298.

CHAPTER 3 THE FOUNDATION

1. Mars Climate Orbiter (MCO) Mishap Investigation Board, NASA, *Phase I Report*, November 10, 1999.

CHAPTER 4   NEW VOLATILITY INDICATOR DESIGN

1. Andrew W. Lo and Archie Craig Mackinlay, *A Non-Random Walk Down Wall Street*, 5th ed. (Princeton, NJ: Princeton University Press, 2002), 4–40.

2. David Aronson, *Evidence-Based Technical Analysis* (Hoboken, NJ: John Wiley & Sons, 2007), 50.

CHAPTER 6   THE FRAMEWORK

1. Richard Bandler and John Grinder, *Frogs into Princes: Neuro-Linguistic Programming* (Moab, UT: Real People Press, 1979).

2. Charles D. Kirkpatrick, CMT, and Julie R. Dahlquist, Ph.D., *Technical Analysis* (Upper Saddle River, NJ: Financial Times Press, 2006), 216.

CHAPTER 7   TRADITIONAL TECHNICAL ANALYSIS

1. Thomas N. Bulkowski, *Encyclopedia of Chart Patterns* (Hoboken, NJ: John Wiley & Sons, 2005) and Thomas N. Bulkowski, *Trading Classic Chart Patterns* (Hoboken, NJ: John Wiley & Sons, 2002).

2. Sharon Yamanaka, "Counting Crows," *Working Money* (June 2007).

PART THREE   TRADING THE INVISIBLE

1. Richard L. Peterson, *Inside the Investor's Brain* (Hoboken, NJ: John Wiley & Sons, 2007), 187.

CHAPTER 9   TRADING THE SHORT-TERM REVERSAL WITH VOLATILITY-BASED TECHNICAL ANALYSIS—THE ADEO

1. Dr. Alexander Elder, *Sell & Sell Short* (Hoboken, NJ: John Wiley & Sons, 2008), 174.

2. U. A. Müller, M. M. Dacorogna, R. D. Davé, O. V. Pictet, R. B. Olsen, and J. R. Ward, *Fractals and Intrinsic Time—A Challenge to Econometricians* (Zürich, Switzerland: Olsen & Associates Research Group, 1995), 1–3.

CHAPTER 10   TRADING THE TREND WITH THE 1-2-3

1. Martin J. Pring, *Technical Analysis Explained*, 4th ed. (New York: McGraw-Hill, 2002), 66.

2. Charles D. Kirkpatrick, CMT, and Julie R. Dahlquist, Ph.D., *Technical Analysis* (Upper Saddle River, NJ: Pearson Education, Inc., 2007), 313–316.

CHAPTER 11 HIDDEN MOMENTUM WITH ADEO HIGH SLOPE

1. John A. Bollinger, *Bollinger on Bollinger Bands* (New York: McGraw-Hill, 2002), 72.

CHAPTER 12 DESIGNING THE EXIT

1. Charles D. Kirkpatrick, CMT, and Julie R. Dahlquist, Ph.D., *Technical Analysis* (Upper Saddle River, NJ: Pearson Education, Inc., 2007), 222.

CHAPTER 13 CORRECTION AND SURGE

1. Martin J. Pring, *Technical Analysis Explained*, 4th ed. (New York: McGraw-Hill, 2002), 492.

CHAPTER 14 TRADING SYSTEM DESIGN

1. Carl von Clausewitz, *On War* (Oxford, England: Oxford University Press, 2007).
2. David Aronson, *Evidence-Based Technical Analysis* (Hoboken, NJ: John Wiley & Sons, 2007), 234–243.

APPENDIX A TRADESTATION EXAMPLES AND EASYLANGUAGE CODE

1. The functions that accomplish peak-and-trough measurement were written by Richard Saidenberg, specifically for Northington Trading, LLC. Richard Saidenberg is an independent consultant and an EasyLanguage specialist. He may be reached at Richard Saidenberg, 35 Tamarack Way, Pleasantville, NY 10570-1515, Phone 914-769-5164, ricksaidenberg@spitfire.net.

About the Author

Kirk Northington is the owner of Northington Trading, LLC, and the creator of MetaSwing, a MetaStock Add-On and TradeStation-compatible system. He trades his own money, and uses the technical analysis methods presented in this book exclusively.

Kirk Northington is a technical analyst. He is an associate member of the Market Technicians Association, through which he is participating in the Chartered Market Technician (CMT) Program.

Kirk has a B.S. degree from Nicholls State University, in Thibodaux, Louisiana. He has extensive experience in control system engineering, software engineering, and project management. Kirk, his wife Faith, and his two sons live in Charlotte, North Carolina.

A Special Offer from MetaStock
Learn by Doing

Use MetaStock® while reading *Volatility-Based Technical Analysis*.

Learn to use and customize the volatility-based indicators and algorithms in this book while you are reading it.

Equis International and Northington Trading, LLC, have teamed up to make this special offer. Try MetaStock under these terms:

Free for 30 Days*

and

First Month Free*

Try the MetaStock software and data subscription of your choice with no commitment for 30 days. Regardless of whether you continue your subscription or cancel, your 30-day trial period is free.*

MetaSwing™

Also use the MetaSwing™ Add-on within the 30-day trial period. Enjoy the volatility!

For full details, select the special offer link at:

www.tradingtheinvisible.com

*Applicable Exchange Fees not included in the above offer.

Index

UPC   035094
DESB OVUR.